Understanding Structured Programming in BASIC

IBM®/MS-DOS® Version

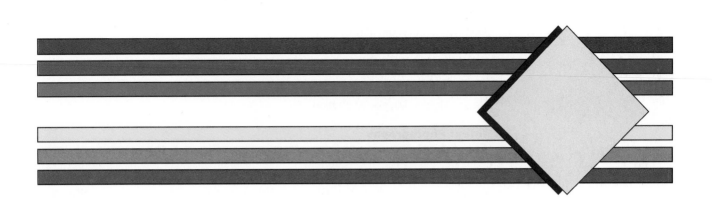

Understanding Structured Programming in BASIC

IBM®/MS-DOS® Version

Susan K. Baumann

B.S., Computer Educator, Computer Programmer

Steven L. Mandell

Bowling Green State University

West Publishing Company

St. Paul   New York   Los Angeles   San Francisco

Copy Editor: Maggie Jarpey
Composition: Carlisle Communications
Artwork: Carlisle Graphics

Cover Image:
Randy Miyake, Miyake Illustration

Intext Photographs
Fig. 1-1 (a)—courtesy of Epson America, Inc.; **Fig. 1-1 (b)**—courtesy of Epson America, Inc.; **Fig. 1-2**—courtesy of International Business Machines Corporation; **Fig. 1-4**—courtesy of International Business Machines Corporation; **Fig. 1-5 (a)**—courtesy of 3M Corporation; **Fig. 1-5 (b)**—courtesy of 3M Corporation; **Fig. 1-5 (c)**—courtesy of Maxtor Corporation; **Fig. 1-6**—courtesy of Los Alamos National Laboratory, LeRoy N. Sanchez; **Fig. 1-7**—courtesy of International Business Machines Corporation; **Fig. 1-8**—courtesy of Digital Equipment Corporation; **Fig. 1-9 (a)**—courtesy of International Business Machines Corporation; **Fig. 1-9 (b)**—courtesy of Apple Computers; **Fig. 1-9 (c)**—courtesy of Epson America, Inc.; **Fig. 10-3**—courtesy of International Business Machines Corporation; **Fig. 10-4**—courtesy of International Business Machines Corporation; **Fig. 11-3**—courtesy of the Huntington National Bank; **Fig. 11-4**—courtesy of BASF Systems Corporation.

IBM® is the registered trademark of International Business Machines Corporation.
MS-DOS® is the registered trademark of Microsoft Corporation.

Library of Congress Cataloging-in-Publication Data

Baumann, Susan K.
  Understanding structured programming in BASIC IBM/MS-DOS version
Susan K. Baumann, Steven L. Mandell.
      p.   cm.
   ISBN 0 314-67029-7
   1. BASIC (Computer program language) 2. Structured programming.
3. IBM Personal Computer—Programming. 4. MS-DOS (Computer
operating system) I. Mandell. Steven L. II. Title.
QA76.73.B3B3973 1991
005.265—dc20   89-25006
                                                  CIP

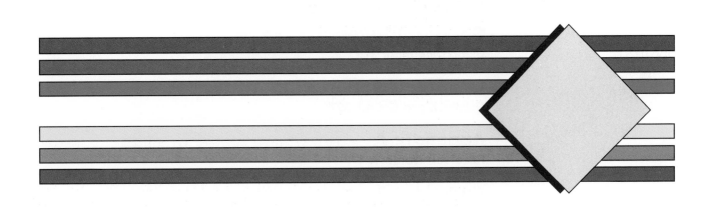

Contents In Brief

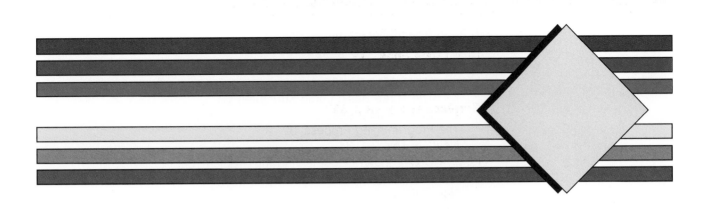

Table of Contents

Chapter Three

The Fundamentals of BASIC Programming 49

Chapter Four

Chapter Five

Chapter Six

Adding Structure by Modularizing Programs 149

Chapter Seven

Loop Structures 185

Chapter Eight

Debugging and Testing Programs and Using Functions 229

Chapter Nine

Chapter Ten

Chapter Eleven

Using Data Files 349

Chapter Twelve

Graphics and Sound 397

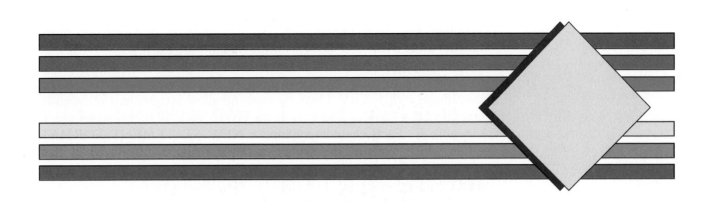

Preface

In our teaching experience, we have discovered that the primary goal of an introductory computer programming course should be to provide students with the thorough understanding of programming principles necessary to create well-designed, well-structured programs. Therefore, the main purpose of this textbook is to establish a basic foundation which will serve the student well during this class and in future programming coursework. Throughout this text, a strong emphasis is placed on designing well-structured programming solutions. The principles of structured programming are introduced early and re-enforced consistently. The student learns to use top-down design in developing solutions. Structure charts are created to functionally decompose solutions by task and to provide guidance in modularizing the final programs. In addition, emphasis is placed on using control structures such as the IF/THEN/ELSE statement and the WHILE/WEND loop to control the flow of program execution instead of unconditional branches (commonly referred to as "GOTO" statements).

Structured programming concepts are particularly important in a textbook such as this one which emphasizes business programming. Many of the programs in this textbook are business oriented. An entire chapter (Chapter 10) discusses software development methodology in business and the principles for creating well-designed business reports. Emphasis is placed on labeling tables, formatting numbers, and handling control breaks. The student learns the importance of designing user-friendly software with the end-user in mind.

Each programming chapter concludes with the development of a programming problem designed to implement the new statements introduced in that chapter. Program specification charts, printer spacing charts, flowcharts, and pseudocode all reinforce the concept of thoroughly designing and documenting the solution before proceeding to the coding phase.

Microsoft GW-BASIC, the language taught in this text, was chosen because it is easily learned and is implemented on the IBM Personal

Computer and IBM-compatibles. An Appendix is provided for those students using Microsoft BASIC on the Macintosh.

Other helpful features of this text include a list of learning objectives at the beginning of each chapter to prepare students for the topics to be covered and NOW TRY THIS exercises to allow intermittent self-testing throughout the chapter. Answers to the NOW TRY THIS exercises are in Appendix E. Each chapter contains a NEW STATEMENT FORMAT section which explains the syntax of the statements introduced in that chapter. The section entitled PROGRAMMING HINTS helps the student avoid common programming pitfalls. End-of-chapter review questions and debugging exercises allow the student to apply new knowledge. The programming problems have been divided into three levels: Level 1, Level 2, and Projects. Level 1 gives the student practice in writing the new statements introduced in the chapter, Level 2 offers problems of medium difficulty, and the projects are longer, more complex problems designed to integrate the ideas learned up to that point.

Color coding has been used in programming examples as follows:

Tan shading	Highlighted Statements	(Used to indicate statement currently being discussed.)
Blue	Computer Output	
Red	User Response	

Acknowledgements

Many professionals have added their expertise to the text. Thanks are owed for the expert contributions of Colleen Kobe, Cheryl Drivdahl and Martin Arthur. The design is a credit to the talents of Janine Wilson. Lastly, a final word of thanks to Carole Grumney for her ever-present support and encouragement.

I was very fortunate to have several outstanding high school educators serve as reviewers for this project. I wish to express my thanks to those people who reviewed the manuscript for this text:

Jill Baker
Greenville High School

Gloria Bales
George Junior High School

Bruce Haan
Jourdanton High School

Jill Knight
West Texas High School

Paul Moore
Refugio High School

Kristi Ray
Floresville High School

Johnnie Wilkins
Waco High School

Brenda Yowell
Burleson High School

Susan K. Baumann
Steven L. Mandell

Understanding Structured Programming in BASIC

IBM®/MS-DOS® Version

CHAPTER 1

Introduction to Computers and the IBM PC

Learning Objectives

After studying this chapter, you should be able to
1. List the three kinds of tasks a computer can perform.
2. Describe the three basic components of all computer systems.
3. Define input and output.
4. Explain the difference between data and information.
5. Name some commonly used input and output devices.
6. List and give the characteristics of the four types of computers.
7. List the basic rules for caring for a computer system and floppy disks.
8. Start your computer.
9. Use the following DOS commands: FORMAT, DISKCOPY, COPY, DEL, and DIR.
10. Access the BASIC system.
11. Type in a BASIC program and execute it.
12. Edit the statements in a BASIC program.
13. List a program on the monitor screen or print it on paper.
14. Save a program on disk and then load it back into the computer's main memory.

Introduction

Computers have become an important force in our society. People use them to perform an ever-increasing variety of tasks, such as banking, locating books in libraries, and making reservations on airline flights. Elementary-school children learn their multiplication tables with the help of computer programs that are entertaining, motivating, and more patient than any human teacher. Everywhere we look, we can find fascinating applications for these versatile machines. The uses for computers are limited only by the creativity of the people who control them. This chapter will present some introductory information about computers and the IBM Personal Computer in particular. You will learn about the parts of a computer system, the different types of computers, how to enter simple BASIC programs, and how to instruct the computer to execute these programs.

What Computers Can Do

Computer
An electronic machine that is capable of processing data in many different ways.

What is it that makes computers different from other machines that we use every day, such as a car or a typewriter? First, a **computer** is an electronic machine that is capable of processing data in a wide variety of ways with an extremely high degree of speed and accuracy. In addition, the computer can combine many simple operations into a single, integrated list of instructions that work together to solve a specific problem. This list of instructions is called a **program.** The programmer uses a **programming language** to instruct the computer to carry out, or execute, these instructions.

Program
A list of step-by-step instructions that a computer can use to solve a problem.

Programming language
A language that a programmer can use to give instructions to a computer.

The actual tasks that computers can perform can be divided into three categories:

1. Arithmetic operations (addition, subtraction, multiplication, and division).
2. Comparison (or logical) operations (determining whether a given value is greater than, equal to, or less than another value).
3. Storage and retrieval operations (such as saving a program on a disk so that it can be used later).

What makes the computer particularly useful to people is its ability to perform these tasks with a high degree of speed and accuracy. With care, a person can add 100 numbers and find the correct result, but the chances of making an error somewhere along the way are considerable. Also, it is a boring job. This is the kind of task that is well suited to the computer. It can perform this task quickly and accurately, and it won't get bored. Moreover, it can store the results for future use.

The Components of a Computer System

Hardware
The physical components of the computer system.

All computers, regardless of their size and complexity, have three basic components: input devices, a central processing unit, and output devices. These physical components are called the **hardware** (Figure 1–1).

FIGURE 1–1 Computers and printers are common types of hardware.

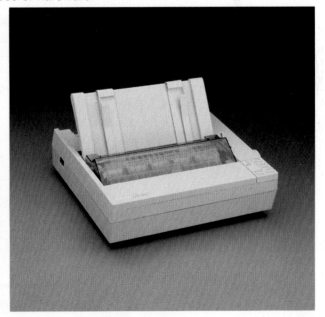

Input Devices

Input
Data that is entered into the computer to be processed.

Data
Facts that have not been organized in a meaningful way.

Information
Data that has been processed so that it is meaningful to the user.

Cursor
The blinking rectangle of light indicating when typing will appear on the screen.

Programs and data that are entered into the computer to be processed are called **input.** The word **data** refers to facts that have not been organized in any meaningful way. When data is processed, or changed into a meaningful form, the result is **information.** For example, in a national election, the records of all the votes cast for the office of president are data. When these votes are tabulated and the final totals are determined, the result is information.

Input devices allow data to be entered into the computer. The most commonly used input device is the keyboard (Figure 1–2). Other devices include joysticks, light pens, mice, graphics tablets, optical disks, and light pens. A joystick, often used with video games or in generating computer art, consists of a stick that pivots freely on a base. Instructions are entered into the computer by pressing one or two buttons on the joystick's base.

A mouse is a hand-movable device that fits into the user's palm. When it is moved across a flat surface, signals are sent through a cable to the computer, and the **cursor** (the block of light indicating where input will appear on the screen) moves in the same direction.

Graphics tablets are flat, board-like pads on which the user draws, using a special pen or a finger. The images traced on the pad appear on the monitor screen.

Optical disks are similar to the compact disks used to record music and can store enormous amounts of data. This area of technology is still in its early stages. These disks will probably become less expensive and more widely used in the near future.

A light pen is a pen-shaped object with a light-sensitive cell at its end. To enter data into the computer, the user touches the device to the screen.

A touch screen looks like a normal computer screen, but it contains sensors that detect the point at which the user's finger touches the screen. The touch screen is especially useful when the user must choose from a list of alternatives. One simply touches the desired alternative, and the computer registers the choice and continues processing accordingly.

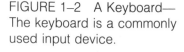

FIGURE 1–2 A Keyboard—
The keyboard is a commonly used input device.

Some devices, such as disk and tape drives, are used as both input and output devices. They can transfer data and programs from magnetic disks or tape to the primary storage unit of the computer. These are discussed more fully in the section on output devices.

The Central Processing Unit

The computer can store data temporarily, and it can also process this data. The part of the computer that performs both functions is the **central processing unit (CPU).** It can be thought of as the "brain" of the computer. As shown in Figure 1–3, the CPU consists of three major components: the control unit, the arithmetic/logic unit, and the primary storage unit.

The **control unit** is in charge of the activities of the CPU. It does not process or store data itself, but instructs various parts of the computer to perform these tasks. Instructions given to the computer by the user are interpreted by the control unit, which then tells the computer how to carry out these instructions. It also tells the computer which input device will be used to enter the data, and it keeps track of what parts of a program have been executed. Finally, it collects the output and sends it to the designated output device, such as a monitor screen or a printer.

The **arithmetic/logic unit (ALU)** performs mathematical computations and logical operations. A logical operation instructs the computer to make a comparison. For example, a program statement might tell the computer to determine whether number X is greater than number Y, and to print X if this condition is true. If the condition is false, the program might specify another course of action.

The **primary storage unit** (also referred to as **main memory**) holds program instructions, data, and the intermediate and final results of processing. It consists of many storage locations, each of which can hold a small amount of information. Each of these storage locations is assigned a unique address. This address allows the computer to locate items that have been stored in its memory. Large computers have millions of these locations.

Output Devices

A computer system can have many different output devices. For example, a programmer may be able to print the results of a program on paper, display them on a screen, or transfer them to a disk to be used later.

Output displayed on a monitor screen (Figure 1–4) is referred to as **soft copy.** It is often convenient and is easy for the user to read, but it is lost as soon as something else replaces it on the screen. Printing the results on paper saves this information permanently so that the user can refer to it later. This type of output is called **hard copy.** A printer is necessary to produce hard copy.

Central processing unit
The "brain" of the computer, composed of three parts: control unit, arithmetic/logic unit, and primary storage unit.

Control unit
The part of the central processing unit that governs the actions of the various components of the computer.

Arithmetic/logic unit
The part of the central processing unit that performs arithmetic and logical operations.

Primary storage unit
The component of the central processing unit that temporarily stores programs, data, and results.

Main memory
The component of the central processing that temporarily stores programs, data, and results.

Soft copy
Output displayed on a monitor screen.

Hard copy
Output printed on paper.

FIGURE 1–3   The Components of a Computer System

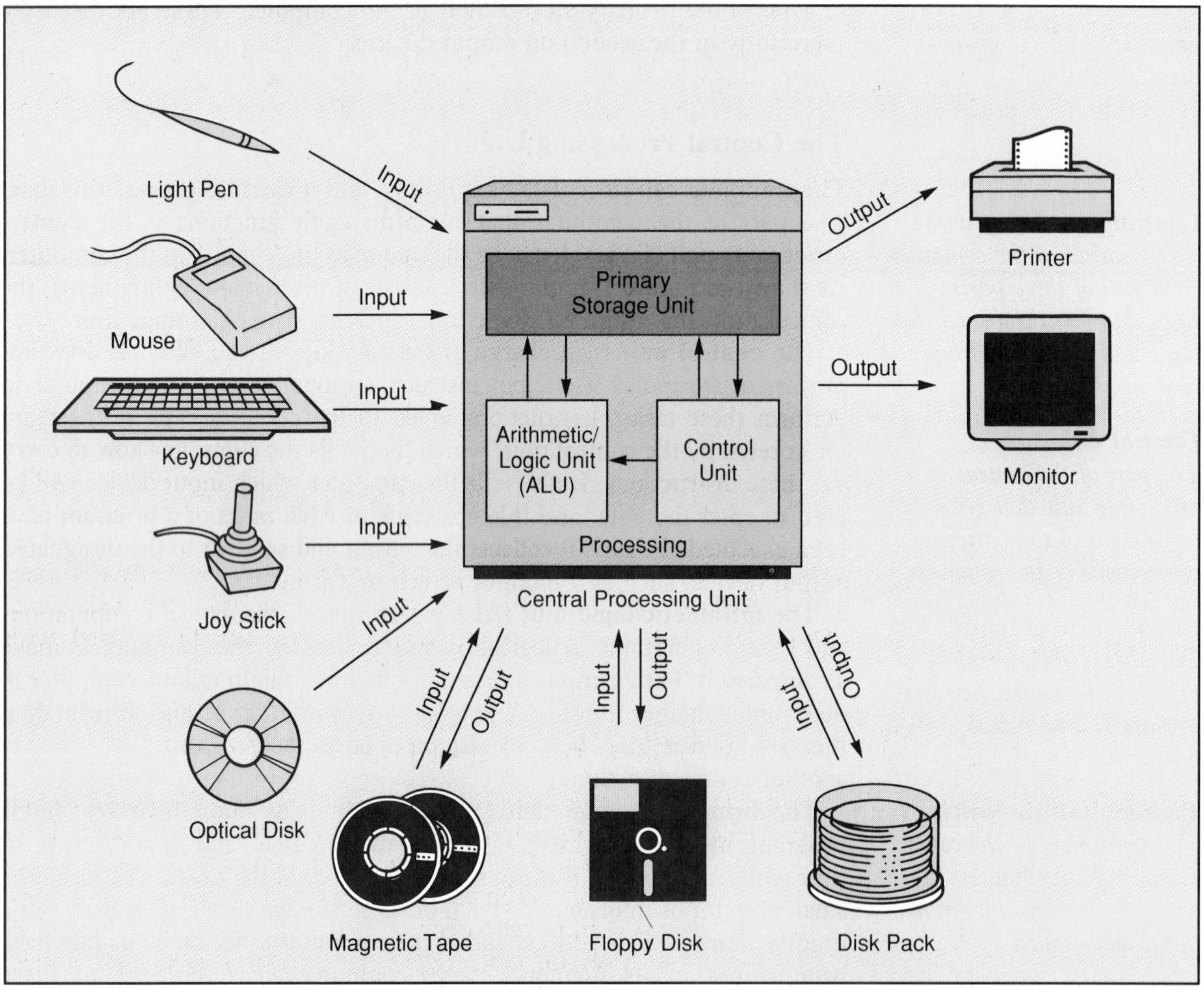

Light Pen

Mouse

Keyboard

Joy Stick

Optical Disk

Input

Primary
Storage Unit

Arithmetic/
Logic Unit
(ALU)

Control
Unit

Processing

Central Processing Unit

Output

Printer

Output

Monitor

Input   Output

Magnetic Tape

Input   Output

Floppy Disk

Input   Output

Disk Pack

Secondary storage
Storage that is supplementary
to the primary storage unit.
It can be easily expanded.
The secondary storage most
commonly used with
microcomputers is floppy or
hard disks.

The primary storage unit has only a limited amount of storage space because this type of memory is relatively expensive and is not easily expanded. Devices such as disk and tape drives are used to transfer data, results, and programs from the primary storage unit to **secondary** (or **auxiliary**) **storage** media such as floppy disks, hard disks, and magnetic tape. When the computer needs to process these items again, they can be copied to the computer's primary storage unit. Although it takes more time to access items in secondary storage than those in main memory, secondary storage can store enormous quantities of data at a reasonable cost. Expanding secondary storage is as easy as going to the store and buying a new disk.

Floppy disks are the most widely used type of storage for microcomputers and come in three sizes: 3½, 5¼, and 8 inches. Hard disks are also

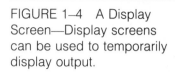

FIGURE 1–4 A Display Screen—Display screens can be used to temporarily display output.

widely used because they can store enormous quantities of data. Unlike floppy disks, most types of hard disks are always left in the disk drive. Figure 1–5 shows the different types of disks commonly used with microcomputers.

Classification of Computer Systems

Computers come in a wide variety of sizes and shapes, ranging from tiny hand-held devices to some that are several feet in height and diameter. Over the years, computers have become smaller and smaller while also becoming increasingly powerful. They can be divided into four categories: supercomputers, mainframes, minicomputers, and microcomputers. These four types differ in price, amount of memory, speed, and processing capabilities.

Supercomputer
The largest, fastest type of computer currently available.

Mainframe
A large computer commonly used in business and industry.

Minicomputer
A computer with many of the capabilities of a mainframe, but generally having a smaller primary storage unit and a lower price than mainframes.

The most powerful machines currently available are the **supercomputers.** They are the fastest and most expensive computers and can perform millions (and even billions) of arithmetic operations each second. The CRAY Y-MP (Figure 1–6), developed by Cray Research, Inc., is a supercomputer system that is used mainly in the scientific areas of weather forecasting, nuclear weapons development, and energy supply and conservation.

For most business applications, the extremely high-speed processing capabilities of a supercomputer are not necessary; a **mainframe** is adequate. Many businesses use mainframes to manage large amounts of data. Figure 1–7 shows a popular mainframe.

The distinction between **minicomputers** and mainframes has gradually become blurred. The minicomputers currently being manufactured are more powerful than the mainframes manufactured just ten years ago. In

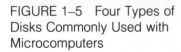

FIGURE 1–5   Four Types of
Disks Commonly Used with
Microcomputers

(a) The 5¼ and 8 inch floppy disks are inexpensive and
have been used for many years.

(b) The 3½ inch floppy disks are protected by
a hard plastic cover.

(c) Hard disks remain inside the hard disk drive. This
photograph of a drive with its cover removed shows the
circular disk inside.

FIGURE 1–6   A
Supercomputer
Configuration

general, minicomputers (Figure 1–8) are lower-priced, have smaller memories, and process data more slowly than mainframes. They are also generally easier to install. Minicomputers are often used in businesses that do not require the capabilities of a mainframe.

Microcomputer
The smallest and least expensive type of computer currently available.

The **microcomputer** is currently the smallest and least costly type of computer. This is the type often found in small businesses and in homes and classrooms. Its primary storage unit is usually smaller than that of the other types of computers. Microcomputers are generally less complex and execute programs at slower speeds than minicomputers. Because of the microcom-

FIGURE 1–7   A Commonly
Used Mainframe

FIGURE 1–8 A
Minicomputer System

puter's low cost and increasing capabilities, and the large number of available *software packages* (commercially written programs that perform specific tasks, such as word processing), its popularity has risen tremendously in the last ten years. Figure 1–9 shows several popular microcomputers.

Now Try This

1. A(n) _____ is a list of instructions that work together to solve a problem.

2. A computer system consists of three main components: _____, _____, and _____ .

3. _____ is facts that have not been organized in any meaningful way.

4. Keyboards, disk drives, and light pens are all examples of _____.

5. Output that is printed on paper is _____.

6. The most powerful computers available today are called _____.

7. _____ are popular because they are relatively inexpensive, small, and easy to use, and can run a wide variety of software.

FIGURE 1–9 Several
Popular Microcomputers

(a) IBM Personal System/2

(b) Macintosh IIcx

(c) Epson Equity Ie

Caring for Your System

Taking good care of your computer will help keep it working properly. Make certain you read any instructions that came with your system on caring for it.

The computer should be set on a sturdy desk or table. The room should be clean and dry. However, if the room is too dry, static electricity may be created that can scramble the data stored on disks. The risk of large amounts of static electricity are greatest when the computer room is carpeted. Therefore, it is best if the floor of the computer room is tile, wood, or some other hard, smooth surface.

Extreme heat and cold can also harm the computer. Keep it away from direct sunlight. Never set any part of the computer system on appliances that get hot, such as televisions, and keep them away from heating ducts and air conditioners.

Eating or drinking around the computer should not be allowed. Crumbs and spilled drinks can make the keyboard keys stick or jam. Dust and dirt from the air can also harm the keyboard or cause static. It is a good idea to keep the computer system covered when it is not being used.

When the computer is on, be careful not to move or jar it. This includes the desk or table on which it is placed. Any movement while the disk drives are being used can be extremely harmful. Make certain that the electrical cord cannot accidently be unplugged. If the cord is unplugged for even a second, the data in the computer's main memory will probably be lost.

Your computer will be only as reliable as the storage media used to store data. The most common type of storage media for microcomputers is floppy disks. Be careful when handling these disks. Never touch the surface of the disk that is exposed through the oval cutout on 5¼ inch floppy disks. When inserting disks, place your thumb on the label and carefully insert the disk into the slot in the front of the drive. Disks can be ruined by extreme temperatures and dirt or even dust. Never leave disks in a car for any length of time, since they may be exposed to extreme heat or cold. Remember that the sun's rays are intensified by the car's windshield. Do not bend or twist the disks. Disks should never be exposed to magnets because the contents will be erased (if you use cassette tapes for music, you may be aware that the "bulk erasers" used to quickly erase cassettes are simply electromagnets).

When making a label for your disk, fill it out before placing it on the disk. The pressure applied when writing on a disk can destroy it. If you must write on a label that is already on a disk, use a felt-tip pen and don't press down.

Being a careful user of your classroom computer system can go a long way to keeping the equipment in good working order. Everyone's schedule is disrupted if the computer system is not working properly.

Getting Started

As previously mentioned, disk drives allow programs and other data to be saved. Your computer system may have one or two floppy disk drives, or a hard disk drive and one floppy disk drive, or any number of different combinations. In addition, the disk drives may use either 5¼ or 3½ inch disks. On systems with two floppy drives, the drives are commonly referred to as drive A and drive B. If the drives are positioned side by side, the left drive is usually drive A; if one drive is above the other one, the top drive is usually the A drive. If the system has one floppy drive and one hard drive, the floppy drive is usually the A drive and the hard drive is usually the C drive. The instructions given here are for a system using two floppy disk drives.

Before starting your computer, carefully insert the *disk operating system* (commonly referred to as *DOS*) disk into drive A and close the drive door. Figure 1–10 presents the steps in inserting a floppy disk. The DOS disk contains programs that the computer will need in order to access the disk drives and run efficiently. Turn on both the power and the monitor switches. The computer whirs for a few seconds and then prompts you for the date and time. Type in the date, press <Enter>, and then type in the time and press <Enter>. Follow the format for the date and time shown on the screen. Note that the time is entered using a 24-hour clock. For example, the following would be entered for 12:30 p.m., March 23, 1990:

```
Current date is Tue  1-01-1980
Enter new date (mm-dd-yy): 3-23-90
Current time is  0:00:48.33
Enter new time: 12:30
```

FIGURE 1–10   Inserting a Floppy Disk

a. Open the door of the drive (the type of latch may vary depending on the computer).

b. Place your thumb on the disk label and remove the disk from its envelope.

c. Carefully slide the disk into the drive opening and close the door.

The computer responds with a display similar to the following:

```
Microsoft(R) MS-DOS(R)  Version 3.30
              (C)Copyright Microsoft Corp 1981-1987
A> ■
```

The symbol at the bottom of the screen (A>) is called the *system prompt*. It indicates that the computer is waiting for your instructions. The rectangle of light after the prompt is called the *cursor* and indicates where the characters you enter will appear. The letter A in the prompt means that drive A is currently being accessed; if you want the computer to read a disk, you must place it in drive A.

DOS Commands

When you are at the system prompt, you can enter commands that allow you to control the disk operating system (or DOS) of the computer. Therefore, these commands are called *DOS commands*. They can be entered using either upper- or lower-case letters. We will discuss some commonly used DOS commands here. Additional ones are introduced throughout the book.

Formatting a Disk   Before you can use a new disk, it must be formatted. The FORMAT command prepares it to store files and, in addition, checks it for defects. If any information was previously stored on the disk, the FORMAT command erases it. If the DOS disk is in the A drive, you can format a disk in drive B by typing the following statement:

```
A>FORMAT B: <Enter>
```

The computer responds with a message similar to the following:

```
Insert new diskette for drive B:
and strike ENTER when ready
```

A whirring noise begins, indicating the disk is being formatted. When the whirring stops, a message resembling the following appears:

```
Formatting...Format complete

   362496 bytes total disk space
   362496 bytes available on disk

Format another (Y/N)?
```

Copying a Disk   Copying files from one disk to another is simple. If you wish to copy an entire disk, place the disk to be copied (the *source disk*) into drive A and the new disk (the *target disk*) into drive B, and enter the following command:

```
A>DISKCOPY A: B: <Enter>
```

Follow the instructions on the screen. After the computer is finished copying, the following message appears:

```
Copy another diskette (Y/N)?
```

If you wish to copy more disks, enter Y; otherwise, enter N. Be careful when using the DISKCOPY command, since any files originally on the target disk will be lost when the source disk is copied to it.

Copying a File   The COPY command allows individual files to be copied from one disk to another. The general format is

```
A>COPY A:file-name B:file-name
```

For example, to copy a file named PROG1.BAS from the disk in drive A to the disk in drive B, type in

```
A>COPY A:PROG1.BAS B:PROG1.BAS <Enter>
```

If the file name of the copy is not specified, it will be given the same name as the original file. Therefore, the following command has the same result as the previous one.

```
A>COPY A:PROG1.BAS B: <Enter>
```

Listing the Files on a Disk   The directory (DIR) command is used to list the names of all of the files on your disk. Enter

```
A>DIR <Enter>
```

A list will be displayed of the names of the files stored on the disk in drive A. If you wish to list the names of the files on the disk in drive B, first change the drive being accessed—

```
A>B:
```

—and then type DIR. The files on the disk in drive B will be displayed.

Erasing a File   The DEL (short for DELete) command removes any unwanted files from your disk. Type in

```
A>DEL PRACTICE.BAS <Enter>
```

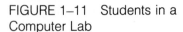

FIGURE 1–11   Students in a Computer Lab

to erase a file named PRACTICE.BAS. Be careful not to delete any files you may want to use later. However, it is a good idea to delete files you no longer need to keep your disk from becoming cluttered.

Now Try This

1. If the system prompt appears as follows:

```
B>
```

what command would you enter to change the drive currently being accessed to drive A?

2. Write a command that copies the entire contents of the disk in drive A to the disk in drive B.

3. Write a command that copies a file named B21.B on the disk in drive A to the disk in drive B.

4. What command will display a list of the files on a disk?

Starting BASIC

To enter the BASIC system, place the BASIC disk in drive A and type in

```
A>BASICA <Enter>
```

(Note: If you are using an IBM-compatible computer, this command might be BASIC or GWBASIC). The BASIC system prompt then appears:

```
Ok
```

You are ready to enter a BASIC program.

You can exit BASIC and return to the DOS prompt at any time with the following BASIC command:

```
SYSTEM <Enter>
```

BASIC Commands

In order to enter, save, execute, or print a program, you must interact with the computer's operating system. BASIC commands are used for this purpose. BASIC commands are entered at the BASIC prompt "Ok" whereas system commands are entered at the system prompt ("A>", if drive A is currently being accessed).

Direct command

A command executed as soon as <Enter> is pressed.

BASIC commands are usually entered in **direct** (or **command**) **mode.** Direct-mode commands are executed as soon as <Enter> is pressed. Some commonly used BASIC commands are discussed here.

Entering a New Program   Before a new program is entered into the computer, a portion of the computer's main memory must be prepared to store it. The NEW command clears a small portion of main memory by telling the computer to erase any program currently in memory and prepare for a new program to be entered. Enter the NEW command as follows:

```
NEW <Enter>
```

A new program can now be typed in. The keyboard has all of the keys on a regular typewriter, plus some additional ones. Table 1-1 shows some of the specialized keys and their purposes. The shift key is marked with the symbol ⇧. While holding it down, you can enter the upper symbol on any key that has two symbols. It also produces uppercase letters when used with the letters A through Z. When the <Caps Lock> key is on, uppercase letters will be produced without the shift key.

When typing in a program, press <Enter> to advance to the beginning of the next line. If you make a mistake, and wish to backspace, the backspace key (←) moves the cursor backwards, a space at a time, deleting the characters as it moves. If you wish to delete the character at the current cursor position, use the <Del> key. The four directional cursor arrows can be used to move the cursor to the location of an error, where it can then be corrected. If you wish to insert one or more characters between two existing characters, press <Ins> and then type the new characters. If <Ins> is not pressed, the new characters will overwrite the old ones. After you correct a

TABLE 1–1   Specialized Keys and Their Functions

Key	Function
< ↵ >	Carriage return key; usually must be pressed to enter information into the computer.
< ← >	Backspace key (located above the carriage return key); moves the cursor one position left and erases that character.
<PrtSc>	Print screen key; when pressed along with the shift key, causes whatever appears on the screen to be printed on the printer.
<Home>	Moves the cursor to the upper left corner of the screen.
< ↑ >	Moves the cursor up one line.
< ↓ >	Moves the cursor down one line.
< ← >	Moves the cursor one character to the left, but does not erase (located on the 4 key on the numeric keyboard).
< → >	Moves the cursor one position to the right.
<End>	Moves the cursor to the end of the line.
<Ins>	Allows characters to be inserted in the statement at the current cursor position. Press it again to return to normal operation mode.
<Del>	Deletes the character at the current cursor position.
<Esc>	Causes the entire line to be erased from the screen; the line is not passed to BASIC for processing.
⟨↹⟩	Tab; moves the cursor to the next tab stop. (Tab stops occur every eight characters.)

statement, be sure to press <Enter> so that the corrected statement will be entered into the computer.

Execute
To carry out the instructions in a program.

Executing a Program   When the computer carries out the instructions in a program, it is said to be running, or **executing,** the program. To execute a program currently in the computer's main memory type in

```
RUN <Enter>
```

Listing a Program   To display the program currently in main memory, use the LIST command:

```
LIST <Enter>
```

The program will appear. If a printer is attached to your computer, the following command prints the program:

```
LLIST <Enter>
```

There are many different options that can be used with the LIST command. They will be discussed in detail in Chapter 3 when you begin programming.

Saving a Program If you do not want to lose your program when the computer is turned off or when you type in another program, you must use the SAVE command to copy it to secondary storage, because the computer's main memory is used only for temporary storage. You must assign the program a file name when you save it. For example,

```
SAVE "PROGRAM1.BAS" <Enter>
```

will save the program under the file name PROGRAM1.BAS. Notice that the file name is in quotation marks. However, because the closing quotation mark is optional, the following command will also work:

```
SAVE "PROGRAM1.BAS <Enter>
```

The part of the name after the period (BAS) is the extension. This part of the name is used to identify the type of program. In this example, the extension BAS is used to identify the program as a BASIC program. You do not have to include the extension when saving a program; the computer will assign it automatically. The statement

```
SAVE "PROGRAM1" <Enter>
```

also saves this file under the name PROGRAM1.BAS.

There are certain rules that must be followed when naming a file. The name may have one to eight characters, and the extension may have from one to three characters. It is a good idea to assign file names that have some meaning to you. This will make it easier to keep track of your programs. The following are examples of valid file names:

```
BOWL4$
#PROG1.B
CHAOS
```

You may wish to save the program on the disk in drive B rather than drive A. To do this, you must specify the drive to be accessed:

```
SAVE "B:PROGRAM1.BAS" <Enter>
```

If you wish to make certain the program has been saved, type in

```
FILES "B:" <Enter>
```

The names of the files stored on the disk in drive B will appear. PROGRAM1.BAS should be one of them. The FILES command performs the same function as the DIR command except it is used in BASIC rather than at the DOS prompt.

Loading a Program At times you will want to transfer a program from secondary storage into the computer's main memory. This is necessary if you wish to edit a program. The following statement loads PROGRAM1.BAS into main memory, erasing any previous program:

```
LOAD "PROGRAM1.BAS" <Enter>
```

The "Ok" prompt appears, indicating the program is loaded. If this program is on the disk in drive B, the following command will load it:

```
LOAD "B:PROGRAM1.BAS" <Enter>
```

As with the SAVE command, the closing quotation mark is optional. The LIST command will display the program on the screen.

Erasing a File Use the KILL command to remove any unwanted BASIC files. The following command erases PROGRAM1.BAS:

```
KILL "PROGRAM1.BAS" <Enter>
```

The KILL command is similar to the DEL command except KILL is used in BASIC and DEL is used at the DOS prompt.

A Practice Program

In this section, you will practice formatting a disk, entering a BASIC program, running it, and so forth. You will need one new disk, a DOS disk, and a disk containing BASIC.

Start by placing the DOS disk in drive A and turning on both the computer and the monitor. Enter today's date and time, following the instructions given on the screen. When the system prompt appears (A>), type in

```
A>FORMAT B: <Enter>
```

Follow the instructions on the screen to format your new disk. After the formatting is completed, enter "N" to indicate there are no more disks to be formatted.

The next step is to enter BASIC. Insert the BASIC disk in drive A and enter the command to start BASIC (as previously mentioned, the exact command may vary).

```
A>BASICA <Enter>
```

The BASIC prompt appears:

```
Ok
```

Enter the NEW command to prepare the computer to accept a new program:

```
NEW <Enter>
```

Type in the following short program, pressing <Enter> at the end of each line (be very careful to enter each statement as it appears below):

```
10 INPUT "ENTER YOUR NAME AND PRESS <ENTER>";NME$
20 PRINT "WELCOME TO BASIC, ";NME$;"."
99 END
```

If you make any typing mistakes, use the cursor movement arrows to move to the location of the mistake. The <←> or <Del> keys can delete any unwanted characters. To insert a new character, position the cursor where the character should be, press < Ins>, and then type whatever needs to be inserted.

After the program is entered, type

```
RUN <Enter>
```

The program is executed, and the following appears:

```
ENTER YOUR NAME AND PRESS <ENTER>?
```

If you type in MATT, the following will appear:

```
WELCOME TO BASIC, MATT.
```

To save the program on your new disk, enter

```
SAVE "B:PROG1.BAS" <Enter>
```

The program is now saved on the disk in drive B so that you can use it again later. Now, return to the DOS prompt:

```
SYSTEM <Enter>
```

To see that your program is actually on the disk in drive B, type

```
A>DIR B: <Enter>
```

The file name PROG1.BAS will appear. Return to BASIC—

```
A>BASICA <Enter>
```

—and load the program from the disk into the computer's main memory (remember, it was lost from main memory when BASIC was exited):

```
LOAD "B:PROG1.BAS" <Enter>
```

The program will not be displayed until you enter the LIST command:

```
LIST <Enter>
```

If you wish, you can execute the program again. If your computer is attached to a printer and the printer is turned on, the following command will output your program to it:

```
LLIST <Enter>
```

Practice using the commands discussed here until you feel comfortable with them.

Now Try This

1. If you are at the BASIC prompt, what command will return you to the DOS prompt?

2. What command prepares the computer to have a new program entered into its main memory?

3. Write a command that will save a program named P21.BAS to a disk in drive B.

4. Write a command that displays the program currently in main memory on the screen. Write a command that outputs this program to the printer.

Programming Hints

■ DOS commands are entered at the system prompt (for example, A>), whereas BASIC commands are entered at the BASIC prompt (Ok).

■ New disks must be formatted before they can be used. It is also possible to format old disks so that they can be reused. However, any previous contents of the disk will be lost.

■ When the DISKCOPY command is used, the previous contents of the target disk are lost. Make certain that there are no files on the target disk that you want to keep.

■ Remember that the NEW command will erase any program currently in the computer's main memory. In addition, when you load a program into

New Statement Review

Statement Format	Explanation
DOS Commands	
FORMAT	Prepares a disk to have files stored on it.
DISKCOPY	Copies the contents of a source disk to a target disk. If the target disk has not been previously formatted, DISKCOPY will also format it.
COPY	Copies a file.
DIR	Lists the names of all the files on a disk.
DEL file-name	Deletes the specified file from the disk.
BASIC Commands	
BASICA	Starts BASIC.
SYSTEM	Returns to DOS from BASIC.
NEW	Prepares the computer to have a new program entered into its main memory.
RUN	Executes the program currently in main memory.
LIST	Displays a program currently in main memory on the monitor screen.
LLIST	Outputs the program currently in main memory to a printer.
SAVE "file-name"	Saves the program currently in main memory on a disk. It is saved under the file name listed in the command.
LOAD "file-name"	Loads the specified file from a disk into the computer's main memory.
FILES	Lists the names of all files on the disk currently being accessed.
KILL "file-name"	Erases the specified file from the disk.

the computer's main memory, any programs previously in memory are lost. If you wish to save the old program, use the SAVE command to copy it to disk before entering NEW or LOAD.

■ When using the SAVE and LOAD commands, the file name must be preceded by a quotation mark.

Summary Points

■ A computer is an electronic machine that can process data with great speed and accuracy.

■ A program is a series of instructions that a computer uses to solve a problem. It must be written in a programming language.

■ Tasks performed by computers can be divided into three categories: arithmetic operations, comparison operations, and storage and retrieval operations.

■ All computer systems have the same basic components: input devices, a central processing unit, and output devices.

■ Common input devices are keyboards, disk drives, and tape drives.

■ The central processing unit consists of the control unit, the arithmetic/logic unit, and the primary storage unit.

■ Common output devices are monitor screens, disk and tape drives, and printers.

■ Computers are classified as supercomputers, mainframes, minicomputers, or microcomputers.

■ DOS commands are executed at the system prompt and allow disks to be formatted, copied, and so forth.

■ BASIC commands are executed at the BASIC prompt ("Ok"). They allow the programmer to manipulate BASIC programs.

■ The NEW command prepares main memory to have a new program entered. A program can then be typed at the keyboard.

■ The RUN command executes a program, and LIST displays the program on the screen. LLIST outputs the program to a printer.

■ Programs can be copied onto a disk by using the SAVE command. LOAD copies a program on disk back into the computer's main memory.

Vocabulary List

Arithmetic/logic unit	Information
Auxiliary storage	Input
Central processing unit (CPU)	Mainframe
Command mode	Main memory
Computer	Microcomputer
Control unit	Minicomputer
Cursor	Primary storage unit
Data	Program
Direct mode	Programming language
Executing	Secondary storage
Hard copy	Soft copy
Hardware	Supercomputer

Questions

Whenever appropriate, use complete sentences in answering the following questions.

1. How is the computer hardware related to the computer software?

2. Into what three categories can all functions performed by a computer be divided?

3. Into which of the three categories of computer functions would each of the following be placed?

    a. Finding the square of a number.

    b. Storing a program so that it can be run at a later time.

    c. Determining which of two letters comes first alphabetically.

    d. Calculating a paycheck by multiplying the hours worked by the hourly rate of pay.

4. What is the purpose of the central processing unit?

5. List the three parts of the central processing unit, and tell what each does.

6. List the four categories of computers, from the largest to the smallest. What kind of computer are you using for this class?

7. What is the FORMAT command used for?

8. Explain the difference between the DISKCOPY and the COPY commands.

9. What is a BASIC command? In what mode are BASIC commands usually executed?

10. Explain how to save a program on disk.

11. Explain how to copy a program from disk into the computer's main memory.

12. What happens when the RUN command is executed?

13. Write a statement that will load a program named EX3.BAS into the computer's main memory.

14. What is the difference between the DIR command and the FILES command?

15. Explain how to erase a file from a disk when you are at the DOS prompt. Explain how to do it in BASIC.

CHAPTER

2

Introduction to Structured Programming and Problem Solving

Learning Objectives

After studying this chapter, you should be able to
1. Describe the three levels of programming languages.
2. Discuss why structured programming was first developed.
3. Explain why structured programs are divided into modules.
4. Give a brief history of BASIC.
5. List the five steps used in problem solving.
6. Determine the needed input and output for simple programming problems.
7. Define algorithm and develop algorithms for problem solutions.
8. List the three basic logic structures.
9. Draw structure charts for simple programming problem solutions.
10. Define top-down design and give three advantages of using top-down design.
11. Define flowchart and pseudocode.
12. List and explain the purpose of the five flowcharting symbols discussed in this chapter.
13. Explain how the three basic logic structures are represented in flowcharts.
14. Create flowcharts and pseudocode for simple programming problems.

Introduction

Software
A program or a series of programs.

The first part of Chapter 1 focused on computer hardware, which consists of the physical components of the system. This chapter focuses on **software,** the programs that the hardware executes. Without software, the hardware is unusable. The software allows the user to tell the computer what tasks to perform. In this chapter, you will learn about the history of software development and a method of problem solving that encourages the writing of well-designed software.

Programming Languages

In order for the computer to be able to carry out instructions, they must be written in a programming language. This section will present a brief overview of programming languages and how they have changed since the early days of computing. There are three broad categories: machine languages, assembly languages, and high-level languages.

Machine Language

Machine language
The only instructions that the computer is able to execute directly; consists of combinations of zeros and ones that represent high and low electrical states.

Machine language is the only language that the computer can directly execute. Programs written in any other type of language must be translated into machine language by the computer before they can be executed. Machine-language statements consist of series of ones and zeros representing "high" and "low" electrical states. A programmer can specify a "high" state with a one (1) and a "low" state with a zero (0). Every operation that the computer is capable of performing (such as addition or storing a value in a given memory location) is indicated by a specific binary code (a sequence of ones and zeros). The programmer must use the proper code for each operation. In addition, memory locations must be accessed by listing their storage address in binary code.

Because these ones and zeros have no intrinsic meaning to humans, writing machine language instructions is very difficult. The programmer must carefully keep track of which values have been stored in which storage locations. It is easy to accidentally reference a wrong location or to store a new value in a location that has already been used for something else, thereby losing the previous contents.

Examples of machine-language statements are shown in Figure 2–1. The equivalent BASIC statement is shown at the top of the figure. These statements perform the task of adding the contents of one storage location to the contents of another. The resulting sum is then stored in a third location.

Because machine language is different for each kind of computer, it is necessary for the programmer to be familiar with the particular computer that will execute the program. Although such programs are tedious to write, they allow the programmer to fully use the computer's potential, because he or she is interacting directly with the computer hardware.

When computers were first developed, machine language was the only way to program them. Programmers quickly realized that this method often led to errors and was extremely time-consuming. The next step was to develop assembly languages.

Assembly Language

Assembly language

A programming language that uses symbolic names instead of the ones and zeros of machine language. It's between machine language and high-level languages.

Assembly languages were developed to make programming easier. Symbolic names (rather than ones and zeros) are used to specify various machine operations. For example, the word ADD might be used to instruct the computer to add the contents of two storage locations. Names are also used to represent storage locations; the programmer does not need to know the address of the storage location in which a particular value is kept.

▬▬▬

FIGURE 2–1   A BASIC Statement and Its Machine-Language Equivalent

HIGH-LEVEL LANGUAGE (BASIC)					
LET C = A + B					
MACHINE LANGUAGE (MOS-TECH 6502 MACHINE LANGUAGE)					
1010	0000	0000	0000	0000	1101
1010	1101	0000	1110	0000	1101
0111	1001	0110	0000	0000	1100
1101	1000				
1000	1101	0011	1111	0000	1100

In general, assembly-language instructions have a one-to-one correspondence with machine-language instructions. The assembly-language instructions to add two numbers might look like this:

```
LOAD  A
ADD   B
STORE C
```

These instructions tell the computer to add the value stored in location B to the value stored in location A and place the sum in location C.

As with machine languages, assembly languages are different for each kind of computer. Although assembly language is easier for people to understand than machine language, it usually does not use computer time as efficiently, because the statements must be translated into machine language before execution. As with machine language, though, assembly-language programs can use the computer hardware efficiently.

High-Level Languages

High-level language
A programming language that uses English-like statements that must be translated into machine language before execution.

Although it is simpler to write a program in assembly language than in machine language, considerable knowledge of the internal operations of the computer is still required. To simplify programming further, other languages have been developed that more closely resemble "natural languages" such as English. These languages do not require that the programmer understand the technical details of the hardware. Because they are oriented toward the programmer rather than the computer, they are termed **high-level languages.** Even a person who does not know a particular high-level language can often determine the general purpose of the program statements. Consider the following BASIC statement:

```
120 LET C = A + B
```

Even a nonprogrammer would have little difficulty in understanding that this statement adds the value of A to B and stores the result in C. It is important to remember, however, that programs written in high-level languages must be translated into machine language before they can be executed. A single high-level language statement may translate into many machine-language statements.

Some of the more popular high-level languages are COBOL, FORTRAN, Pascal, and BASIC.

Structured Programming

When high-level languages were first developed, programs written in them often consisted of long lists of instructions with little organization. We might compare them with a textbook that had no structure or form, no paragraphs or chapters, no introductions or summaries, no table of contents or index.

It would be a time-consuming task for the reader to locate a section dealing with a specific topic in such a book.

Early programs were often like this, making it difficult for anyone but the original programmer to understand them. If changes had to be made at a later date (as they virtually always do in business), it was difficult to locate the section of the program to be altered.

To correct these problems, computer scientists came up with a method of writing programs called **structured programming.** Structured programming encourages the development of programs with easy-to-follow logic. This is accomplished by dividing programs into *subprograms* and using only the three basic logic structures. These two techniques are discussed next. Other characteristics of structured programming will be presented throughout this textbook.

Using Modules

A structured program is divided into subprograms, referred to as **modules,** each performing a specific task. These modules can be compared to the chapters in a textbook. Each chapter deals with a specific topic and has specific goals. The chapters are combined to present a unified whole. Dividing a program into modules makes the program's logic easier to follow, just as dividing a book into chapters (and subsections within those chapters) makes the facts and ideas presented easier to understand. Programs developed in this manner tend to have fewer errors than unstructured programs because the logic is readily apparent. Dividing a program into modules is a very important concept of structured programming and is discussed in detail in Chapter 6.

The Three Basic Logic Structures

Computer scientists have determined that any programming problem can be solved by using the needed combination of three basic logic structures: the sequence, the decision structure, and the loop structure.

A **sequence** is merely a series of statements that the computer executes in the order in which they occur in the program. A program that converts feet to miles is a sequence. It determines the number of feet, divides this number by 5,280, and prints the number of miles.

When a program contains a decision structure or a loop structure, the program statements are no longer executed in the order in which they occur in the program. For example, certain statements may be skipped, or a group of statements may be repeated many times. In a **decision structure,** a comparison is made; what happens next depends on the result of this comparison. The decision structure is similar to decisions people make every day. For example, when you get up in the morning, you may decide to take one action (stay in bed) if it is a weekend and another action (get ready for school) if it is a weekday. An example of a decision that a computer

Structured programming
A method of programming in which programs have easy-to-follow logic, attempt to use only the three basic logic structures, and are divided into subprograms.

Module
A subprogram performing a specific task.

Sequence
A group of statements that are executed in the order in which they occur in the program.

Decision structure
A structure in which a condition is tested. The action taken next depends on the result of this test.

might make would be to compare two numbers named *X* and *Y*. If *X* is larger than *Y*, *X* might be printed; otherwise *Y* might be printed. Decision structures are discussed in detail in Chapter 5.

Loop structures involve performing repetitive tasks. When you do 50 pushups in physical education class, you are executing a loop structure; you are repeatedly performing the same action. Loops are very useful in computer programs for performing tasks such as reading a list of names or adding together a series of numbers. A loop structure allows a series of instructions to be executed as many times as needed. Loop structures are discussed in Chapter 7.

Loop structure
A structure that allows a series of instructions to be executed as many times as needed.

The BASIC Language

BASIC stands for *B*eginner's *A*ll-purpose *S*ymbolic *I*nstruction *C*ode. It was developed in the mid-1960s at Dartmouth College by Professors John Kemeny and Thomas Kurtz. BASIC is a high-level language that uses English-like words and statements such as LET, READ, and PRINT. It is easy to learn and is useful for writing programs that perform many different kinds of tasks. There are many different versions of BASIC. The BASIC taught in this textbook is commonly referred to as IBM PC BASIC or Microsoft GW-BASIC. IBM PC BASIC runs on the IBM family of personal computers, and Microsoft GW-BASIC runs on IBM-compatible computers.

Just like English and other languages used for communication, BASIC has rules for spelling, grammar, and punctuation. In BASIC, however, these rules are very precise and allow no exceptions. They enable the programmer to tell the computer what to do.

Interpreter
A language-translation program that translates each statement in the source program into machine language and executes it before continuing on to the next statement.

Because BASIC is a high-level language, BASIC instructions must be translated into machine language before they can be executed. The BASIC system contains a special program, called an **interpreter,** that performs this task. When the programmer instructs the computer to execute the BASIC program, the interpreter translates the program, a statement at a time, and the computer executes it a statement at a time. Figure 2–2 graphically shows this process.

The Programming Process

People who are good programmers are also good problem solvers. Writing a program is a way of using a computer to solve a problem. The last half of this chapter will examine problem-solving methods that can help you arrive at solutions in an efficient, logical manner.

People solve problems every day of their lives. Most problems have a number of possible solutions, and usually there is more than one way to arrive at an acceptable answer to a problem. For example, how many ways are there to clean a room? It is usually possible to vary the method and order in which the tasks are performed and still achieve the desired result. For

FIGURE 2–2 Translating and Executing a BASIC Program

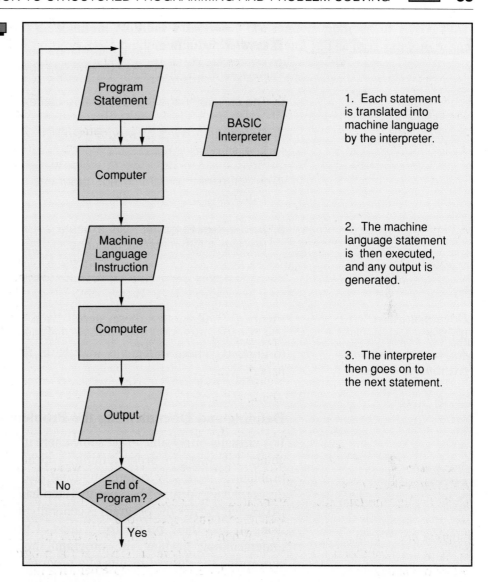

1. Each statement is translated into machine language by the interpreter.

2. The machine language statement is then executed, and any output is generated.

3. The interpreter then goes on to the next statement.

example, either window washing or furniture dusting can be done first. The floor can be cleaned by sweeping it with a broom or with a vacuum cleaner.

The same is true in designing computer programs. There may be many paths that lead to the same solution. Your job will be to find the most practical way to get there.

To use the computer effectively as a problem-solving tool, the programmer performs several steps, which together are called the **programming process:**

Programming process
The steps used to develop a solution for a programming problem.

1. Define and document the problem.
2. Design and document a solution.
3. Write and document the program.
4. Debug and test the program, revising the documentation if necessary.

Now Try This

1. _____ is the programs that are executed by the computer's _____.

2. The only language that computers can execute directly is _____.

3. Of the three levels of programming languages discussed here, the most English-like one is _____.

4. In structured programming, programs are divided into _____, each performing a specific task.

5. Before the computer can execute a BASIC program, the _____ must translate it into machine language.

Documentation
Written statements or instructions explaining programs to humans.

Figure 2–3 illustrates these steps. Each step includes **documentation,** which consists of the instructions or statements written to explain a program to humans. These statements may be in the program itself or written on paper.

Defining and Documenting the Problem

It is virtually impossible to get somewhere if you do not know where you are going. Likewise, in programming, a clear and concise statement of the problem is necessary before anything else is done. Many programming disasters have occurred because this step has been ignored. In business, the person who writes the program is generally not the same person who will be using it, and these people (or groups of people) may not have the same understanding of how the program should work. Misunderstandings concerning the desired results of a program often lead to programs that do not meet the user's needs. Therefore, before the programmer begins work, the problem must be clearly defined and documented in writing. Documentation is very important, because people often believe they understand how a task is to be performed, but when they take time to write it down, they realize that certain steps are missing. This documentation of the problem definition must be agreed upon by all parties involved. It includes a description of the program input and output:

1. What data is necessary to obtain the desired output? From where will this data be obtained? How will this data be entered? The programmer should make it as easy as possible for the user to enter the needed data.
2. All output and the manner in which it is to be formatted must be described. *Formatting* refers to the way in which the output is to be displayed or printed to make it easy for the user to read and use. For

FIGURE 2–3   The Steps in
the Programming Process

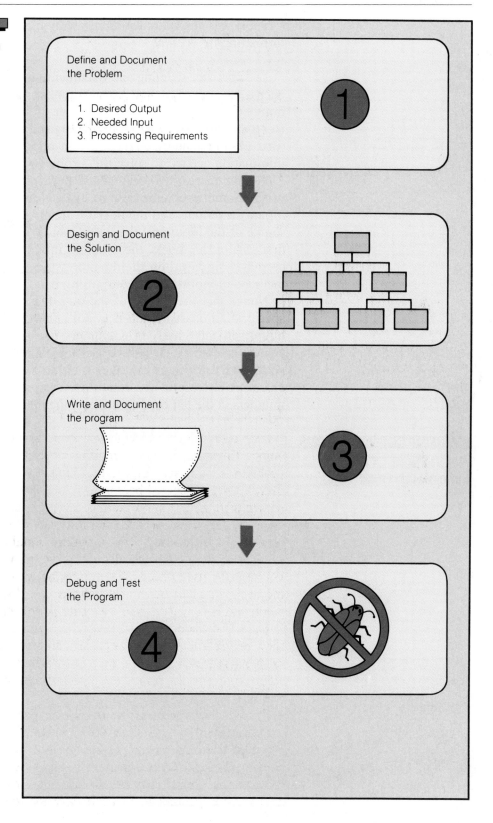

example, placing output in tables with appropriate headings is one way of formatting it.

Let's practice defining and documenting a simple problem. Suppose you need a program to convert a given number of feet to miles. The output is the number of miles in the stated number of feet. The input is the number of feet to be converted. In addition, you need to know the conversion formula (that is, how many feet there are in one mile). You now have all of the information needed to solve this problem.

Programmers often create *program specification charts* when documenting programming problems (Figure 2–4). Notice in the figure that the needed input, the output, and the purpose are stated in this chart. In addition, the source of the input and the destination of the output are specified. In the first part of this book, the program input is entered at the keyboard and output is displayed on the monitor screen. Later on, you will learn other methods of inputting and outputting data.

Notice that the format of the output is also requested on the program specification chart. When it is not convenient to show the format of the output on this chart, programmers use printer spacing charts like that shown in Figure 2–5. Notice that the chart has 80 horizontal spaces. The width of most printer carriages is either 80 or 132 spaces. Printer spacing charts are also useful in formatting output on monitor screens. The vertical numbers in the left column indicate the lines. The output of the conversion

FIGURE 2–4   A Program
Specification Chart

PROGRAM SPECIFICATION CHART		
PROGRAM NAME: FEET TO MILES	**PROGRAMMER'S NAME:** S. Baumann	**DATE:** 9/19/91
INPUT: Number of feet to be converted.	**OUTPUT:** Printer spacing chart attached.	
SOURCE OF INPUT: Keyboard	**DESTINATION OF OUTPUT:** Monitor screen	
PURPOSE: Converts a specified number of feet to miles.		

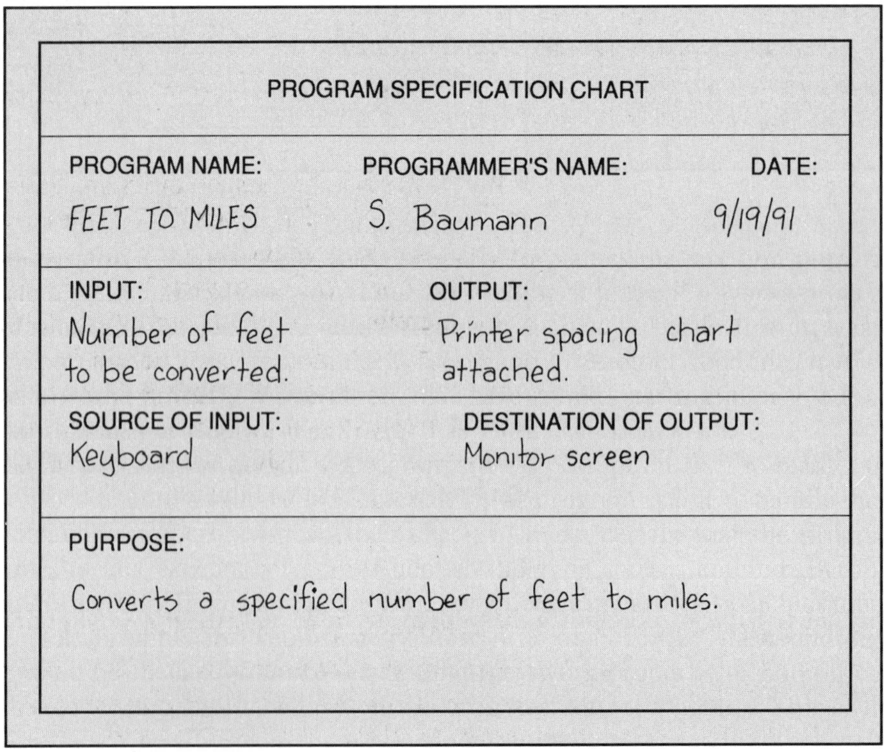

FIGURE 2–5   A Printer Spacing Chart

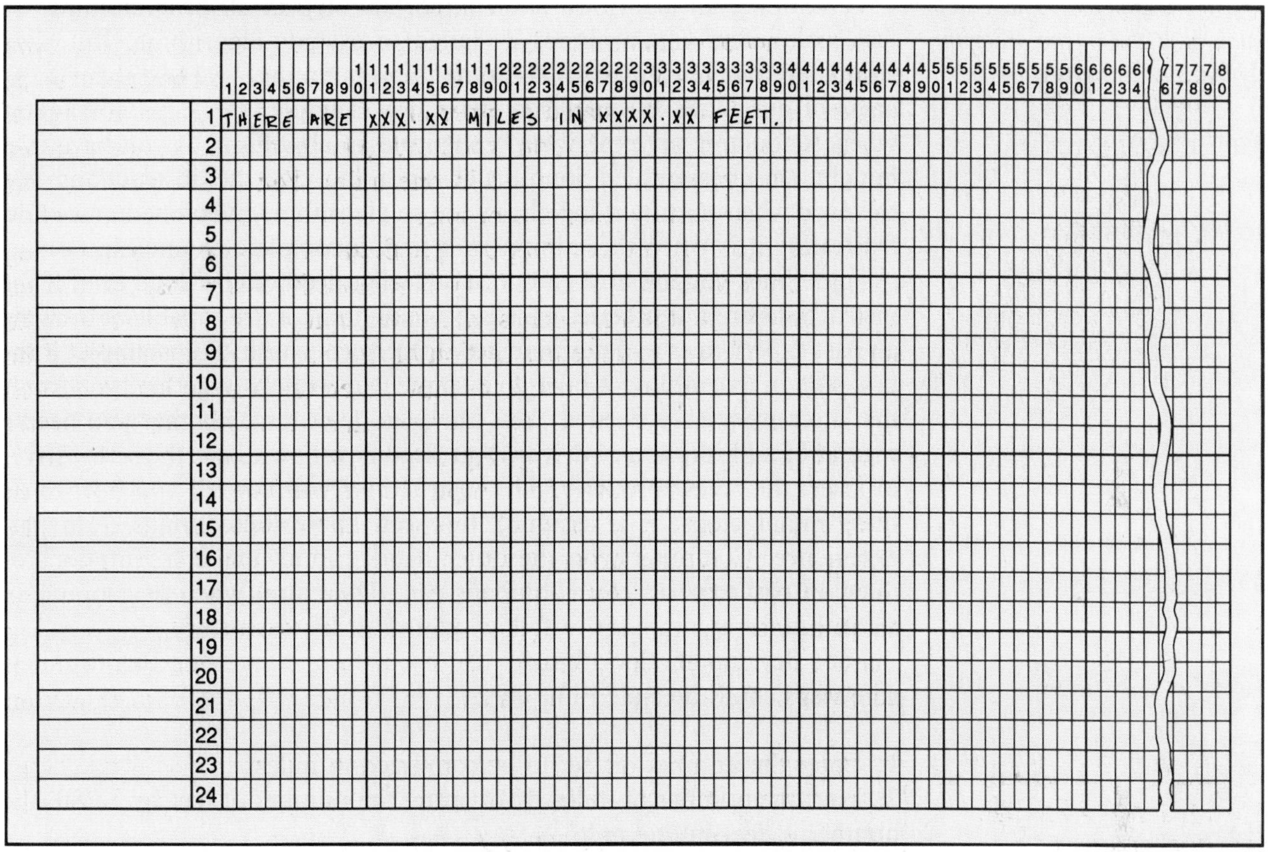

problem has been written on the chart, the number of feet and miles marked by Xs (XXXX.XX feet, XXX.XX miles), with each X representing a digit. Xs are used because the values of these numbers will vary depending on the number of feet being converted. However, the rest of the output will not vary; therefore, it is written exactly as it will appear.

This printer spacing chart should be attached to the program specification chart. Because this output is very simple, it was not necessary to fill out a printer spacing chart. However, later you will be writing programs that generate reports. Using printer spacing charts will help you in creating attractive, easy-to-read output.

Designing and Documenting a Solution

Once the programming problem is thoroughly understood and the necessary input and output has been determined, it is time to determine the steps needed to obtain the correct output from the input. A sequence of steps

Algorithm

The sequence of steps needed to solve a problem. Each step must be listed in the order in which it is to be performed.

needed to solve a problem is called an **algorithm.** In an algorithm, each step must be listed in the order in which it is to be performed.

Developing an algorithm is an important step in all programming. In fact, computers are machines designed to execute algorithms. But algorithms are not only used in computer programming—we use them in all areas of our lives. In chemistry class, for example, the steps you follow when conducting an experiment constitute an algorithm. If you have ever bought an unassembled item, such as a bicycle, the instructions you followed when putting it together were an algorithm. Everyone knows how frustrating it is when these instructions are incomplete or unclear.

Sometimes you are able to figure out what needs to be done even if the instructions are not precise. This is because humans are capable of drawing on past experiences to determine how to perform a task. For example, if the first step in assembling a bike is to screw two sections together, you know that a screwdriver is needed. You can even determine whether you need a regular or a Phillips screwdriver. You also know how to use the screwdriver to insert the screw properly. The instructions will not tell you how to do these minor steps; it is assumed that you know these things from past experience. Computers, on the other hand, cannot make assumptions or draw on past experiences as humans can. Therefore, when developing an algorithm for a computer to follow, you must list each step.

Let's develop an algorithm for the problem of converting feet to miles. The steps could be stated like this:

1. Enter the number of feet to be converted to miles.
2. Find the number of miles by dividing the number of feet by 5,280 (the number of feet in one mile).
3. Output the number of miles.

The importance of taking time to carefully design a solution cannot be overemphasized. A well-designed solution can save countless hours in writing a program and correcting errors. The following section describes some methods of arriving at a clear and efficient solution.

Now Try This

1. Any given problem has only one correct solution. True or false?

2. What is the first step in solving a problem?

3. What is the second step in solving a problem?

4. A(n) _____ is a sequence of steps needed to solve a problem.

5. The steps in an algorithm can be listed in any order. True or false?

Top-down design
A method of solving a problem that proceeds from the general to the specific. The major problems are dealt with first, and the details are left until later.

Top-Down Design   The most difficult aspect of programming is learning to organize solutions in a clear, concise way. Structured programming uses **top-down design,** which proceeds from the general to the specific, attempting to solve the major problem first and worry about the details later. This process of gradually dividing a problem into smaller and smaller subproblems often is referred to as the divide-and-conquer method, because it is easier to deal with a large job by completing it a small step at a time. Top-down design prevents the programmer from becoming overwhelmed by the size of the job.

Top-down design can be applied to tasks people perform every day. Cleaning a car is a good example. The basic steps involved in cleaning a car might be listed as follows:

1. Collect cleaning supplies.
2. Clean exterior of car.
3. Clean interior of car.
4. Put away supplies.

These steps are a basic algorithm for cleaning a car. This algorithm can be further subdivided by breaking each step into smaller substeps. For example, Step 2 (clean exterior of car) could be divided like this:

1. Wash body and tires.
2. Clean windows.
3. Clean chrome.

Even these steps could be divided further. For example, Step 1 (wash body and tires) contains many substeps. Figure 2–6 illustrates the input and output for cleaning a car. The box labeled "Processing" would contain all of the tasks necessary to complete the job.

Structure chart
A diagram that visually illustrates how a problem solution has been divided into subparts.

Figure 2–7 shows a **structure chart**, which graphically illustrates the results of the top-down design process. Each level represents a further subdividing of the tasks into smaller subtasks. Level 0 contains the general statement of the problem, and Level 1 contains the first level subtasks. In Figure 2–7, only one step in Level 1, clean exterior, has been broken down further. Of course, each of these steps could be further subdivided.

FIGURE 2–6   Input and Output for Cleaning a Car

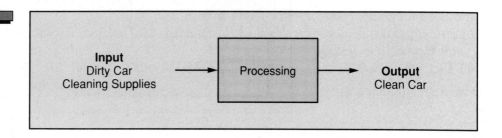

FIGURE 2–7   Structure Chart for Cleaning a Car

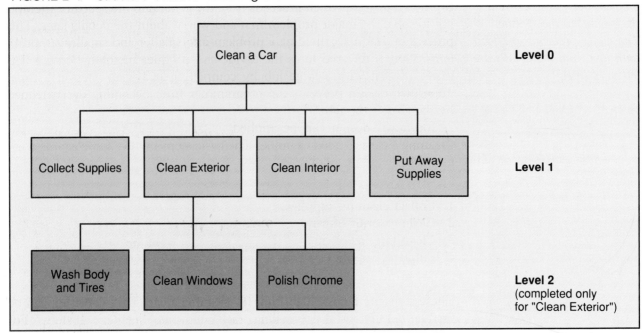

The structure chart for the problem of converting feet to miles is shown in Figure 2–8. The three subtasks are the same as the steps listed in the algorithm. Because each subtask is fairly simple, there is no need to have more than one level in the structure chart.

Flowchart
A graphic representation of the solution to a programming problem.

Flowcharts   One way of graphically representing the steps needed to solve a programming problem is by using a **flowchart.** A flowchart shows the actual flow of the logic of a program whereas a structure chart simply shows

FIGURE 2–8   Structure Chart for Converting Feet to Miles

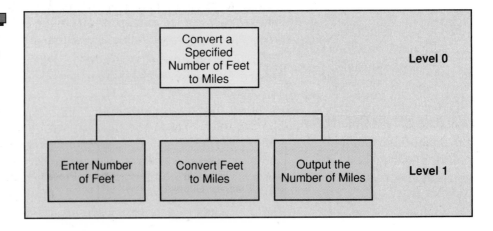

how the program can be divided into subtasks. The meanings of several flowcharting symbols are shown below:

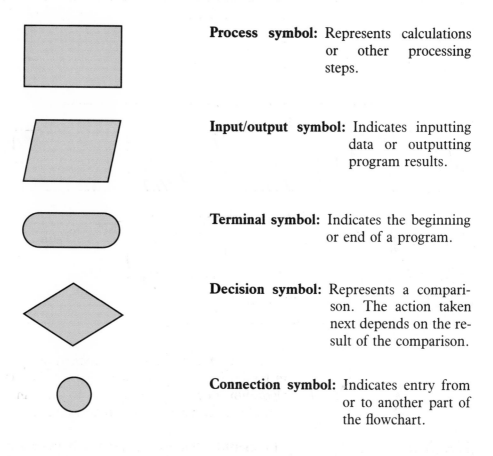

Process symbol: Represents calculations or other processing steps.

Input/output symbol: Indicates inputting data or outputting program results.

Terminal symbol: Indicates the beginning or end of a program.

Decision symbol: Represents a comparison. The action taken next depends on the result of the comparison.

Connection symbol: Indicates entry from or to another part of the flowchart.

Additional symbols will be explained throughout this textbook as they are needed.

Figure 2–9 explains how the three basic logic structures can be represented using flowchart symbols. The flowchart for the problem of converting feet to miles is shown in Figure 2–10. It begins and ends with the terminal symbol. Two input/output symbols are used: one when the number of feet is entered and another when the number of miles is printed. A processing symbol indicates the arithmetic step of dividing the feet by 5,280.

Pseudocode
An English-like description of a program's logic.

Pseudocode **Pseudocode** is an English-like description of the logic of a programming problem solution. The prefix "pseudo" means "similar to." Therefore, pseudocode is similar to the actual statements (or code) in the program. It is a type of algorithm in that all steps needed to solve the problem must be listed. However, algorithms can be written to solve all types of problems, whereas pseudocode is used specifically for program-

FIGURE 2–9   The Three
Basic Logic Structures

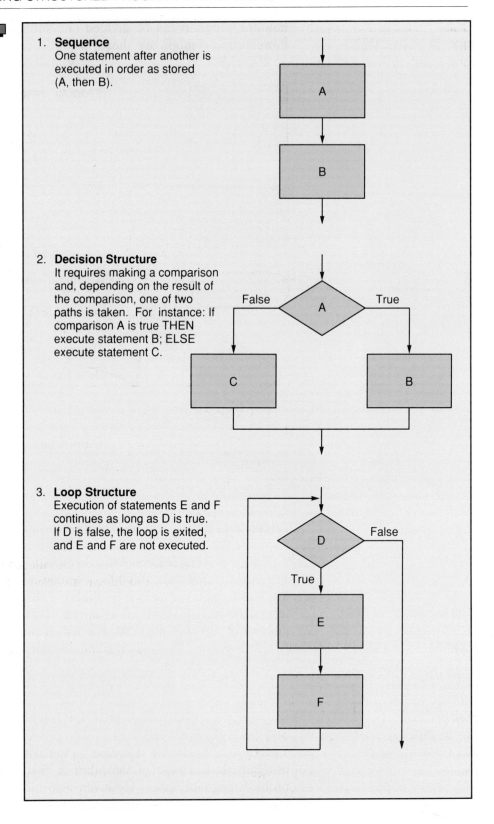

1. **Sequence**
   One statement after another is
   executed in order as stored
   (A, then B).

2. **Decision Structure**
   It requires making a comparison
   and, depending on the result of
   the comparison, one of two
   paths is taken. For instance: If
   comparison A is true THEN
   execute statement B; ELSE
   execute statement C.

3. **Loop Structure**
   Execution of statements E and F
   continues as long as D is true.
   If D is false, the loop is exited,
   and E and F are not executed.

FIGURE 2–10   Flowchart
for Converting Feet to Miles

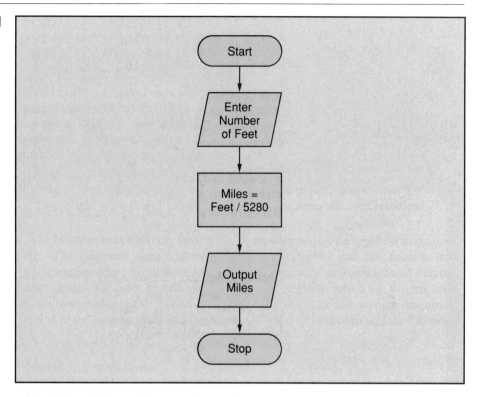

ming problems. The pseudocode for the problem to convert feet to miles
could be written as follows:

```
Begin
Enter the number of feet
Miles = feet / 5,280
Print the number of miles
End
```

There are no rigid rules for writing pseudocode. However, once you have
developed a style, you should use it consistently.

Writing and Documenting a Program

Code

*To write a problem solution
in a programming language.*

Desk check

*To trace through a program
by hand to try to locate any
errors.*

Once a solution to a programming problem has been developed and
documented with a structure chart, flowchart, and/or pseudocode, the
actual writing, or **coding,** of the solution in a programming language should
be fairly simple. Before entering it into the computer, the programmer
should spend some time **desk checking** the program, that is, making sure
each statement follows the syntax rules of the language. This book explains
the syntax of BASIC. These rules may be hard to understand at first, like
the rules of any foreign language, but they will quickly become second
nature to you. When a programmer desk checks a program, he or she also

traces through the program to determine whether the logic is correct. This simple process often locates many errors that can easily be corrected before the program is entered into the computer.

Like the original problem, the program must be thoroughly documented. This type of documentation consists of comments placed within the program to explain it to humans; the computer simply ignores these comments. Documenting a program thoroughly is especially important in business where many different programmers may have to modify, or alter, the program over a period of time.

Figure 2–11 shows the final program that converts feet into miles. Do not worry if you do not completely understand it at this point. However, notice the similarity between the final program and the pseudocode for this problem.

Debugging and Testing the Program

Structured programming techniques encourage the development of programs with easy-to-follow logic and fewer errors than unstructured pro-

FIGURE 2–11   Program to Convert Feet to Miles

```
10   REM ***            PROGRAM FEET TO MILES              ***
20   REM ***                                               ***
30   REM *** THIS PROGRAM PROMPTS THE USER TO ENTER        ***
40   REM *** A SPECIFIC NUMBER OF FEET AND THEN            ***
50   REM *** CONVERTS IT TO MILES.                         ***
60   REM
70   INPUT "ENTER NUMBER OF FEET   ";FEET
80   LET MILES = FEET / 5280
90   PRINT "THERE ARE";MILES; "MILES IN";FEET;"FEET."
99   END
```

```
RUN
ENTER NUMBER OF FEET   ? 10560
THERE ARE 2 MILES IN 10560 FEET.
```

grams. Nonetheless, programs of any significant length virtually always contain some errors, and correcting them can account for a large portion of time spent in program development.

Debug
To locate and correct program errors.

Debugging is the process of locating and correcting program errors. The most common errors made by a beginning programmer are **syntax errors,** which occur when the programmer violates the grammatical rules of the language (which are as strict as, or stricter than, those of English). Most syntax errors are caused by simple typing mistakes and could have been prevented by careful proofreading.

Syntax error
A violation of the grammar rules of a language.

Once the computer is able to run your program, you will need to test it with a variety of data to determine whether the results are always correct. A program may yield correct results with one set of data but not with another.

Logic error
A mistake in the algorithm developed to solve the problem.

How the programmer is able to determine that a program contains an error depends on the type of error that has been made. If a syntax error is made, the computer usually will not be able to execute the program, and an error message will be displayed. If the programmer makes a **logic error**, the program may stop executing prematurely, or it may execute properly but yield incorrect results. Once errors are corrected, the programmer must remember to also revise any corresponding documentation.

2-3 ▷ Now Try This

1. _____ is the process of writing a problem solution in a programming language.

2. Tracing through a program by hand, attempting to locate errors, is called _____.

3. A violation of the grammatical rules of a programming language generally results in a(n) _____error.

4. _____is the process of locating and correcting program errors.

5. The computer uses comments to tell it how to execute a program. True or false?

Summary Points

- Software consists of the programs that are executed on the computer hardware.
- The three levels of programming languages are machine languages, assembly languages, and high-level languages.

■ Machine language is the only language that the computer can execute directly. All other languages must be translated into machine language before execution. Machine language is different for each type of computer.

■ High-level languages are the most English-like, while assembly language is between machine language and high-level languages.

■ Structured programming was developed to encourage the writing of easy-to-understand, more error-free programs. A structured program is divided into modules, each performing a specific task.

■ BASIC (Beginner's All-purpose Symbolic Instruction Code) was developed in the mid-1960s by Professors John Kemeny and Thomas Kurtz. BASIC is translated into machine language by an interpreter. Each statement is translated and then executed before the interpreter continues on to the next statement.

■ There are four basic steps in the programming process:
–Define and document the problem.
–Design and document a solution.
–Write and document the program.
–Debug and test the program, revising the documentation if necessary.

■ Before a problem can be solved, it must be thoroughly understood. A clear statement of the problem is written, including the needed input and output.

■ An algorithm is developed that lists all steps necessary to solve the problem.

■ Top-down design is an efficient way of developing a problem solution. This method proceeds from the general to the specific. Thus, the programmer can concentrate on major problems first and leave the details until later.

■ Structure charts graphically represent how a problem solution has been broken down into subtasks.

■ Flowcharts graphically represent the logic flow of a solution to a programming problem.

■ Pseudocode is an English-like description of a solution to a programming problem.

■ The actual process of writing a program is called coding. Coding should be fairly simple if the programmer has already developed a clear solution. After a program is coded, it should be desk checked.

■ Debugging is the process of finding and correcting program errors. After a program is running, it must be executed with a wide variety of data to determine whether it always yields correct results.

Vocabulary List

Algorithm	Loop structures
Assembly languages	Machine language
Coding	Modules
Debugging	Programming process
Decision structure	Pseudocode
Desk checking	Sequence
Documentation	Software
Flowchart	Structure chart
High-level languages	Structured programming
Interpreter	Syntax errors
Logic error	Top-down design

Questions

Whenever appropriate, use complete sentences in answering the following questions.

1. Why is computer hardware of little use without software?

2. Give two reasons why writing programs in machine language is a difficult process. What is an advantage of using machine language?

3. Why is it difficult to use assembly language, even though it has advantages over machine language?

4. What were some early difficulties in writing programs that led to the development of structured programming?

5. Explain the steps in the translation and execution of a BASIC program.

6. Think of a task you have performed. What input was needed to complete this task? What was the output? Develop an algorithm for the task.

7. The first step in the programming process is to define and document the problem. What is meant by defining the problem?

8. What is the purpose of using a printer spacing chart?

9. Write an algorithm that will evaluate the following expression:

$$\frac{14 + 8}{2} \times \frac{3}{16}$$

10. Create an algorithm that contains all the steps necessary to access BASIC on your computer.

11. How is top-down design used in developing a programming problem solution?

12. Explain how you might write a term paper for a class using top-down design. Create a structure chart for the problem.

13. List and explain the purpose of the flowchart symbols discussed in this chapter.

14. If the programmer has properly followed the steps listed in the programming process, why should the actual coding of the program be fairly simple (assuming the programmer is familiar with the programming language being used)?

15. Why is it important to test a program by executing it with a wide variety of data?

The Fundamentals
of BASIC Programming

Learning Objectives

After studying this chapter, you should be able to
1. Explain the difference between direct and indirect mode.
2. Identify reserved words in programs.
3. Differentiate between numeric and character string constants and give examples of each.
4. Use numeric and character string constants correctly in programs.
5. Explain how variables are used to store values in the computer's main memory.
6. List the rules for naming variables.
7. Assign values to variables.
8. Perform arithmetic operations using both constants and variables.
9. Evaluate arithmetic expressions according to the hierarchy of operations.
10. Display program output on the monitor screen.

Introduction

Chapter 1 discussed several BASIC commands by which the programmer instructs the computer to perform certain functions. One command was to save a program on disk. Another was to clear a portion of the computer's main memory so that a new program could be entered. The types of commands discussed in this chapter are called BASIC statements. They are placed in the program itself to instruct the computer to perform tasks such as displaying output on the screen or performing arithmetic. The four BASIC statements covered in this chapter, REM, LET, PRINT, and END, form the foundation of program writing. Therefore, it is important that you clearly understand how to use them.

Line Numbers

Indirect mode
A mode in which statements are not executed until the RUN command is executed.

Line numbers
Integer values placed at the beginning of a statement to indicate its order of execution. In Microsoft BASIC, line numbers must be between 0 and 65529.

As previously mentioned, BASIC commands are normally executed in immediate or direct mode. These commands are executed as soon as <Enter> is pressed. BASIC statements, or instructions, may be executed in either direct mode or **indirect (or programming) mode.** In indirect mode, the statements are not executed until the RUN command is given. **Line numbers** tell the computer that the statements following them are to be executed in indirect mode. Therefore, the computer does not execute these statements until it is instructed to do so.

Line numbers also determine the sequence of execution of statements. Execution starts at the lowest line number and continues in ascending numerical order to the highest number. (Later on, you will learn ways to alter the order in which statements are executed.) Line numbers must be integers from 0 through 65529. Table 3–1 contains some examples of valid and invalid line numbers. The program in Figure 3–1 contains three statements with the line numbers 10, 20, and 99.

TABLE 3–1   Valid and Invalid Line Numbers

Valid	Invalid	(and Reason Why)
10	10.5	(No decimal points allowed)
1230	2,000	(No commas allowed)
99	9 99	(No spaces allowed)
65529	65530	(Maximum number is 65529)
100	− 100	(Negative numbers not allowed)

FIGURE 3–1   Program Demonstrating Line Numbers

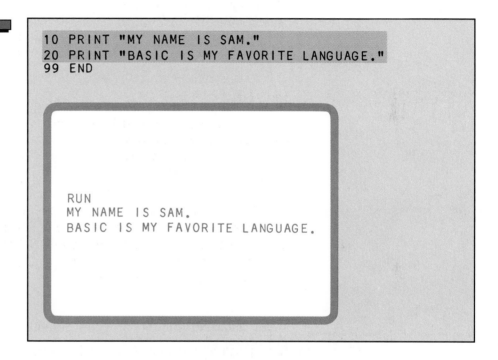

```
10 PRINT "MY NAME IS SAM."
20 PRINT "BASIC IS MY FAVORITE LANGUAGE."
99 END




RUN
MY NAME IS SAM.
BASIC IS MY FAVORITE LANGUAGE.
```

Scroll
To move vertically off the top of the monitor screen.

Line numbers are useful when using the LIST command. The typical monitor screen can display 24 lines at a time. If a program has more than 24 lines, the lines **scroll** (move vertically) off the top of the screen. For example, if your program has 80 lines, the first 56 lines will scroll off the top of the screen before you get a chance to read them. You can solve this problem in one of two ways. One is to suppress the scrolling, that is, to "freeze" the listing temporarily by pressing <Ctrl><Num Lock> (hold down the <Ctrl> key and then press <Num Lock>). Pressing any other key will resume the scrolling. The second method is to display only part of a program at a time by specifying the line numbers of the statements to be displayed. For example,

```
LIST 150-170
```

displays only lines 150 through 170 of the program currently in main memory.

Line numbers do not have to be in increments of 1. In fact, it is best to use increments of 10 or 20 so that if needed, new statements can be inserted at a later time. In addition, the statements need not be entered in ascending numerical order; the BASIC system will rearrange them in this order for execution. For example, if you type

```
10 LET NAM$ = "SAM"
20 PRINT MESS$,NAM$
```

and then realize you forgot a statement that should go between lines 10 and 20, you can simply add the needed statement like this:

```
15 LET MESS$ = "MY NAME IS"
```

If the program is listed again, it appears like this:

```
10 LET NAM$ = "SAM"
15 LET MESS$ = "MY NAME IS"
20 PRINT MESS$,NAM$
```

If the statements had been numbered in increments of 1 instead of 10, inserting a new line would have been more difficult. For this reason, programmers generally use increments of at least 10. If the following command is entered—

```
RENUM
```

—the statements in the program automatically will be renumbered in increments of 10:

```
10 LET NAM$ = "SAM"
20 LET MESS$ = "MY NAME IS"
30 PRINT MESS$,NAM$
```

If you find that you have made a typing mistake, you can retype the line number and the correct statement. This procedure corrects the error, because if two lines are entered with the same line number, the computer saves and executes the most recent one. Assume that line 160 should print SUM, but the following was typed instead:

```
160 PRINT SUN
```

One way of correcting this error is to retype the line:

```
160 PRINT SUM
```

The computer discards the old line 160 and replaces it with the new version. However, it is important to remember that the new statement is not entered into the computer until the <Enter> key is pressed. If you enter the command

```
AUTO
```

before typing in a program, a line number will be generated automatically each time you press <Enter>. The new numbers will be in increments of 10. Pressing <Ctrl><Break> stops the automatic numbering.

BASIC Statement Components

A program is a sequence of instructions that tells the computer how to solve a problem. Figure 3–2 is an example of a program that calculates the gross pay of an employee who worked 40 hours at $4.50 per hour. This program has eight statements. All BASIC statements are composed of special programming commands, called *reserved words*, that have specific meanings to the BASIC system, and of the following elements of the language: constants, variables, and operators.

Constants

Constant

A value that does not change during program execution.

Constants are values that do not change during the execution of a program. There are two kinds: numeric constants and character string constants.

FIGURE 3–2 Program Gross Pay

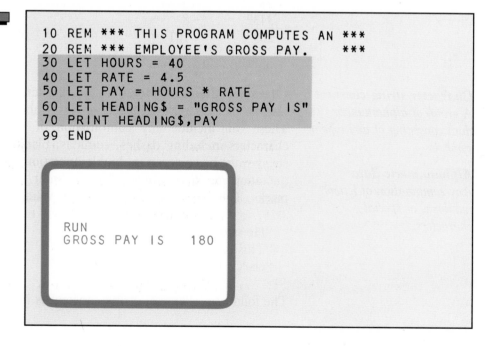

```
10 REM *** THIS PROGRAM COMPUTES AN ***
20 REM *** EMPLOYEE'S GROSS PAY.    ***
30 LET HOURS = 40
40 LET RATE = 4.5
50 LET PAY = HOURS * RATE
60 LET HEADING$ = "GROSS PAY IS"
70 PRINT HEADING$,PAY
99 END


RUN
GROSS PAY IS    180
```

Numeric constant
A number (other than the line number) contained in a statement.

Numeric Constants   A number included in a BASIC statement (other than the line number) is called a **numeric constant**. Numbers can be represented in two ways in BASIC: as *real numbers*, which include a decimal point, or as *integers*, which do not. When using numbers in BASIC, remember these rules:

1. No commas can be included in numbers. The computer interprets the digits before and after a comma as two separate numbers. For example, the computer would interpret 3,751 as the number 3 *and* the number 751. The valid form of the number is 3751.

2. If a number has no sign, the computer assumes it is positive. For example, 386 is the same as +386.

3. If a number is negative, the negative sign must precede the digits, as in −21.

4. Fractions must be written in decimal form. For example, 2.75 is the correct representation for 2¾.

A *real constant* has a decimal portion. The following are all valid real constants:

6.0	6.782
.95	0.58
−7.234	−0.09

An *integer constant* is a number with no decimal portion. The following numbers are integer constants:

29	123434
3432	−8
205	−101

Character string constant
A group of alphanumeric data consisting of any type of symbols.

Alphanumeric data
Any combination of letters, numbers, or special characters.

Character String Constants   A **character string constant** (or *string constant*, for short) is a collection of symbols called **alphanumeric data.** These can include any combination of letters, numbers, and special characters including dashes, commas, blanks, and others. The character string must be enclosed in double quotation marks. You can include single quotation marks within a string constant delimited by double quotation marks. The following are examples of valid character string constants:

"He said, 'Good morning.' "
"This is a string constant."
"Gary's tennis racket."

The following character string constant is invalid:

"The letter "A" is a vowel."

The system will recognize the double quotation mark before the letter A as indicating the end of the string. Actually, the quotation mark at the end of the line is supposed to indicate the end of the string.

The length of a string constant is determined by counting all its characters. For example, here is a character string 8 characters long:

"SATURDAY"

Now here is one 10 characters long, because it has two blank spaces at the end:

"SATURDAY "

The computer can store a blank just as it can store any other character. The maximum length of a character string is 255 characters.

Now Try This

1. _____ tell the BASIC system that the commands following them are to be executed in indirect mode.

2. The line numbers 101 and 20 are valid in BASIC. True or false?

3. Write a LIST statement that displays lines 120–300 of the program currently in main memory.

4. Which of the following are not valid numeric constants?
   a. 354–6957
   b. 1360
   c. 109,493
   d. 12.817

5. Which of the following are not valid character string constants?
   a. "May 16, 1990"
   b. "Miami, Florida"
   c. '123"
   d. George Smith

6. If two statements are entered with the same line number, the computer retains only the second. True or false?

Variables

Before BASIC programming is explained further, it is important that you understand how data is stored in the primary storage unit of the computer. Imagine a block of post office boxes, each with an assigned number that acts as an address for that particular box (see Figure 3–3). The addresses of these boxes always remain the same, but their contents will almost certainly change over a period of time. Similarly, the primary storage unit in a computer is divided into many separate storage locations, each with a specific address. A storage location containing a value that can change during program execution is referred to as a **variable.** A variable can contain only one value at a time; when a new value is assigned to a variable, the old value is lost.

These storage locations can be referred to by their addresses, just as post office boxes can be referred to by the numbers assigned to them. In machine-language programming, a storage location is always referenced by its actual address. It is a difficult task for the programmer to keep track of these addresses. Fortunately, in BASIC (and other high-level languages) the programmer is allowed to use names for storage locations. Names are much easier than addresses to remember. HOURS and RATE are **variable names** in Figure 3–4. The values (or contents) of the locations they specify are 40 and 4.50, respectively.

Variable names can have any number of characters; however, BASIC recognizes only the first 40 characters. This means that if the first 40 characters of two names are identical, BASIC sees the names as being identical, even if the forty-first character is different. The first character

Variable

A storage location whose value may change during program execution.

Variable name

A name that identifies a specific storage location. It must start with a letter and may contain any combination of letters, numbers, or periods.

FIGURE 3–3 Variables Are Similar to Post Office Boxes

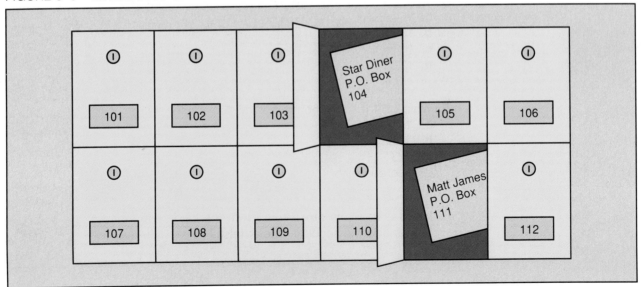

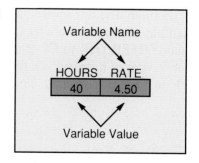

FIGURE 3–4   Variables in Storage

Descriptive variable name
A variable name that describes the storage location it represents.

Reserved word
A word that has a predefined meaning to the BASIC interpreter.

Numeric variable
A variable that stores a number.

must be a letter. The remaining characters may be letters, numbers, or periods. Good programming habits include the use of **descriptive variable names,** that is, names that describe the values they identify. Such names make the logic of programs easier to understand. For example, a variable named EMPLOYEE has more meaning than EM.

Certain words have specific meanings to the BASIC interpreter. These are **reserved words** (or **keywords**), and they cannot be used as variable names. Table 3–2 contains a list of the common ones. See Appendix A for a complete list.

Variables are also classed as numeric or string. Each of these types will be discussed here.

Numeric Variables   Numbers supplied to the computer by the programmer or internally calculated during program execution are stored in **numeric variables.** A numeric variable name must begin with a letter, followed by letters and/or digits and periods, with no embedded blanks.

TABLE 3–2   Commonly Used Reserved Words

ABS	DIM	INPUT	MKD$	PRINT#	SPC(
AND	DRAW	INPUT#	MKI$	PSET	SQR
ATN	EDIT	INT	MKS$	PUT	STEP
AUTO	ELSE	KEY	MOD	RANDOMIZE	STOP
BEEP	END	KILL	NAME	READ	STR$
CHR$	EOF	LEFT$	NEW	REM	SWAP
CIRCLE	ERASE	LEN	NEXT	RENUM	TAB(
CLEAR	EXP	LET	NOT	RESET	THEN
CLOSE	FIELD	LIST	OFF	RESTORE	TO
CLS	FILES	LLIST	ON	RETURN	VAL
COLOR	FNxxx	LOAD	OPEN	RIGHT$	WEND
COS	FOR	LOG	OR	RND	WHILE
CVD	GET	LPRINT	OUT	RUN	WIDTH
CVI	GOSUB	LSET	PEEK	SAVE	WRITE
CVS	GOTO	MERGE	POKE	SCREEN	WRITE#
DATA	IF	MID$	PRINT	SGN	XOR
DEF					

Periods are often useful in dividing a variable name in order to make it more readable. For example, the amount of city taxes owed could be represented by the variable name CITY.TAX rather than CITYTAX.

There are several types of numeric variables. *Integer variable* names have a percent sign (%) as the last character. For example,

```
DAY%
COUNT%
QUANTITY%
```

Real numeric variables can be single- or double-precision variables. The difference between the two is somewhat complex. A single-precision variable can have up to seven digits. However, if the number is printed, the seventh digit may not be accurate (this possible inaccuracy is caused by the way in which the computer internally stores the number). For example, if a variable has the value

```
7.654321
```

the digit "1" may not be correct. However, the first six digits will always be correct. A single-precision variable name can have an exclamation point (!) as its last character. For example:

```
CITY.TAX!
```

However, if a variable name is written with no symbol at the end, the BASIC interpreter assumes that it is a single-precision variable. Therefore, the following two variable names are identical:

```
RATE!    RATE
```

In this textbook we will not use the exclamation point at the end of single-precision numeric variable names. Double-precision variables can store real numbers with up to 17 digits; however only the first 16 can be printed. These variable names must have a number sign (#) as their last character. For example:

```
CITY.TAX#
```

Double-precision variables take up more space in the computer's main memory than single-precision ones. Because this type of accuracy is not needed for the programs in this text, we will only be using single-precision variables. We will refer to single-precision variables as simply *real variables*.

It is possible to store an integer value in a real variable. The BASIC interpreter simply converts the integer to a real number by adding zeros after the decimal point. Therefore, programmers often store integer values in real variables. In this text, we will store integer values in real variables.

Table 3–3 shows some examples of valid and invalid numeric variable names.

String Variables   A character string, such as a name, an address, or a date, is stored in a **string variable.** Like numeric variables, string variables can store only one value at a time. A string variable name must have a dollar sign ($) as the last character. The BASIC system recognizes the variable as a string variable because of the $ symbol. Table 3–4 gives examples of valid and invalid string variable names.

In the sample program in Figure 3–2, lines 60 and 70 contain the string variable named HEADING$:

```
60 LET HEADING$ = "GROSS PAY IS"
70 PRINT HEADING$,PAY
```

In line 60, the character string GROSS PAY IS is stored in the location named HEADING$; in line 70, the value stored in location HEADING$ is printed.

String variable

A variable that stores a character string.

TABLE 3–3   Valid and Invalid Numeric Variable Names

Valid	Invalid	(and Reason Why)
SUM! (real)	225	(Variable name must start with a letter)
M1% (integer)	M2&	(Ampersand not allowed)
D6E7 (real)	RT%DAY	(The percent sign must be the last symbol)
BIG47 (real)	B2$	($ symbol cannot be used with a numeric variable)
AMT% (integer)	D M6	(Variable name cannot include a blank)
ROOM.LENGTH (real)	ROOM__LENGTH	(Only period can separate characters)

TABLE 3–4   Valid and Invalid String Variable Names

Valid	Invalid	(and Reason Why)
C$	$	(First character must be a letter)
HEADING$	4$	(First character must be a letter)
DAY$	E2%	(A string variable name must have a $ as the last character)
EMP$	EM$P	(The $ symbol must be the last character)
M1$	M 1$	(No blanks allowed)
SSNO$	SS-NO$	(Hyphen not allowed)

Now Try This

1. The two types of constants are _____ constants and _____ constants.

2. A _____ is a storage location whose value can change during program execution.

3. A _____ variable name must have a "$" as its last character.

4. Identify the type of variable that could be stored in each of the following:
   a. DISCOUNT
   b. STATE$
   c. NUMBER#
   d. MONTH2!

5. What is the difference between the following two variable names?

   `TOTAL.YARDS`   `TOTAL.YARDS!`

6. Reserved words are also referred to as _____ .

Simple BASIC Statements

The remainder of this chapter discusses four elementary programming statements: REM, LET, PRINT, and END.

Documenting a Program

The REM, or remark, statement provides information for the programmer or anyone else reading the program. It is ignored by the computer; in other words, it is a nonexecutable statement. This information is referred to as documentation, and its function is to explain to humans the purpose of the program, what variables are used in the program, and anything else of importance. Because documentation does not affect program execution, it can be placed anywhere in the program. The following is a REM statement:

```
10 REM *** THIS PROGRAM ADDS 3 NUMBERS. ***
```

It must begin with the reserved word REM. Placing asterisks before and after the remark is optional. It is used simply to set the documentation apart from the rest of the program. It is also possible to place a remark on the same line as an executable statement:

```
10 LET A = B + C     'DETERMINE THE SUM OF THE 2 NUMBERS.
```

In this situation, the single apostrophe indicates to the BASIC interpreter where the remark starts. However, most programmers feel it is better programming practice to use separate REM statements because the documentation is placed on a separate line, making it easier to locate. REM statements also can be used alone to create a blank line to separate one part of a program from another.

Assigning Values to Variables

Assignment statement
A statement used to assign a value to a variable.

The LET statement is an **assignment statement,** that is, a statement that stores a value in main memory in the location allotted to the stated variable. In a flowchart, an assignment statement is illustrated by a processing symbol (□). The general format of the assignment statement is

line# LET variable = expression

The variable can be a numeric or string variable. If it is a numeric variable, the expression can be a numeric constant, an arithmetic formula or another numeric variable. If it is a string variable, the expression can be either a string constant or another string variable.

The LET statement can be used to assign values to numeric or string variables directly or to assign the result of a calculation to a numeric variable. In either case, the expression on the right side of the equal sign is assigned to the variable on the left side. This operation causes the value of the expression to be placed in the memory location identified by the variable name on the left side of the LET statement.

The program in Figure 3–2 has four assignment statements:

```
30 LET HOURS = 40
40 LET RATE = 4.5
50 LET PAY = HOURS * RATE
60 LET HEADING$ = "GROSS PAY IS"
```

Lines 30 and 40 assign three numeric constants (in this case, the hours worked and the pay rate) to two numeric variables. Line 50 assigns the result of an arithmetic calculation to the numeric variable PAY, which represents the gross pay, and line 60 assigns an appropriate character string to HEADING$.

Some additional examples of how the LET statement assigns values to variables follow.

Example 1

```
20 LET NME$ = "AARON"
```

The character string "AARON" is stored in location NME$ (remember, however, that the quotation marks are not stored):

AARON

NME$

Example 2

```
20 LET HOURS = 30.5 + 10
```

The storage location named HOURS now has the value of 40.5:

40.5

HOURS

Example 3

```
30 LET AMOUNT$ = "30.5 + 10"
```

The character string "30.5 + 10" is stored in location AMOUNT$.

30.5 + 10

AMOUNT$

Because this value is stored as a character string, it is stored exactly as it appears inside the quotation marks. Because AMOUNT$ is a string variable, it cannot be used in arithmetic operations.

Example 4

```
40 LET CNT = 10
50 LET CNT = CNT + 1
```

First, the value 10 is stored in CNT:

10

CNT

Then CNT is incremented by 1:

11

CNT

Only a variable name is permitted on the left side of the LET statement. For example,

```
130 LET A + 1 = B
```

is *not* a valid statement. The word LET is optional. BASIC treats the following two statements as being identical.

```
10 LET TEST1 = 36
20 TEST1 = 36
```

For simplicity's sake, we will discontinue using LET after this chapter.

Arithmetic Operations   In BASIC, arithmetic expressions are composed of numeric constants, numeric variables, and arithmetic operators. The arithmetic operators that can be used are defined in the following table.

Operator	Operation	BASIC Expression
+	Addition	A + B
−	Subtraction	A − B
/	Division	A / B
*	Multiplication	A * B
^	Exponentiation	A ^ B

For example, in the statement

```
50 LET X = Y ^ 3
```

Y is cubed (Y * Y * Y), and the result is stored in the location identified by X. Note that a space has been left on each side of the operators. This spacing is not necessary, but it greatly improves the readability of the program. Table 3–5 contains some statements using these arithmetic operators.

Hierarchy of operations
Rules that determine the order in which operations are performed.

Hierarchy of Operations   When more than one operation is performed in a single arithmetic expression, the computer follows a **hierarchy of**

TABLE 3–5   Statements Using Arithmetic Operators

Statement	Result
X = 4 + 5 − 1	X = 8
Y = 5 * 10 + 2	Y = 52
Z = 6 + 4 ^ 2	Z = 22
M = 12 / 4 − 5	M = −2

operations that states the order in which arithmetic expressions are to be evaluated. Operations are performed as follows:

Priority	Operation	Symbol
First	Exponentiation	^
Second	Multiplication, division	*, /
Third	Addition, subtraction	+, −
Fourth	Any operations on the same level are performed left to right	

In this statement,

```
20 LET X = 10 + 4 * 2
```

X is assigned the value of 18 because the multiplication is performed before the addition.

When parentheses are used in an expression, the operations inside the parentheses are performed before the operations outside the parentheses. If parentheses are nested, the operations inside the innermost set are done first. Thus, in the expression

```
(6 + (5 * 2) / 3.12) + 10
```

the first operation to be performed is to multiply 5 by 2.

Operations of high priority are performed before operations of lower priority. If several operations are on the same level, they are performed from left to right. Table 3–6 gives some examples of how BASIC evaluates expressions.

TABLE 3–6 Examples of Evaluating Expressions

Expression	Evaluation Process
1. $Y = 2 * 5 + 1$	
First: $2 * 5 = 10$	Process highest priority
Second: $10 + 1 = 11$	Process next priority
Result: $Y = 11$	
2. $Y = 2 * (5 + 1)$	
First: $5 + 1 = 6$	Perform process within parentheses
Second: $2 * 6 = 12$	Perform next priority
Result: $Y = 12$	
3. $Y = (3 + (6 + 2)/ 4) + 10\,\hat{}\,2$	
First: $6 + 2 = 8$	Process innermost parentheses
Second: $8/4 = 2$	Perform next priority
Third: $3 + 2 = 5$	Process rest of outer parentheses
Fourth: $10\,\hat{}\,2 = 100$	Perform next priority
Fifth: $5 + 100 = 105$	Perform lowest priority

Now Try This

1. Write a REM statement that places a blank line in a program to separate two sections of the program.

2. Write a REM statement that tells the reader the variable SUBTOTAL is being multiplied by 10.

3. Write an assignment statement to do each of the following:
   a. Assign your age to an appropriate variable.
   b. Assign the value 8 cubed to a numeric variable.
   c. Assign the total calories in your lunch to an appropriate variable. (Assume you had three items for lunch containing 100, 65, and 305 calories.)

4. Write assignment statements for the following mathematical expressions.
   a. $X = \dfrac{(14 - 10) \times 3}{2 + 2}$
   b. $Y = 6^3 + 17 / 2$

Displaying Results

The PRINT statement is used to display the results of computer processing. It is flowcharted using the input/output symbol ($\square$). If more than one item is listed in a PRINT statement, the items can be separated by commas. There are many different ways the output of the PRINT statement can be formatted. This topic will be discussed in detail in Chapter 4. For now, we will use commas, which automatically space the items across the output line.

Displaying the Value of a Variable   You can tell the computer to output values assigned to storage locations simply by using the reserved word PRINT with the variable name after it. In Figure 3–2, the following statement displays the program results on the monitor screen:

```
70 PRINT HEADING$,PAY
```

HEADING$ displays the character string "GROSS PAY IS " and PAY displays the amount owed, which in this example is 180. Therefore, the output appears as follows:

```
GROSS PAY IS    180
```

Printing has no effect on the contents of the storage location being printed. The PRINT statement accesses only the value of a variable and displays it on the screen.

Literal

A group of characters containing any combination of alphabetic, numeric, and/or special characters.

Displaying Literals A **literal** is a group of characters containing any combination of alphabetic, numeric, and/or special characters. It is essentially the same as a constant, but the term is applied to constants used in PRINT statements. There are two types: character string and numeric.

A character-string literal is a group of letters, numbers, and/or special characters enclosed in quotation marks. Everything inside the quotation marks is printed exactly as it is. For example,

```
190 PRINT "SAMPLE @%OUTPUT 12"
```

would appear on the screen as

```
SAMPLE @%OUTPUT 12
```

Note that the quotation marks are not printed.

Literals can be used to print headings in output. To print column headings, for example, put each heading in quotation marks and separate them with commas. Here is an example:

```
40 PRINT "NAME","RANK","SERIAL NO."
```

When this statement is executed, the following output will appear on the screen:

```
NAME           RANK           SERIAL NO.
```

Headings can be set off from the rest of the output by underlining and/or by using a blank line. One way to underline headings is by including a separate PRINT statement that contains the necessary underscore lines, as follows:

```
40 PRINT "NAME","RANK","SERIAL NO."
50 PRINT "____","____","_____"
```

The output would be

```
NAME           RANK           SERIAL NO.
____           ____           _____
```

Note that the underline is slightly separated from the heading. This is caused by using a separate PRINT statement.

A blank line in output makes the output more readable, and can be achieved by using a PRINT statement alone:

```
140 PRINT
```

Numeric literals, placed within the PRINT statement, are numbers that are to be printed in the output. They do not have to be enclosed in quotation marks. For example, the statement

```
100 PRINT 103
```

will print

```
103
```

Displaying the Value of an Expression   The computer can print not only literals and the values of variables, but also the values of arithmetic expressions. Look at the following program:

```
10 LET A = 15
20 LET B = 26
30 PRINT (A + B) / 2, A / B
99 END
```

The computer will evaluate each expression in line 30 (according to the hierarchy of operations) and then print the results:

```
20.5            .5769231
```

The computer can print only a certain number of digits for each value. Look at the second value printed. In this case, the computer cannot print more than seven digits. If the computer did not have this limit, an infinite number of digits would have been printed, because the full answer is as follows:

```
.576923076923076923076 . . .
```

Using the END Statement

The END statement instructs the computer to stop program execution. In a flowchart, it is indicated by the termination symbol ($\bigcirc$). The END statement is always the last line to be executed in a program. To make the END statement readily identifiable, many programmers give it a line number of all nines, as follows:

```
999 END
```

All programs in this book will follow this practice.

A Programming Problem

Problem Definition

The Carmichael Manufacturing Company makes three items. It would like a program to calculate both the wholesale and the retail prices of these items. The cost of manufacturing each of the three items is:

Item 1	$102.40
Item 2	$87.51
Item 3	$34.18

The company calculates the wholesale prices of these items by adding on 38 percent of the manufacturing costs. The retail prices are calculated by adding on 62 percent of the wholesale cost. A report, with appropriate headings, should be displayed on the monitor screen. Figure 3–5 contains the program specification chart, and the format of the needed report is shown in Figure 3–6.

Solution Design

The tasks this program must perform are as follows:

1. Assign the manufacturing cost of each item to a variable.
2. Add on 38 percent of the manufacturing cost to obtain the wholesale cost.
3. Add on 62 percent of the wholesale cost to obtain the retail cost. Figure 3–7 shows the structure chart.

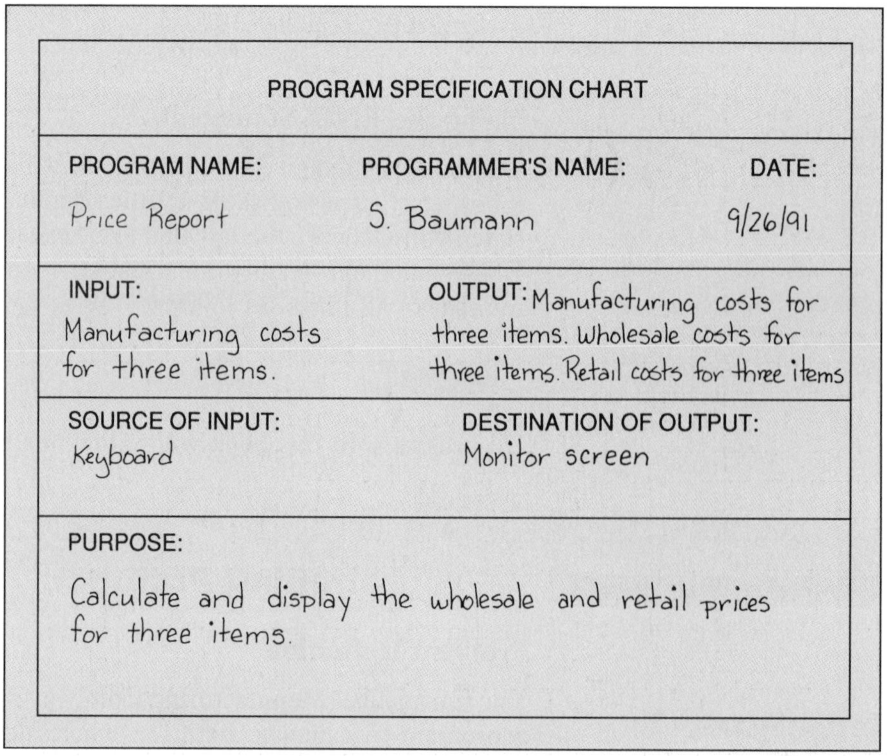

FIGURE 3–5   Program Specification Chart for Price Report

PROGRAM SPECIFICATION CHART

PROGRAM NAME:	PROGRAMMER'S NAME:	DATE:
Price Report	S. Baumann	9/26/91

INPUT:
Manufacturing costs for three items.

OUTPUT: Manufacturing costs for three items. Wholesale costs for three items. Retail costs for three items

SOURCE OF INPUT:
Keyboard

DESTINATION OF OUTPUT:
Monitor screen

PURPOSE:

Calculate and display the wholesale and retail prices for three items.

Now Try This

1. Write a PRINT statement that displays your age, with an appropriate label, on the monitor screen.

2. Write a PRINT statement that displays the numbers 10, 20, 30, and 40, evenly spaced across a line.

3. Rewrite Exercise 2 so that the numbers 10, 20, 30, and 40 are placed on separate lines.

4. Write a statement that will terminate program execution.

The first part of the processing will use assignment statements to assign each of the manufacturing costs to a variable. Each wholesale and retail price can be determined by using simple arithmetic operations. The report

FIGURE 3–6   Printer Spacing Chart for Price Report

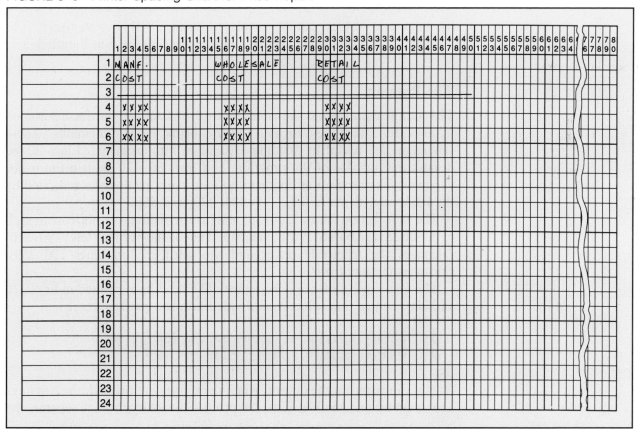

FIGURE 3–7   Structure Chart for Price Report

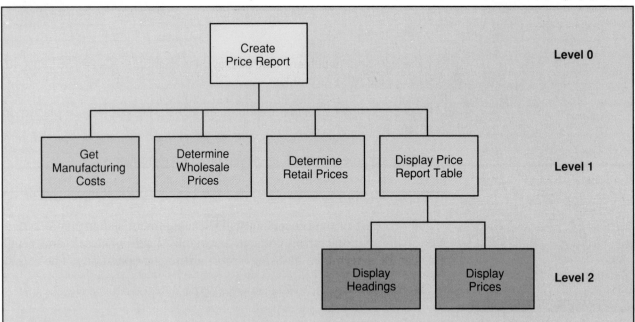

headings and values can be displayed using PRINT statements. The flowchart and pseudocode for this solution are contained in Figure 3–8.

The Program

The complete program is shown in Figure 3–9. Examine the documentation in lines 10–120. Lines 20 and 130 are blank REM statements. These statements are useful in dividing a program into segments. Lines 30–80 discuss the purpose of the program, and lines 90–120 explain the major variables. The program is divided into four major sections, as indicated by the REM statements in lines 140, 180, 220, and 260.

The first section (lines 150–170) assigns the manufacturing cost to each of the three variables M1, M2, and M3. The second section (lines 190–210) calculates the wholesale price, and the third section (lines 230–250), calculates the retail price.

The final section displays the report. The heading is printed in lines 270 and 280. Notice that it has been divided into two parts:

```
270 PRINT "MANUF.","WHOLESALE","RETAIL"
280 PRINT "COST","COST","COST"
```

As you can see from the output, when these lines are printed, the headings line up under one another. Line 290 prints a row of hyphens to separate the

FIGURE 3–8   Flowchart and Pseudocode for Price Report

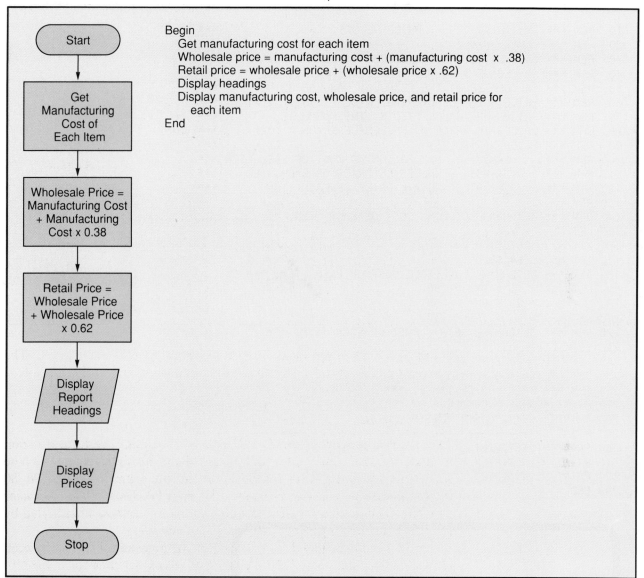

heading from the prices. The cost, wholesale price, and retail price of each item is printed on a separate line. The program concludes with an END.

Programming Hints

- Be careful not to use reserved words as variable names.
- Check carefully to make sure that the variable name type matches the type of value being assigned to it.

FIGURE 3–9   Price Report Program

```
10   REM ***                    PRICE REPORT                   ***
20   REM
30   REM *** CALCULATES THE WHOLESALE PRICES AND RETAIL   ***
40   REM *** PRICES OF 3 ITEMS.  WHOLESALE PRICES ARE      ***
50   REM *** CALCULATED BY THE FORMULA: MANUFACTURING      ***
60   REM *** PRICE + (MANUFACTURING PRICE * .38). RETAIL   ***
70   REM *** PRICES ARE CALCULATED BY THE FORMULA:         ***
80   REM *** WHOLESALE PRICE + (WHOLESALE PRICE * .62)     ***
90   REM *** MAJOR VARIABLES:                              ***
100  REM ***     M1-M3      MANUFACTURING COST OF EACH ITEM ***
110  REM ***     WS1-WS3    WHOLESALE PRICE OF EACH ITEM    ***
120  REM ***     RTL1-RTL3  RETAIL PRICE OF EACH ITEM       ***
130  REM
140  REM *** GET MANUFACTURING COST OF EACH ITEM. ***
150  LET M1 = 102.4
160  LET M2 =  87.51
170  LET M3 =  34.18
180  REM *** DETERMINE WHOLESALE COST OF EACH ITEM. ***
190  LET WS1 = M1 + (M1 * .38)
200  LET WS2 = M2 + (M2 * .38)
210  LET WS3 = M3 + (M3 * .38)
220  REM *** DETERMINE RETAIL COST OF EACH ITEM. ***
230  LET RTL1 = WS1 + (WS1 * .62)
240  LET RTL2 = WS2 + (WS2 * .62)
250  LET RTL3 = WS3 + (WS3 * .62)
260  REM *** PRINT PRICE TABLE. ***
270  PRINT "MANUF.","WHOLESALE","RETAIL"
280  PRINT "COST","COST","COST"
290  PRINT "----------------------------------------------------"
300  PRINT M1,WS1,RTL1
310  PRINT M2,WS2,RTL2
320  PRINT M3,WS3,RTL3
999  END
```

```
RUN
MANUF.          WHOLESALE       RETAIL
COST            COST            COST
----------------------------------------------------
102.4           141.312         228.9254
87.51           120.7638        195.6374
34.18           47.1684         76.41281
```

- Be certain that all expressions appear to the right of an assignment operator. Only variables may appear on the left side.
- Remember that your program concludes with an END statement.
- Remember that line numbers must be from 0 through 65529. Do not use the same line number more than once unless you want to replace a line with a new one.
- Increment your line numbers by a large enough margin to allow for insertions if necessary.
- Always enclose character strings in quotation marks.
- When the reserved word REM is used to indicate a remark, it must always be placed at the beginning of the line.
- Double-check any mathematical expressions to make certain they will be evaluated correctly. Remember that the computer always follows the hierarchy of operations when evaluating arithmetic expressions.
- Adding parentheses, even when they are not needed, can often make mathematical expressions easier for people to understand.

New Statement Review

Statement Format	Explanation
line# REM remark	Allows the programmer to enter documentation. Remarks are ignored by the computer. Also, an apostrophe (') may be used to indicate the beginning of a remark.
line# LET variable = expression	Assigns the value of the expression on the right to the variable on the left.
line# PRINT expression-list	Displays the values in the expression list on the monitor screen.
line# END	Indicates the end of program execution.

Summary Points

- Line numbers are placed at the beginning of BASIC statements to indicate they are to be executed in indirect mode. They must be integers from 0 through 65529.
- Using line numbers in large increments, such as 10, permits easy insertion of new statements.
- BASIC statements contain special programming commands (reserved words), constants, variables, and operators.
- Constants are values that do not change during program execution. A valid numeric constant is any integer or real number. Character strings are alphanumeric data enclosed in quotation marks.

■ Variable names are programmer-supplied names that identify storage locations where data values may be stored. Numeric variable names represent numbers. String variables contain alphanumeric values; their names are distinguished from numeric names by the $ symbol used as the last character.

■ REM statements are nonexecutable statements that provide information for the programmer or reader. These statements can be placed anywhere in a program.

■ The LET statement is used to assign values and results of arithmetic calculations to variables. The word LET is optional on most systems.

■ Arithmetic expressions are evaluated according to the following hierarchy of operations: (1) operations in parentheses, (2) exponentiation, (3) multiplication or division, and (4) addition or subtraction. Multiple operations at the same level are evaluated from left to right.

■ The PRINT statement enables the user to see the results of a program. It can be used to print the values of variables, literals, arithmetic expressions, or a combination of these.

■ The END statement causes program execution to stop.

Vocabulary List

Alphanumeric data	Literal
Assignment statement	Numeric constant
Character string constant	Numeric variable
Constant	Programming mode
Descriptive variable name	Reserved word
Hierarchy of operations	Scroll
Indirect mode	String variable
Keywords	Variable
Line number	Variable name

Questions

Whenever appropriate, use complete sentences in answering the following questions.

1. What are the two main purposes of line numbers?
2. What is the advantage of incrementing line numbers by 10?
3. What is a constant? Name two types.
4. What is a variable? Name two types and explain how they differ from each other.
5. How does the BASIC interpreter distinguish a string variable from a numeric variable?
6. Which of the following are illegal variable names and why?
    a. 7$
    b. DOWN.ONE
    c. SB
    d. H$

e. M$

f. RT

g. 2009

h. W*

i. 25 cent

j. $FACT

7. What is the purpose of the REM statement?

8. In an assignment statement, what are the three forms that the expression on the right side of the equal sign can take if the variable on the left side is a numeric variable?

9. List the arithmetic operators in BASIC. In what order are these operators evaluated?

10. Define a literal and give three examples.

11. Evaluate the following expressions.

```
a. 3 * 6 - 12 / 3
b. 4 ^ (8 / 4)
c. 3 ^ 2 ^ 2
d. 4 + 6 / (3 * (10 - 9))
```

12. Convert each of the following arithmetic expressions into a BASIC expression.

a. $\dfrac{9 \times B + 4^2}{5 + A}$

b. $\dfrac{A + B + C + (D \times E)}{F}$

c. $\dfrac{X^2}{Y/Z + 5}$

d. $A + 3C - D^2$

e. $(A + 4) \div 6 + (B \times C)$

f. $\dfrac{(X^2 \div 4) + 6}{(L \div M)\,N}$

Refer to the following program to answer Questions 13 through 15.

```
100 REM *** COMPUTE PERCENTAGE ***
110 REM *** FROM FRACTION.      ***
120 REM *** MAJOR VARIABLES:    ***
130 REM ***    N  NUMERATOR     ***
140 REM ***    D  DENOMINATOR   ***
150 REM ***    P  PERCENT       ***
160 LET N = 3
170 LET D = 4
180 LET P = (N / D) * 100
190 PRINT "PERCENT"
200 PRINT -
210 PRINT P
999 END
```

13. Find and correct the single error in the program above.

14. Draw a flowchart to represent this program.
15. Write a REM statement that would be appropriate to include between lines 170 and 180.

Debugging Exercises

Identify the following programs or program segments that contain errors, and debug them.

```
1. 10 REM *** ASSIGN CHARACTER STRINGS TO N$ AND L$. ***
   20 LET N$ = NANCY
   30 LET L$ = LINDA
   40 REM *** OUTPUT N$ AND L$.
   50 PRINT N$,L$
   99 END
```

```
2. 10 REM *** THIS PROGRAM PRINTS
   20 A NAME AND AGE OF A PERSON.
   30 REM
   40 LET A = 21
   50 LET N$ = "STACY"
   60 PRINT N$,A
   99 END
```

```
3. 30 REM *** CONVERT A DISTANCE FROM KILOMETERS TO MILES. ***
   40 LET X = 15.5
   50 LET K = "DISTANCE IN KILOMETERS"
   60 LET Y = X * 1.6
   70 LET M = "DISTANCE IN MILES"
   80 PRINT K,X
   90 PRINT M,Y
   99 END
```

```
4. 410 LET AGE% = 17.5
```

Programming Problems

Level 1

1. Write a program to cube the digits 1 through 9, and display the results with appropriate labels.
2. Write a program to display the following design on the monitor screen. Use asterisks to make the design.

```
*******
*  *  *
*******
```

3. Write a program that displays the United States flag on the monitor screen. Use asterisks and/or other special characters to print the design.

4. Write a program that displays the names and telephone numbers of the following people:

Linda Jones	818–7081
Peter Szabo	223–8764
Leroy Price	449–6062

The output should have the following format:

```
NAME            TELEPHONE #
XXXXXXXXX       XXX-XXXX
```

5. Write a program that computes the current balance in a checking account. At the beginning of the month the balance was $46.19. During the month, checks were written for the following items: record − $8.93, jeans − $15.60, and a book– $14.89. A deposit of $25.00 was made. The program should display the final balance.

6. The local sporting goods store has monthly specials on sporting equipment. The manager has asked you to write a program to calculate the total days' sales for these items:

Item	Sales Price	Units Sold
Hockey stick	$ 9.95	12
Soccer ball	12.95	5
Baseball gloves	17.95	20

Level 2

1. Write a program that converts your weight from pounds to kilograms and your height from inches to centimeters. (There are 2.54 centimeters in an inch and 0.45359 kilograms in a pound.)

2. Your physical education class went on a three-mile hike yesterday. You want to know how many feet you walked. (Remember, there are 5,280 feet in one mile.) Create a flowchart to solve this problem. Then write a program to find the total number of feet you walked.

3. Johnny Thurn wants to know how much it will cost for gas to Miami, Florida, and back home. Miami is 2,340 miles from his home. His car gets 28 miles per gallon, and he estimates that gas will cost an average of $1.21 a gallon. Write a program that produces output similar to the following:

```
DISTANCE        TOTAL COST
XXXX            XXX.XX
```

4. The Igloo Ice Cream Store would like you to write a program that will calculate the quantities of ice cream, nuts, sauce, and cones that are used on a given day. The following is a list of items sold and the quantities of ingredients used in each item:

Sundaes	8 oz. ice cream
	1 oz. nuts
	2 oz. sauce
Cones	6 oz. ice cream
	1 cone
Shakes	10 oz. ice cream
	1 oz. sauce

On a given day, the store sold 104 sundaes, 94 shakes, and 96 cones. Output should be stated in terms of quarts (32 fluid ounces per quart) of ice cream and sauce, pounds of nuts, and units of cones.

5. Tuition at Famous University is $3,000 per year and room and board fees are $6,500 per year. Next fall, tuition is expected to rise by 15 percent; room and board fees by 10 percent. Karl Perry wants to know what the fees will be and whether he will have enough money to cover them. Karl earns approximately $10,000 a year working part-time and summers and gets no additional help for his college expenses. Write a program for Karl. The output should have the following format:

```
TUITION          ROOM/BOARD      TOTAL          EXCESS
XXXX.XX          XXXX.XX         XXXX.XX        XXX.XX
```

6. Frank Mendelle is the father of two teenagers, and lately his telephone bills have been extremely high. To control this expense, he is charging each child $1.00 for every 10 minutes for long-distance calls and $.25 for every 10 minutes for local calls. The following calls were made:

Tom	2 long-distance calls (30 minutes each)
	6 local calls (20 minutes each)
Jenny	3 long-distance calls (10 minutes each)
	8 local calls (20 minutes each)

Compute how much each child owes Frank, and the total for the two children. Assume the telephone bill totaled $73.62. How much of his own money does Frank owe the telephone company?

Projects

For each project, complete the following:

- Fill out a program specification chart.
- Develop a structure chart.
- Create a flowchart or pseudocode.
- Thoroughly document the final program.
- Test your program using a variety of data.

1. The Rich Rug Company's top salesperson is Emmet Mitchell. He earns a base salary of $95 per week. In addition, he earns 6 percent commission on all Oriental rugs sold and 4 percent on all other items. The total salary is calculated as follows:

Total Salary = Base Salary + Commission

Write a program to calculate his salary. Then print his total weekly salary with an appropriate label. Use the following data: Oriental rugs sold, $3,892; all other sales, $989.

2. Linda Thurston is considering buying a new sports car. Calculate the monthly payment for an installment purchase, using the following formula:

$$P = I(T - D) \left[\frac{(1 + I)^m}{(1 + I)^m - 1} \right]$$

where

P is the monthly payment in dollars.
T is the purchase price in dollars.
D is the down payment in dollars.
I is the monthly interest rate (determine this value by dividing the annual rate by 12).
M is the number of months.

The price of the car is $10,000, to be paid for within five years at 15 percent interest. The down payment is 10 percent of the sale price.

CHAPTER 4

Reading and Writing Data

Learning Objectives

After studying this chapter, you should be able to
1. Enter data into a program during execution.
2. Store data within a program to be used during execution.
3. Use prompts to tell the user when data should be entered into a program.
4. Discuss the advantages of the various methods of placing data in variables.
5. Format program results appropriately.
6. Print the results of a program on paper.

Introduction

As we discussed in Chapter 3, variables are storage locations that contain values that can change during program execution. The values depend on the needs of your program. All programming languages have a variety of methods of assigning values to variables. For example, the value can be placed directly in a program statement, as is done in the LET (or assignment) statement. However, this method has only limited use because if the value needs to be changed, you must rewrite the assignment statement. In this chapter, you will learn two additional methods of assigning data to variables. The first one is extremely useful and allows the user to enter data at the keyboard while the program is executing. The second one allows the programmer to place the data in separate statements within the program itself.

Chapter 3 also discussed displaying program results by using the PRINT statement. However, outputting the results of a program is only the beginning. In order to be truly useful to people, these results must be displayed on the monitor (or printed on paper) in a manner that makes them easy to read and understand, such as in report or table form. This is called **formatting** the output, and it is discussed in the second half of this chapter.

Format
To control the arrangement of output.

More on Storing Data in Variables

Entering Data During Execution

In many programs, the data changes each time the program is executed. For example, think of a program that calculates the gas mileage for your car. Each time you run this program, you will want to be able to enter new values for the number of miles traveled and the amount of gas used. If such a program used assignment statements to assign these values to variables, these statements would have to be rewritten every time you wanted to calculate your gas mileage. A more practical approach to this programming problem is to use the INPUT statement.

The INPUT statement allows the user to enter data at the keyboard while the program is executing. The format of the INPUT statement is

```
line# INPUT variable1[,variable2]. . .
```

Take a minute to study the method used to present the format of this statement. This method will be used whenever a new statement is introduced in this text. Let's look at each part of this format description:

line#	A valid line number, such as 210, must be placed here. (In a format description, anything in lowercase represents a value to be inserted in the actual statement. In this case, "line#" represents an actual line number.)
INPUT	The statement must begin with the reserved word INPUT. (Uppercase words must be placed in the statement exactly as they appear in the format description.)
variable1	The reserved word INPUT must be followed by the name of a variable. (Because "variable1" is in lowercase, we know that it is used here to represent something else, in this case an actual variable name.)
[,variable2]. . .	Additional variables are optional. (Anything placed in brackets is optional.) The dots indicate that as many variable names as are needed may be listed in this statement.

Therefore, by examining this format description, we can determine that the following are all valid INPUT statements:

```
100  INPUT  STUDENT$,GPA,YEAR
110  INPUT  ADDRESS$
250  INPUT  TOTAL.PAY,NET.PAY,TAX
300  INPUT  MONTH$,DAY$,YEAR%
```

The following INPUT statements are not valid:

```
100  INPUT  CITY$ ST$
110  TABLES,INPUT  CHAIRS
```

Note that one or more variables may be listed in a single INPUT statement. If there is more than one, the variables must be separated by commas. The programmer places INPUT statements in a program at the point at which user-entered data is needed, as determined by the logic of the program.

When an INPUT statement is encountered while a program is running, the program temporarily stops executing, and a question mark appears on the monitor screen. The user must then enter the required data and press <Enter>. After each value entered is stored in its corresponding variable, program execution continues to the next statement.

Consider the following program:

```
10 INPUT CITY$
20 INPUT STATE$
30 INPUT PEOPLE
40 PRINT CITY$,STATE$,PEOPLE
99 END
```

When this program is executed, the monitor screen looks like this:

```
RUN
? CEDAR RAPIDS
? IOWA
? 125000
CEDAR RAPIDS   IOWA              125000
```

Let's trace through what happens as this program is executing. First, the computer executes line 10 and, upon encountering the INPUT statement, prints a question mark and stops. Next, the user enters the value CEDAR RAPIDS and presses <Enter>. The computer then continues execution, assigning the character string CEDAR RAPIDS to the character string variable CITY$. Execution proceeds to line 20, where another INPUT statement is encountered. Again the computer prints a question mark and stops until the user enters a value and presses <Enter>. This process is repeated for the last INPUT statement in this program, which assigns the value 125000 to the numeric variable PEOPLE. The values of these three variables are then printed by the PRINT statement to line 40, and the program ends. Note that quotation marks are not needed when using the INPUT statement to enter character strings.

The three INPUT statements in the program could be combined into a single statement like this:

```
10 INPUT CITY$,STATE$,PEOPLE
```

Because of the single INPUT statement, only one question mark appears on the screen when the program is run. In this case, the user enters the data in the following format:

```
RUN
? CEDAR RAPIDS,IOWA,125000
```

Note that when more than one data value is entered on a single line, the values must be separated by commas. After the user enters these values and presses <Enter>, CEDAR RAPIDS is assigned to CITY$, IOWA to STATE$, and 125000 to PEOPLE.

The user must enter the exact number of values needed by the INPUT statement. If fewer values are entered than there are variables in the INPUT statement, an error message is printed. For example, if line 10 in the preceding program is executed and the user enters only two values, the following appears on the screen:

```
RUN
? CEDAR RAPIDS, IOWA

?Redo from start
?
```

The system prompts the user to reenter the data because not enough data has been entered. The program will continue executing when the user enters the correct data.

If the user attempts to enter a character string to a numeric variable, the "Redo from start" message again appears:

```
RUN
? CEDAR RAPIDS,IOWA,USA

?Redo from start
?
```

The BASIC interpreter cannot assign the string USA to the numeric variable PEOPLE, and therefore an error occurs.

The user can, however, assign a numeric value to a character string variable. BASIC treats the numeric value as a string of characters and stores it in the corresponding string variable, but it cannot perform calculations with this value.

Displaying Prompts for the User

Prompt

A statement telling the user that data should be entered at this point.

In the previous example, when the INPUT statement was executed, only a question mark (?) appeared on the monitor screen when it was time for the user to enter data. The user was not told what type of data or how many data items to enter. Therefore, the programmer should also include a **prompt** to tell the user what is to be entered. A prompt can consist of a PRINT statement, placed before the INPUT statement in the program, which tells the user the type and quantity of data to be entered.

Figure 4–1 shows a short program that calculates the volume of a box. The length, width, and height of the box are entered, and the volume is displayed.

Line 40 of the program in Figure 4–1 contains the prompt,

```
40 PRINT "ENTER THE LENGTH, WIDTH, AND HEIGHT OF THE BOX."
```

Line 50 is the INPUT statement,

```
50 INPUT LENGTH, WDTH, HEIGHT
```

FIGURE 4–1   Program Demonstrating the INPUT Statement

```
10 REM *** THIS PROGRAM USES THE INPUT STATEMENT TO READ THE    ***
20 REM *** DIMENSIONS OF A BOX AND CALCULATE ITS VOLUME.        ***
30 REM
40 PRINT "ENTER THE LENGTH, WIDTH, AND HEIGHT OF THE BOX."
50 INPUT LENGTH,WDTH,HEIGHT
60 VOLUME = LENGTH * WDTH * HEIGHT
70 PRINT "VOLUME OF THE BOX IS ";VOLUME
99 END
```

```
RUN
ENTER THE LENGTH, WIDTH, AND HEIGHT OF THE BOX.
? 2.75,4.5,8.2
VOLUME OF THE BOX IS  101.475
```

After line 50 is executed, the computer stops and waits for the user to enter the desired length, width, and height. Then execution continues, and the volume of the box is calculated and displayed on the screen.

The prompt can also be contained within the INPUT statement itself. If this were done for the program in Figure 4–1, lines 40 and 50 could be replaced with a single statement:

```
40 INPUT "ENTER THE LENGTH, WIDTH, AND HEIGHT OF THE BOX";LENGTH,WDTH,HEIGHT
```

When this program is run, the question mark and the prompt appear on the same line:

```
RUN
ENTER THE LENGTH, WIDTH, AND HEIGHT OF THE BOX? 2.75,4.5,8.2
VOLUME OF THE BOX IS  101.475
```

Using this format simplifies the writing of the program and makes the logic easy to follow.

Inquiry-and-response mode
A mode of operation in which the system asks a question and the user types in a response.

This method of data entry, in which the user enters a response to a prompt printed on the monitor screen, is called **inquiry-and-response** or **conversational mode.**

Placing Data in the Program

A second method of entering data to a BASIC program is to use the READ and DATA statements. The READ and DATA statements differ from the INPUT statement in that data values are not entered by the user during program execution, but instead are assigned by the programmer within the program itself.

The general formats for the READ and DATA statements are

> line# READ variable1[,variable2]. . .
> line# DATA value1[,value2]. . .

The values in the DATA statement are assigned to the corresponding variables in the READ statement. The following is a list of rules explaining the use of the READ and DATA statements.

- A program may contain any number of READ and DATA statements.
- The placement of READ statements is determined by the logic of a given program. The programmer places them in the program at the point at which data needs to be read.
- DATA statements are nonexecutable and can therefore be placed anywhere in the program before the END statement. This book follows the common practice of placing all data statements immediately before the END statement, so that they are easy to locate.

Data list
A list containing all the values in the DATA statements in a program. The values are read to variables in the order in which they occur in the list.

- The computer collects the values from all of the DATA statements in a program and places them in a single list, referred to as the **data list.** This list is formed by taking the values from the DATA statements in order, from the lowest to the highest line number and from left to right within a single statement.
- When more than one data value is placed in a single DATA statement, the values are separated by commas. Character string values may or may not be placed in quotes. However, if the character string contains leading or trailing blanks, commas, or semicolons, it must be enclosed in quotation marks.
- When the program encounters a READ statement, it goes to the data list and assigns the next value from that list to the corresponding variable in the READ statement. If the variable is numeric, the data value must also be

numeric. If it is a character string variable, however, the computer will allow a numeric value to be assigned to it, as previously explained for the INPUT statement. Again, computations cannot be performed with numbers that have been assigned to character string variables.

■ If there is inadequate data for a READ statement (that is, if there are no more data values in the data list), an error message appears stating the line at which the program ran out of data, and execution terminates. For example:

```
Out of DATA in 130
```

■ If there are more data values than variables, these extra data values simply remain unread.

Figure 4–2 shows a program segment containing READ and DATA statements. When the computer executes this program, it first encounters the READ statement in line 100. The statement instructs it to read four data values from the data list and assign these values to the corresponding variables. Therefore, the values JACOBS, 48, 60, and 53 are assigned to the variables NME$, S1, S2, and S3 respectively. After this task is completed, program execution continues to line 110, where the next value in the data list, GUINARD, is assigned to the variable NME$. This new value of NME$ replaces JACOBS, which was the previous value.

Note that the computer "remembers" where it is in the data list. Whenever it encounters another READ statement, it assigns the next value in the list to that variable. Study Figure 4–2 to make certain you understand how the READ and DATA statements are used in reading data values. Notice that the columns on the right side of the figure state the current values of each of the variables for lines 100 through 130.

The program in Figure 4–3 shows how READ and DATA statements can be used to read the dimensions of a box and to calculate and display the volume. Note that line 40 contains a single READ statement that reads all

FIGURE 4–2 Examples Using the READ and DATA Statements

		CURRENT VALUE OF VARIABLES			
	AT LINE #:	NME$	S1	S2	S3
100 READ NME$,S1,S2,S3	100	JACOBS	48	60	53
110 READ NME$	110	GUINARD	48	60	53
120 READ S1,S2	120	GUINARD	62	58	53
130 READ S3	130	GUINARD	62	58	54
140 DATA JACOBS,48					
150 DATA 60,53,GUINARD					
160 DATA 62,58					
170 DATA 54					

FIGURE 4–3   Program Demonstrating the READ and DATA Statements

```
10 REM *** THIS PROGRAM USES THE READ AND DATA STATEMENTS TO   ***
20 REM *** READ THE DIMENSIONS OF A BOX AND CALCULATE ITS      ***
24 REM *** VOLUME.                                             ***
30 REM
40 READ LENGTH, WDTH, HEIGHT
50 VOLUME = LENGTH * WDTH * HEIGHT
60 PRINT "VOLUME OF THE BOX IS ";VOLUME
70 DATA 2.75,4.5,8.2
99 END
```

```
RUN
VOLUME OF THE BOX IS   101.475
```

three dimensions of the box. The DATA statement in line 70 contains the three values to be assigned to the three variables in the READ statement.

Comparing the INPUT and the READ/DATA Statements

The INPUT statement is more suitable for some situations and the READ/DATA statements for others. As you become adept at programming in BASIC, you will easily be able to choose the more appropriate data-entry method for a given situation. Some guidelines follow:

■ The INPUT statement is ideal when data values change frequently, because it allows the data to be entered at the keyboard during program execution.

■ The READ and DATA statements are well suited for programs using large quantities of data, because the user does not have to enter a long list of data values during program execution, as would be necessary with the INPUT statement.

■ The READ and DATA statements are most useful when data values will remain the same for each program execution. The main disadvantage of using the READ and DATA statements is that the program itself must be altered when the data values change.

Now Try This

1. Write a program segment containing two statements. The first statement should prompt the user to enter his or her graduation year. The second statement should assign that value to a variable named GRAD.YEAR.

2. Rewrite Question 1 so that only a single INPUT statement is used.

3. Write an INPUT statement that prompts users to enter the names of the classes they are currently taking (assume all students are taking five classes).

4. Rewrite Question 3 so that READ and DATA statements are used to read the names of the classes.

5. Write a program segment that uses READ and DATA statements to read the names of five companies and the number of employees each company has. Use the following data:

E & J Electronics	8
Best Commercial Cleaning	21
Toledo Plumbing	13
M & J Accounting	109
SKB Communications	34

Formatting Results

Chapter 3 explained that the PRINT statement lets us display the results of processing on the monitor screen. When more than one item is to be printed on a line, a variety of methods can be used to control the spacing and format of the output.

Semicolon

The semicolon is often used to separate two or more variables in a single PRINT statement. It signals the computer to print the next item starting at the next available print position. The following example shows the result when two strings are separated by a semicolon in a PRINT statement.

```
10 PRINT "JOHN";"DRAKE"
```

```
RUN
JOHNDRAKE
```

The first string is outputted, and then the semicolon indicates that the next item should be printed in the next available print position, which is the next column.

To display these strings with a space between them, you can enclose a blank within the quotation marks of one of the strings:

```
10 PRINT "JOHN";" DRAKE"
```

```
RUN
JOHN DRAKE
```

A preceding space is printed if a number has no sign, such as 104 or 48. If the number has a sign, such as −176 or +32, no preceding space is printed, because the sign is printed in that position. In either case, a space is left after the number for greater readability. Therefore, when numeric values are separated by a semicolon, the printed digits are not adjacent the way they are in character strings. The following example demonstrates this point:

```
10 PRINT 100;-200;300
```

```
RUN
 100 -200  300
```

Notice that the output shows only one space before −200. This is because the computer left a space after printing the number 100. But there are two spaces before 300: Not only was a space left after −200 was printed, but a space was left for the sign (an assumed positive) of the number 300.

A semicolon appearing after the *last* item in a PRINT statement prevents the output of the next PRINT statement from starting on a new line. Instead, the next item printed will appear on the same line at the next available print position:

```
10 PRINT 3567;
20 PRINT "YVONNE";" DRAKE"
```

```
RUN
 3567 YVONNE DRAKE
```

The semicolon at the end of line 10 causes the print position to remain on the same line. When line 20 is encountered, YVONNE DRAKE is printed at the first position after the blank that follows 3567.

Print Zones

A maximum of 80 characters can be displayed on each line of the monitor screen. Each line is divided into sections called *print zones*, which are 14 characters wide, with five zones per line. The beginning columns of the five print zones are as follows:

ZONE 1:	ZONE 2:	ZONE 3:	ZONE 4:	ZONE 5:
COL 1	COL 15	COL 29	COL 43	COL 57

Commas, like semicolons, can be used within a PRINT statement to control the format of output. A comma indicates that the next item to be printed will start at the beginning of the next print zone. The following example shows how this works:

```
10 READ W1$,W2$,W3$
20 PRINT W1$,W2$,W3$
30 DATA "BE","SEEING","YOU"
```

The first item in the PRINT statement is printed at the beginning of the line, which is the start of the first print zone. The comma between W1$ and W2$ causes the system to space over to the next print zone; then the value in W2$ is printed. The second comma directs the system to space over to the next zone (Zone 3) and print the value in W3$. The output is as follows:

```
RUN
BE            SEEING       YOU
```

If there are more items listed in a PRINT statement than there are print zones in a line, the print zones of the next line are also used, starting with the first zone. Notice the output of the following example.

```
10 READ SEX$,AGE,CLASS$,MAJOR$,HOURS,GPA
20 PRINT SEX$,AGE,CLASS$,MAJOR$,HOURS,GPA
30 DATA "M",19,"JR","CS",18,2.5
```

```
RUN
M             19           JR           CS           18
 2.5
```

Note that 2.5 starts in column 2 because it is a positive number and has no sign. If the value to be printed exceeds the width of the print zone, the entire value is printed, regardless of how many zones it occupies. A following comma causes printing to continue in the next print zone, as shown in the following example:

```
10 SPOT$ = "BAGHDAD"
20 PRINT "YOUR NEXT DESTINATION WILL BE",SPOT$
```

```
RUN
YOUR NEXT DESTINATION WILL BE            BAGHDAD
```

A print zone can be skipped by typing consecutive commas:

```
10 PRINT "ARTIST",,"ALBUM"
```

The literal ARTIST will be printed in Zone 1, the second zone will be blank, and the literal ALBUM will be printed in Zone 3:

```
RUN
ARTIST                            ALBUM
```

If a comma appears after the last item in a PRINT statement, the output of the next PRINT statement encountered will begin at the next available print zone. Thus, the statements

```
10 READ NME$,AGE,SEX$,VOICE$
20 PRINT NME$,AGE,
30 PRINT SEX$,VOICE$
40 DATA "SHICOFF",32,"M","TENOR"
```

produce the following output:

```
RUN
SHICOFF        32            M              TENOR
```

TAB Function

We have seen that the semicolon causes data to be printed in the next position on the output line, and that the comma causes data to be printed according to predefined print zones. Both formats are easy to use, and many reports can be formatted in this fashion. However, there are times when a report should be structured more precisely.

The TAB function allows output to be printed in any column in an output line, thus giving you greater flexibility in formatting. As with the comma and semicolon, one or more TAB functions can be used in a PRINT statement. The general format of the TAB function is

TAB(expression)

The expression may be a numeric constant, a variable, or an arithmetic expression. When a TAB function is encountered in a PRINT statement, the computer spaces over to the column number indicated in the expression. The next variable value or literal found in the PRINT statement is printed, starting in that column. For example, the statement

```
50 PRINT TAB(10) "HI THERE!";TAB(25) "BYE!"
```

causes the literal HI THERE! to be printed starting in column 10. Then, starting in column 25, the literal BYE! is printed.

```
RUN
        HI THERE!        BYE!
```

When using the TAB function in Microsoft BASIC, there cannot be a space between TAB and the left parenthesis. This is because the reserved word that this system recognizes is TAB(. Without the opening parenthesis following it, TAB is taken as a variable name TAB, and the value in parentheses is taken as an array subscript. (Arrays will be discussed in Chapter 9.) Therefore, the following statement is invalid:

```
10 PRINT TAB (5) "ITEM";TAB (25) "GALLONS"
```

The statement is correctly written like this:

```
10 PRINT TAB(5) "ITEM";TAB(25) "GALLONS"
```

The TAB function can be used only to advance the print position from left to right; backspacing is not possible. Therefore, if more than one TAB function appears in a single PRINT statement, the column numbers specified should increase from left to right. An example illustrates this point:

Correct Use of TAB function:

```
20 PRINT TAB(5) 3;TAB(15) 4;TAB(25) 5

RUN
    3         4         5
```

Incorrect Use of TAB function:

```
20 PRINT TAB(25) 5;TAB(15) 4;TAB(5) 3


RUN
                          5
              4
    3
```

The program in Figure 4–4 prints a simple table by using the TAB function to place the printed values in columns. Examine the CLS statement in line 60:

```
60 CLS
```

This statement clears the screen of any output and places the cursor in the upper left corner. It is a good idea to clear the screen before displaying program results such as tables and reports.

FIGURE 4–4   Program Demonstrating the TAB Function

```
10   REM ***                          INVENTORY REPORT                        ***
20   REM ***                                                                  ***
30   REM *** THIS PROGRAM DISPLAYS AN INVENTORY REPORT FOR AN                 ***
40   REM *** ICE CREAM STORE.                                                 ***
50   REM
60   CLS
70   PRINT
80   REM *** GET THE DATA. ***
90   INPUT "ENTER ITEM AND QUANTITY";ITEM1$,QUANTITY1
100  INPUT "ENTER ITEM AND QUANTITY";ITEM2$,QUANTITY2
110  INPUT "ENTER ITEM AND QUANTITY";ITEM3$,QUANTITY3
120  REM
130  REM  *** DISPLAY THE REPORT. ***
140  CLS
150  PRINT TAB(11) "INVENTORY REPORT"
160  PRINT
170  PRINT TAB(8) "ITEM";TAB(24) "GALLONS"
180  PRINT
190  PRINT TAB(5) ITEM1$;TAB(25) QUANTITY1
200  PRINT TAB(5) ITEM2$;TAB(25) QUANTITY2
210  PRINT TAB(5) ITEM3$;TAB(25) QUANTITY3
999  END
```

```
ENTER ITEM AND QUANTITY? ICE CREAM,50
ENTER ITEM AND QUANTITY? TOPPINGS,4
ENTER ITEM AND QUANTITY? CHERRIES,1.5
```

```
          INVENTORY REPORT

      ITEM           GALLONS

   ICE CREAM           50
   TOPPINGS            4
   CHERRIES            1.5
```

SPC Function

The SPC (an abbreviation for SPACE) function is similar to TAB in that it is used in controlling the printing of output. However, instead of instructing the computer to print output in a specified column, it tells the computer how many spaces to move over before printing the output. For example:

```
40 PRINT "WORD";SPC(10) "LETTER"
```

```
RUN
WORD            LETTER
```

When line 40 is executed, WORD is printed in columns 1 through 4; then the computer leaves ten blank spaces between the end of WORD and the beginning of LETTER. Therefore, LETTER is printed starting in column 15. Figure 4–5 shows how the program in Figure 4–4 could be rewritten using the SPC function. Notice that the numbers do not line up. This is because the SPC function causes output to "move over" a specified number of spaces rather than to begin in a specified column.

Now Try This

1. Write a statement that displays your name and address on the screen. Your name should start in column 4 and your address in column 25. Use the TAB function.

2. Rewrite Exercise 1 so that your name starts in the first column and there is one blank space between it and your address.

3. Rewrite Exercise 1 so that your name starts in column 4 and your address starts 20 spaces over from the end of your name. Use the SPC function.

4. Rewrite Exercise 1 so that your name starts in the first print zone and your address starts in the third print zone.

Sending Output to the Printer

As previously mentioned, you can print an entire program (or specified lines in it) on paper by using the LLIST command. For example, the following statement sends lines 100–200 to the printer:

```
LLIST 100-200
```

FIGURE 4–5   Program Demonstrating the SPC Function

```
10   REM ***                        INVENTORY REPORT                    ***
20   REM ***                                                            ***
30   REM *** THIS PROGRAM DISPLAYS AN INVENTORY REPORT FOR AN           ***
40   REM *** ICE CREAM STORE.                                           ***
50   REM
60   CLS
70   PRINT
80   REM *** GET THE DATA. ***
90   INPUT "ENTER ITEM AND QUANTITY";ITEM1$,QUANTITY1
100  INPUT "ENTER ITEM AND QUANTITY";ITEM2$,QUANTITY2
110  INPUT "ENTER ITEM AND QUANTITY";ITEM3$,QUANTITY3
120  REM
130  REM  *** DISPLAY THE REPORT. ***
140  CLS
150  PRINT SPC(14) "INVENTORY REPORT"
160  PRINT
170  PRINT SPC(8) "ITEM";SPC(16) "GALLONS"
180  PRINT
190  PRINT SPC(5)  ITEM1$;SPC(18) QUANTITY1
200  PRINT SPC(5)  ITEM1$;SPC(18) QUANTITY2
210  PRINT SPC(5)  ITEM3$;SPC(18) QUANTITY3
999  END
```

```
ENTER ITEM AND QUANTITY? ICE CREAM,50
ENTER ITEM AND QUANTITY? TOPPINGS,4
ENTER ITEM AND QUANTITY? CHERRIES,1.5
```

```
              INVENTORY REPORT

        ITEM               GALLONS

     ICE CREAM                50
     ICE CREAM                4
     CHERRIES                 1.5
```

In addition, there are times when you will want the results of a program printed on paper. You can instruct output to be sent to the printer by using the LPRINT statement. It is used in the same way you would use the PRINT statement. In this program segment,

```
10 INPUT "ENTER EMPLOYEE'S NAME AND SALARY";NME$,SALARY
20 LPRINT "EMPLOYEE'S NAME IS ";NME$
30 PRINT "EMPLOYEE'S SALARY IS $";SALARY
```

the statement in line 20 is printed on paper while line 30 is displayed on the screen. Remember that in order to use the LPRINT statement, your computer must be attached to a printer and the printer must be turned on.

Centering Output Lines

Often, when writing programs, you may wish to center output on a line—for example, the headings of a report. If you have ever centered headings using a typewriter, you will be familiar with the method we use here. First, use a printer spacing chart to format the report to be created. Then, follow these steps to center a heading:

1. Determine the width of the report (that is, count the number of spaces in the longest line).
2. Count the number of characters in the heading.
3. Subtract the length of the heading from the entire width of the report.
4. Divide the result of Step 3 by 2.
5. Use this value in a TAB statement to indicate the column where the heading should start.

For example, if you want to center the heading INVENTORY REPORT in the program shown in Figure 4–4, perform the following steps.

1. Determine the width of the report, which is 31 spaces.
2. Count the number of characters in the heading, which is 16.
3. Subtract 16 from 31, getting 15.
4. Divide 15 by 2, getting 7.5.
5. The final statement is

```
130 PRINT TAB(7.5) "INVENTORY REPORT"
```

When a real number is used in a TAB statement, the number is rounded to the nearest integer. Therefore, the heading will start in column 8. The actual program segment could be written like this:

```
30 WDTH = 31
40 HDG = 16
50 POSITION = WDTH - HDG
60 PRINT TAB(POSITION / 2) "INVENTORY REPORT"
```

The PRINT USING Statement

Another convenient feature for formatting output is the PRINT USING statement. It is especially useful when formatting reports or columns of numbers. Like any PRINT statement, the PRINT USING statement displays the values of expressions, such as variables and constants. However, the PRINT USING statement tells the system to display these values using a specified format. Special control characters are used to indicate the format (see Table 4–1). For example:

```
70 X = 15.673
80 PRINT USING "###.##";X
```

The value of X (15.673) is displayed using the format ###.##. Each number sign (#) represents a single digit. Because there are only two number signs to the right of the decimal point, the number 15.673 is

TABLE 4–1   PRINT USING Format Control Characters

String Format Characters

!	Only the first character in the string is displayed.
\ \	The characters between the slash marks +2 are displayed. For example, if there are 10 spaces between the slash marks, a maximum of 12 characters are displayed. If the character string has fewer than 12 characters, it is right-justified (any blank spaces are placed on the left side of the field).

Numeric Format Characters

#	A # symbol is used to represent each digit in the number to be displayed. If the number of digits is fewer than the number of these symbols, the number is right-justified (any blank spaces are placed to the left of the number).
.	A period indicates the position of the decimal point in a real number.
+	A plus sign causes the sign of the number (either positive or negative) to be displayed.
**	Any leading blank spaces are filled with asterisks.
$	A dollar sign ($) is displayed in the specified position.
$$	The dollar sign floats; it will appear immediately to the left of the first digit of the number.
,	A comma is inserted between each group of three numbers.

rounded to two decimal places. When these statements are executed, the output is

```
15.67
```

One blank space appears at the beginning of the line, because the control characters allow for a maximum of three digits to the left of the decimal point.

PRINT USING statements are useful in aligning columns of numbers. Consider the following program segment:

```
10  READ V1,V2,V3,V4
20  PRINT USING "#####.##";V1,V2,V3,V4
30  READ V1,V2,V3,V4
40  PRINT USING "#####.##";V1,V2,V3,V4
50  READ V1,V2,V3,V4
60  PRINT USING "#####.##";V1,V2,V3,V4
70  READ V1,V2,V3,V4
80  PRINT USING "#####.##";V1,V2,V3,V4
90  DATA 14.56,78.90,104.1,0.03,6.73,322.4,943.05,17.65
100 DATA 65.56,945.7,447.80,0.17,175.35,78.92,319.00,4.56
```

The output of this program segment is

```
RUN
    14.56    78.90   104.10     0.03
     6.73   322.40   943.05    17.65
    65.56   945.70   447.80     0.17
   175.35    78.92   319.00     4.56
```

Notice that the columns of numbers are aligned at the decimal points. When formatting numbers, make certain that you use enough format characters for the largest possible number. For example, ###.## can hold any number up to 999.99.

The following statement places a dollar sign in front of dollar amounts:

```
40 PRINT USING "$####.##";AMT
```

If the value of AMT is 3.67, the output is

```
RUN
$    3.67
```

Because this number has only one digit to the left of the decimal point, and the format allows for four digits, there are three blank spaces between the dollar sign and the first digit. If you want to have the dollar sign immediately in front of the first digit, you can make it "float" by using two dollar signs ($$):

```
40 PRINT USING "$$####.##";AMT
```

Now the output is

```
$3.67
```

A second method of using the PRINT USING statement is to assign the format control characters to a string variable. This variable can then be referred to in the PRINT USING statement. The previous program segment could be rewritten using this method as follows:

```
10   FMT$ = "#####.##"
20   READ V1,V2,V3,V4
30   PRINT USING FMT$;V1,V2,V3,V4
40   READ V1,V2,V3,V4
50   PRINT USING FMT$;V1,V2,V3,V4
60   READ V1,V2,V3,V4
70   PRINT USING FMT$;V1,V2,V3,V4
80   READ V1,V2,V3,V4
90   PRINT USING FMT$;V1,V2,V3,V4
100  DATA 14.56,78.90,14.1,0.03,6.73,322.4,943.05,17.65
110  DATA 65.56,945.7,447.80,0.17,175.35,78.92,319.00,4.56
```

Line 10 assigns the format control characters to the string variable FMT$. FMT$ is then referenced in the PRINT USING statements in lines 30, 50, 70, and 90. This method is particularly helpful when a number of output lines need to be formatted in the same way.

Another set of useful control characters is the slash marks (\). They are used to format character strings. The string is left-justified in the output field. For example:

```
10 PRINT USING "\    \ $$###.##";ITEM$,COST
```

There are four spaces between the slash marks. Therefore, the maximum size of a string that can be output is 4 + 2, or 6. If the string is any longer, it is *truncated* (cut off). If it is any shorter, it is left-justified in the field (that is, the first character of the string is output at the left margin). Any blank spaces are placed at the end of the string. Therefore, if ITEM$ equals BICYCLE, and COST equals 149.50, the output is

```
RUN
BICYCL  $149.50
```

The last letter in BICYCLE is truncated because the string has more than six characters. However, if the statement is rewritten with ten spaces between the slash marks (allowing for a 12-character string)—

```
10 PRINT USING "\          \ $$###.##";ITEM$,COST
```

—there will be five blank spaces after BICYCLE because it is five spaces shorter than the maximum space allowed (12 − 7 = 5).

```
RUN
BICYCLE        $149.50
```

To make numbers more readable, commas can be inserted between each group of three digits:

```
10 PRINT USING "##,###.##";NUMBER
```

If NUMBER equals 1381.80, the output is

```
RUN
1,381.80
```

However, if the number is only 381.80, no comma is displayed:

```
RUN
 381.80
```

A plus sign (+) causes the sign of a number to be displayed. If the PRINT USING looks like this:

```
100 PRINT USING "+###.##";NUMBER
```

and NUMBER is 310.20, the output is

```
RUN
+310.20
```

If NUMBER is −310.20, the output is

```
RUN
-310.20
```

Figure 4–6 illustrates how the PRINT USING statements can be used to display a table. The LPRINT USING statement works the same as the PRINT USING except output is sent to the printer.

Placing Multiple Statements on a Single Physical Line

It is possible to place several statements on the same line, separating them with colons. For example, the following line actually contains three statements:

```
100 V1 = 10 : V2 = 20 : V3 = 30
```

However, this can make the logic of the program more difficult to follow. Therefore, it is generally considered good programming practice to place each statement on a separate line.

FIGURE 4–6   Program Demonstrating the PRINT USING Statement

```
10   REM *** PROGRAM DEMONSTRATING THE PRINT USING STATEMENT. ***
20   REM
30   PRINT
40   PRINT USING "\           \         \     \     \       \";"ITEM","TOTAL","SALES"
50   PRINT USING "\         \     \     \       \     \";"PURCHASED","PRICE","TAX"
60   PRINT
70   READ A$,X
80   Y = X * .06
90   PRINT USING "\         \      $$##.##      $$##.##";A$,X,Y
100  READ A$,X
110  Y = X * .06
120  PRINT USING "\         \      $$##.##      $$##.##";A$,X,Y
130  READ A$,X
140  Y = X * .06
150  PRINT USING "\         \      $$##.##      $$##.##";A$,X,Y
160  READ A$,X
170  Y = X * .06
180  PRINT USING "\         \      $$##.##      $$##.##";A$,X,Y
190  READ A$,X
200  Y = X * .06
210  PRINT USING "\         \      $$##.##      $$##.##";A$,X,Y
220  REM
230  REM *** DATA STATEMENTS ***
240  DATA TOASTER,27.50,BLENDER,18.45
250  DATA BLANKET,9.90,KNIVES,34.99,FAN,29.99
999  END
```

```
RUN

ITEM            TOTAL        SALES
PURCHASED       PRICE        TAX

TOASTER         $27.50       $1.65
BLENDER         $18.45       $1.11
BLANKET          $9.90       $0.59
KNIVES          $34.99       $2.10
FAN             $29.99       $1.80
```

A Programming Problem

Problem Definition

Baymont High School needs a program to generate the percentage of students absent in each of the grades 9 through 12. The input is the current date, the total number of students in each class, and the number of students absent in each class. The output should be an attendance report listing each

Now Try This

4-3

1. Use the PRINT USING statements to display the following numbers in two columns, each ten spaces wide. Each number should be rounded to two decimal places.

148.073	70.514
16.1	100.00
2576.905	3609.95

2. Rewrite the statements in Question 1 so that the output is sent to the printer.

3. Write a PRINT USING statement that displays the number 4,190.03 (be sure the comma is inserted as indicated).

4. Write an LPRINT USING statement that prints a dollar amount (AMT) up to $999.99. The dollar sign should always be immediately to the left of the number.

---

of these values plus the percentage of students absent from each class. The report should be sent to the printer. Figure 4–7 contains the program specification chart and Figure 4–8 the printer spacing chart.

FIGURE 4–7 Program Specification Chart for Attendance Report

PROGRAM SPECIFICATION CHART

PROGRAM NAME: Attendance Report

PROGRAMMER'S NAME: S. Baumann

DATE: 10/10/91

INPUT:
Enrollment per class
Number absent per class

OUTPUT: Printer report formatted as shown in printer spacing chart (Figure 4-8)

SOURCE OF INPUT: Keyboard

DESTINATION OF OUTPUT: Printer

PURPOSE:
Creates and prints hard copy of daily attendance report, listing class enrollments, absences, and percentage of students absent.

FiGURE 4–8   Printer Spacing Chart for Attendance Report

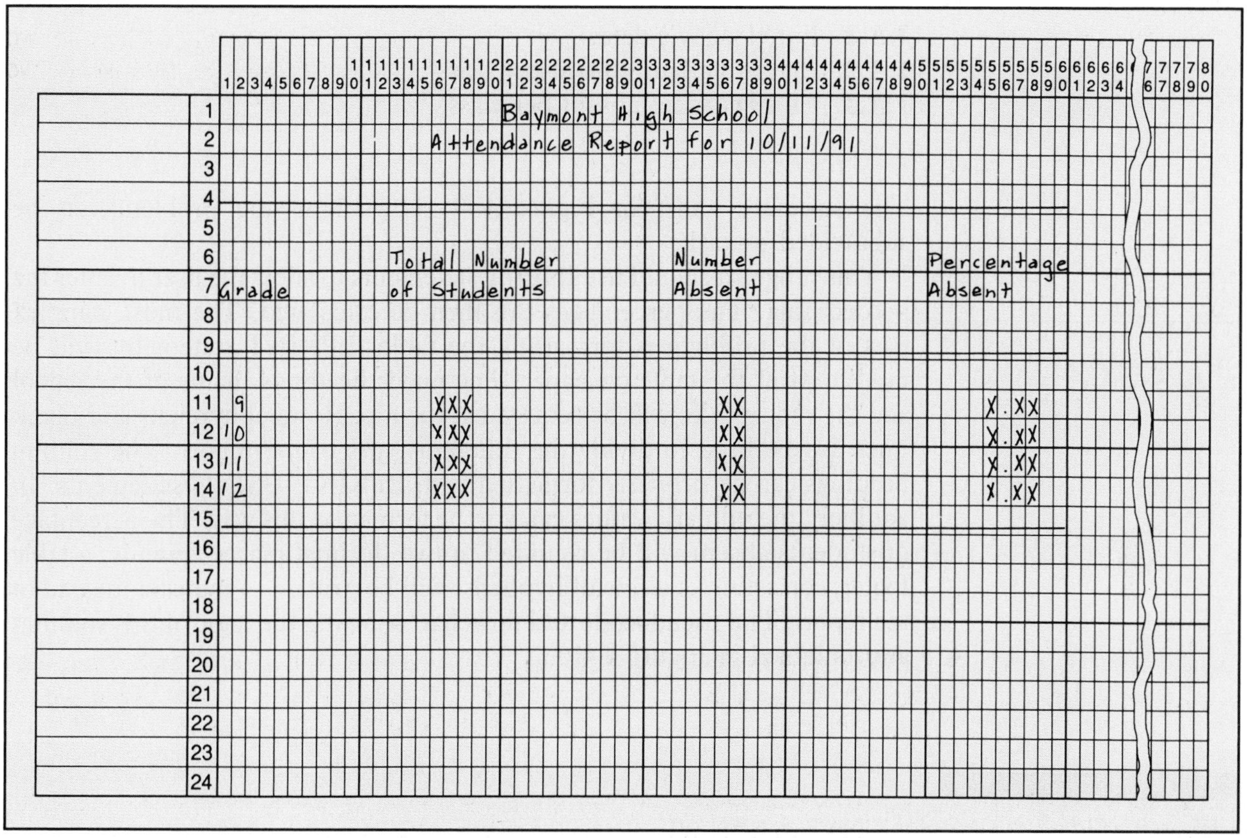

Solution Design

The general problem of generating an attendance report can be divided into two subproblems—the task of processing each class, and the task of printing the information in a report format:

1. Process each class.
2. Print report.

Step 1 can be further divided into several smaller tasks that must be performed for each class:

1.A. Enter the data.
1.B. Calculate the percentage absent per class.

Step 2 can also be broken down into smaller steps:

2.A. Center and print the headings.
2.B. Print information for each class.

Step 1.A, "Enter the data," can be further divided as well:

1.A.1. Enter today's date.
1.A.2. Enter total enrollment per class.
1.A.3. Enter number absent per class.

The structure chart in Figure 4–9 shows how the problem can be subdivided by task.

This program should use INPUT statements to allow the user to enter the needed data. The percentages can then be calculated. The most complex part of the problem is formatting the table. LPRINT statements will be used to print the table on paper. The major headings (name of the school and the report title) will be centered at the top. Rows of hyphens and blank lines can be used to divide the different parts of the report. The column headings can be properly formatted with LPRINT USING statements. In addition, the numeric values can also be formatted this way. The percentage of students absent will be rounded to two decimal places. Finally, a table footer, consisting of a row of hyphens, will be printed to indicate the end of the report. The pseudocode and flowchart showing the logic of this solution are contained in Figure 4–10.

FIGURE 4–9   Structure Chart for Attendance Report

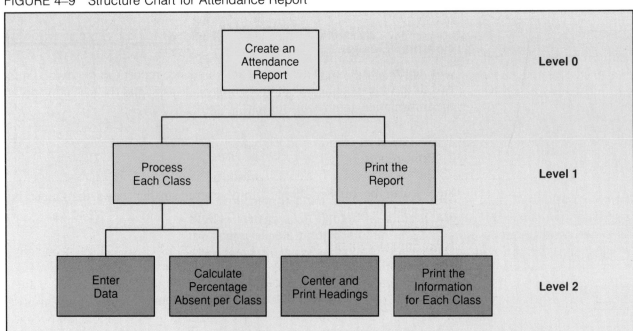

FIGURE 4–10   Pseudocode
and Flowchart for
Attendance Report

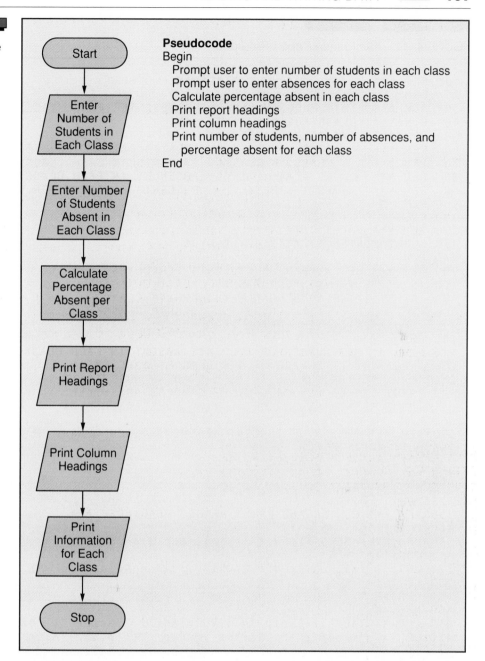

Pseudocode
Begin
  Prompt user to enter number of students in each class
  Prompt user to enter absences for each class
  Calculate percentage absent in each class
  Print report headings
  Print column headings
  Print number of students, number of absences, and
    percentage absent for each class
End

Start

Enter
Number of
Students in
Each Class

Enter Number
of Students
Absent in
Each Class

Calculate
Percentage
Absent per
Class

Print Report
Headings

Print Column
Headings

Print
Information
for Each
Class

Stop

The Program

Figure 4–11 contains the program that prints the attendance report. It prompts the user to enter today's date, the number of students enrolled in each class, and the number absent in each class. Lines 280–310 calculate the percentage absent in each class. Lines 350–520 print the final report. Notice that LPRINT and LPRINT USING statements are used so that the output goes to the printer. The two report headings are centered and printed in

FIGURE 4–11   Attendance Report Program

```
10   REM ***                   ATTENDANCE REPORT                    ***
20   REM
30   REM ***   THIS PROGRAM GENERATES ABSENTEE PERCENTAGES PER ***
40   REM ***   CLASS FOR ANY GIVEN DAY.                        ***
50   REM ***     MAJOR VARIABLES:                              ***
60   REM ***       DTE$              TODAY'S DATE              ***
70   REM ***       CLASS 1- CLASS4   STUDENTS IN EACH CLASS    ***
80   REM ***       A1 - A4           ABSENCES IN EACH CLASS    ***
90   REM ***       PCT1 - PCT4       PERCENTAGE ABSENT PER CLASS ***
100  REM
110  CLS
120  REM *** INPUT DATE. ***
130  INPUT "ENTER TODAY'S DATE";DTE$
140  REM
150  REM *** GET NUMBER OF STUDENTS PER CLASS. ***
160  INPUT "ENTER 9TH GRADE ENROLLMENT";CLASS1
170  INPUT "ENTER 10TH GRADE ENROLLMENT";CLASS2
180  INPUT "ENTER 11TH GRADE ENROLLMENT";CLASS3
190  INPUT "ENTER 12TH GRADE ENROLLMENT"; CLASS4
200  REM
210  REM *** GET NUMBER OF STUDENTS ABSENT IN EACH CLASS. ***
220  INPUT "ENTER NUMBER OF 9TH GRADERS ABSENT";A1
230  INPUT "ENTER NUMBER OF 10TH GRADERS ABSENT";A2
240  INPUT "ENTER NUMBER OF 11TH GRADERS ABSENT";A3
250  INPUT "ENTER NUMBER OF 12TH GRADERS ABSENT";A4
260  REM
270  REM *** DETERMINE PERCENT ABSENT IN EACH CLASS. ***
280  PCT1 = (A1 / CLASS1) * 100
290  PCT2 = (A2 / CLASS2) * 100
300  PCT3 = (A3 / CLASS3) * 100
310  PCT4 = (A4 / CLASS4) * 100
320  REM
330  REM *** CENTER AND PRINT REPORT HEADINGS. ***
340  POSITION = 60 - 19
350  LPRINT TAB(POSITION / 2) "Baymont High School"
360  POSITION = 60 - 28
370  LPRINT TAB(POSITION / 2) "Attendance Report for ";DTE$
380  LPRINT
390  LPRINT "_____"
400  LPRINT
410  LPRINT TAB(13) "Total Number";TAB(33) "Number";TAB(51);"Percentage"
420  LPRINT "Grade";TAB(13) "of Students";TAB(33) "Absent";TAB(51) "Absent"
430  LPRINT "_____"
440  LPRINT
450  F$ = "##            ###              ##           ##.##"
460  REM
470  REM *** PRINT REPORT FIGURES. ***
480  LPRINT USING F$;9,CLASS1,A1,PCT1
490  LPRINT USING F$;10,CLASS2,A2,PCT2
500  LPRINT USING F$;11,CLASS3,A3,PCT3
510  LPRINT USING F$;12,CLASS4,A4,PCT4
520  LPRINT "_____"
999  END
```

FIGURE 4–11 Continued

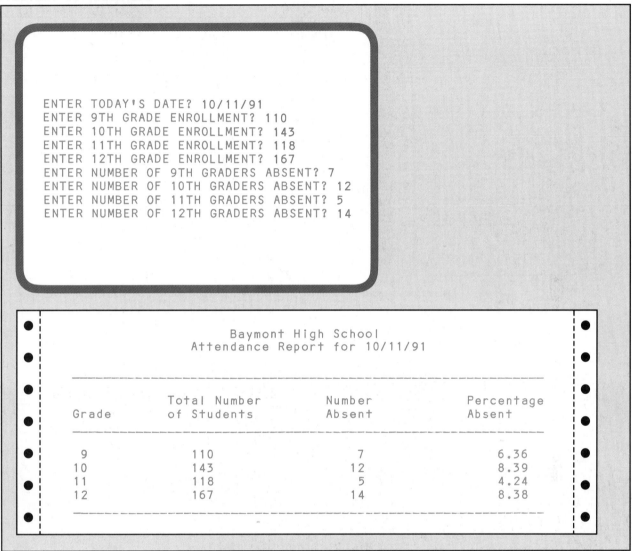

```
ENTER TODAY'S DATE? 10/11/91
ENTER 9TH GRADE ENROLLMENT? 110
ENTER 10TH GRADE ENROLLMENT? 143
ENTER 11TH GRADE ENROLLMENT? 118
ENTER 12TH GRADE ENROLLMENT? 167
ENTER NUMBER OF 9TH GRADERS ABSENT? 7
ENTER NUMBER OF 10TH GRADERS ABSENT? 12
ENTER NUMBER OF 11TH GRADERS ABSENT? 5
ENTER NUMBER OF 12TH GRADERS ABSENT? 14
```

```
                    Baymont High School
              Attendance Report for 10/11/91

       _____

              Total Number      Number         Percentage
       Grade  of Students       Absent         Absent
       _____

         9        110              7              6.36
        10        143             12              8.39
        11        118              5              4.24
        12        167             14              8.38

       _____
```

lines 340–370. Next, the underscore (___) is printed with a blank line before and after the headings. Lines 410 and 420 print the two rows of column headings. Each line of numbers is printed using the format control characters assigned to variable F$. Finally, a row of underscores is printed to indicate the end of the table.

Programming Hints

■ Wherever your program contains an INPUT statement, be sure to include a prompt telling the user the number of data values to be entered and the kind of values (numeric or string).

▪ Make certain that each data value in the DATA statements of a program will be assigned to the correct variable in a READ statement.

▪ Remember that if a PRINT statement contains more commas than there are print zones, the print zones of the next line will be used.

▪ Do not use commas in a TAB statement. TAB will work properly only if the items are separated by semicolons.

▪ Remember that the TAB function can be used only to advance the print position. Therefore, each column number in the statement should be larger than the previous one. Also, there can be no space between the reserved word TAB and the left parenthesis.

▪ When using the PRINT USING statement, remember to place the control characters in quotation marks.

▪ If you want a control character, such as a dollar sign, to "float," be sure to use two symbols in the PRINT USING statement.

New Statement Review

Statement Format	Explanation
line# INPUT variable1 [,variable2] . . .	Allows the user to enter values while the program is executing. Each value is assigned to the corresponding variable.
line# READ variable1 [,variable2] . . .	Allows data to be placed in the program itself. A value is read from the data list and assigned to each variable.
line# DATA value1 [,value2] . . .	Contains the values assigned to each of the variables in the READ statement(s).
TAB(expression)	The next value output will appear in the column number specified by the value of *expression*.
SPC(expression)	The next output will be spaced over the number of positions specified by the value of *expression*.
line# LPRINT expression-list	Works the same as the PRINT statement except output is sent to the printer.
PRINT USING "format characters"; expression-list	The values of the expressions are outputted using the formatting specified by the format characters.

Summary Points

- This chapter introduced two methods of entering data to a program: the INPUT statement and the READ and DATA statements.
- The INPUT statement allows the user to enter data while the program is running. Therefore, the values used can change each time the program is run.
- When an INPUT statement is encountered during program execution, the program stops running until the user enters the needed data and presses <Enter>. Each data value entered is then assigned to the corresponding variable in the INPUT statement.
- When data must be entered by the user, the program should display a prompt telling exactly what data is to be entered.
- The READ and DATA statements are a second method of entering data. The READ statement causes values contained in the DATA statements to be assigned to the variables listed in the READ statement.
- DATA statements are nonexecutable and can be located anywhere in the program. For consistency, they are generally placed at the end of the program. When a program is executed, all of the data values in all of the DATA statements are combined into one listing, called the data list.
- READ and INPUT statements are located in a program where the logic of the program dictates.
- Numeric values can be assigned to character variables, but character strings cannot be assigned to numeric variables.
- The INPUT statement is ideally suited for programs in which the data changes often, whereas the READ and DATA statements are particularly useful when it is necessary to read large quantities of data.
- When more than one item is to be printed on a single output line, the spacing can be controlled by the use of commas and semicolons.
- The semicolon causes the next item output to be placed in the next available print position, whereas the comma causes output to begin in the next print zone.
- The TAB function instructs output to begin at a specified column number.
- The SPC function causes the specified number of spaces to be left between output items.
- Output can be formatted in a variety of ways such as aligning numbers at the decimal point by using the PRINT USING statement.

Vocabulary List

Conversational mode   Inquiry-and-response mode
Data list   Prompt
Formatting

Questions

Whenever appropriate, use complete sentences in answering the following questions.

1. What are the advantages of the INPUT statement? What is a disadvantage?
2. What does the computer do when it encounters an INPUT statement?

3. What is a prompt used for? What two things should a prompt tell the user?

4. When are READ and DATA statements best used?

5. How does the programmer determine where to place INPUT and READ/DATA statements in a program?

6. What is a data list, and how is it created?

7. What happens if a program attempts to read a data value when there are no more data values in the data list?

8. What will be the output of the following program segment?

```
230 X$ = "MOUNTAIN"
240 Y$ = "MOLEHILL"
250 PRINT X$;Y$
```

9. In which zone will the word RETURNS appear if the following statement is executed?

```
70 PRINT "HAPPY",,"RETURNS"
```

10. When using commas, what happens if there are more items listed in a PRINT statement than there are print zones?

11. What will be the output of the following program segment?

```
100 READ W1$,W2$,W3$,W4$
110 PRINT,,W2$
120 PRINT W3$;" ";W4$
130 DATA "WE","WANT","INFORMATION","!"
```

12. What will be the output of the following statement (be sure to indicate spacing)?

```
30 PRINT TAB(20) 10;TAB(35) "TIMES";TAB(45); 8
```

13. Explain the difference between the TAB and the SPC functions.

14. Explain the purpose of three format control characters that can be used with the PRINT USING statement.

15. Explain the difference between these two statements:

```
20 PRINT USING "$$###.##";PRICE
30 PRINT USING "$###.##";PRICE
```

Debugging Exercises

Identify the following programs or program segments that contain errors and debug them.

```
1. 10 REM *** PROMPT THE USER TO ENTER A COUNTRY. ***
   20 PRINT "INPUT THE NAME OF A COUNTRY";CTRY$
```

```
2. 90   REM *** TOTAL 3 SCORES AND GET PERCENTAGE. ***
   100  READ P1,P2,P3
   110  AMT = (P1 + P2 + P3) / 100
   120  DATA 14,77
```

```
3. 50   READ W1$,W2$,W3$
   60   READ X,Y,Z
   70   X = X - 10
   80   Y = Y + 5
   90   PRINT W1$;TAB(X);W2$;TAB(Y);W3$
   100  DATA "WHAT","IS","LIFE?",8,5,15
```

```
4. 40 REM *** READ AND PRINT LIST OF EMPLOYEES AND SALARIES. ***
   50   READ NME$,SAL
   60   F$  = \           \  $$######
   70   PRINT USING F$;NME$,SAL
   80   READ NME$,SAL
   90   PRINT USING F$;NME$,SAL
   100  ERICSON, 3100,LING,4050
```

Programming Problems

Level 1

1. Write a program segment that asks for the name of an object and its weight in pounds. The program should then calculate the weight in kilograms (1 pound = 0.453592 kilograms) and display the name, weight in pounds, and weight in kilograms, each in a different print zone.

2. Rewrite Problem 1 using READ and DATA statements rather than an INPUT statement.

3. Write a program that uses the INPUT statement to enable the user to enter any two numbers. The program should then display the sum, difference, product, and quotient of these two numbers. Your output should be similar to the following:

```
ENTER ANY TWO NUMBERS.
(SEPARATE THE NUMBERS WITH A COMMA) XXX,XXX
XXX + XXX = XXXX
XXX - XXX = XXX
XXX * XXX = XXXXX
XXX / XXX = XXX
```

4. The Persian Pots Co. is running a sale of 10 percent off all plants for Arbor Day. Write a program that uses READ/DATA and the TAB function to print a table containing the sale prices of the following plants:

Plant	Regular Price
Swedish Ivy	1.50
Boston Fern	2.00
Poinsettia	5.40
Cactus	1.70

The columns in the table should be 20 spaces apart.

```
PLANT               SALE PRICE
XXXXXXXX            X.XX
XXXXXXXX            X.XX
XXXXXXXX            X.XX
XXXXXXXX            X.XX
```

5. Alter Problem 4 so that it uses the SPC function instead of the TAB function. Place 20 spaces between the longest item in the first column and the second column.

6. Write a program segment using the PRINT USING to duplicate the following table.

COMPANY	ASSETS	SALES	MARKET VALUE
CHRYSLER	7,074,365	15,537,788	1,227,533
AT&T	86,716,989	32,815,582	38,570,218
BURROUGHS	2,539,319	1,870,845	3,707,422

Level 2

1. Write a program that calculates the batting average of a baseball player. Use INPUT statements to allow the necessary data to be entered. The program should read the times at bat, the number of walks, and the number of hits. Subtract the number of walks from the times at bat, and then divide the number of hits by this value to calculate the batting average. Output this batting average with an appropriate label.

2. Write a program to compute an individual's typing speed. The program should prompt the user to enter the following data: person's name, number of words typed, number of minutes spent typing, and the number of errors. The formula to be used for calculating words typed per minute is:

$$\text{WPM} = \frac{\text{Number of Words Typed} - (\text{Number of Errors} * 5)}{\text{Number of Minutes Spent Typing}}$$

3. Write a program to list several activities and the number of calories expended during 15, 30, and 60 minutes of each activity. Use the following data:

Activity	Calories Burned per Minute
Sleeping	2.3
Jogging	15.0
Sitting	1.7

Use READ and DATA statements to place the data in variables. Then use commas to space the output so that it looks similar to the following:

```
ACTIVITY        15 MINUTES      30 MINUTES      60 MINUTES
SLEEPING        XXX.XX          XXX.XX          XXX.XX
JOGGING         XXX.XX          XXX.XX          XXX.XX
SITTING         XXX.XX          XXX.XX          XXX.XX
```

4. Jim and Bob have decided to stop smoking and would like to know how much money they will save per week and per year. Bob smokes one and one-half packs a day at $1.25 a pack, and Jim smokes one pack a day at $1.32 a pack. Format your output as follows:

```
SMOKER'S     NO. PACKS        COST        AMT. SAVED      AMT. SAVED
  NAME        PER DAY       PER PACK       PER WEEK        PER YEAR
XXXXXX          XX           $X.XX          $X.XX          $XXX.XX
```

5. The Rainbow Paint Shop would like a program to determine the cost and number of gallons of paint needed to paint one room, based on the room's width, length, and height. Assume that each gallon of paint covers approximately 250 square feet and the cost is $15.95 a gallon. Write a program that will enable the user to enter the dimensions of the room during program execution and print (on paper) a table containing the desired output. Create your own input to use when testing the program.

6. Martha's Dance School charges a flat hourly rate of $6.75. Martha would like a program to determine the total amount owed by each student and the dance school's total income. The output should be in table form. Use READ and DATA statements to read the following data to the program:

	Hours				
Name	**Monday**	**Tuesday**	**Wednesday**	**Thursday**	**Friday**
Karen	2	3	3	4	2
Alex	3	2	2	2	3

Projects

For each project, complete the following:

- Fill out a program specification chart.
- Develop a structure chart.
- Create a flowchart or pseudocode.
- Thoroughly document the final program.
- Test your program using a variety of data.

1. The Acme Concrete Company has bought a new computer and would like a program to compute the cost of a given amount of concrete and the cost of the labor to pour it. The input should be the length, width, and depth, in feet, of the concrete to be poured. Concrete costs $32 per cubic yard, and labor costs $20 per cubic yard (a cubic yard has 27 cubic feet). The output should appear similar to the following:

```
                       CONCRETE COSTS

IN FEET:              CUBIC   CONCRETE AT   LABOR AT      TOTAL
LEN    WID    DEP     YARDS   $32/CU. YD.   $20/CU. YD.   COST
XX     XX     XX      XXX     $XXX.XX       $XXX.XX       $XXXX.XX
```

2. The Thriftway Company wants to generate a monthly report for each of its salespeople. The report should print a salesperson's total sales for each item, and his or her total sales overall (on three items). The output should look similar to the following (place three asterisks after total):

```
                  THRIFTWAY COMPANY
                SALES ANALYSIS REPORT

SALESPERSON       PRODUCT       QNTY SOLD   UNIT PRICE   SALE AMT
XXXXXXXXXXX       XXXXXXXXX      XXX         XX.XX        XXX.XX
XXXXXXXXXXX       XXXXXXXXX      XXX         XX.XX        XXX.XX
XXXXXXXXXXX       XXXXXXXXX      XXX         XX.XX        XXX.XX

                                            TOTAL     XXXXXX.XX***
```

CHAPTER 5

Introduction to Control Structures

Learning Objectives

After studying this chapter, you should be able to
1. Discuss how control statements alter the order in which program statements are executed.
2. Explain how the GOTO statement works.
3. Explain why GOTO statements should be avoided in structured programming.
4. Explain the difference between the single-alternative and double-alternative decision statements.
5. Explain how IF statements are used to implement the decision structure in structured programming.
6. Draw flowcharts representing decision structures.
7. Explain how relational operators are used to test for conditions.
8. Write programs using single- and double-alternative decision statements.
9. Explain how nested IF statements function.
10. Write programs using nested IF statements.

Introduction

Control statement
A statement allowing the programmer to control the order in which statements are executed.

This chapter introduces the control statement, a powerful programming tool that will be used in virtually all programs from this point on. **Control statements** allow the programmer to control the order in which program statements are executed.

Unconditional Transfer: The GOTO Statement

All of the programs we have written so far have been executed in a simple sequential manner. That is, the lowest-numbered line is executed first, then control passes to the next-lowest-numbered line, and so on from the beginning to the end of the program. To solve many programming problems, however, it is necessary to alter the order in which statements are executed. Changing the normal path or flow of program execution is known as **branching,** and a statement that can make such a change is called a *branch.*

Branch
To change the normal flow of program execution.

An example of a branch is the GOTO statement. Its general format looks like this:

line# GOTO transfer line#

The transfer line number tells the computer the line number of the next statement to be executed, and control transfers to that line regardless of its location in the program.

When a GOTO statement is executed, three possible actions may be taken:

- If the statement indicated by the transfer line number is executable, it is executed, and execution continues from that point forward.
- If the statement indicated by the transfer line number is nonexecutable (such as a REM or DATA statement), control passes to the first line following it.
- If the transfer line number is not a line number contained in the program, an error message is displayed, and program execution is terminated.

The following is an example of a GOTO statement:

```
100 GOTO 60
```

This statement causes program execution to branch, or "go to," line 60, execute it if possible, and continue execution with the line following line 60.

Unconditional transfer
A transfer that always takes place.

Because control of the execution path always changes when the GOTO statement is encountered, such a statement is known as an **unconditional transfer.** Figures 5–1 and 5–2 show how execution paths are controlled with GOTO statements.

In Figure 5–1, the GOTO statement in line 50 causes control to pass to line 70. Therefore, only the value of Y is printed; line 60 is skipped and left unexecuted. In Figure 5–2, control is transferred to line 50 by the GOTO statement in line 20. Line 50 contains a nonexecutable statement, so control passes to line 60. Notice that lines 30 and 40 are skipped and left unexecuted.

At this point a word of caution is in order. Although the GOTO statement gives the programmer increased control over the logic flow of a program, unconditional transfers can produce an execution path so complex and unreadable that the logic is virtually impossible to follow, and debugging becomes a nightmare. Programs with large numbers of GOTO statements

FIGURE 5–1 GOTO
Statement: Example 1

```
 ┌─ 30 X = 10
 ├─ 40 Y = 20
 ├─ 50 GOTO 70
 │  60 PRINT X
 └─ 70 PRINT Y
    99 END
```

FIGURE 5–2 GOTO
Statement: Example 2

```
 ┌─ 10 X = 20
 └→ 20 GOTO 50
    30 Y = X * 2
    40 PRINT Y
 ┌─ 50 REM *** THIS ISN'T EXECUTED. ***
 └─ 60 PRINT X
    99 END
```

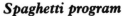

Spaghetti program
A program with difficult-to-follow logic caused by the use of a large number of unconditional transfers.

Conditional transfer statement
A statement in which control is transferred to different locations depending on specific conditions.

are referred to as **spaghetti programs.** Tracing through these programs is as difficult as following a single strand in a large platter of spaghetti. Later in this chapter and in other chapters, you will be introduced to control statements that are preferable to the GOTO statement. The GOTO should be used only when these other statements cannot be used.

Conditional Transfer: The ON/GOTO Statement

The ON/GOTO, or computed GOTO, statement transfers control to other statements in a program based on how a mathematical expression evaluates. The ON/GOTO is a **conditional transfer statement;** control is transferred to different locations depending on specified conditions. Its general format is

```
line# ON expression GOTO line#1[,line#2]. . .
```

The expression must be arithmetic. If it evaluates as a real number, it is rounded to the nearest integer. The steps in executing the ON/GOTO statement are as follows:

1. The expression is evaluated as an integer (real numbers are rounded).
2. Depending on the value of the expression, control passes to the corresponding line number.

> **a.** If the value of the expression is 1, control passes to the first line number listed.
> **b.** If the value of the expression is 2, control passes to the second line number listed.
> **c.** If the value of the expression is n, control passes to the nth line number listed.

The following examples demonstrate how three ON/GOTO statements are executed.

Statement	Value of Variable	Execution
`10 ON X GOTO 30,50,70`	X = 1	Control passes to line 30.
	X = 2	Control passes to line 50.
	X = 3	Control passes to line 70.
`10 ON X - 2 GOTO 100,150`	X = 3	3 − 2 = 1. Control passes to line 100.
`20 ON X / 3 GOTO 40,60,80`	X = 7	7/3 = 2.33. Result of 2.33 is rounded to 2. Control passes to line 60.

Two additional rules apply to the ON/GOTO statement:

- If the value of the expression is zero or greater than the number of transfer lines, the ON/GOTO statement is ignored, and control passes to the next statement. Therefore, because there are not five transfer line numbers in the following ON/GOTO statement,

```
20 COUNT = 5
30 ON COUNT GOTO 70,85,100
40 COUNT = COUNT - 1
```

program control simply continues on with line 40.

- If the value of the expression is negative, or if it is greater than 255, an error message is displayed, and execution stops. Consider the following program segment:

```
20 COUNT = 5 - 7
30 ON COUNT GOTO 70,85,100
```

Because the value of COUNT is negative (-2), the following error message is displayed when this program segment is executed:

```
Illegal function call in 30
```

The next section demonstrates how the ON/GOTO statement is used when a program needs to perform one of a number of tasks.

Creating Menus

Menu
A list of the functions a program can perform.

A **menu** is a displayed list of program functions. Just as a customer in a restaurant looks at the menu to choose a meal, so a program user looks at a menu displayed on the screen to choose a desired function. The user makes a selection by entering a code, usually a simple number or letter, at the keyboard. Here is an example of a menu:

```
            MONEY CONVERSION MENU

ENTER NUMBER OF DOLLARS TO BE CONVERTED
? 300

PLEASE ENTER ONE OF THE FOLLOWING NUMBERS:
    1   TO CONVERT TO POUNDS
    2   TO CONVERT TO MARKS
    3   TO CONVERT TO FRANCS
    4   TO CONVERT TO LIRA

?
```

This menu allows the user to choose the desired conversion by entering a number from 1 through 4. The complete program is shown in Figure 5–3. Line 60 clears the screen before the menu is displayed. After entering the

FIGURE 5–3   A Menu Using the ON/GOTO Statement

```
10   REM ***                    MONEY CONVERSION PROGRAM                    ***
20   REM
30   REM *** CONVERT DOLLARS TO FOREIGN CURRENCY ACCORDING      ***
40   REM ***  TO THE MENU.                                      ***
50   REM
60   CLS
70   PRINT , "MONEY CONVERSION MENU"
80   PRINT
90   PRINT "ENTER NUMBER OF DOLLARS TO BE CONVERTED"
100  INPUT DOLLARS
110  PRINT
120  PRINT "PLEASE ENTER ONE OF THE FOLLOWING NUMBERS: "
130  PRINT "    1   TO CONVERT TO POUNDS"
140  PRINT "    2   TO CONVERT TO MARKS"
150  PRINT "    3   TO CONVERT TO FRANCS"
160  PRINT "    4   TO CONVERT TO LIRA"
170  PRINT
180  INPUT CODE
190  ON CODE GOTO 220,260,300,340
200  REM
210  REM CONVERT TO POUNDS.
220  RESULT = DOLLARS * .94
230  GOTO 370
240  REM
250  REM CONVERT TO MARKS.
260  RESULT = DOLLARS * 2.4
270  GOTO 370
280  REM
290  REM CONVERT TO FRANCS.
300  RESULT = DOLLARS * 7.2
310  GOTO 370
320  REM
330  REM CONVERT TO LIRA.
340  RESULT = DOLLARS * 1439
350  REM
360  REM DISPLAY THE RESULT.
370  PRINT USING "\            \ $$#####.##";"THE AMOUNT IS";RESULT
999  END
```

FIGURE 5–3 Continued

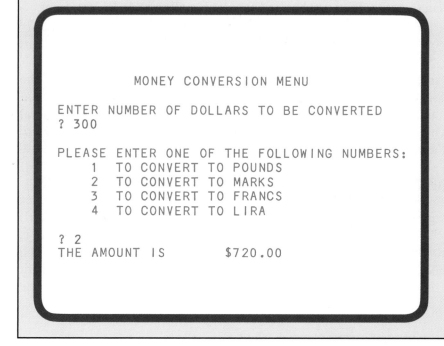

```
          MONEY CONVERSION MENU

ENTER NUMBER OF DOLLARS TO BE CONVERTED
? 300

PLEASE ENTER ONE OF THE FOLLOWING NUMBERS:
     1   TO CONVERT TO POUNDS
     2   TO CONVERT TO MARKS
     3   TO CONVERT TO FRANCS
     4   TO CONVERT TO LIRA

? 2
THE AMOUNT IS          $720.00
```

number of dollars to be converted, the user enters a 1, 2, 3, or 4 to indicate the desired currency. The ON/GOTO statement in line 190 branches to the statement that performs the correct conversion. Control is then transferred to line 370 so the result can be displayed. However, notice that there is no GOTO statement after the statement converting dollars to lira (line 340). Because this is the last conversion made, the normal flow of program execution will cause line 370 to be the next statement executed.

 5-1

Now Try This

1. Write a statement that always transfers program control to line 580.

2. Write a statement that transfers program control to line 400 if V is 4, line 500 if V is 5, and line 800 if V is 6.

3. Write a statement that transfers program control to line 100 if PRCNT is 100 or 400, to line 200 if PRCNT is 200, and line 300 if PRCNT is 300.

Decision Structures

As previously mentioned, any programming problem can be solved using the needed combination of three structures: the sequence, the decision structure, and the loop. In this section, you will learn to write programs that use the *decision structure*, which is used to test a condition. In BASIC, decision structures are written using two variations of the IF statement: the single-alternative IF statement and the double-alternative IF statement.

The Single-Alternative IF Statement

Single-alternative IF statement
A decision statement in which an action is taken if the specified comparison is true. Otherwise, control continues to the next statement.

The **single-alternative IF** (IF/THEN) **statement** tests a condition: if the condition is true, an action is taken; if it is false, no action is taken, and program execution simply continues on to the next statement. The general flowchart and pseudocode for this statement are shown in Figure 5–4. Here is an example of an IF/THEN statement:

```
20 IF NMBR = 10 THEN PRINT "THIS IS A LARGE SIZE."
```

In this example, the THEN clause—PRINT "THIS IS A LARGE SIZE"—is executed only if NMBR is equal to 10. Otherwise, no action is taken. Execution then continues on to the next program statement. The THEN clause can contain any number of statements by separating them with colons. The IF/THEN statement below executes two statements if the expression is true:

```
20 IF NMBR = 10 THEN PRINT "THIS IS A LARGE SIZE." : LRGE = LRGE + 1
```

The expression after the THEN can be a transfer to another line number:

```
20 IF NMBR = 10 GOTO 120
      .
      .
      .
120 PRINT "THIS IS A LARGE SIZE."
130 LRGE = LRGE + 1
```

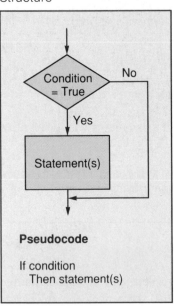

FIGURE 5–4 Flowchart and Pseudocode for Single-Alternative Decision Structure

Therefore, there are two general formats for the IF statement:

line# IF expression THEN clause
line# IF expression {GOTO / THEN} line#

Notice that when braces ({ }) are used in a format statement, the programmer must choose one of the options listed.

It is better structured programming practice to use the first format because the actions are taken within the statement itself, avoiding an unnecessary GOTO statement. However, if the second format is used, the IF statement can be written in several ways. The following statements both transfer control to line number 300.

```
40 IF SCORE$ = "A" THEN 300
40 IF SCORE$ = "A" THEN GOTO 300
```

Relational operators
Operators used to compare two expressions.

Comparisons in IF statements are made by using **relational operators,** which determine whether one expression is greater than, equal to, or less than another expression. Table 5–1 shows the relational operators used in BASIC. The values of the expressions can be either numeric or character strings. However, both expressions must be of the same type. Therefore, the following statement comparing two character strings is valid:

```
40 IF "SAL" < "SALLY" THEN PRINT "THIS IS A NICKNAME."
```

However, the next statement is invalid because it attempts to compare a character string to a number:

```
40 IF "SAL" < 5 THEN PRINT "WRONG NAME"
```

Collating sequence
The internal ordering that the computer assigns to the characters it can recognize. This ordering allows the computer to make comparisons between different character values.

It is easy to understand how the computer can compare numbers, but you may be wondering how it compares character strings. When comparing characters, the computer makes use of a code that assigns an integer value to each character according to its order in the computer's **collating sequence.** There are many different collating sequences depending on the type of computer being used. The collating sequence used in IBM (and IBM-compatible) personal computers is ASCII (American Standard Code for Information Interchange). Table 5–2 shows part of the ASCII collating sequence. From examining it, you can determine that "A" is less than "D" because 65 is less than 68. In addition, notice that uppercase letters are always less than lowercase letters.

When the computer compares two character strings, it compares each character, from left to right. The first character of one string is compared to the first character of the other string, then the second character of each string is compared, and so on until a character of one string is found to be less than the corresponding character of the other string. For example, the expression

```
"MAN" < "MAT"
```

is true because N is less than T.

When two strings of unequal length are compared, and all the letters of the shorter string match the corresponding letters of the longer string, the shorter string is considered to be less than the longer string. Thus, the following condition is true:

```
"HOPE" < "HOPEFUL"
```

TABLE 5–1   Relational Operators

Operator	Meaning	Example
<	Less than	1 < 10
< =	Less than or equal to	"Y" < = "Z"
>	Greater than	1043.4 > 1042
> =	Greater than or equal to	"SAMUEL" > = "SAM"
=	Equal to	10 + 4 = 14
<>	Not equal to	"Jones" <> "Done"

TABLE 5–2   ASCII Chart

Code	Character	Code	Character	Code	Character
32	SPC	64	@	96	´
33	!	65	A	97	a
34	"	66	B	98	b
35	#	67	C	99	c
36	$	68	D	100	d
37	%	69	E	101	e
38	&	70	F	102	f
39	'	71	G	103	g
40	(	72	H	104	h
41	)	73	I	105	i
42	*	74	J	106	j
43	+	75	K	107	k
44	,	76	L	108	l
45	-	77	M	109	m
46	.	78	N	110	n
47	/	79	O	111	o
48	0	80	P	112	p
49	1	81	Q	113	q
50	2	82	R	114	r
51	3	83	S	115	s
52	4	84	T	116	t
53	5	85	U	117	u
54	6	86	V	118	v
55	7	87	W	119	w
56	8	88	X	120	x
57	9	89	Y	121	y
58	:	90	Z	122	z
59	;	91	[	123	{
60	<	92	\	124		
61	=	93	]	125	}
62	>	94	∧	126	~
63	?	95	_	127	⌂

Be aware also that leading and trailing blanks are significant. Because a blank has a smaller ASCII value than any letter or digit, the following conditions are true:

```
"  CAT < "CAT" (blank < C)
"PAY" < "PAY  "
```

The second string is longer because it ends with a blank.

Let's write a program using the IF/THEN statement. The local music store is having a sale. All of the cassettes are marked down to $5. If you buy six or more cassettes, you get 10 percent off the total price. The flowchart for this problem is shown on the left side of Figure 5–5. In the program, the number of cassettes being purchased must be read first. Next, the program must determine whether the number of cassettes being bought is greater than or equal to 6. If it is, the price charged will be only 90 percent of the total (100% − 10%). The needed IF/THEN statement could be written like this:

```
130 IF NMBR >= 6 THEN CST = CST * .9
```

It also could be written as

```
130 IF NMBR > 5 THEN CST = CST * .9
```

Either way, 10 percent is subtracted from the total price if six or more cassettes are purchased. The complete program is on the right side of Figure 5–5.

Now Try This

1. Write the pseudocode for a single-alternative decision structure specifying that you will take an American literature course only if it is being taught by Mr. Ericson.

2. Write an IF/THEN statement that compares a variable NME$ to the character string "NORMA JEAN." If they are equal, the statement "THE NAME IS FOUND" should be displayed.

3. Write an IF statement that prints the statement "IT'S FREEZING OUTSIDE" if the temperature (TEMP) is less than or equal to 32.

4. Write a program segment that prompts the user to enter a password. If the password entered is "OPEN SAYS ME," the statement "PLEASE ENTER" should be displayed.

FIGURE 5–5   Program Using Single-Alternative Decision Structure

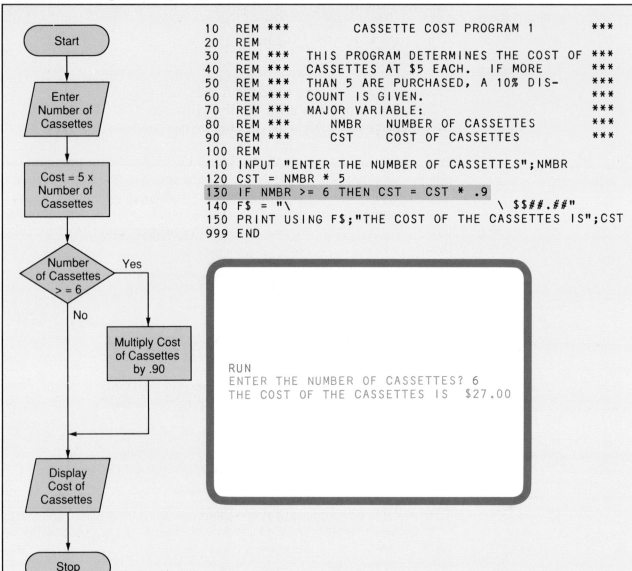

The Double-Alternative IF Statement

An extension of the IF/THEN statement is the IF/THEN/ELSE statement. It is referred to as a **double-alternative IF statement** because one action is taken if the comparison is true and another if it is false. As with the IF/THEN statement, either statements or line numbers can be specified:

Double-alternative IF statement

A decision statement in which one action is taken if the specified condition is true and another action if it is false.

$$\text{line\# IF expression THEN } \begin{Bmatrix} \text{clause} \\ \text{line\#} \end{Bmatrix} \text{ ELSE } \begin{Bmatrix} \text{clause} \\ \text{line\#} \end{Bmatrix}$$

The IF/THEN/ELSE statement is executed as follows:

■ If the condition is true, the THEN clause is executed and the ELSE clause is ignored.
■ If the condition is false, the THEN clause is ignored and the ELSE clause is executed.

The basic flowchart and pseudocode are shown in Figure 5–6.

As with the single-alternative IF statement, the statements following the THEN and ELSE can be replaced by transfer line numbers as shown here:

```
20 IF NMBR > 10 THEN 60 ELSE 100
```

If NMBR is greater than 10, program control transfers to line 60; otherwise, it transfers to line 100.

Let's write a program using the IF/THEN/ELSE statement by altering the pricing arrangement used in the music store sale:

1 to 5 cassettes	$5.00 each
6 or more cassettes	$4.85 each

Look at the flowchart for this problem at the top of Figure 5–7. The easiest way to write this program is by using an IF/THEN/ELSE statement:

FIGURE 5–6 Flowchart and Pseudocode for Double-Alternative Decision Structure

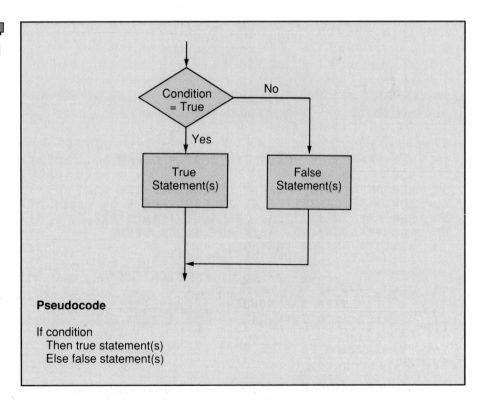

Pseudocode

If condition
    Then true statement(s)
    Else false statement(s)

FIGURE 5–7   Program Using Double-Alternative Decision Structure

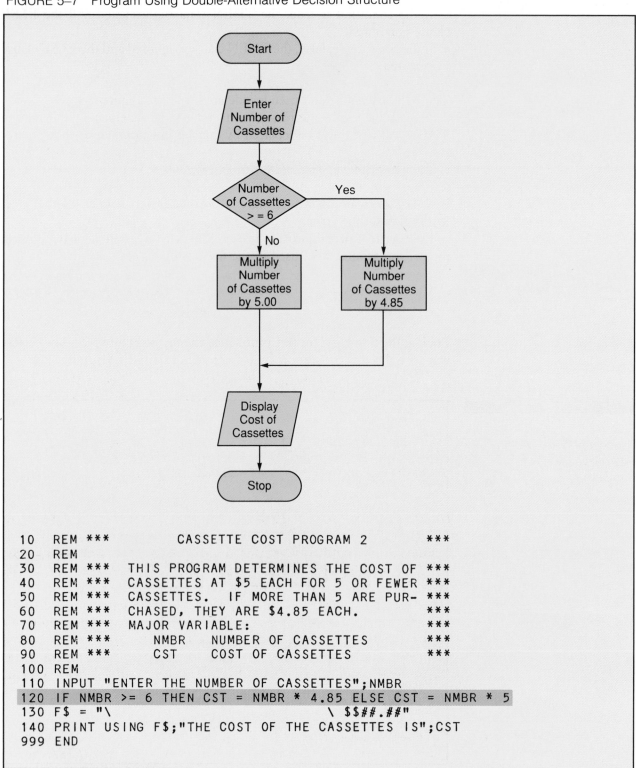

```
10   REM ***              CASSETTE COST PROGRAM 2          ***
20   REM
30   REM ***   THIS PROGRAM DETERMINES THE COST OF ***
40   REM ***   CASSETTES AT $5 EACH FOR 5 OR FEWER ***
50   REM ***   CASSETTES.  IF MORE THAN 5 ARE PUR- ***
60   REM ***   CHASED, THEY ARE $4.85 EACH.        ***
70   REM ***   MAJOR VARIABLE:                     ***
80   REM ***      NMBR    NUMBER OF CASSETTES       ***
90   REM ***      CST     COST OF CASSETTES         ***
100  REM
110  INPUT "ENTER THE NUMBER OF CASSETTES";NMBR
120  IF NMBR >= 6 THEN CST = NMBR * 4.85 ELSE CST = NMBR * 5
130  F$ = "\                        \ $$##.##"
140  PRINT USING F$;"THE COST OF THE CASSETTES IS";CST
999  END
```

FIGURE 5–7   Continued

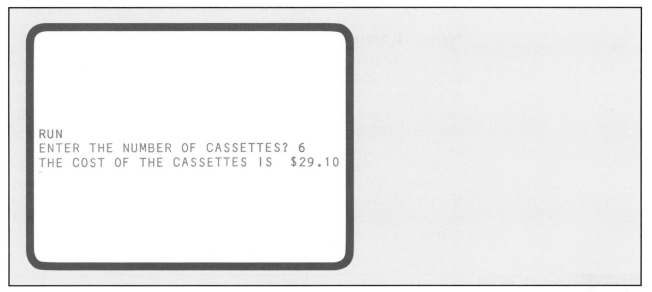

```
RUN
ENTER THE NUMBER OF CASSETTES? 6
THE COST OF THE CASSETTES IS   $29.10
```

```
120 IF NMBR >= 6 THEN CST = NMBR * 4.85 ELSE CST = NMBR * 5
```

If six or more cassettes are purchased, the price is $4.85 each; otherwise, the price is $5.00 each. The bottom of Figure 5–7 contains the complete program. Notice that it is similar to Figure 5–5 except for line 120.

IF/THEN/ELSE statements can become long, particularly when the THEN or ELSE clauses contain more than one statement as follows:

```
10 IF X > Y THEN Y = 0 : X = X + 5 ELSE X = 0 : Y = Y + 5
```

Both the THEN and the ELSE clauses contain two statements. The entire IF/THEN/ELSE statement must appear on a single physical line (a physical line always ends when the <Enter> key is pressed). If a statement is longer than 80 characters (the width of the screen), the computer system causes the statement to "wrap around" to the next line without the use of the <Enter> key. Because <Enter> has not been pressed, the BASIC system correctly sees the statement as being on a single physical line. Many programmers like to use the space bar to insert blanks so that the second line of a statement is indented below the first line, making the program more readable. The previous IF/THEN/ELSE statement could be made to wrap around as shown:

```
10 IF X > Y THEN Y = 0 : X = X + 5
         ELSE X = 0 : Y = Y + 5
```

Inserting blanks so that the ELSE clause appears on the second line makes the logic of the IF/THEN/ELSE easier to understand.

Nested IF Statements

It is possible to nest two or more IF/THEN or IF/THEN/ELSE statements by placing another IF statement in either the THEN or the ELSE portion of a statement. Figure 5–8 contains an example of an IF/THEN/ELSE statement nested in the ELSE portion of an outer IF/THEN/ELSE statement. The last clause—ELSE PRINT "ZERO"—is executed only if neither of the two previous clauses is true.

Nesting statements in this manner can quickly make a program difficult to follow. To avoid errors in logic, make certain that nested IF/THEN/ELSE statements contain the same number of ELSE and THEN clauses; on execution, each ELSE is matched with the closest unmatched THEN.

FIGURE 5–8 A Nested IF Statement

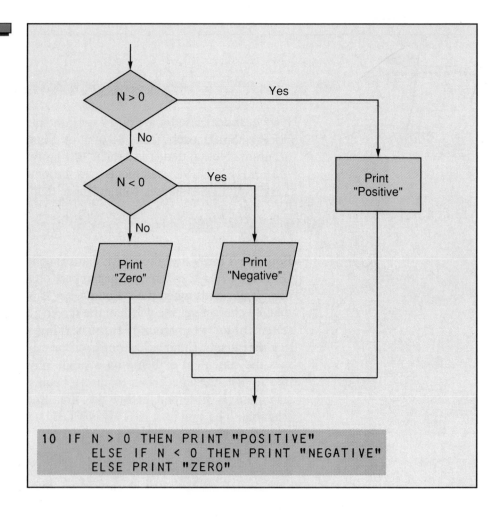

```
10 IF N > 0 THEN PRINT "POSITIVE"
   ELSE IF N < 0 THEN PRINT "NEGATIVE"
   ELSE PRINT "ZERO"
```

Once again, let's alter the sale prices for the music store cassettes:

1 to 5 cassettes	$5.00
6 to 9 cassettes	$4.85
10 or more cassettes	$4.50

The top of Figure 5–9 contains the flowchart for this problem. The following nested IF statement is an efficient solution.

```
110 IF NMBR >= 10 THEN CST = NMBR * 4.5
    ELSE IF NMBR >= 6 THEN CST = NMBR * 4.85
    ELSE CST = NMBR * 5
```

Notice that the statement begins by checking for the largest range (10 or more), then checks for the middle range (6 to 9). Any amount less than 6 will be assigned the highest price, which is $5. The complete program is shown at the bottom of Figure 5–9.

Now Try This

1. Refer to Figure 5–7. Can you think of two alternate ways of writing the IF/THEN/ELSE statement in this program?

2. Write a nested IF/THEN/ELSE statement that determines the largest of three numbers and assigns it to the variable LRGE.

3. Write a nested IF statement to determine whether a student is a likely candidate for Coach Wilson's football team. According to Coach Wilson, students are likely candidates if (1) they are male, (2) they weigh over 140, and (3) they have a grade point average of at least 2.5.

4. Write a program segment that prompts the user to enter a password. If the password entered is "OPEN SAYS ME," the statement "PLEASE ENTER" should be displayed. If the user entered an incorrect password, the statement "ACCESS DENIED" should be displayed.

A Programming Problem

Problem Definition

The Acme Car Rental Company charges customers for the use of its rental cars based on the type of car, number of days, miles traveled, and type of

FIGURE 5–9   Program Using a Nested IF Statement

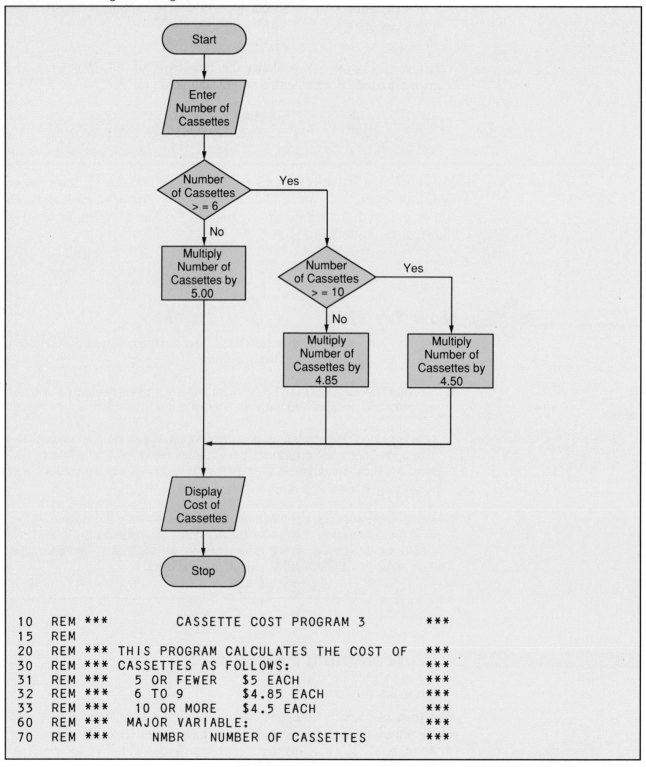

```
10   REM ***          CASSETTE COST PROGRAM 3       ***
15   REM
20   REM *** THIS PROGRAM CALCULATES THE COST OF   ***
30   REM *** CASSETTES AS FOLLOWS:                 ***
31   REM ***   5 OR FEWER    $5 EACH               ***
32   REM ***   6 TO 9        $4.85 EACH            ***
33   REM ***   10 OR MORE    $4.5 EACH             ***
60   REM ***   MAJOR VARIABLE:                     ***
70   REM ***      NMBR   NUMBER OF CASSETTES        ***
```

FIGURE 5–9   Continued

```
80   REM ***      CST     COST OF CASSETTES          ***
90   REM
100  INPUT "ENTER THE NUMBER OF CASSETTES";NMBR
110  IF NMBR >= 10 THEN CST = NMBR * 4.5
         ELSE IF NMBR >= 6 THEN CST = NMBR * 4.85
         ELSE CST = NMBR * 5
120  F$ = "\                                    \ $$##.##"
130  PRINT USING F$;"THE COST OF THE CASSETTES IS",CST
999  END
```

```
RUN
ENTER THE NUMBER OF CASSETTES? 10
THE COST OF THE CASSETTES IS  $45.00
```

insurance chosen. The company would like a program to calculate customers' bills. Acme leases three types of cars:

Type	Daily Charge	Mileage Charge
1	$8.00	.06
2	$10.00	.08
3	$15.00	.12

The company offers two insurance plans:

Plan	Cost
1	20 percent of the daily and mileage charges
2	$4 per day of use

The program should prompt the user to enter the type of car rented, the number of days, the mileage, and the type of insurance plan. A billing report should then be displayed. Figure 5–10 contains the program

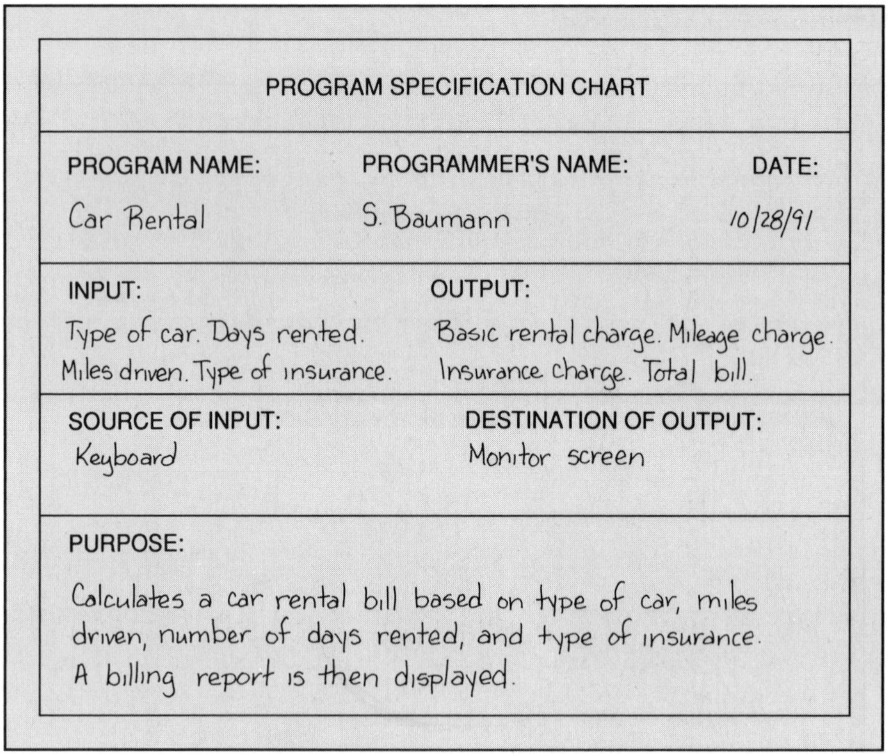

FIGURE 5–10 Program
Specification Chart for Car
Rental

PROGRAM SPECIFICATION CHART

PROGRAM NAME:	PROGRAMMER'S NAME:	DATE:
Car Rental	S. Baumann	10/28/91

INPUT:
Type of car. Days rented.
Miles driven. Type of insurance.

OUTPUT:
Basic rental charge. Mileage charge.
Insurance charge. Total bill.

SOURCE OF INPUT:
Keyboard

DESTINATION OF OUTPUT:
Monitor screen

PURPOSE:

Calculates a car rental bill based on type of car, miles
driven, number of days rented, and type of insurance.
A billing report is then displayed.

specification chart. The format of the needed report is shown in Figure
5–11.

Solution Design

There are five basic tasks to be performed here:

1. Determine the basic rental charge.
2. Determine the mileage charge.
3. Determine the insurance charge.
4. Determine the total bill.
5. Display the billing report.

Several of these tasks can be broken down further. Step 1 can be divided as
follows:

1.A. Determine the type of car and days rented.
1.B. Multiply daily rate × days rented.

Step 2 can also be divided into two subtasks:

FIGURE 5–11   Format for Car Rental Report

2	ACME CAR RENTAL	
5	BASIC CHARGE:	$XXX.XX
6	MILEAGE CHARGE:	$XXX.XY
7	INSURANCE CHARGE:	$XXX.XX
8	TOTAL AMOUNT OWED:	$XXX.XX

2.A. Determine miles driven.
2.B. Multiply mileage charge × miles driven.

Step 5, "Display the billing report," contains three subtasks:

5.A. Display report headings.
5.B. Display basic, mileage, and insurance charges.
5.C. Display total amount due.

The structure chart for this problem is shown in Figure 5–12. Now let us examine the data-processing flow to determine what types of statements we need. In calculating the basic charge and the mileage charge, we must choose between three rates. Therefore, we can use nested IF/THEN/ELSE statements to determine the appropriate charges.

Selecting the insurance rate is simpler. Because there are only two rates, a simple IF/THEN/ELSE statement can assign the desired rate. The

FIGURE 5–12 Structure Chart for Car Rental

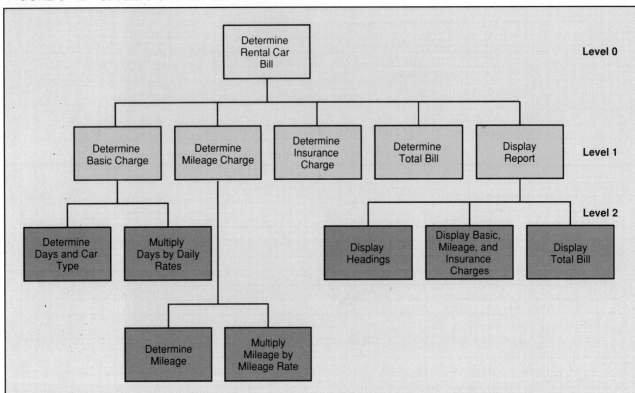

insurance rate can then be added to the basic charge and the mileage charge. The flowchart and pseudocode are shown in Figure 5–13.

The Program

Examine the program in Figure 5–14. The needed data is entered in lines 180, 190, 220, and 260. Lines 200 and 230 contain nested IF statements to calculate the basic charge and the mileage charge. Line 250 adds these two values together and stores the result in the variable COST. It is necessary to obtain this subtotal because its value is needed in calculating the cost of the first type of insurance. Then, line 280 calculates the total bill. The billing report is output in lines 310–390.

FIGURE 5–13   Flowchart and Pseudocode for Car Rental

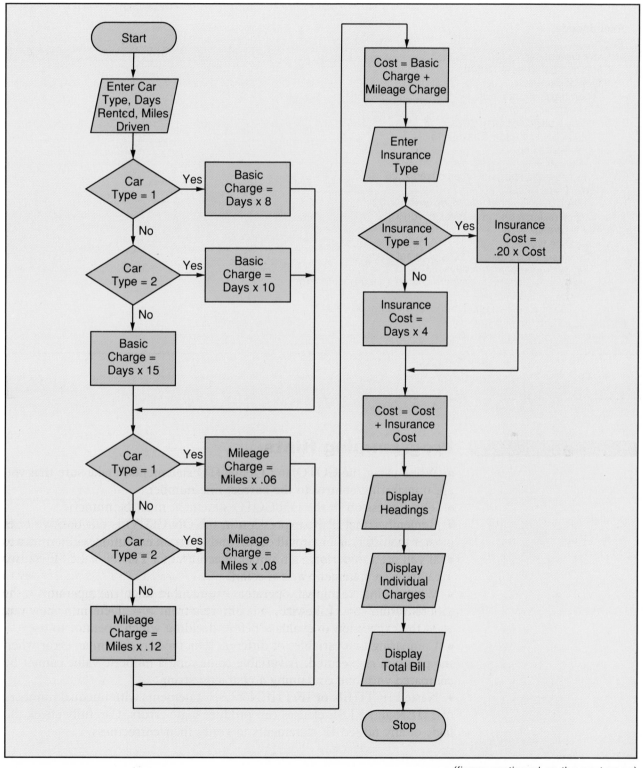

(figure continued on the next page)

FIGURE 5–13 Continued

Pseudocode
```
Begin
    Enter type of car
    Enter number of days rented
    If type of car = 1
        Then basic charge = days x 8
        Else if type of car = 2
            Then basic charge = days x 10
            Else basic charge = days x 15
    Enter miles driven
    If type of car = 1
        Then mileage charge = miles driven x .06
        Else if type of car = 2
            Then mileage charge = miles driven x .08
            Else mileage charge = miles driven x .12
    Enter insurance type
    If insurance type = 1
        Then insurance charge = 20% of rental charges
        Else insurance charge = days x 4
    Total bill = basic charge + mileage charge + insurance charge
    Print billing report heading
    Print basic charge, mileage charge, and insurance charge
    Print total amount of bill
End
```

Programming Hints

■ When using the GOTO and ON/GOTO statements, make sure that you are transferring control to the correct line number.

■ The expression in the ON/GOTO statement must be numeric.

■ Remember that if the expression in the ON/GOTO is not positive or is greater than 255, an error will occur, and program execution will terminate.

■ If you need to perform a number of actions in a THEN or ELSE clause, separate each statement with a colon.

■ When using relational operators, remember that the operator $<$ is different from $<=$. Likewise, $>$ is different from $>=$. Determine how you want the expression to evaluate before deciding which operator to use.

■ Comparing two variables of different data types results in an error when the program is executed. A variable containing a numeric value cannot be compared with one containing a character string.

■ Nested IF/THEN or IF/THEN/ELSE statements with unequal numbers of THEN and ELSE clauses can produce logic errors. Carefully check the logic of any nested IF statements to verify their correctness.

FIGURE 5–14   Car Rental Program

```
10   REM ***                    CAR RENTAL PROGRAM              ***
20   REM ***                                                    ***
30   REM *** DETERMINES A RENTAL CAR BILL DEPENDING ON THE TYPE ***
40   REM *** OF CAR, DAYS RENTED, AND MILES TRAVELED.           ***
50   REM *** MAJOR VARIABLES:                                   ***
60   REM ***     TYPE         TYPE OF CAR RENTED                ***
70   REM ***     DAYS         THE NUMBER OF DAYS RENTED         ***
80   REM ***     MILES        MILES DRIVEN                      ***
90   REM ***     INSURANCE    TYPE INSURANCE                    ***
100  REM ***     COST         TOTAL AMOUNT OWED                 ***
110  REM ***     BCHARGE      BASIC CHARGE                      ***
120  REM ***     MCHARGE      MILEAGE CHARGE                    ***
130  REM ***     ICHARGE      INSURANCE CHARGE                  ***
140  REM
150  CLS
170  REM *** DETERMINE BASIC CHARGE. ***
180  INPUT "ENTER THE TYPE OF CAR (1, 2, OR 3)";TYPE
190  INPUT "ENTER THE NUMBER OF DAYS";DAYS
200  IF TYPE = 1 THEN BCHARGE = DAYS * 8
        ELSE IF TYPE = 2 THEN BCHARGE = DAYS * 10
        ELSE BCHARGE = DAYS * 15
210  REM *** DETERMINE MILEAGE CHARGE. ***
220  INPUT "ENTER THE MILES TRAVELED";MILES
230  IF TYPE = 1 THEN MCHARGE = MILES * .06
        ELSE IF TYPE = 2 THEN MCHARGE = MILES * .08
        ELSE MCHARGE = MILES * .12
240  COST = BCHARGE + MCHARGE
250  REM *** DETERMINE INSURANCE CHARGE. ***
260  INPUT "ENTER THE TYPE OF INSURANCE (1 OR 2)";INSURANCE
270  IF INSURANCE = 1 THEN ICHARGE = .2 * COST
        ELSE ICHARGE = 4 * DAYS
280  COST = COST + ICHARGE
290  REM *** DISPLAY THE RENTAL BILL. ***
300  CLS
310  PRINT
320  PRINT USING "          \                    \";"ACME CAR RENTAL"
330  PRINT USING "          \                    \";"_____"
340  PRINT
350  F$ = "\                    \ $###.##"
360  PRINT USING F$;"BASIC CHARGE:",BCHARGE
370  PRINT USING F$;"MILEAGE CHARGE:",MCHARGE
380  PRINT USING F$;"INSURANCE CHARGE:",ICHARGE
390  PRINT USING F$;"TOTAL AMOUNT OWED:",COST
999  END
```

(figure continued on the next page)

FIGURE 5–14 Continued

```
ENTER THE TYPE OF CAR (1, 2, OR 3)? 2
ENTER THE NUMBER OF DAYS? 10
ENTER THE MILES TRAVELED? 280
ENTER THE TYPE OF INSURANCE (1 OR 2)? 2
```

```
            ACME CAR RENTAL
         _____

BASIC CHARGE:        $100.00
MILEAGE CHARGE:      $ 22.40
INSURANCE CHARGE:    $ 40.00
TOTAL AMOUNT OWED:   $162.40
```

New Statement Review

Statement Format	Explanation
line# GOTO line#	Always transfers control to the specified line number.
line# ON expression GOTO line#1 [,line#2]. . .	Transfers control to the line number corresponding to the value of the expression.
line# IF expression THEN { clause / line# }	Executes the clause following the THEN if the expression is true.
line# IF expression THEN { clause / line# } ELSE { clause / line# }	Executes the clause following the THEN if the expression is true; otherwise, the clause following the ELSE is executed.

Summary Points

■ An unconditional transfer statement, such as the GOTO, *always* passes control to the specified program line.

■ A conditional transfer statement, such as the ON/GOTO, transfers control depending on how an expression evaluates.

■ The single-alternative decision structure (IF/THEN statement) compares two expressions. If the comparison is true, the clause following the THEN is executed; otherwise, control continues to the next statement.

■ Relational operators such as <, >, and = are used to compare expressions. The result of these comparisons is either true or false.

■ The double-alternative decision structure (IF/THEN/ELSE statement) is similar to the IF/THEN statement. If the comparison is true, the THEN clause is executed. If it is false, the ELSE clause is executed.

■ IF statements can be *nested* within one another so that multiple conditions can be checked for.

Vocabulary List

Branching
Collating sequence
Conditional transfer statement
Control statement
Double-alternative IF statement

Menu
Relational operator
Single-alternative IF statement
Spaghetti program
Unconditional transfer

Questions

Whenever appropriate, use complete sentences in answering the following questions.

1. What is meant by branching?

2. Why are control statements useful to programmers?

3. Why is the GOTO statement called an unconditional transfer statement?

4. What happens if the expression in an ON/GOTO statement is a real number?

5. Control passes to what line number when the following statement is executed (assuming SUM = 21)?

```
10 ON SUM / 17 GOTO 50,80,110
```

6. What is a menu?

7. Why is the IF/THEN statement a type of control structure?

8. Which of the following are valid IF/THEN statements?

```
a. 10 IF X$ = "FRANCO" THEN M = M + 1
b. 10 IF Y$ <> "YES" THEN 40
c. 20 IF Z = "NIENTE" GOTO 100
d. 70 IF Y THEN 20
e. 60 IF "HOPELESS" >= "HOPEFUL" THEN 999
```

9. List each of the relational operators discussed in this chapter and explain its meaning.

10. Evaluate the following expressions as true or false:

```
a. 12 + 6 > 18
b. 99 * 2 <> 99
c. 16 / 4 + 2 < 6
d. 2 ^ 2 = 4
```

11. What is printed when the following statements are executed?

```
20 X = 100
30 IF X > 50 THEN PRINT "HUGE"
        ELSE IF X < 50 THEN PRINT "SMALL"
        ELSE PRINT "FIFTY"
```

12. Explain the difference between the single-alternative and the double-alternative decision structures.

13. Draw a flowchart for the following statement:

```
20 IF SIZE > 20 THEN PRINT "LARGE"
        ELSE IF SIZE > 12 THEN PRINT "AVERAGE"
        ELSE PRINT "SMALL"
```

14. Given the statement in Question 13, what will be printed for the following values of SIZE?

```
a. 52
b. −5
c. 12
d. 20
```

15. Write the statement(s) corresponding to the following flowchart:

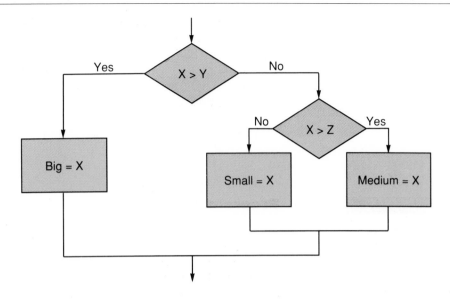

Debugging Exercises

Identify the following programs or program segments that contain errors and debug them.

1.
```
20   X = -100
30   ON X / 50 GOTO 100,200,300
     .
     .
     .
100 PRINT X * 10
     .
     .
     .
200 PRINT X * 20
     .
     .
     .
300 PRINT X * 30
     .
     .
     .
```

2.
```
10   REM *** THIS PROGRAM CALCULATES A GRADE   ***
20   REM *** AS FOLLOWS:                       ***
30   REM ***      GOOD       80 - 100          ***
40   REM ***      AVERAGE    60 - 79           ***
50   REM ***      POOR       BELOW 60          ***
60   REM
70   INPUT "ENTER THE SCORE";SCR
80   IF SCR > 80 THEN G$ = "GOOD" ELSE IF SCR > 60
        THEN G$ = "AVERAGE" ELSE G$ = "POOR"
90   PRINT G$
99   END
```

3. 10 REM *** IF X > 10, PRINT X. ***
20 INPUT X
30 IF X THEN PRINT X
99 END

4. 10 REM *** READ DATA AND PRINT NAME AND AGE IF OVER 18. ***
20 READ NAM$,AGE
30 IF AGE >= 18 THEN PRINT NAM$
40 DATA IRENA,23

Programming Problems

Level 1

1. Write a statement that will transfer program control to line 70, 140, 210, or 280 depending on whether a variable NUM is equal to 1, 2, 3, or 4.

2. Write a statement that transfers control to line 100 if X is 2, to line 300 if X is 4, and to line 200 if X is 6.

3. Write a program segment that reads and compares two numbers. Place the larger in a variable named LARGE and the smaller in a variable named SMALL.

4. Write a program segment that will display the name of the teacher for a class when the name of that class is entered. Use the following data:

American History	Ms. Mansfield
Calculus	Ms. Mueller
Spanish	Mr. Johnson
English	Mr. Ramirez
Algebra II	Mr. Svenson

Use a series of IF/THEN statements to display the appropriate teacher's name.

5. Write a program to determine the cost of a movie ticket. The program prompts the user to enter the customer's age. If the age is 12 or less, the ticket is $2. If the age is 13 or more, the cost is $3.50. Display the cost of the ticket on the monitor with an appropriate label.

6. Write a program segment to determine whether a student is eligible for honors on graduation day. The student must be a senior with at least a 3.5 cumulative grade point average out of a possible 4.0. The user should be prompted to enter the student's name, class, and grade point average. If the student is eligible, a message similar to the following should be displayed:

ELAINE PAULETTE IS ELIGIBLE FOR HONORS.

Level 2

1. The local paint store wants a program that will conveniently list its best-selling shades of a specified color. Use a menu to display the colors available. Prompt the user to enter the number of the color in front of the following choices:

1. Blue
2. Brown
3. Green
4. Yellow

An ON/GOTO statement should be used to display the shades for the chosen color. Use the following data:

Color	Shades
Blue	Cote d'Azur, Periwinkle, Cornflower
Brown	Mocha, Sandalwood
Green	Kelly, Forest, Key Lime
Yellow	Mellow, Iced Lemon, True Saffron

2. Write a program to compute how much a person would weigh on the moon and on the planets listed in the following table:

Planet	Percentage of Earth Weight
1. Moon	16
2. Jupiter	264
3. Venus	85
4. Mars	38

Allow the user to choose the number of a planet from a menu. Then use an ON/GOTO statement to display the appropriate weight.

3. Marilyn Cavanaugh works for Uptown Lumber Company on weekends and evenings. She receives $3.60 an hour for the first 15 hours and $3.75 for any hours over 15. Write a program that Marilyn can use to display how much she has earned in a week. Marilyn should be prompted to enter the number of hours worked, and an IF/THEN/ELSE statement should be used to calculate the earnings.

4. Rewrite Problem 2 using nested IF/THEN/ELSE statements instead of the ON/GOTO statement.

5. Write a program that uses nested IF/THEN/ELSE statements to determine whether an employee is eligible for promotion. An employee is eligible if he or she has been with the company for more than four years and is employed as a salesperson. Have the program output a message that states whether the employee is eligible for a promotion.

6. The Wastenot Utility Company charges $20.00 a month for electricity. In addition, the customer is charged 3 cents for each kilowatt hour over 300. Write a program that prompts the user to enter the old and new electricity meter readings. The number of kilowatt hours and the total bill should be displayed.

Projects

For each project, complete the following:

- Fill out a program specification chart.
- Develop a structure chart.

- Create a flowchart or pseudocode.
- Thoroughly document the final program.
- Test your program using a variety of data.

1. Steve Hoffman works weekends at a carpet-cleaning business. Write a program that he can use to determine how much to bill a customer. The charges are as follows:

a. $1.00 per square yard for normal carpets.
b. $1.20 per square yard for extra dirty carpets.
c. $0.10 extra per square yard if the carpet is to be deodorized.

Allow Steve to enter the length and width of a room in feet, and have the program compute the number of square yards. Assume that the room is rectangular. Prompt the user to answer the needed questions to determine the total cost. Display a report on the screen specifying the following:

a. The total yards of carpet cleaned.
b. Was it extra dirty?
c. Was it deodorized?
d. The total amount due.

2. The Drake Encyclopedia Company is processing the monthly checks for its door-to-door sales agents. Each agent receives a 35 percent commission on his or her monthly sales. An agent whose sales exceed $800 receives a $50 bonus, and an agent whose sales are less than $300 must pay a $25 processing charge, which is subtracted from that month's check. Each set of encyclopedias sells for $150. Write a program that will calculate an agent's total sales, straight commission, bonus or deduction if necessary, and the total amount to be paid. The program should display a report containing all of the preceding, except total sales, for each agent.

CHAPTER

6

Adding Structure by Modularizing Programs

Learning Objectives

After studying this chapter, you should be able to

1. Explain the importance of using modules in structured programming.

2. Use the GOSUB statement to unconditionally transfer control to a subroutine.

3. Use the RETURN statement to return program control back to the calling program.

4. Use structure charts to determine how programs should be modularized by task.

5. Explain the single-entry, single-exit point principle and follow it when writing subroutines.

6. Use the ON/GOSUB statement to conditionally transfer control to the needed subroutine.

7. Develop and test programs in a structured manner by using stubs.

Introduction

Subroutine

A module designed to perform a specific task; subroutines are usually placed after the main program.

As discussed in Chapter 2, a major feature of structured programming is that programs are divided into modules, called **subroutines** in BASIC, each performing a specific task. A subroutine is a sequence of statements typically located after the main body of the program.

Dividing a program into modules is useful for three basic reasons:

1. It makes the program easier to write because it is simpler to accomplish a large task by dividing it into smaller subtasks. For example, if you are cleaning your car, it is most efficient to complete one job (such as washing the outside) before proceeding to the next job (such as vacuuming the inside). Not only is your time used more efficiently, but you are more likely to do a thorough job on each of the subtasks.

2. It makes the logic of the finished program easier to follow. As previously mentioned, dividing a textbook into chapters by topic makes the book's logic easier to follow. The same principle is true for programs.

3. The same module can be executed any number of times. For example, if a program needs to perform the same task at two different points, the subroutine that performs this task may be executed two times.

This chapter will help you develop the skills needed to write well-modularized programs. There are two methods of executing a subroutine in BASIC: the GOSUB statement and the ON/GOSUB statement.

Unconditional Transfer: The GOSUB Statement

Call

To cause a subroutine to be executed.

The GOSUB statement is used to execute (or **call**) a subroutine. The format is line# GOSUB transfer line#

For example, the statement

60 GOSUB 1000

calls the subroutine starting at line 1000. This GOSUB statement will always cause program control to transfer to line 1000. Therefore, the GOSUB statement is an unconditional transfer statement.

Subroutines are ordinarily placed after the main body of a program. Below is a short program that uses a subroutine to convert a length in inches to the corresponding yards and feet.

```
10    REM *** THIS PROGRAM CONVERTS A SPECIFIED NUMBER OF   ***
20    REM *** INCHES TO THE CORRESPONDING NUMBER OF YARDS   ***
30    REM *** AND FEET.                                     ***
40    REM
50    INPUT "ENTER THE NUMBER OF INCHES";INCHES
60    GOSUB 1000
70    PRINT INCHES;"INCHES EQUALS";YARDS;"YARDS."
80    PRINT INCHES;"INCHES EQUALS";FEET;"FEET."
99    END
1000  REM *** SUBROUTINE TO CONVERT INCHES TO YARDS AND FEET. ***
1010  REM
1020  YARDS = INCHES / 36
1030  FEET = INCHES / 12
1040  RETURN
```

The main program is contained in lines 10–99 and the subroutine in lines 1000–1040. The transfer line number (in this case, 1000) should be the first line number of the subroutine. The system will not detect an error if it is instructed to branch to an incorrect line. It will detect an error only if the transfer line number does not exist in the program. Let's trace through what happens when this program is executed. First, line 50 prompts the user to enter the number of inches. Then line 60 calls the subroutine, causing lines 1000–1040 to be executed. When the RETURN statement in line 1040 is executed, program control is returned to the first statement after the GOSUB. Therefore, lines 70 and 80 are executed, outputting the program results. Finally, execution stops when line 99 is executed.

Every subroutine must have a RETURN statement to return control to the line following the one that contains the GOSUB statement. Note that no transfer line number is used in the RETURN statement. The computer automatically returns control to the statement immediately following the GOSUB statement that called the subroutine. If the line returned to is a nonexecutable statement, such as a REM statement, the computer simply skips it.

In Figure 6–1, the program previously presented in Figure 4–4 has been rewritten so that it is modularized. This program displays an inventory

FIGURE 6–1   Modularized Inventory Report

```
10    REM ***                         INVENTORY REPORT                    ***
20    REM ***                                                             ***
30    REM *** THIS PROGRAM DISPLAYS AN INVENTORY REPORT FOR AN            ***
40    REM *** ICE CREAM STORE.                                            ***
50    REM
60    REM *** GET DATA. ***
70    GOSUB 1000
80    REM *** DISPLAY TABLE. ***
90    GOSUB 2000
99    END
1000  REM ***************************************************************
1010  REM ***                 SUBROUTINE GET INVENTORY                  ***
1020  REM ***************************************************************
1030  REM
1040  REM *** THIS SUBROUTINE PROMPTS THE USER TO ENTER THE NAME ***
1050  REM *** AND QUANTITY IN INVENTORY FOR EACH ITEM.           ***
1060  REM
1070  INPUT "ENTER ITEM AND QUANTITY";ITEM1$,QUANTITY1
1080  INPUT "ENTER ITEM AND QUANTITY";ITEM2$,QUANTITY2
1090  INPUT "ENTER ITEM AND QUANTITY";ITEM3$,QUANTITY3
1100  RETURN
2000  REM ***************************************************************
2010  REM ***              SUBROUTINE DISPLAY INVENTORY TABLE           ***
2020  REM ***************************************************************
2030  REM *** THIS SUBROUTINE DISPLAYS THE QUANTITY OF EACH      ***
2040  REM *** ITEM CURRENTLY IN THE INVENTORY.                   ***
2050  REM
2060  CLS
2070  PRINT TAB(11) "INVENTORY TABLE"
2080  PRINT
2090  PRINT TAB(8) "ITEM";TAB(24); "GALLONS"
2100  PRINT
2110  PRINT TAB(5)  ITEM1$;TAB(25) QUANTITY1
2120  PRINT TAB(5)  ITEM2$;TAB(25) QUANTITY2
2130  PRINT TAB(5)  ITEM3$;TAB(25) QUANTITY3
2140  RETURN
```

FIGURE 6–1 Continued

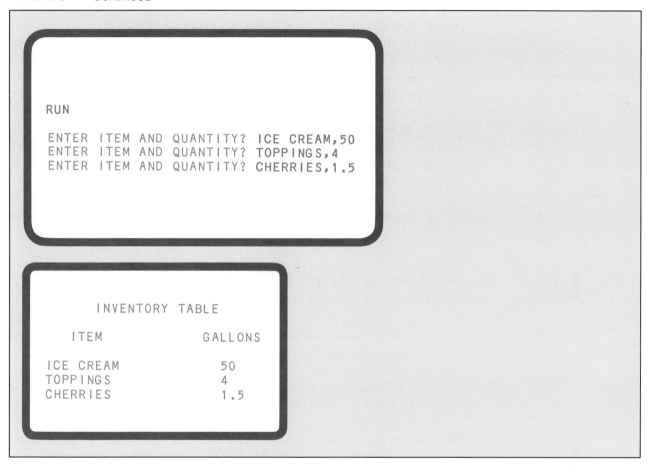

```
RUN

ENTER ITEM AND QUANTITY? ICE CREAM,50
ENTER ITEM AND QUANTITY? TOPPINGS,4
ENTER ITEM AND QUANTITY? CHERRIES,1.5
```

```
        INVENTORY TABLE

    ITEM              GALLONS

ICE CREAM               50
TOPPINGS                4
CHERRIES                1.5
```

report for an ice cream store. Spend a few minutes examining Figure 6–1. Lines 10–99 contain the main program. It calls two subroutines. The first one starts at line 1000 and prompts the user to enter the inventory data. The second subroutine starts at line 2000 and displays the final inventory report. To make subroutines easier to locate, programmers often start them at line numbers that are multiples of 1000. For example, the subroutines in this program start at 1000 and 2000. In addition, each subroutine has been given a title that is surrounded by asterisks. These asterisks are optional; again, they serve merely to make it easier to locate the start of a subroutine. Examine line 70:

```
70 GOSUB 1000
```

This statement calls the subroutine starting at line 1000. When line 70 is executed, program control branches to line 1000, and execution continues from that point. When the RETURN statement in line 1100 is executed, program control transfers back to the first statement following GOSUB,

Driver program

A main program that consists largely of calls to subroutines. The actual processing of the program is performed in the subroutines.

which in this case is line 80. Because line 80 is nonexecutable, control continues on to line 90. This line calls the second subroutine, and control branches to line 2000. When line 2140 is executed, control returns to the END statement in line 99, which stops program execution.

Notice that the main program in Figure 6–1 contains only three executable statements, two of which are calls to subroutines; the third is the END statement. This is an example of a **driver program,** in which the main program calls subroutines, and the processing is then performed in these subroutines.

The difference between the GOSUB and the GOTO statements is that when a GOSUB is used, the BASIC system keeps track of the line number to which program control will branch when the RETURN statement is encountered. Therefore, it is good structured programming practice to use the GOSUB statement whenever possible. Not only does it make the logic of the program easier to follow, but it is less error-prone than using the GOTO statement.

Using Structure Charts to Modularize Programs

So far in this textbook, we have been using structure charts to help analyze the steps necessary to solve programming problems. These charts enable us to visualize the specific tasks a program must perform to achieve the desired overall result. Because structure charts represent the subtasks involved in solving a problem, they are very useful in developing modularized programs. Once the tasks of a program are identified, each of these can be implemented in the program as a separate subroutine.

To demonstrate how to modularize a program using a structure chart, we will rewrite the program developed at the end of Chapter 4 (the original program is shown in Figure 4–11). The structure chart is shown again in Figure 6–2. Spend a minute examining this chart. Level 1 contains two subtasks. Each of these subtasks is then further subdivided. The chart serves as a guide in dividing the program into subroutines. Each of the four modules at Level 2 can be written as a separate subroutine. Figure 6–3 shows how this program containing four subroutines could be written.

A Program Containing Multiple Calls to the Same Subroutine

One of the advantages of using subroutines that was mentioned at the beginning of this chapter was that they can be called as many times as needed. For example, if you had a program that needed to calculate the interest on a savings account many times, you could call a subroutine to perform this task each time it was needed. The program in Figure 6–3 prints a dividing line in the report three times (in lines 3090, 3130, and 4140). Figure 6–4 shows how this task could be performed in a subroutine. Each time a dividing line is needed, the subroutine starting in line 5000 is called. Subroutines can be called either from the main program or from other subroutines. In Figure 6–4, subroutine PRINT DIVIDER is called

FIGURE 6–2   Structure Chart for Attendance Report

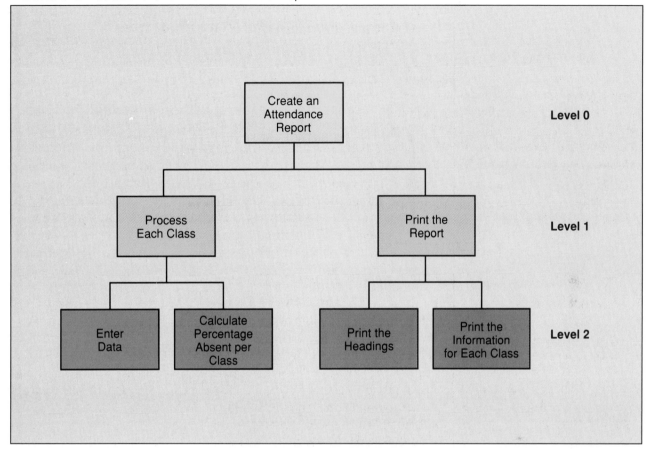

from two different subroutines. Subroutine PRINT DIVIDER not only prints the dividing line, but it also prints a blank line. In this example, subroutine PRINT DIVIDER is very short. However, when a subroutine is longer, considerable space can be saved if it is used many times. In addition, the program's logic is easier to follow.

The Single-Entry, Single-Exit Point Principle

Single-entry, single-exit point principle

The structured programming principle that states a subroutine should have only one entry point and one exit point.

An important principle of structured programming is the **single-entry, single-exit point principle,** which requires that every structure in a program, such as a subroutine or a loop (loops are covered in Chapter 7), should be entered at the beginning and exited at the end.

A subroutine may be called any number of times in a given program, but it should always be entered at the first line of the subroutine. Branching to the middle of a subroutine makes program logic virtually impossible to follow and often leads to errors.

Figure 6–5 contains two program segments, both of which perform the same task. The top segment is incorrectly written, because the

FIGURE 6–3   Modularized Attendance Report

```
10    REM ***                        ATTENDANCE REPORT                  ***
20    REM
30    REM ***   THIS PROGRAM GENERATES ABSENTEE PERCENTAGES PER ***
40    REM ***   CLASS FOR ANY GIVEN DAY.                         ***
50    REM ***   MAJOR VARIABLES:                                 ***
60    REM ***      DTE$                TODAY'S DATE              ***
70    REM ***      CLASS1- CLASS4   STUDENTS IN EACH CLASS       ***
80    REM ***      A1 - A4           ABSENCES IN EACH CLASS       ***
90    REM ***      PCT1 - PCT4       PERCENTAGE ABSENT PER CLASS ***
100   REM
110   REM *** GET NEEDED DATA. ***
120   GOSUB 1000
130   REM
140   REM *** DETERMINE PERCENT ABSENT IN EACH CLASS. ***
150   GOSUB 2000
160   REM
170   REM *** PRINT HEADINGS FOR REPORT. ***
180   GOSUB 3000
190   REM
200   REM *** PRINT REPORT COLUMNS. ***
210   GOSUB 4000
999   END
1000  REM *****************************************************************
1010  REM ***                  SUBROUTINE GET DATA                  ***
1020  REM *****************************************************************
1030  REM *** THIS SUBROUTINE PROMPTS THE USER TO ENTER THE    ***
1040  REM *** DATE, NUMBER OF STUDENTS IN EACH CLASS, AND AB-  ***
1050  REM *** SENCES PER CLASS.                                ***
1060  CLS
1070  INPUT "ENTER TODAY'S DATE";DTE$
1080  REM
1090  REM *** GET NUMBER OF STUDENTS PER CLASS. ***
1100  INPUT "ENTER 9TH GRADE ENROLLMENT";CLASS1
1110  INPUT "ENTER 10TH GRADE ENROLLMENT";CLASS2
1120  INPUT "ENTER 11TH GRADE ENROLLMENT";CLASS3
1130  INPUT "ENTER 12TH GRADE ENROLLMENT"; CLASS4
1140  REM
1150  REM *** GET ABSENCES PER CLASS. ***
1160  INPUT "ENTER NUMBER OF 9TH GRADERS ABSENT";A1
1170  INPUT "ENTER NUMBER OF 10TH GRADERS ABSENT";A2
1180  INPUT "ENTER NUMBER OF 11TH GRADERS ABSENT";A3
1190  INPUT "ENTER NUMBER OF 12TH GRADERS ABSENT";A4
1200  RETURN
2000  REM *****************************************************************
2010  REM ***            SUBROUTINE CALCULATE PERCENTAGES.          ***
2020  REM *****************************************************************
2030  REM *** THIS SUBROUTINE CALCULATES THE PERCENTAGE OF     ***
2040  REM *** STUDENTS ABSENT IN EACH CLASS.                   ***
2050  REM
2060  PCT1 = (A1 / CLASS1) * 100
2070  PCT2 = (A2 / CLASS2) * 100
2080  PCT3 = (A3 / CLASS3) * 100
2090  PCT4 = (A4 / CLASS4) * 100
```

FIGURE 6–3   Continued

```
2100 RETURN
3000 REM ****************************************************************
3010 REM ***          SUBROUTINE PRINT REPORT HEADINGS          ***
3020 REM ****************************************************************
3030 REM *** THIS SUBROUTINE PRINTS THE REPORT TITLES AND     ***
3040 REM *** COLUMN HEADINGS.                                 ***
3050 REM
3060 LPRINT TAB(21) "Baymont High School"
3070 LPRINT TAB(16) "Attendance Report for ";DTE$
3080 LPRINT
3090 LPRINT "_____"
3100 LPRINT
3110 LPRINT TAB(13) "Total Number";TAB(33) "Number";TAB(51) "Percentage"
3120 LPRINT "Grade";TAB(13) "of Students";TAB(33) "Absent";TAB(51) "Absent"
3130 LPRINT "_____"
3140 LPRINT
3150 RETURN
4000 REM ****************************************************************
4010 REM ***               SUBROUTINE PRINT TABLE              ***
4020 REM ****************************************************************
4030 REM *** THIS SUBROUTINE PRINTS THE INFORMATION FOR THE   ***
4034 REM *** ATTENDANCE REPORT.                               ***
4050 REM
4060 LPRINT
4070 F$ = "##              ###              ##              ##.##"
4080 REM
4090 REM *** PRINT REPORT FIGURES. ***
4100 LPRINT USING F$;9,CLASS1,A1,PCT1
4110 LPRINT USING F$;10,CLASS2,A2,PCT2
4120 LPRINT USING F$;11,CLASS3,A3,PCT3
4130 LPRINT USING F$;12,CLASS4,A4,PCT4
4140 LPRINT "_____"
4150 RETURN
```

```
ENTER TODAY'S DATE? 11/14/91
ENTER 9TH GRADE ENROLLMENT? 110
ENTER 10TH GRADE ENROLLMENT? 143
ENTER 11TH GRADE ENROLLMENT? 118
ENTER 12TH GRADE ENROLLMENT? 107
ENTER NUMBER OF 9TH GRADERS ABSENT? 7
ENTER NUMBER OF 10TH GRADERS ABSENT? 12
ENTER NUMBER OF 11TH GRADERS ABSENT? 5
ENTER NUMBER OF 12TH GRADERS ABSENT? 14
```

(figure continued on the next page)

FIGURE 6–3   Continued

```
                        Baymont High School
                    Attendance Report for 11/14/91


          _____


                     Total Number        Number          Percentage
          Grade      of Students         Absent           Absent
          _____


             9          110                 7                6.36
            10          143                12                8.39
            11          118                 5                4.24
            12          107                14               13.08
          _____
```

IF/THEN/ELSE statement in line 110 can allow control to be passed either to the first line of the subroutine (line 1000) or to the middle of the subroutine (line 1060). The bottom example shows this segment correctly written. Note that an IF/THEN statement within the subroutine is used to control execution.

Likewise, a subroutine should contain only one RETURN statement, which should be the last statement of the subroutine. This rule is referred to as the single-exit point principle. At the top of Figure 6–6 is a program segment that is incorrectly written because it contains two RETURN statements, one in line 1040 and one in line 1070. The bottom program segment accomplishes the same task by using an IF/THEN statement (line 1040) to branch to the RETURN statement at the end of the subroutine.

Now Try This

1. Write a statement that transfers program control to a subroutine starting at line 12000.

2. Write a subroutine that converts a specified number of ounces to pounds. (Hint: There are 16 ounces in a pound).

3. Write a subroutine that calculates the gross pay for an employee. The subroutine should prompt the user to enter the hours worked and hourly rate. The gross pay should be assigned to a variable named GROSS.PAY.

4. Write a subroutine that calculates your grade point average.

FIGURE 6–4 Multiple Calls to a Single Subroutine

```
10 REM ***                        ATTENDANCE REPORT                    ***
20 REM ***                                                             ***
30 REM *** THIS PROGRAM GENERATES ABSENTEE PERCENTAGES PER ***
40 REM *** CLASS FOR ANY GIVEN DAY.                                    ***
50 REM *** MAJOR VARIABLES:                                            ***
60 REM ***     DTE$                TODAY'S DATE                        ***
70 REM ***     CLASS1 - CLASS4     STUDENTS IN EACH CLASS              ***
80 REM ***     A1 - A4             ABSENCES IN EACH CLASS              ***
90 REM ***     PCT1 - PCT4         PERCENTAGE ABSENT PER CLASS ***
100 REM
110 REM *** GET NEEDED DATA. ***
120 GOSUB 1000
130 REM
140 REM *** DETERMINE PERCENT ABSENT IN EACH CLASS. ***
150 GOSUB 2000
160 REM
170 REM *** PRINT HEADINGS FOR REPORT. ***
180 GOSUB 3000
190 REM
200 REM *** PRINT REPORT COLUMNS. ***
210 GOSUB 4000
999 END
1000 REM ************************************************************
1010 REM ***               SUBROUTINE GET DATA                    ***
1020 REM ************************************************************
1030 REM *** THIS SUBROUTINE PROMPTS THE USER TO ENTER THE    ***
1040 REM *** DATE, NUMBER OF STUDENTS IN EACH CLASS, AND AB-  ***
1050 REM *** SENCES PER CLASS.                                ***
1060 CLS
1070 INPUT "ENTER TODAY'S DATE";DTE$
1080 REM
1090 REM *** GET NUMBER OF STUDENTS PER CLASS. ***
1100 INPUT "ENTER 9TH GRADE ENROLLMENT";CLASS1
1110 INPUT "ENTER 10TH GRADE ENROLLMENT";CLASS2
1120 INPUT "ENTER 11TH GRADE ENROLLMENT";CLASS3
1130 INPUT "ENTER 12TH GRADE ENROLLMENT"; CLASS4
1140 REM
1150 REM *** GET ABSENCES PER CLASS. ***
1160 INPUT "ENTER NUMBER OF 9TH GRADERS ABSENT";A1
1170 INPUT "ENTER NUMBER OF 10TH GRADERS ABSENT";A2
1180 INPUT "ENTER NUMBER OF 11TH GRADERS ABSENT";A3
1190 INPUT "ENTER NUMBER OF 12TH GRADERS ABSENT";A4
1200 RETURN
2000 REM ************************************************************
2010 REM ***          SUBROUTINE CALCULATE PERCENTAGES.        ***
2020 REM ************************************************************
2030 REM *** THIS SUBROUTINE CALCULATES THE PERCENTAGE OF    ***
2040 REM *** STUDENTS ABSENT IN EACH CLASS.                  ***
2050 REM
2060 PCT1 = (A1 / CLASS1) * 100
2070 PCT2 = (A2 / CLASS2) * 100
2080 PCT3 = (A3 / CLASS3) * 100
2090 PCT4 = (A4 / CLASS4) * 100
```

(figure continued on the next page)

FIGURE 6–4 Continued

```
2100 RETURN
3000 REM *********************************************************
3010 REM ***              SUBROUTINE PRINT REPORT HEADINGS        ***
3020 REM *********************************************************
3030 REM *** THIS SUBROUTINE PRINTS THE REPORT TITLES AND        ***
3040 REM *** COLUMN HEADINGS.                                     ***
3050 REM
3060 LPRINT TAB(21) "Baymont High School"
3070 LPRINT TAB(16) "Attendance Report for ";DTE$
3080 LPRINT
3090 GOSUB 5000
3100 LPRINT TAB(13) "Total Number";TAB(33) "Number";TAB(51);"Percentage"
3110 LPRINT "Grade";TAB(13) "of Students";TAB(33) "Absent";TAB(51) "Absent"
3120 GOSUB 5000
3130 RETURN
4000 REM *********************************************************
4010 REM ***                 SUBROUTINE PRINT TABLE               ***
4020 REM *********************************************************
4030 REM *** THIS SUBROUTINE PRINTS THE INFORMATION FOR THE      ***
4040 REM *** ATTENDANCE REPORT.                                   ***
4050 REM
4060 F$ = "##              ###                 ##            ##.##"
4070 REM
4080 REM *** PRINT REPORT FIGURES. ***
4090 LPRINT USING F$;9,CLASS1,A1,PCT1
4100 LPRINT USING F$;10,CLASS2,A2,PCT2
4110 LPRINT USING F$;11,CLASS3,A3,PCT3
4120 LPRINT USING F$;12,CLASS4,A4,PCT4
4130 GOSUB 5000
4140 RETURN
5000 REM *********************************************************
5010 REM ***                 SUBROUTINE PRINT DIVIDER            ***
5020 REM *********************************************************
5030 REM ***    THIS SUBROUTINE PRINTS A SINGLE LINE TO DIVIDE   ***
5040 REM ***    DIFFERENT SECTIONS OF THE REPORT.                ***
5050 REM
5060 LPRINT "_____"
5070 LPRINT
5080 RETURN
```

FIGURE 6–4 Continued

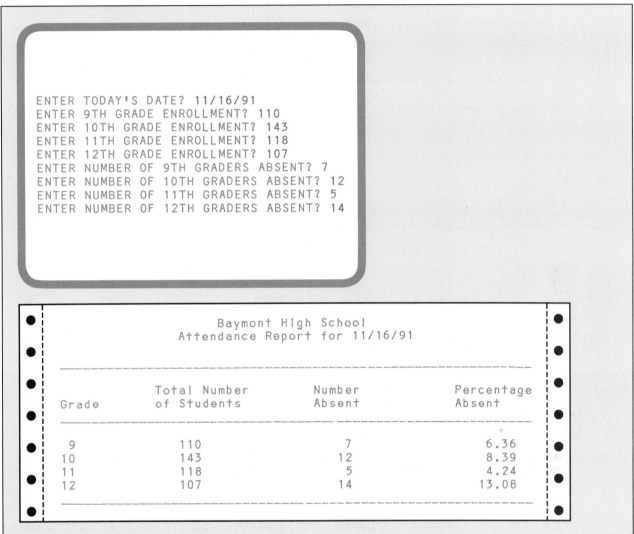

```
ENTER TODAY'S DATE? 11/16/91
ENTER 9TH GRADE ENROLLMENT? 110
ENTER 10TH GRADE ENROLLMENT? 143
ENTER 11TH GRADE ENROLLMENT? 118
ENTER 12TH GRADE ENROLLMENT? 107
ENTER NUMBER OF 9TH GRADERS ABSENT? 7
ENTER NUMBER OF 10TH GRADERS ABSENT? 12
ENTER NUMBER OF 11TH GRADERS ABSENT? 5
ENTER NUMBER OF 12TH GRADERS ABSENT? 14
```

```
                    Baymont High School
                 Attendance Report for 11/16/91
     _____

                 Total Number        Number          Percentage
     Grade       of Students         Absent          Absent
     _____

       9             110                7               6.36
      10             143               12               8.39
      11             118                5               4.24
      12             107               14              13.08
     _____
```

Conditional Transfer: The ON/GOSUB Statement

Because the GOSUB statement is an unconditional transfer statement, it always transfers program control to the subroutine starting at the indicated line number. Sometimes, however, it is necessary to branch to one of several subroutines, depending on existing conditions. The ON/GOSUB statement allows for such conditional transfer of program control. The following statement transfers control to line 2000, 3000, or 1000 depending on whether AMT is 1, 2, or 3.

```
150 ON AMT GOSUB 2000,3000,1000
```

FIGURE 6–5   Program Segments Demonstrating the Single-Entry Point Principle

```
100   INPUT "ENTER YOUR SCORE";PTS
110   IF PTS > 80 THEN GOSUB 1000 ELSE GOSUB 1060
120   GOTO 9999
1000  REM
1010  REM *********************************************
1020  REM ***                SUBROUTINE             ***
1030  REM *********************************************
1040  REM
1050  PRINT "YOU DID VERY WELL!"
1060  PRINT "YOU PASSED THE COURSE."
1070  RETURN
9999  END
```

Incorrectly Written Program Segment with Branch to the Middle of Subroutine

```
100   INPUT "ENTER YOUR SCORE";PTS
110   GOSUB 1000
120   GOTO 9999
1000  REM *********************************************
1010  REM ***                SUBROUTINE             ***
1020  REM *********************************************
1030  REM
1040  IF PTS > 80 THEN PRINT "YOU DID VERY WELL!"
1050  PRINT "YOU PASSED THE COURSE."
1060  RETURN
9999  END
```

Correctly Written Program Segment with a Single Entry Point to the Subroutine

The ON/GOSUB is similar to the ON/GOTO statement (Chapter 5) in that it uses an expression to determine the line number to which program control will transfer. This expression must be arithmetic. The transfer line numbers in the ON/GOSUB statement, however, are not within the calling program. Each transfer line number indicates the beginning of a subroutine.

The general execution of the ON/GOSUB proceeds as follows:

1. The expression is evaluated as an integer. If the expression is a real number, it is rounded to the nearest integer.
2. Depending on the value of the expression, control passes to the subroutine starting at the corresponding line number. For example, given the following statement

```
40 ON X / 10 GOSUB 2000,5000,4000
```

program execution continues as follows:

FIGURE 6–6 Program Segments Demonstrating the Single-Exit Point Principle

```
100   INPUT "ENTER YOUR SCORE";PTS
110   GOSUB 1000
999   END
1000  REM ********************************************
1010  REM ***                SUBROUTINE            ***
1020  REM ********************************************
1030  REM
1040  IF PTS < 80 THEN PRINT "YOU FAILED" : RETURN   ELSE PRINT "YOU PASSED"
1050  CREDITHR = CREDITHR + 4
1060  ST$ = "OK"
1070  RETURN
```

Incorrectly Written Program Segment with Multiple RETURNs

```
100   INPUT "ENTER YOUR SCORE";PTS
110   GOSUB 1000
999   END
1000  REM ********************************************
1010  REM ***                SUBROUTINE            ***
1020  REM ********************************************
1030  REM
1040  IF PTS < 80 THEN PRINT "YOU FAILED" : GOTO 1070 ELSE PRINT "YOU PASSED"
1050  CREDITHR = CREDITHR + 4
1060  ST$ = "OK"
1070  RETURN
```

Correctly Written Program Segment with a Single RETURN

If $X / 10 = 1$, control is passed to the subroutine at line 2000.
If $X / 10 = 2$, control is passed to the subroutine at line 5000.
If $X / 10 = 3$, control is passed to the subroutine at line 4000.

3. After the specified subroutine is executed, control is transferred back to the line following the ON/GOSUB statement by a RETURN statement at the end of the subroutine.

The ON/GOSUB statement provides a more structured approach to programming than the ON/GOTO statement, because the location of the return of control is determined by the BASIC system and not by the programmer. This eliminates the chance of the programmer stating the incorrect line number in the GOTO statement.

If the expression in an ON/GOSUB statement evaluates as a number larger than the number of transfer line numbers indicated, program execution skips to the next executable statement.

Figure 6–7 demonstrates the ON/GOSUB statement. The user enters an integer value representing his or her year in high school (1, 2, 3, or 4). This

▬▬▬▬▬▬

FIGURE 6–7   Program Using the ON/GOSUB Statement

```
10    REM ***                GRADUATION PROGRAM              ***
20    REM ***                                                ***
30    REM *** THIS PROGRAM DISPLAYS THE CLASS A STUDENT ***
40    REM *** BELONGS TO (FRESHMAN, SOPHOMORE, JUNIOR,  ***
50    REM *** SENIOR) AND THE YEAR OF GRADUATION WHEN    ***
60    REM *** THE CORRESPONDING INTEGER (1, 2, 3, OR 4)  ***
70    REM *** IS ENTERED.                                ***
80    REM *** MAJOR VARIABLES:                           ***
90    REM ***    STUDENT$          STUDENT'S NAME        ***
100   REM ***    YR                YEAR                  ***
110   REM
120   REM *** ENTER THE NECESSARY DATA. ***
130   INPUT "ENTER THE STUDENT'S NAME";STUDENT$
140   INPUT "ENTER THE STUDENT'S YEAR (1, 2, 3, OR 4)";YR
150   REM
160   REM *** BRANCH TO SUBROUTINE TO DISPLAY MESSAGE. ***
170   ON YR GOSUB 1000,2000,3000,4000
999   END
1000  REM *****************************************************
1010  REM ***              SUBROUTINE FRESHMAN            ***
1020  REM *****************************************************
1030  REM
1040  PRINT STUDENT$;" IS A FRESHMAN"
1050  PRINT "AND WILL GRADUATE IN 1994."
1060  RETURN
2000  REM *****************************************************
2010  REM ***              SUBROUTINE SOPHOMORE           ***
2020  REM *****************************************************
2030  REM
2040  PRINT STUDENT$;" IS A SOPHOMORE"
2050  PRINT "AND WILL GRADUATE IN 1993."
2060  RETURN
3000  REM *****************************************************
3010  REM ***              SUBROUTINE JUNIOR              ***
3020  REM *****************************************************
3030  REM
3040  PRINT STUDENT$;" IS A JUNIOR"
3050  PRINT "AND WILL GRADUATE IN 1992."
3060  RETURN
4000  REM *****************************************************
4010  REM ***              SUBROUTINE SENIOR              ***
4020  REM *****************************************************
4030  REM
4040  PRINT STUDENT$;" IS A SENIOR"
4050  PRINT "AND WILL GRADUATE IN 1991."
4060  RETURN
```

FIGURE 6–7   Continued

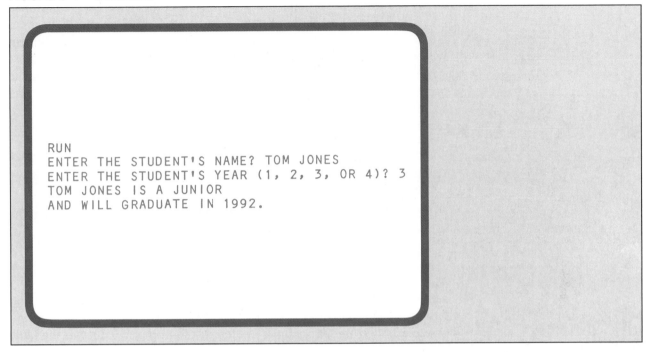

```
RUN
ENTER THE STUDENT'S NAME? TOM JONES
ENTER THE STUDENT'S YEAR (1, 2, 3, OR 4)? 3
TOM JONES IS A JUNIOR
AND WILL GRADUATE IN 1992.
```

integer value is assigned to the variable YR, which is then used to determine which subroutine will be executed. If YR = 1, the subroutine starting at line 1000 will be executed; if YR = 2, the subroutine starting at line 2000 will be executed; if YR = 3, the subroutine starting at line 3000 will be executed; and if YR = 4, the subroutine starting at line 4000 will be executed. After the appropriate subroutine is executed, control is returned to the main program, which then stops executing.

Using Stubs to Develop Programs

So far, considerable attention has been given to top-down development of programming problem solutions. It is also possible to use a top-down method when entering a program to the computer. Indeed, when writing a large program that contains many subroutines, it is poor programming practice to enter the entire program at one time. A far wiser approach is to start by entering the main program (the driver) and one or two subroutines.

Subroutines that are not yet implemented are called, but each of these nonimplemented subroutines consists merely of a **stub.** A stub contains a PRINT statement that indicates a given subroutine has been called but is not yet implemented. The stub must also contain a RETURN statement to return control to the main program. The idea is to enter the program in manageable segments, which can then be executed and tested for errors in

Stub

A subroutine containing only a print statement indicating that the subroutine has not yet been implemented and a RETURN statement.

an orderly way. As segments of the program work properly, more can gradually be added and tested.

Let's see how the program in Figure 6–4 could have been developed using stubs. First, the main program must be typed into the computer (lines 10–999). At this point we need to decide which subroutines to implement now and which to add later. Generally, it is easiest to implement those subroutines that output the results first. We then can run the program to determine whether the table is properly formatted. Therefore, we will implement subroutines PRINT REPORT HEADINGS and PRINT TABLE first. GET DATA and CALCULATE PERCENTAGES will be implemented as stubs; for example:

```
1070 PRINT "SUBROUTINE GET DATA CALLED BUT NOT YET IMPLEMENTED."
```

The program, as it looks at this point, is shown in Figure 6–8. Notice the statement in line 105:

```
105 CLEAR
```

The CLEAR statement sets all the numeric variables in a program to 0 and all the string variables to the empty string (also called the *null string*). Therefore, when this program is executed, the numeric values in the table will all be zero. When we run the program in Figure 6–8, the following messages appear on the screen:

```
SUBROUTINE GET DATA CALLED BUT NOT YET IMPLEMENTED.
SUBROUTINE CALCULATE PERCENTAGES CALLED BUT NOT IMPLEMENTED.
SUBROUTINE PRINT DIVIDER CALLED BUT NOT IMPLEMENTED.
SUBROUTINE PRINT DIVIDER CALLED BUT NOT IMPLEMENTED.
SUBROUTINE PRINT DIVIDER CALLED BUT NOT IMPLEMENTED.
```

At this point, the report sent to the printer looks like this:

```
                    Baymont High School
              Attendance Report for


              Total Number      Number         Percentage
   Grade      of Students       Absent         Absent

     9             0              0               0.00
     10            0              0               0.00
     11            0              0               0.00
     12            0              0               0.00
```

The PRINT statement in subroutine PRINT DIVIDER is displayed three times because this subroutine was called three times. Even though no data is in the table, we can determine that the headings and the layout of the table are correct. If there are any problems, they must be corrected before more subroutines are added. The subroutine to print the dividing lines in

FIGURE 6–8   Program with Stubs

```
10   REM ***                    ATTENDANCE REPORT              ***
20   REM ***                                                   ***
30   REM ***   THIS PROGRAM GENERATES ABSENTEE PERCENTAGES PER ***
40   REM ***   CLASS FOR ANY GIVEN DAY.                        ***
50   REM ***   MAJOR VARIABLES:                                ***
60   REM ***     DTE$              TODAY'S DATE                ***
70   REM ***     CLASS1 - CLASS4   STUDENTS IN EACH CLASS      ***
80   REM ***     A1 - A4           ABSENCES IN EACH CLASS      ***
90   REM ***     PCT1 - PCT4       PERCENTAGE ABSENT PER CLASS ***
100  REM
105  CLEAR
110  REM *** GET NEEDED DATA. ***
120  GOSUB 1000
130  REM
140  REM *** DETERMINE PERCENT ABSENT IN EACH CLASS. ***
150  GOSUB 2000
160  REM
170  REM *** PRINT HEADINGS FOR REPORT. ***
180  GOSUB 3000
190  REM
200  REM *** PRINT REPORT COLUMNS. ***
210  GOSUB 4000
999  END
1000 REM *******************************************************
1010 REM ***                 SUBROUTINE GET DATA           ***
1020 REM *******************************************************
1030 REM *** THIS SUBROUTINE PROMPTS THE USER TO ENTER THE ***
1040 REM *** DATE, NUMBER OF STUDENTS IN EACH CLASS, AND AB- ***
1050 REM *** SENCES PER CLASS.                              ***
1060 REM
1070 PRINT "SUBROUTINE GET DATA CALLED BUT NOT YET IMPLEMENTED."
1080 RETURN
2000 REM *******************************************************
2010 REM ***          SUBROUTINE CALCULATE PERCENTAGES.    ***
2020 REM *******************************************************
2030 REM *** THIS SUBROUTINE CALCULATES THE PERCENTAGE OF  ***
2040 REM *** STUDENTS ABSENT IN EACH CLASS.                ***
2050 REM
2060 PRINT "SUBROUTINE CALCULATE PERCENTAGES CALLED BUT NOT IMPLEMENTED."
2070 RETURN
2080 RETURN
3000 REM *******************************************************
3010 REM ***                PRINT REPORT HEADINGS.         ***
3020 REM *******************************************************
3030 REM *** THIS SUBROUTINE PRINTS THE REPORT TITLES AND  ***
3040 REM *** COLUMN HEADINGS.                              ***
3050 REM
3060 LPRINT TAB(21) "Baymont High School"
3070 LPRINT TAB(16) "Attendance Report for ";DTE$
3080 LPRINT
3090 GOSUB 5000
3100 LPRINT TAB(13) "Total Number";TAB(33) "Number";TAB(51);"Percentage"
3110 LPRINT "Grade";TAB(13) "of Students";TAB(33) "Absent";TAB(51) "Absent"
```

(figure continued on the next page)

FIGURE 6–8 Continued

```
3120 GOSUB 5000
3130 RETURN
4000 REM **********************************************************
4010 REM ***                 SUBROUTINE PRINT TABLE             ***
4020 REM **********************************************************
4030 REM *** THIS SUBROUTINE PRINTS THE INFORMATION FOR THE     ***
4040 REM *** ATTENDANCE REPORT.                                 ***
4050 REM
4060 F$ = "##              ###                ##              ##.##"
4070 REM
4080 REM *** PRINT REPORT FIGURES. ***
4090 LPRINT USING F$;9,CLASS1,A1,PCT1
4100 LPRINT USING F$;10,CLASS2,A2,PCT2
4110 LPRINT USING F$;11,CLASS3,A3,PCT3
4120 LPRINT USING F$;12,CLASS4,A4,PCT4
4130 GOSUB 5000
4140 RETURN
5000 REM **********************************************************
5010 REM ***                 SUBROUTINE PRINT DIVIDER           ***
5020 REM **********************************************************
5030 REM
5040 PRINT "SUBROUTINE PRINT DIVIDER CALLED BUT NOT IMPLEMENTED."
5050 LPRINT
5060 RETURN
```

the table can be added at this point. Again, the program must be run to make certain the table layout is correct. Next, we can add the subroutine GET DATA and run the program to determine that the data is properly outputted. The subroutine CALCULATE PERCENTAGES, which performs the arithmetic operations, is added last. After the program is executed this time, we must check the percentages to determine whether they have been properly calculated. Following this method of implementing programs allows the programmer to enter and test programs in a structured manner.

A Programming Problem

Problem Definition

The public library needs a program to calculate the total cost of the books it adds to its collection. This cost includes not only the purchase price of the book but also the cost of processing the book. The program should be interactive, allowing the librarians to enter the data at the keyboard. The total book cost should then be printed on the monitor screen.

Processing costs are dependent upon two factors: (1) the type of book (reference, circulating, or paperback) and (2) whether or not the book is a

Now Try This

1. Write an ON/GOSUB statement that transfers control to line 1000 if X equals either 2 or 8, to line 2000 if X equals 4, and to line 3000 if X equals 6.

2. Rewrite Question 1 using IF/THEN and GOSUB statements instead of the ON/GOSUB statement.

3. Rewrite the following program segment using a single ON/GOSUB statement.

```
350 IF X = 1 THEN GOSUB 2000
360 IF X = 2 THEN GOSUB 3000
370 IF X = 3 THEN GOSUB 4000
```

4. Rewrite the following statements using an ON/GOSUB statement:

```
400 IF QUANTITY * 4 = 20 THEN GOSUB 8000
500 IF QUANTITY * 4 = 24 THEN GOSUB 6000
600 IF QUANTITY * 4 = 28 THEN GOSUB 8000
700 IF QUANTITY * 4 = 32 THEN GOSUB 4000
```

---

duplicate of one already in the library. It is cheaper to process books that are duplicates of those already in the library's collection, because cards for these books are already in the card catalog and the cost of card production is saved. Processing costs are as follows:

Reference Book

not a duplicate	$8.50
duplicate	$7.40

Circulating Book

not a duplicate	$7.82
duplicate	$6.60
bestseller	$1.75 additional

Paperback

not a duplicate	$4.60
duplicate	$3.10

The type of book should be entered using an integer code:

1—Reference
2—Circulating
3—Paperback

Note the additional $1.75 cost for processing circulating books that are also bestsellers. This cost is for a plastic cover to give the book extra protection. Figure 6–9 contains the program specification chart.

Solution Design

Each time this program is executed, it will calculate the total cost (purchase price plus processing cost) of one book. The program needs four input variables: one numeric variable for the price of the book, another numeric variable to represent the book code, a character string variable to store a Y if the book is a duplicate and an N if it is not, and, if the book code entered is a 2, a character string variable to indicate whether the book is a bestseller. The output variable will be a numeric variable containing the total cost. The needed variables are summarized in the following table:

Input Variables

price of book	(PRICE)
code for type of book	(CODE)
duplicate indicator	(DUP$)
bestseller indicator	(SELLER$)

FIGURE 6–9 Program Specification Chart for Book Cost

PROGRAM SPECIFICATION CHART

PROGRAM NAME:	PROGRAMMER'S NAME:	DATE:
Book Cost Program	S. Baumann	11/20/91

INPUT:	OUTPUT:
Book price. Book type. Duplicate (Yes/No). Bestseller (Yes/No).	***TOTAL COST: $XXX.XX

SOURCE OF INPUT:	DESTINATION OF OUTPUT:
Keyboard	Monitor screen

PURPOSE:

This program calculates the total cost of a book to a library based on the purchasing price and the processing costs.

Output Variables

total cost   (TTCST)

Program Variables

processing cost   (PRCST)

Three basic steps are necessary to determine the total book costs:

1. Enter the data for the book.
2. Calculate the correct processing cost.
3. Determine the total cost.

Step 1 can be divided into three substeps that ask the user to enter the price of the book, the code for the type of book, and the duplicate indicator. Since each of these substeps is relatively simple, we will include them all in a single subroutine when we write the program.

Step 2 is the most difficult part of this problem. It involves performing one of three options, depending on whether a reference, circulating, or paperback book is being processed. Because only one of these options will be executed, this is an ideal solution for a conditional branch to one of three subroutines, each of which will calculate the cost for a particular type of book. The book-type code can be used as the controlling expression in an ON/GOSUB statement to transfer program control from the main program to the appropriate subroutine.

Step 3 involves adding the processing cost to the purchase price of the book and displaying this total. The structure chart is shown in Figure 6–10 and the flowchart and pseudocode in Figure 6–11.

The Program

Study the complete program as shown in Figure 6–12. Note that the main body of the program is a driver program and is therefore quite short.

The first subroutine enables the user to enter the necessary data. The value entered for the book type code must be a 1, 2, or 3. This value is then used in the ON/GOSUB statement in line 310 to determine which one of the three subroutines will be executed. Each of the subroutines calculates the processing cost for one type of book. The circulating-book subroutine is a little more complicated than the other two, because it must ask the user if the book is a bestseller and include an additional charge if it is. After the processing cost of the book has been determined, control returns to the main program, where the final subroutine is called to add the processing cost to the purchase price and display the total cost.

FIGURE 6–10   Structure Chart for Book Cost

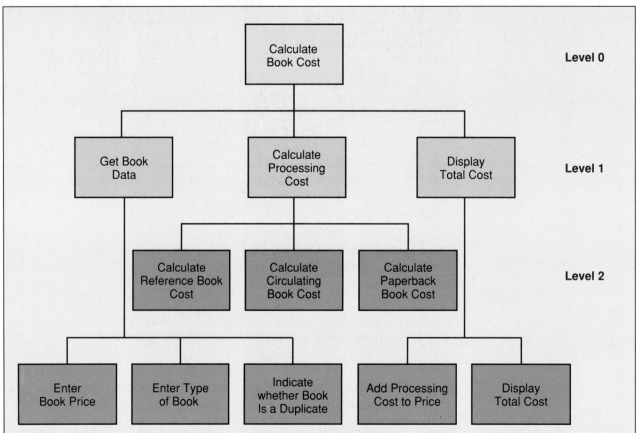

Programming Hints

- When branching to a subroutine, be careful that program control is being transferred to the correct line number. A common programming error is to place incorrect line numbers in GOSUB and ON/GOSUB statements. This error can lead to unpredictable behavior when the program is executed.
- When using the ON/GOSUB statement, make certain that the numerical expression will evaluate as expected. Test the program using a variety of data.
- All subroutines must have a single exit point and a single entry point. This rule is fundamental to good structured programming.
- Take the time to use stubs when developing programs. In the long run, it will make programming simpler and more enjoyable.

FIGURE 6–11 Flowchart and Pseudocode for Book Cost

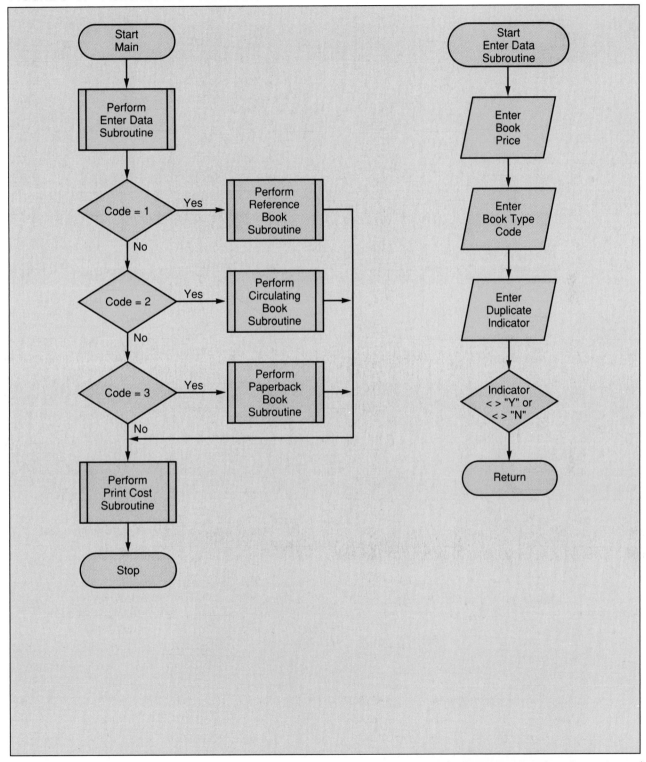

(figure continued on the next page)

FIGURE 6–11 Continued

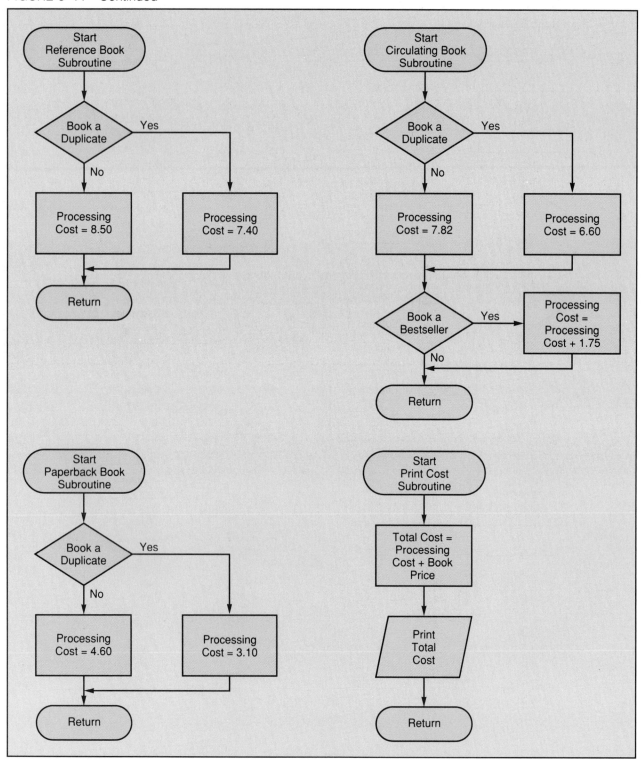

FIGURE 6–11 Continued

Pseudocode

Begin main program
Perform enter data subroutine
If type code = 1 perform reference book subroutine
If type code = 2 perform circulating book subroutine
If type code = 3 perform paperback book subroutine
Perform print cost subroutine
End main program

Begin enter data subroutine
Prompt user to enter price
Prompt user to enter type code
Prompt user to enter duplicate indicator
End enter data subroutine

Begin reference book subroutine
If book is duplicate
    Then processing cost = 7.40
    Else processing cost = 8.50
End if
End reference book subroutine

Begin circulating book subroutine
If book is duplicate
    Then processing cost = 6.60
    Else processing cost = 7.82
End if
Prompt user to enter bestseller indicator
If book is a bestseller
    Then add 1.75 to processing cost
End if
End circulating book subroutine

Begin paperback book subroutine
If book is duplicate
    Then processing cost = 3.10
    Else processing cost = 4.60
End if
End paperback subroutine

Begin print cost subroutine
Total cost = processing cost + book price
Print total cost
End print cost subroutine

FIGURE 6–12   Book Cost Program

```
10    REM ***                    PROGRAM BOOKCOST              ***
20    REM
30    REM *** THIS PROGRAM CALCULATES THE TOTAL COST OF A      ***
40    REM *** BOOK.   THE TOTAL COST IS OBTAINED BY ADDING     ***
50    REM *** THE PRICE OF THE BOOK TO THE PROCESSING COST,    ***
60    REM *** WHICH IS BASED ON THE TYPE.                      ***
70    REM ***      1.   REFERENCE BOOK                         ***
80    REM ***              NOT A DUPLICATE     $8.50           ***
90    REM ***              DUPLICATE           $7.40           ***
100   REM ***      2.   CIRCULATING BOOK                       ***
110   REM ***              NOT A DUPLICATE     $7.82           ***
120   REM ***              DUPLICATE           $6.60           ***
130   REM ***              BESTSELLER          $1.75    EXTRA  ***
140   REM ***      3.   PAPERBACK                              ***
150   REM ***              NOT A DUPLICATE     $4.60           ***
160   REM ***              DUPLICATE           $3.10           ***
170   REM
180   REM *** MAJOR VARIABLES:                                 ***
190   REM ***      PRICE        PRICE OF THE BOOK              ***
200   REM ***      CODE         TYPE OF BOOK AS ABOVE          ***
210   REM ***      DUP$         IS BOOK A DUPLICATE(Y/N)?      ***
220   REM ***      PRCST        PROCESSING COST                ***
230   REM ***      SELLER$      IS BOOK A BESTSELLER (Y/N)?    ***
240   REM ***      TTCST        TOTAL COST OF BOOK             ***
250   REM
260   REM *** CALL SUBROUTINE TO ENTER DATA.                   ***
270   GOSUB 1000
280   REM
290   REM *** CALL APPROPRIATE SUBROUTINE TO CALCULATE.        ***
300   REM *** THE PROCESSING COST.                             ***
310   ON CODE GOSUB 2000,3000,4000
320   REM
330   REM *** CALL SUBROUTINE TO ADD PROCESSING COST TO        ***
340   REM *** BOOK PRICE AND PRINT TOTAL COST.                 ***
350   GOSUB 5000
999   END
1000  REM ********************************************************
1010  REM ***                  SUBROUTINE ENTER DATA            ***
1020  REM ********************************************************
1030  REM *** SUBROUTINE TO ALLOW USER TO ENTER DATA.          ***
1040  REM
1050  CLS
1060  INPUT "ENTER PRICE OF THE BOOK";PRICE
1070  PRINT
1080  PRINT "1 - REFERENCE BOOK"
1090  PRINT "2 - CIRCULATING BOOK"
1100  PRINT "3 - PAPERBACK"
1110  INPUT "ENTER TYPE CODE FOR THE BOOK, USING THE CODE LISTED ABOVE";CODE
1120  PRINT
1130  INPUT "IS BOOK A DUPLICATE (Y/N)";DUP$
1140  RETURN
```

FIGURE 6–12   Continued

```
2000 REM ****************************************************
2010 REM ***              SUBROUTINE REFERENCE BOOK         ***
2020 REM ****************************************************
2030 REM *** SUBROUTINE TO CALCULATE PROCESSING COST OF    ***
2040 REM *** REFERENCE BOOK.                               ***
2050 REM
2060 IF DUP$ = "Y" THEN PRCST = 7.4 ELSE PRCST = 8.5
2070 RETURN
3000 REM ****************************************************
3010 REM ***              SUBROUTINE CIRCULATING BOOK       ***
3020 REM ****************************************************
3030 REM *** SUBROUTINE TO CALCULATE PROCESSING COST OF    ***
3040 REM *** CIRCULATING BOOK.                             ***
3050 REM
3060 IF DUP$ = "Y" THEN PRCST = 6.6 ELSE PRCST = 7.82
3070 INPUT "IS THE BOOK A BESTSELLER (Y/N)";SELLER$
3080 IF SELLER$ = "Y" THEN PRCST = PRCST + 1.75
3090 RETURN
4000 REM ****************************************************
4010 REM ***              SUBROUTINE PAPERBACK BOOK         ***
4020 REM ****************************************************
4030 REM *** SUBROUTINE TO CALCULATE PROCESSING COST OF    ***
4040 REM *** PAPERBACK BOOK.                               ***
4050 REM
4060 IF DUP$ = "Y" THEN PRCST = 3.1 ELSE PRCST = 4.6
4070 RETURN
5000 REM ****************************************************
5010 REM ***              SUBROUTINE PRINT COST            ***
5020 REM ****************************************************
5030 REM *** SUBROUTINE TO CALCULATE AND PRINT TOTAL COST. ***
5040 REM
5050 TTCST = PRCST + PRICE
5060 PRINT
5070 PRINT USING "\                    \ $$###.##";"*** TOTAL COST:",TTCST
5080 RETURN
```

(figure continued on the next page)

FIGURE 6–12 Continued

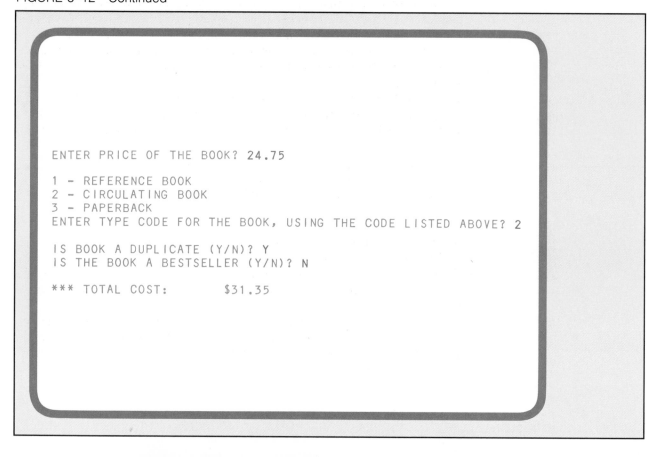

```
ENTER PRICE OF THE BOOK? 24.75

1 - REFERENCE BOOK
2 - CIRCULATING BOOK
3 - PAPERBACK
ENTER TYPE CODE FOR THE BOOK, USING THE CODE LISTED ABOVE? 2

IS BOOK A DUPLICATE (Y/N)? Y
IS THE BOOK A BESTSELLER (Y/N)? N

*** TOTAL COST:        $31.35
```

New Statement Review

Statement Format	Explanation
line# GOSUB transfer line#	Transfers control to the specified line number. Also, keeps track of where control branched from so that when a RETURN statement is encountered, control can be transferred back to the correct location.
line# RETURN	Returns control to the first executable statement following the GOSUB statement.
line# ON expression GOSUB line#1[,line#2]...	Control branches to the line number corresponding to the value of the expression. If the expression equals 3, control transfers to the third line number listed.

Summary Points

- Modularizing programs involves dividing them into modules, each of which performs a specific task. In BASIC, these modules are referred to as subroutines.
- The use of subroutines makes program logic easier to follow and the program easier to develop. Also, a given subroutine can be called any number of times.
- The two BASIC statements that can be used to call subroutines are GOSUB and ON/GOSUB.
- The GOSUB statement is an unconditional branch that causes the flow of execution to be passed to the line number contained in the GOSUB statement.
- The RETURN statement causes control to be transferred back to the statement after the one that called the subroutine.
- The ON/GOSUB statement allows for a conditional branch to one of several stated subroutines. The expression in the ON/GOSUB statement is evaluated and control is passed to the appropriate subroutine. For example, if the value of the expression is 4, control passes to the subroutine starting at the fourth line number listed.
- An important rule in structured programming is that all subroutines should have a single entry point and a single exit point. Otherwise, the possibility of an error in the program is greatly increased. Also, entering or exiting from the middle of a subroutine makes the logic of the program convoluted and difficult to follow.
- Stubs allow a program to be developed in a methodical fashion. Rather than entering a program to the computer all at once, the programmer can add and test subroutines gradually. Once the parts already entered work properly, more of the program can be entered. This procedure makes it easier to locate program errors.
- Structure charts are helpful in determining how to modularize programs.

Vocabulary List

Call	Stub
Driver program	Subroutine
Single-entry, single-exit point principle	

Questions

Whenever appropriate, use complete sentences in answering the following questions.

1. Name three advantages of modularizing programs.
2. Where are subroutines usually placed in a program?
3. Why is the GOSUB statement referred to as an unconditional branching statement?
4. Explain the format of the statement used to call a subroutine.
5. What happens if the transfer line number in a GOSUB statement is a nonexecutable statement?
6. Where are RETURN statements placed in programs?
7. Why doesn't the RETURN statement contain a transfer line number? That is, how is it possible that program control can be transferred back to the correct statement even though no transfer line number is specified in the RETURN statement?
8. What is a driver program?

9. How can a structure chart help in modularizing a program?

10. Why is it important that a subroutine have only one entry point and one exit point?

11. Explain how the ON/GOSUB statement works. How is it different from the GOSUB statement?

12. Where will program control be transferred if the following statements are executed?

```
260 X = 4 + 23
270 N = X / 8 + 1
280 ON N GOSUB 1000,2000,3000,4000
```

13. What subroutine will be executed by this statement,

```
410 ON TTL / 2 GOSUB 2000,3000,5000,7000
```

for each of the values of TTL given in parts a through c?

    a. `400 LET TTL = 8 / 2`
    b. `400 LET TTL = 4 + 2`
    c. `400 LET TTL = 4 * 2`

14. What is a stub?

15. How can stubs be used when entering programs into the computer?

Debugging Exercises

Identify the following programs or program segments that contain errors and debug them.

```
1. 90   REM *** IF SIZE IS SMALL, INCREMENT ***
   100  REM *** APPROPRIATE COUNTER.        ***
   110  IF SIZE < 45 THEN GOSUB 1030
             .
             .
             .
   1000 REM *** THIS PACKAGE IS A SMALL SIZE. ***
   1010 REM
   1020 SMALL = SMALL + 1
   1030 PRINT "THIS PACKAGE IS A SMALL SIZE"
   1040 RETURN
```

```
2. 10   REM *** EXECUTE SUBROUTINE TO DETERMINE ***
   20   REM *** TOTAL QUANTITY.                 ***
   30   GOSUB 1000
   40   PRINT X
             .
             .
             .
   99   END
   1000 REM ***    SUBROUTINE     ***
   1010 REM
   1020 X = 12 * 77
```

```
3. 90   REM *** EXECUTE APPROPRIATE SUBROUTINE ***
   100 REM *** DEPENDING ON GRADE.           ***
   110 INPUT "ENTER THE STUDENT'S GRADE";GD$
   120 ON GD$ GOSUB 2000,3000,4000,5000
         •
         •
         •


4. 20 SALARY = 3000
   30 ON GOSUB SALARY / 1000 1000,2000,3000,4000
         •
         •
         •
```

Programming Problems

Level 1

1. Write a subroutine that calculates the new balance of a checking account. The user should be prompted to enter the old balance, deposits, and total amount of checks written.

2. Write a subroutine that determines the unit price (cents per ounce) of different boxes of laundry detergent. The input should include the weight in pounds and ounces and the total price. The output should state the price per ounce.

3. Alter the program in Figure 5–14 so that it uses subroutines.

4. Assume that numeric variable AMT can contain the value 1, 2, or 3. Write a program segment that asks the user to enter a value to AMT. The program should then call one of three subroutines, depending on the value of AMT. If the value of AMT is 1, the subroutine starting at line 1000 should be executed. If the value of AMT is 2, the subroutine starting at line 2000 should be executed. If the value of AMT is 3, the subroutine starting at line 3000 should be executed.

5. Assume that the numeric value of a variable named DIST can be 200, 400, or 600. Write an ON/GOSUB statement that will cause program control to transfer to the subroutine starting at line 2000 if DIST is 200, to line 3000 if DIST is 400, and to line 4000 if DIST is 600.

6. Write a program segment to accomplish the same task as in Problem 5, but this time use IF/THEN and GOSUB statements to do the job.

Level 2

1. Think of a song you know that contains a refrain. Write a program that will display the words to this song. Use a different subroutine for each of the verses and a subroutine for the refrain. Then, after each verse is displayed, call the refrain subroutine to print the refrain.

2. Rewrite the program for Problem 2 of Level 2 in Chapter 5, using ON/GOSUB statements.

3. The Interior Furniture Company wants you to write a program that will help them color-coordinate furniture with room color for their customers. Three main colors can be used as room colors: blue, yellow, and tan. The program should allow the user to enter the room color and should then print appropriate color schemes for that room. The following coordinating colors should be printed on paper, depending on the room color entered:

Room Color	Coordinating Colors
Blue	Soft Peach, Sunshine Yellow, Passionate Purple, Creamy Beige
Yellow	Halo Blue, Soft Peach, Spring Green, Burnt Orange
Tan	Amber Brown, Crimson, Soft Peach, Sierra Blue

4. Urbank's Well Drilling Company drills water and oil wells for businesses and individuals. A water well costs $15 a foot to drill. An oil well costs $20 a foot to drill for the first 10,000 feet; below that, it costs $35 a foot. Write a subroutine that calculates the cost of drilling a given well.

5. Write a program that will print the number of days in a given month. The user should enter the name of the month, and the program should call a subroutine to print the correct number of days in that month.

6. Write a program that will tell a bicyclist how long it will take to travel a given distance under certain weather conditions. The bicyclist is able to travel at the following rates:

Weather	Speed
EXCELLENT	25 miles an hour
GOOD	18 miles an hour
POOR	14 miles an hour

The program should be written so that the user enters the current weather conditions (EXCELLENT, GOOD, or POOR) and the number of miles to be traveled. The program should use subroutines to determine the approximate time needed to complete the trip. This time should then be printed with an appropriate label.

Projects

For each project, complete the following:

- Develop the program by using stubs.
- Fill out a program specification chart.
- Develop a structure chart.
- Create a flowchart or pseudocode.
- Thoroughly document the final program.
- Test your program using a variety of data.

1. Shangri-La Realty needs a program to assist its agents in keeping track of the various apartments available for rent. Write a program using subroutines that will give the user a choice of a studio, one-bedroom, or two-bedroom apartment. The monthly rent depends on the size of the apartment and whether it is to be furnished or unfurnished (this data should also be entered by the user). Use the following data:

| | | Rent | |
Type	Deposit	Furnished	Unfurnished
Studio	$ 75	$150	$135
One-bedroom	150	275	250
Two-bedroom	200	325	315

The program should display the apartment description, required deposit, and monthly rent according to the choices entered, using the following format:

Description: One-bedroom furnished
Deposit: $150
Rent: $275

2. Stan's Television Corporation needs a program to help with the billing of its customers. The user should be able to enter the due date for the bill to be processed. For each customer, enter a name, address, and the applicable charges selected from the following list:

Standard Service	$7.00
Cable Service	4.00
Home Cinema Channel	2.00
Continual Cartoon Channel	2.00

All customers receive the standard service. The program should display an itemized bill showing the total amount due and the amount owed for late payment, which is the total plus 5 percent. Your output should resemble the following:

Name:
Address: Due Date:

Services:

Standard service	$7.00
Cable service	4.00
Continual Cartoon Channel	2.00
Total amount due:	$13.00
After due date:	$13.65

CHAPTER 7

Loop Structures

Learning Objectives

After studying this chapter, you should be able to
1. Explain the importance of loop structures in structured programming.
2. Draw flowcharts representing loops.
3. Explain how the WHILE loop functions.
4. Write programs using WHILE loops.
5. Use trailer values to control loops.
6. Write counting loops.
7. Explain how the FOR/NEXT loop functions.
8. Write programs using FOR/NEXT loops.
9. Create nested loops.
10. Use the single-entry, single-exit point principle in creating loops.
11. Determine which type of loop is more appropriate in a particular situation.
12. Use the logical operators NOT, AND, and OR to check for specific conditions.

Introduction

As discussed in Chapter 2, structured programs have easy-to-understand logic, partly due to the use of modules, or subroutines. In addition, they should contain only the three basic program structures: the sequence, the decision structure, and the loop structure. The unconditional branch (or GOTO statement) should be avoided whenever possible. So far you have learned to write programs that use sequences and decision structures. This chapter introduces the loop structure. This structure is very useful when performing repetitive tasks because a specified group of statements can be executed as many times as needed. In BASIC, loops can be written using the WHILE or the FOR/NEXT statements. At the end of this chapter, a new type of operator, the *logical operator,* is explained. It allows you to combine expressions to form new, more complex expressions.

Using Loop Structures

Often a situation arises where a task must be performed several times. For example, a teacher may need a program to find the average test score of all the students in a class. The job of processing one student's data is simple enough:

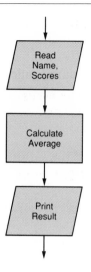

However, consider the problem of repeating these steps for a class of 30 students:

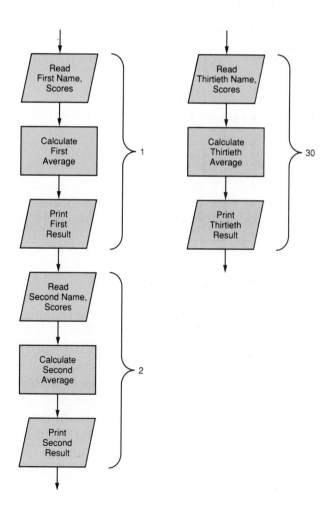

The same three statements used to process one student's data would have to be written 30 times—a tedious job for the programmer. To simplify the problem, the statements could be written once, then executed as many times as necessary. This procedure, called *looping*, is shown here in a flowchart:

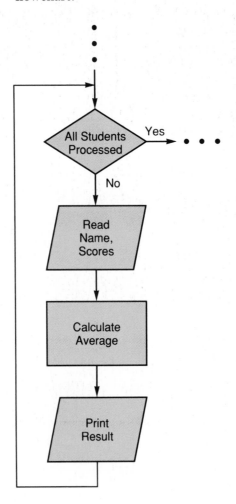

The loop is an extremely useful programming tool. Several loop structures exist among the many programming languages used today, but all share some basic components. They all use a **loop control variable,** which is a variable whose value is used to determine whether a loop will be repeated. In the example of the student test scores, the loop control variable could contain the current number of students processed. All loops contain some action to be performed repeatedly; the statements that perform such an action make up the **loop body**. In the student test score example, the loop body consists of three steps: (1) read the name and scores, (2) calculate the average, and (3) print the result.

Execution of the basic loop structure consists of the following five steps:

Loop control variable
A variable whose value determines whether a loop will execute.

Loop body
The statement(s) that make up the action to be performed by the loop.

1. The loop control variable is initialized to a particular value before loop execution begins.

2. The program tests the loop control variable to determine whether to execute the loop body or exit from the loop.

3. The loop body, consisting of any number of statements, is executed.

4. At some point during loop execution, the value of the loop control variable is modified to allow an exit from the loop.

5. The loop is exited when the decision of Step 2 determines that the right number of loop repetitions has been made. Execution continues with the next statement following the loop.

Figure 7–1 pictures the elements of a loop in the form of a flowchart. Keep in mind the five loop elements as the next section presents one way to form a loop in BASIC: using the WHILE and WEND statements.

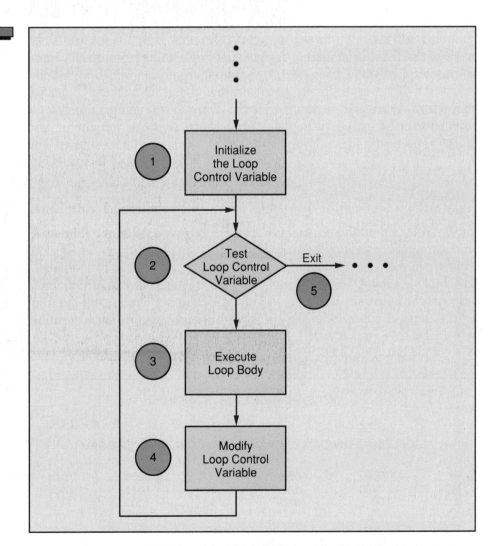

FIGURE 7–1 Flowchart of Loop Elements

The WHILE Loop

In a WHILE loop, the condition controlling loop execution is placed at the top of the loop. The loop continues executing as long as this condition is true. Spend a minute examining the WHILE loop in Figure 7–2. Notice that each part of the loop is labeled. The WHILE loop is executed as follows:

1. The expression is evaluated as true or false. In Figure 7–2, as long as the expression "NUMBER <> − 1" is true, the body of the loop is executed.
2. If the expression is true, the loop body statements are executed until the WEND statement is encountered; if the expression is false, control passes to the first statement after the WEND. The body of the WHILE loop in Figure 7–2 contains two statements:

```
50        SUM = SUM + NUMBER
60        INPUT "ENTER THE NEXT NUMBER (-1 TO QUIT)";NUMBER
```

FIGURE 7–2   Program Demonstrating a WHILE Loop

```
10 REM *** THIS PROGRAM ADDS A LIST OF POSITIVE INTEGERS. ***
20 SUM = 0
30 INPUT "ENTER THE FIRST NUMBER (-1 TO QUIT)";NUMBER      Initialize loop control
                                                           variable
40 WHILE NUMBER <> -1
50     SUM = SUM + NUMBER                                   Test loop control variable
60     INPUT "ENTER THE NEXT NUMBER (-1 TO QUIT)";NUMBER
70 WEND                                                     Modify loop control
80 PRINT "THE SUM IS";SUM                                   variable
99 END
```

```
RUN
ENTER THE FIRST NUMBER (-1 TO QUIT)? 32
ENTER THE NEXT NUMBER (-1 TO QUIT)? 14
ENTER THE NEXT NUMBER (-1 TO QUIT)? 8
ENTER THE NEXT NUMBER (-1 TO QUIT)? 40
ENTER THE NEXT NUMBER (-1 TO QUIT)? -1
THE SUM IS 94
```

3. When the WEND is encountered, control passes back to the WHILE statement, and the condition is checked again.

4. If the condition is still true, the loop is executed again; if false, the loop is exited and program execution skips to the first statement after the WEND. When the loop in Figure 7–2 is exited, control transfers to line 80, and the sum of the numbers is outputted. Examine line 30:

```
30 INPUT "ENTER THE FIRST NUMBER (-1 TO QUIT)";NUMBER
```

Priming read

A READ or INPUT statement that is placed immediately before a loop; it assigns a value to the loop control variable.

You may be wondering why the first number is read before the loop is entered. This first INPUT statement is referred to as a **priming read**. The variable NUMBER should be initialized to a starting value before the condition in the WHILE statement is evaluated the first time. For this reason it is necessary to use two INPUT statements: one to initialize the variable the first time and one at the bottom of the loop to get the remaining numbers. This second INPUT statement should appear as the last statement in the loop body. If the second INPUT statement occurred before NUMBER was added to SUM, the first value of NUMBER would be lost before it was added.

The general format of the WHILE statement is

```
line# WHILE expression
         .
         .
         .
line# WEND
```

Controlling Loops

One of the most difficult aspects of using loops is making them stop execution at the proper time. In this section, we will discuss two methods of controlling loop repetition: using trailer values and counting loops.

Trailer value

A data value indicating that a loop should stop executing. It must be a value that would not ordinarily occur in the input data.

Trailer Values   A **trailer value** is a "dummy" value that follows, or trails, the data items being processed. It is sometimes referred to as a **sentinel value**. The trailer value signals to the program that all data has been entered. The loop in Figure 7–2 uses a trailer value of −1. When the user enters that value, the loop stops, and the sum is displayed. The trailer value can be either a numeric value or a character string, depending on the type of data being input, but it should always be a value outside the range of the actual data. For example, if a program reads people's ages, a good trailer value might be −1. If names are being read, an example of a good trailer value would be "FINISHED."

As previously mentioned, a priming read should be used to assign a value to the loop control variable before loop repetition begins. Subsequent values are read to the loop control variable at the bottom of the loop. If the loop control variable's value does not equal the trailer value, the loop is repeated. The program in Figure 7–3 shows another loop using a trailer value. Figure 7–4 contains the corresponding flowchart with the loop elements identified. This program calculates the wages of employees of The Village Hotel. After

FIGURE 7–3   Loop Controlled by a Trailer Value

```
10   REM ***                    THE VILLAGE PAYROLL.              ***
20   REM
30   REM *** THIS PROGRAM CALCULATES EMPLOYEE SALARIES.           ***
40   REM
50   RATE = 5
60   INPUT "ENTER FIRST NAME AND NUMBER OF HOURS";NME$,HOURS
70   WHILE NME$ <> "FINISHED"
80      WAGE = RATE * HOURS
90      PRINT "NAME","WAGE"
100     PRINT NME$,WAGE
110     PRINT
120     INPUT "ENTER NEXT NAME AND NUMBER OF HOURS";NME$,HOURS
130     PRINT
140  WEND
150  PRINT "FINISHED"
999  END
```

```
RUN
ENTER FIRST NAME AND NUMBER OF HOURS? FETTERMAN,78
NAME            WAGE
FETTERMAN       390

ENTER NEXT NAME AND NUMBER OF HOURS? HOSSLER,32

NAME            WAGE
HOSSLER         160

ENTER NEXT NAME AND NUMBER OF HOURS? BULAS,25

NAME            WAGE
BULAS           125

ENTER NEXT NAME AND NUMBER OF HOURS? FINISHED,0

FINISHED
```

FIGURE 7–4   Flowchart of a Loop Using a Trailer Value

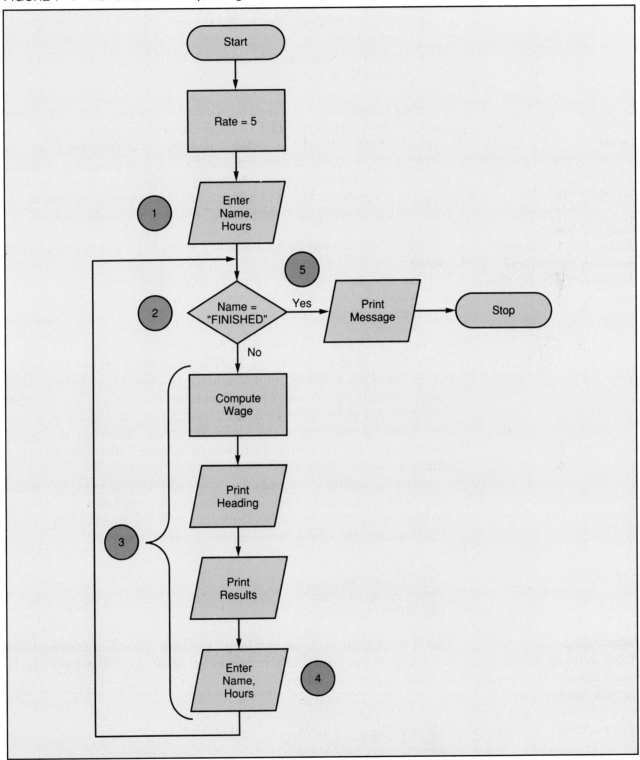

each employee's data is entered, the following statement tests for the trailer value:

```
70   WHILE NME$ <> "FINISHED"
```

If the condition is false, control passes out of the loop to line 150. Otherwise, the loop body is executed.

Counter

A variable that keeps track of how many times a loop has been executed.

Counting loop

A loop in which the exact number of repetitions is determined before the loop begins executing.

Counting Loops   A second method of controlling a loop is to create a loop control variable that keeps track of the number of times the loop has been executed. Such a variable is called a **counter**. In a **counting loop,** the counter is incremented or decremented during each repetition. When it reaches a specified value, loop execution stops. A counting loop is useful when the programmer knows in advance how many times a loop should be performed. The following steps are used to set up a counting loop:

1. Initialize the counter by setting it to a beginning value before entering the loop.
2. Increment the counter each time the loop is executed.
3. Test the counter each time the loop is executed to see if the loop has been performed the desired number of times.

The program from Figure 7–3 has been rewritten in Figure 7–5 to use a counter rather than a trailer value. The corresponding flowchart is shown in Figure 7–6. Data on three employees must be read, so the loop must be executed exactly three times. The counter is initialized to 1 in line 60 before loop execution starts. Line 70 determines whether the counter is greater than 3 and exits the loop if the condition is true. Otherwise, the loop is executed, and the counter is incremented in Line 130 before execution returns to the top of the loop.

Always be careful to initialize the loop control variable to the starting value before entering the loop. In addition, make certain that at some point the loop control variable reaches the value needed to stop the loop. In the following loop, the loop control variable is never modified:

```
10 CNT = 1
20 WHILE CNT < 50
30    PRINT CNT
40 WEND
```

Infinite loop

A loop in which the loop control variable never reaches the value needed to stop the loop; therefore, the loop never stops executing.

This is an example of an **infinite loop.** The loop will execute infinitely (or at least until the computer's resources are used up). This loop can be correctly written as follows:

```
10 CNT = 1
20 WHILE CNT < 50
30    PRINT CNT
40    CNT = CNT + 1
50 WEND
```

FIGURE 7–5   Program Demonstrating a Counting Loop

```
10    REM ***                    THE VILLAGE PAYROLL             ***
20    REM
30    REM *** THIS PROGRAM CALCULATES EMPLOYEE SALARIES.         ***
40    REM
50    RATE = 5
60    COUNTER = 1
70    WHILE COUNTER <= 3
80        INPUT "ENTER NEXT NAME AND NUMBER OF HOURS";NME$,HOURS
90        WAGE = RATE * HOURS
100       PRINT "NAME","WAGE"
110       PRINT NME$,WAGE
120       PRINT
130       COUNTER = COUNTER + 1
140   WEND
150   PRINT "FINISHED"
999   END
```

```
RUN
ENTER NEXT NAME AND NUMBER OF HOURS? FETTERMAN,78
NAME            WAGE
FETTERMAN        390


ENTER NEXT NAME AND NUMBER OF HOURS? HOSSLER,32
NAME            WAGE
HOSSLER          160


ENTER NEXT NAME AND NUMBER OF HOURS? BULAS,25
NAME            WAGE
BULAS            125


FINISHED
```

The FOR/NEXT Loop

The FOR and NEXT statements are used together to form a counting loop.
For example, this loop,

```
10 FOR COUNTER = 1 TO 8 STEP 1
20    PRINT COUNTER;
30 NEXT COUNTER
```

FIGURE 7–6   Flowchart Showing Elements of a Loop with Counter

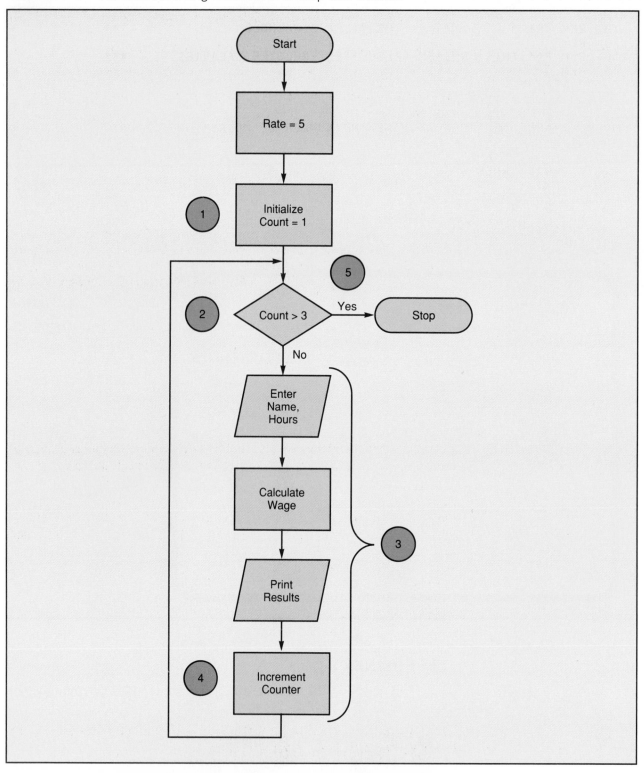

Now Try This

1. Write a WHILE loop that reads data until it encounters the trailer value 9999.

2. Write a WHILE loop that displays all the multiples of 3 between 1 and 100 (3, 6, 9 . . .).

3. Write a program segment that prompts the user to enter a positive integer, I, and calculates the following:

$$I + I - 1 + I - 2 \ldots + 1$$

For example, if the integer read is six, the calculation should look like this:

$$6 + 5 + 4 + 3 + 2 + 1 = 21$$

4. Write a program segment that prompts the user to enter the amount in a savings account. Assuming that 7.5 percent interest is calculated annually, use a WHILE loop to determine how much will be in the account after six years.

---

executes eight times and outputs the following:

```
RUN
 1   2   3   4   5   6   7   8
```

The loop control variable starts at 1 and is incremented by 1 at the end of each repetition until its value is greater than 8. The FOR statement marks the beginning of the loop, and the NEXT statement marks its end. Any statements between the two make up the loop body. Figure 7–7 shows this loop with its components labeled. The step value determines the amount by which the loop control variable is incremented. If the step value is changed to 2,

```
10 FOR COUNTER = 1 TO 8 STEP 2
20    PRINT COUNTER;
30 NEXT COUNTER
```

The following is outputted:

```
RUN
 1   3   5   7
```

If no step value is specified, BASIC assumes a value of 1. Therefore, the following two statements work the same:

FIGURE 7–7 Labeled Parts
of a FOR/NEXT Loop

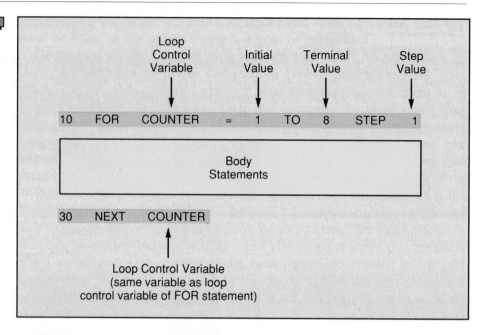

```
10 FOR COUNTER = 1 TO 8 STEP 1
```

```
10 FOR COUNTER = 1 TO 8
```

The loop control variable of a FOR/NEXT loop can be any numeric variable. The initial and terminal values and the optional step value, taken together, determine the number of times the loop body is executed. These values must all be numeric. They can consist of any of the following:

Value Type	Examples
constants	`FOR I = 1 TO 3 STEP 1`
variables	`FOR I = SMALL TO BIG STEP X`
expressions	`FOR I = (A + B) TO (C - D) STEP (K + 1)`

Figure 7–8 shows how the WHILE loop in Figure 7–5 can be rewritten using a FOR/NEXT loop. The general format of the FOR/NEXT loop is

```
line# FOR loop control variable = initial value TO terminal value
    [STEP value]
    .
    .
    .
line# NEXT loop control variable
```

FIGURE 7–8   Payroll Program with a FOR/NEXT Loop

```
10   REM ***                THE VILLAGE PAYROLL.            ***
20   REM
30   REM *** THIS PROGRAM CALCULATES EMPLOYEE SALARIES.     ***
40   REM
50   RTE = 5
60   FOR COUNTER = 1 TO 3
70      INPUT "ENTER NEXT NAME AND NUMBER OF HOURS";NME$,HOURS
80      WAGE = RTE * HOURS
90      PRINT "NAME","WAGE"
100     PRINT NME$,WAGE
110     PRINT
120  NEXT COUNTER
130  PRINT "FINISHED"
999  END
```

```
RUN
ENTER NEXT NAME AND NUMBER OF HOURS? FETTERMAN,78
NAME          WAGE
FETTERMAN     390

ENTER NEXT NAME AND NUMBER OF HOURS? HOSSLER,32
NAME          WAGE
HOSSLER       160

ENTER NEXT NAME AND NUMBER OF HOURS? BULAS,25
NAME          WAGE
BULAS         125

FINISHED
```

A number of actions are taken when a FOR statement is first encountered:

1. The initial, terminal, and (if given) step value expressions are evaluated.
2. The loop control variable is assigned the initial value.
3. The value of the loop control variable is tested against the terminal value.
4. If the loop control variable is less than or equal to the terminal value, the loop body is executed.

5. If the loop control variable is greater than the terminal value, the loop body is skipped, and control passes to the first statement following the NEXT statement. This means that the loop will not be executed at all.

Here is what happens when the NEXT statement is found:

1. The step value indicated in the FOR statement is added to the loop control variable. If the step value is omitted, + 1 is added.
2. A check is performed to determine if the value of the loop control variable exceeds the terminal value.
3. If the loop control variable is less than or equal to the terminal value, control transfers back to the statement after the FOR statement, and the loop is repeated. Otherwise, the loop is exited, and execution continues with the statement following the NEXT statement.

The step value of the FOR statement can be negative rather than positive. In this case, the loop control variable is decremented, rather than incremented, after each loop execution. The following statement is valid:

```
FOR I = 8 TO -4 STEP -2
```

When a negative step value is used, the loop body is executed if the loop control variable is greater than or equal to the terminal value. When the NEXT statement is encountered, the step value is added to the loop control variable as usual; and because this value is negative, the loop control variable is decremented. The program in Figure 7–9 demonstrates a FOR/NEXT loop with a negative step value.

Rules for Using the FOR/NEXT Loop   To avoid errors in using the FOR and NEXT statements, become familiar with the following rules:

■ The body of the loop is not executed if the initial value is greater than the terminal value when using a positive step, or if the initial value is less than the terminal value when using a negative step. For example, a loop containing either of the following statements would not be executed at all:

```
10 FOR X = 10 TO 5 STEP 2
20 FOR COUNT = 4 TO 6 STEP -1
```

■ The initial, terminal, and step values cannot be modified in the loop body.
■ It is possible to modify the loop control variable in the loop body, *but this should never be done*. Note how unpredictable the execution of the following program loop would be. The value of I is dependent on the integer entered by the user.

FIGURE 7–9   A FOR/NEXT Loop with a Negative Step Value

```
10 REM *** DISPLAY A COUNTDOWN FROM 10 TO 1. ***
20 REM
30 FOR I = 10 TO 1 STEP -1
40    PRINT I;
50 NEXT I
60 PRINT "** IGNITION! **"
99 END
```

```
RUN
 10  9  8  7  6  5  4  3  2  1 ** IGNITION! **
```

```
30 FOR I = 1 TO 10
40    INPUT "ENTER AN INTEGER";X
50    I = X
60 NEXT I
```

■ If the step value is zero, an infinite loop is created, as in the following example:

```
10 FOR X = 10 TO 20 STEP 0
```

This loop could be written correctly so that it would execute eleven times as follows:

```
10 FOR X = 10 TO 20 STEP 1
```

- Although it is perfectly correct to transfer control from one statement to another within the loop body, transferring from a loop body statement to the FOR statement is incorrect. Such a transfer resets the loop control variable rather than continuing the looping process. In the following segment, line 30 is a proper branch, but line 40 is not:

```
10 FOR K = 1 TO 10
20    READ AGE
30    IF AGE < 20 THEN 50
40    IF AGE > 20 THEN 10
50    PRINT AGE
60 NEXT K
```

To skip the remainder of the loop body and continue looping, a transfer should be made to the NEXT statement, as in line 40 of the following example:

```
10 FOR K = 1 TO 10
20    READ AGE
30    IF AGE < 20 THEN 50
40    IF AGE > 20 THEN 60
50    PRINT AGE
60 NEXT K
```

- Each FOR statement should be associated with a corresponding NEXT statement.

Single-Entry, Single-Exit Point Principle

As previously mentioned, an important principle of structured programming is that a program structure (such as a loop or a subroutine) must have only one entry point and only one exit point. The entry point should be the first statement of the structure, and the exit point should be the last statement. Restricting the entry and exit points in this way limits the number of different execution paths the program can follow, thus making the logic easier to follow and errors easier to detect.

In FOR/NEXT loops, the FOR statement is the proper entry point. In other words, no statement outside the loop should branch around the FOR statement to a statement in the loop body. The program and flowchart shown in Figure 7–10 demonstrate a poorly designed FOR/NEXT loop with multiple entry points. When X is greater than 10, control passes from line 60 directly to line 90 within the loop body, skipping the FOR statement. Because I is initialized in the FOR statement, it may not have a valid value when a branch like this takes place. Also, an error will occur when the NEXT statement is encountered, because no corresponding FOR statement has been found.

Similarly, the NEXT statement should be the only exit point for the loop. That is, no statement within the loop body should branch out of the loop,

FIGURE 7–10   Incorrectly Written Loop with Multiple Entry Points

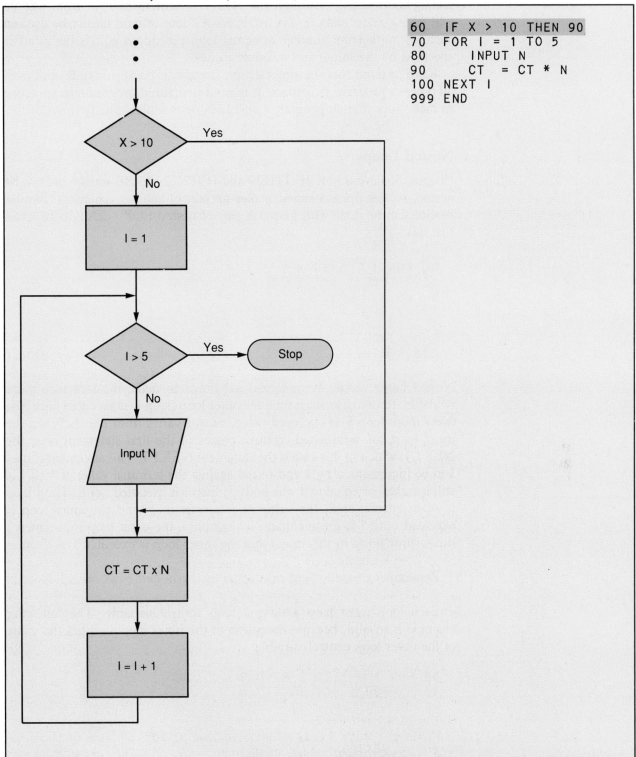

```
60   IF X > 10 THEN 90
70   FOR I = 1 TO 5
80      INPUT N
90      CT  = CT * N
100 NEXT I
999 END
```

bypassing the NEXT statement. Figure 7–11 shows an example of a poorly designed loop with multiple exit points. Note that there are two ways of exiting the loop: (1) through the NEXT statement and (2) from line 70 when J is greater than 6. The FOR/NEXT loop should ideally be used in such a way that the number of actual loop executions equals the number specified by the initial and terminal values.

Keep in mind that the single-entry, single-exit point principle applies to all types of program structures. It is good structured programming practice to make sure that all program structures, or modules, satisfy this rule.

Nested Loops

Chapter 5 showed how IF/THEN and IF/THEN/ELSE statements can be nested, so that one statement makes up part of another statement. Similar nesting can be done with loops. A pair of nested FOR/NEXT loops looks like this:

```
 50 FOR I = 1 TO 4
 60     FOR J = 1 TO 2
            .
            .
            .
100     NEXT J
110 NEXT I
```

Nested loops should be indented as shown to make the structure more readable. In this case, each time the outer loop (loop I) is executed once, the inner loop (loop J) is executed twice, since J varies from 1 to 2. When the inner loop has terminated, control passes to the first statement after the NEXT J, which in this case is the statement NEXT I. This statement causes I to be incremented by 1 and tested against the terminal value of 4. If I is still less than or equal to 4, the body of loop I is executed again. The J loop is again encountered, the value of J is reset to 1, and the inner loop is executed until J is greater than 2. Altogether, the outer loop is executed I times (four times in this case), and the inner loop is executed I × J times (4 × 2 = 8 times).

Remember the following rules when using nested FOR/NEXT loops.

■ Each loop must have a unique loop control variable. The following example is invalid, because execution of the inner loop modifies the value of the outer loop control variable:

```
30 FOR I = 1 TO 2 STEP 2
40     FOR I = 1 TO 4
           .
           .
           .
80     NEXT I
90 NEXT I
```

FIGURE 7–11 Incorrectly Written Loop with Multiple Exit Points

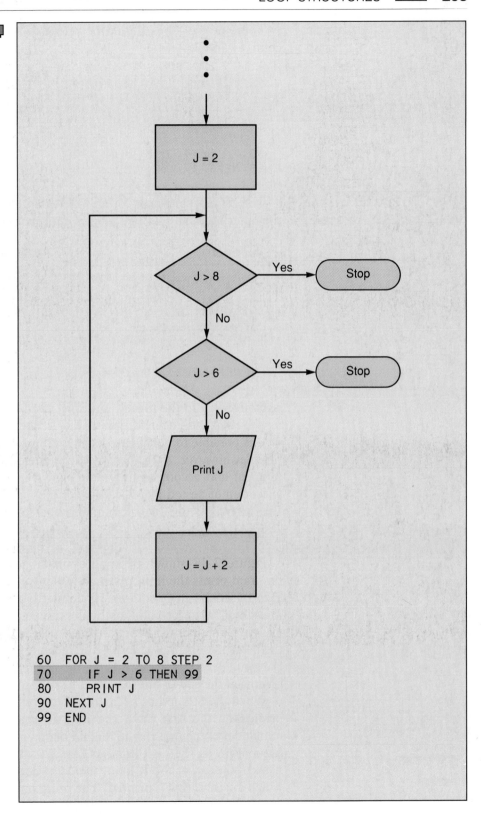

```
60   FOR J = 2 TO 8 STEP 2
70      IF J > 6 THEN 99
80      PRINT J
90   NEXT J
99   END
```

These nested loops should be rewritten so that each uses a unique loop control variable:

```
30 FOR I = 1 TO 2 STEP 2
40     FOR J = 1 TO 4
             .
             .
             .
80     NEXT J
90 NEXT I
```

■ The NEXT statement for an inner loop must appear within the body of the outer loop, so that one loop is entirely contained within another.

Incorrect	Correct

```
FOR I = 1 TO 5              FOR I = 1 TO 5
    FOR J = 1 TO 10             FOR J = 1 TO 10
        .                           .
        .                           .
        .                           .
NEXT I                         NEXT J
    NEXT J                     NEXT I
```

Notice that in the invalid example, the J loop is not entirely inside the I loop but extends beyond the NEXT I statement.

■ It is possible to nest many loops within each other. (Beware of improper nesting, however, as in the preceding "incorrect" example.) The program segment and accompanying table shown in Figure 7–12 demonstrate the execution of nested loops. The outer loop is executed three times, because I varies from 1 to 3, and the inner loop is executed twelve times (3 × 4 = 12).

Figure 7–13 shows an application of nested FOR/NEXT loops. The program prints the multiplication tables for the numbers 1, 2, and 3, with each table in a single column. The inner loop, loop S, controls the printing in each of the three columns, while the outer loop R controls the printing of rows. The first time the outer loop is executed, the first row is printed; the inner loop prints three statements on that row. The first time the S loop is executed, R = 1 and S = 1, so the printed statement is "1 * 1 = 1". The comma at the end of line 90 causes a space to appear before the next output.

When the S loop has been completed (when three statements have been printed on the first row), the PRINT statement in line 110 causes the remainder of the first row to remain blank, and the next output starts on the left margin on the next line. As line 120 increments R and passes control back to the top of the R loop, this loop begins a second execution, during which a second row is printed. The program ends when the R loop has been executed ten times and ten rows have been printed. Check the output of the

FIGURE 7–12   Example of Nested Loops

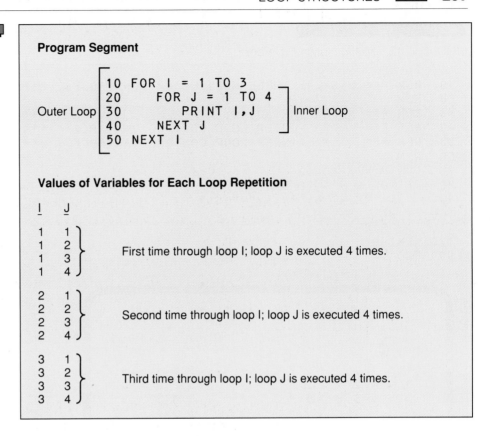

Program Segment

```
10 FOR I = 1 TO 3
20     FOR J = 1 TO 4
30         PRINT I,J
40     NEXT J
50 NEXT I
```

Outer Loop / Inner Loop

Values of Variables for Each Loop Repetition

I	J
1	1
1	2
1	3
1	4

First time through loop I; loop J is executed 4 times.

I	J
2	1
2	2
2	3
2	4

Second time through loop I; loop J is executed 4 times.

I	J
3	1
3	2
3	3
3	4

Third time through loop I; loop J is executed 4 times.

program by following the execution from beginning to end, performing each statement by hand. (As previously mentioned, this is referred to as *desk checking* the program.)

Comparing Loop Structures

The WHILE loop can always be used in place of the FOR/NEXT loop, but the reverse is not true. The FOR/NEXT loop is used for counting loops that execute a prespecified number of times, as stated by the initial and terminal values of the loop control variable. The WHILE loop can also execute a given number of times, if the programmer initializes the loop control variable before the loop begins and tests for the given value in the WHILE statement. However, the WHILE loop can also be used when the final number of desired loop executions is not known, such as when a trailer value is used. In such a situation, a properly structured FOR/NEXT loop would not be appropriate.

When writing counting loops, there are several advantages to using the FOR/NEXT loop. The loop control variable is automatically initialized and incremented. In addition, it is compared to the terminal value. When using a WHILE loop, the programmer must write statements to perform these tasks. Because the FOR/NEXT loop does them automatically, it is easier to use and less error-prone.

FIGURE 7–13 Multiplication Program

```
10   REM *** DISPLAY THREE MULTIPLICATION TABLES. ***
20   REM
30   REM *** MAJOR VARIABLES:                        ***
40   REM ***     R    OUTER LOOP CONTROL VARIABLE   ***
50   REM ***     S    INNER LOOP CONTROL VARIABLE   ***
60   REM
70   FOR R = 1 TO 10
80       FOR S = 1 TO 3
90           PRINT S;"*";R;"=";S * R,
100      NEXT S
110      PRINT
120  NEXT R
999  END
```

```
RUN
1 * 1  = 1       2 * 1  = 2       3 * 1  = 3
1 * 2  = 2       2 * 2  = 4       3 * 2  = 6
1 * 3  = 3       2 * 3  = 6       3 * 3  = 9
1 * 4  = 4       2 * 4  = 8       3 * 4  = 12
1 * 5  = 5       2 * 5  = 10      3 * 5  = 15
1 * 6  = 6       2 * 6  = 12      3 * 6  = 18
1 * 7  = 7       2 * 7  = 14      3 * 7  = 21
1 * 8  = 8       2 * 8  = 16      3 * 8  = 24
1 * 9  = 9       2 * 9  = 18      3 * 9  = 27
1 * 10 = 10      2 * 10 = 20      3 * 10 = 30
```

Logical Operators

Logical operator
An operator that acts on one or more expressions to create a new expression that will evaluate as either true or false.

In addition to arithmetic operators ($^\wedge$, $*$, $/$, $+$, $-$) and relational operators ($=$, $<>$, $<$, $>$, $<=$, $>=$), there is a third group of operators, **logical operators**. A logical operator acts on one or more expressions that evaluate as true or false to produce a statement with a true or false value. The three most commonly used logical operators are AND, OR, and NOT.

The operator AND combines two expressions and produces a value of true only when both of these conditions are true. For example, the combined logical expression in the statement

```
20 IF (HEIGHT > 72) AND (WEIGHT > 150) THEN PRINT NME$
```

Now Try This

1. Assume that your state charges a sales tax of 5 percent on goods purchased. Create a FOR/NEXT loop to print (on paper) a tax table for the even dollar amounts from $1 to $50.

2. Rewrite the following program segment using a FOR/NEXT loop instead of a WHILE loop.

```
10 X = 200
20 Y = 4
30 WHILE X >= 100
40    X = X - Y
50 WEND
```

3. Write a program segment that determines how much money companies owe on overdue accounts. A FOR/NEXT loop should prompt the user to enter the name and amount owed by each of 10 companies. A 10 percent late penalty should be added to each account and the amount of the total bill displayed.

---

evaluates as true only if the expressions HEIGHT $>$ 72 and WEIGHT $>$ 150 are both true. If one or the other is false, the entire statement is false, and the THEN clause of the statement is ignored. The parentheses in the preceding statement are not necessary, but they improve the readability of the statement.

The logical operator OR also combines two expressions, but only one of these expressions needs to evaluate as true for the entire statement to be true. Thus, the statement

```
20 IF (HEIGHT > 72) OR  (WEIGHT > 150) THEN PRINT NME$
```

evaluates as true if either HEIGHT $>$ 72 *or* WEIGHT $>$ 150 is true, or if both are true. The entire condition is false only if the expressions HEIGHT $>$ 72 and WEIGHT $>$ 150 are both false.

Unary operator

An operator with only one operand. The logical operator NOT is a unary operator.

The third logical operator, NOT, is a **unary operator** (an operator used with only one operand) and therefore is used with a single expression. The effect of NOT is to reverse the logical value of the expression it precedes. For example, if the variable PET$ has the value DOG, the condition of the following statement is false:

```
20 IF NOT (PET$ = "DOG") THEN 90
```

Because the condition PET$ = "DOG" evaluates as true, the NOT operator reverses this value to false, making the final result of the entire condition false. If PET$ contained any other value, the condition PET$ = "DOG" would evaluate as false, and the NOT would make the value of the entire condition true.

Logical operators can be combined in a single statement, and they are evaluated in the following sequence:

1. NOT
2. AND
3. OR

For example, the following statement combines AND and OR:

```
50 IF (PET$ = "DOG") OR (AGE = 3) AND (WT = 10) THEN 90
```

Given the predefined order of evaluation, the following diagram shows how the preceding statement would be evaluated if PET$ = "DOG", AGE = 3, and WT = 9:

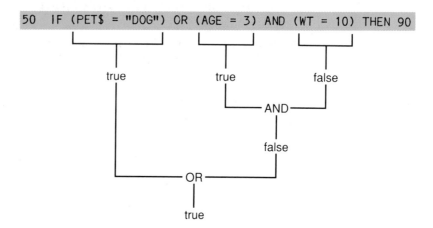

The AND portion of the IF/THEN statement is evaluated first. That result is then combined with the OR portion of the statement to determine the final value of the entire condition. In this case, the statement condition is true, so control is passed to line 90.

The precedence of logical operators (like that of arithmetic operators) can be altered using parentheses. The previous example, using the same variable values as before, could be rewritten as

```
50 IF ((PET$ = "DOG") OR (AGE = 3)) AND (WT = 10) THEN 90
```

In this example, the OR portion of the expression is evaluated before the AND portion. Thus, the parentheses can change the final result of the evaluation, as shown in the following diagram. Compare the evaluation of this statement with the previous diagram.

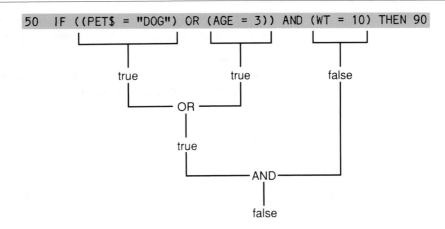

Even if the order of evaluation desired in a condition is the same as the predefined order, it is good programming practice to use parentheses in order to make the logic easier to follow.

NOT can also be combined with AND and OR in a single statement, as shown in the following diagram. Study the evaluation of the condition, making sure that you understand how the use of parentheses and the predefined order of operators has determined the final result of the evaluation. Assume that PET$ = "PIG", AGE = 6, and WT = 1500.

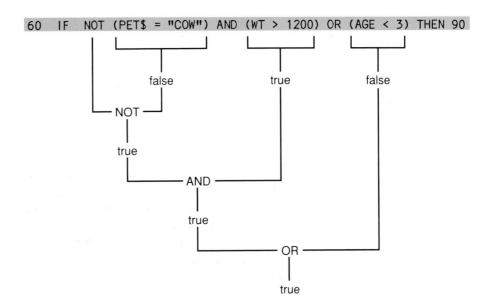

Table 7–1 shows the order in which all types of BASIC operators are evaluated. Further examples involving these operators are shown in Table 7–2.

The program shown in Figure 7–14 demonstrates how logical operators can be used to determine if a triangle is scalene, isosceles, or equilateral. A

TABLE 7–1   Hierarchy of Operations for all Operators

1. Anything in parentheses
2. Exponentiation (^)
3. Unary plus and minus (+, −)
4. Multiplication and division (*, /)
5. Addition and subtraction (+, −)
6. Relational operators (=, <>, <, >, <=, >=)
7. NOT
8. AND
9. OR

Note: Operators on the same level are evaluated left to right.

TABLE 7–2   Examples of Conditions Using Logical Operators

Condition	Evaluates As
NOT (1 * 4 = 5)	TRUE
(18 < 16) OR (7 + 2 = 9)	TRUE
(18 < 16) AND (7 + 2 = 9)	FALSE
((2 + 8) <= 11) AND (17 * 2 = 34)	TRUE
NOT (12 > 8 − 2)	FALSE

triangle is scalene if it has no equal sides, isosceles if it has two equal sides, and equilateral if all three sides are equal. Notice that the condition of the first test uses the AND operator to determine if all three sides are equal:

```
80 IF (S1SIDE = S2SIDE) AND (S2SIDE = S3SIDE)
```

The test for an isosceles triangle is more complex and involves checking for three different conditions. Only one of these conditions needs to be true for the triangle to be isosceles; therefore, this test involves the OR operator. If none of these conditions is true, the triangle must be scalene. As shown by this program, logical operators allow for a variety of conditions to be checked efficiently and simultaneously.

A Programming Problem

Problem Definition

The book reviewer for the local newspaper would like a program that prints her weekly book review ratings. She wants to be able to enter each book's title, author, and rating (a number from 1 through 5) at the keyboard. Then a ratings report should be printed on paper. The program should allow her to enter data for as many books as she wants. The printed listing should

▬▬▬▬▬

FIGURE 7–14   Program Demonstrating the Use of Logical Operators

```
10 REM *** DETERMINE THE TYPE OF A TRIANGLE:    ***
20 REM *** SCALENE, ISOSCELES, OR EQUILATERAL. ***
30 REM
40 INPUT "ENTER THE THREE SIDES";SIDE1,SIDE2,SIDE3
50 PRINT "TRIANGLE IS ";
60 REM
70 REM *** CHECK FOR EQUILATERAL. ***
80 IF (SIDE1 = SIDE2) AND (SIDE2 = SIDE3)
      THEN PRINT "EQUILATERAL" : GOTO 999
90 REM *** CHECK FOR ISOSCELES; IF NOT, THEN IT'S SCALENE. ***
100 IF (SIDE1 = SIDE2) OR (SIDE1 = SIDE3) OR (SIDE2 = SIDE3)
      THEN PRINT "ISOSCELES" ELSE PRINT "SCALENE"
999 END
```

```
RUN
ENTER THE THREE SIDES? 7,9,7
TRIANGLE IS ISOSCELES
```

include each book's title, author, and from 1 through 5 asterisks, depending on the book's rating. Sample input is shown below:

Title	Author	Rating
Learning to Love C.	Lord, P.	5
The Survivor	Bulas, I.	3
Don't Look Now	Poirot, H.	1
Neon Sun	Rainer, A.	4

The specifications for this problem are given in Figure 7–15. Figure 7–16 shows the format of the report.

Solution Design

The input variables for this program are the data items given for each book; the program must output the values of those items. In addition, a variable

FIGURE 7–15   Program
Specification Chart for Book
Review

PROGRAM SPECIFICATION CHART

PROGRAM NAME:	PROGRAMMER'S NAME:	DATE:
Book Review Program	S. Baumann	12/17/91

INPUT:	OUTPUT:
Books' titles. Authors. Ratings (1-5).	Printed book review formatted as shown in Figure 7-16.

SOURCE OF INPUT:	DESTINATION OF OUTPUT:
Keyboard	Printer

PURPOSE:

Prints a chart for a book review, including each book's title, author, and asterisks received.

7-3

Now Try This

1. Write a statement that uses logical operators to determine whether the month (MNTH$) equals APRIL and the date (DTE) equals 15. If both of these conditions are true, the following message should be displayed:

    TAXES ARE DUE.

2. Write a program segment that determines whether a person is eligible to vote. To vote, a person must be 21 or over and be a resident. Prompt the user to get this information and then display an appropriate message.

3. Rewrite the following statement so that it evaluates in the same way without using the NOT operator:

    ```
    100 IF NOT (DISTANCE > 800) THEN PRINT "DRIVE CAR."
              ELSE PRINT "TAKE PIPER CUB."
    ```

4. Write an IF statement that displays the message "SEND BILL" if the amount owed on an account is over $1,000 or if the account is more than 30 days overdue.

FIGURE 7–16 Printer Spacing Chart for Book Review Problem

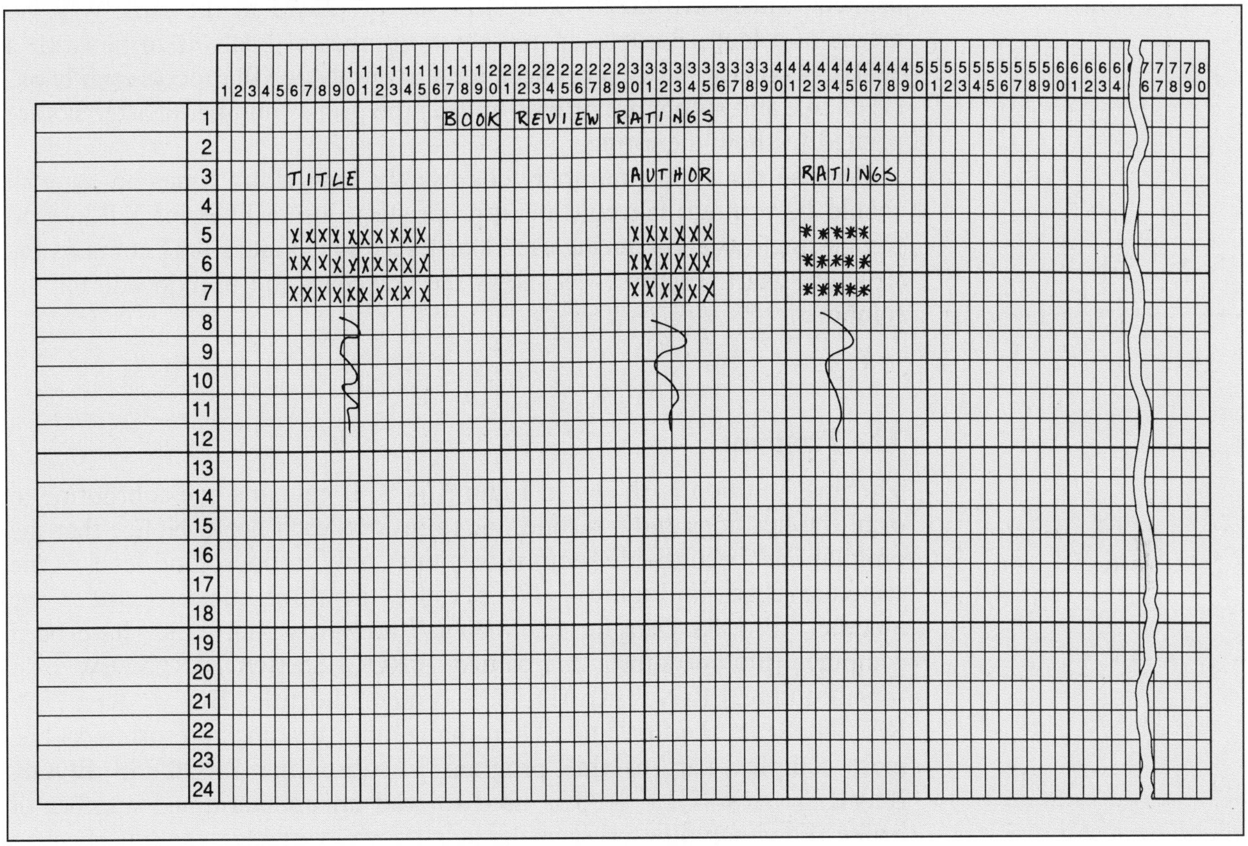

is needed to assign a number to each book in the list. The problem also specifies that a row of asterisks should be printed that corresponds to the book's numeric rating. This task is well suited to a loop, so a program variable will be needed to control that loop. The following variables are to be used:

Input Variables

title	(TITLE$)
author	(AUTHR$)
rating number	(RTG)

Program Variables

loop control variable for asterisks	(POSITION)

Output Variables

title	(TITLE$)
author	(AUTHR$)

What operations are needed to produce the list? First, an appropriate heading must be centered above the output. Column headings must also be printed. Then each book's data must be processed in the same way, by means of a loop. Because an unknown number of books is to be read, a WHILE loop can be used to check for a trailer value. To process each book, (1) its title and author are printed and (2) the proper number of asterisks are printed to show the rating.

Because the rating number tells exactly how many times an asterisk should be printed, it would be appropriate to use a FOR/NEXT loop to print a single asterisk during each loop execution. Figure 7–17 contains the structure chart. Figure 7–18 shows the flowchart and pseudocode for the solution.

The Program

The final solution is shown in Figure 7–19. It contains one subroutine to print the headings and a second one to process each book. Notice that the program has been divided into subroutines only to the second level of the structure chart in Figure 7–17. Because the three substeps under the module, "Process Data for Each Book," are fairly short, they have been combined into one subroutine named "PROCESS BOOK REVIEW."

Subroutine PRINT HEADINGS centers the title, BOOK REVIEW RATINGS, on the first line. Then the column headings are printed. The most complex part of this program is subroutine PROCESS BOOK REVIEW. A WHILE loop is used to read an undetermined number of books. The book title serves as the loop control variable, which is checked for the trailer value "DONE" in the WHILE statement of line 2110. The loop control variable TITLE$ is initialized to the first book title in line 2080. Within the loop body the title and author are printed. To print the rating, a FOR/NEXT loop is set up in line 2180 that uses the rating number as the terminal value and prints a single asterisk for each loop execution. The loop control variable of the main loop is modified by reading the next book's title in line 2230; control then branches to the top of the loop.

Programming Hints

- The loop control variable of the WHILE loop must be initialized before entering the loop.
- If the loop control variable is not modified within the WHILE loop body, an infinite loop is created.
- The WEND statement of the WHILE loop does *not* contain the name of the loop control variable.
- Care must be taken that the initial, terminal, and step values of the FOR statement are all numeric, and that the proper values have been specified to produce the desired number of loop executions.

FIGURE 7–17   Structure Chart for Book Review Problem

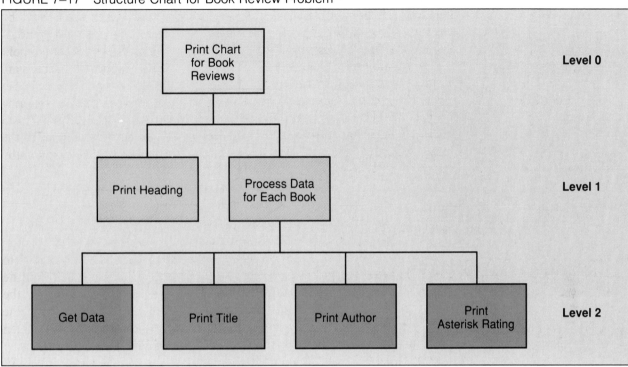

- Branching from within the loop body to the FOR statement resets the value of the loop control variable, which upsets the logic of the loop.
- Special care should be given to nested FOR/NEXT loops; overlapping loops or missing FOR or NEXT statements result in an error.
- When using logical operators, it is best to use parentheses to control the order of evaluation. Parentheses also make the logic of the program easier to follow.
- Some rules to remember for using FOR and NEXT loops follow:
  —The initial value must be less than or equal to the terminal value when using a positive step value. Otherwise, the loop will never be executed.
  —The step value can be negative, but if it is, the initial value must be greater than or equal to the terminal value in order for the loop to execute at least once.
  —The step value should never be zero; this creates an infinite loop.
  —The loop control variable in the NEXT statement must be the same loop control variable that was used in the corresponding FOR statement.
  —Transfer can be made from one statement to another within a loop. However, transfer from a statement in the loop body to the FOR statement is poor programming practice.
  —The value of the loop control variable should not be modified by program statements within the loop.

FIGURE 7–18   Flowchart and Pseudocode for Book Review Problem

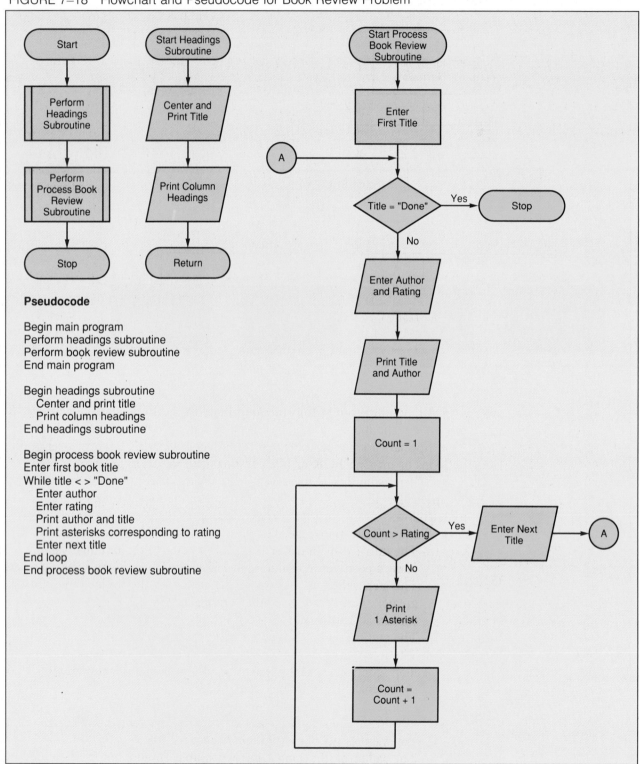

Pseudocode

Begin main program
Perform headings subroutine
Perform book review subroutine
End main program

Begin headings subroutine
   Center and print title
   Print column headings
End headings subroutine

Begin process book review subroutine
Enter first book title
While title < > "Done"
   Enter author
   Enter rating
   Print author and title
   Print asterisks corresponding to rating
   Enter next title
End loop
End process book review subroutine

FIGURE 7–19   Book Review Program

```
10    REM ***                    BOOK REVIEW PROGRAM                    ***
20    REM
30    REM *** THIS PROGRAM ALLOWS THE USER TO ENTER THE TITLE, ***
40    REM *** AUTHOR, AND RATING OF EACH BOOK BEING REVIEWED. ***
50    REM *** A GRAPH, SHOWING THE TITLE, AUTHOR, AND NUMBER ***
60    REM *** OF STARS RECEIVED BY EACH BOOK IS PRINTED ON ***
70    REM *** PAPER.                                          ***
80    REM *** MAJOR VARIABLES:                                ***
90    REM ***      TITLE$    BOOK TITLE                        ***
100   REM ***      AUTHR$    BOOK'S AUTHOR                     ***
110   REM ***      RTG       BOOK'S RATING (1-5)               ***
120   REM
130   REM *** CALL SUBROUTINE TO PRINT HEADINGS. ***
140   GOSUB 1000
150   REM *** CALL SUBROUTINE TO PROCESS EACH BOOK. ***
160   GOSUB 2000
999   END
1000  REM *************************************************************
1010  REM ***              SUBROUTINE PRINT HEADINGS              ***
1020  REM *************************************************************
1030  REM *** SUBROUTINE TO PRINT MAIN HEADING AND COLUMN ***
1040  REM *** HEADINGS.                                    ***
1050  REM
1060  REM *** CENTER HEADING. ***
1070  WDTH = 52
1080  HDG = 19
1090  START = WDTH - HDG
1100  LPRINT TAB(START/2) "BOOK REVIEW RATINGS"
1110  LPRINT
1120  REM *** PRINT COLUMN HEADINGS.***
1130  LPRINT TAB(6);"TITLE";TAB(30);"AUTHOR";TAB(42);"RATING"
1140  LPRINT
1150  RETURN
2000  REM *************************************************************
2010  REM ***              SUBROUTINE PROCESS BOOK REVIEW         ***
2020  REM *************************************************************
2030  REM *** SUBROUTINE TO READ TITLE, AUTHOR, AND RATING ***
2040  REM *** FOR EACH BOOK AND PRINT TITLE, AUTHOR, AND ***
2050  REM *** RATING STARS.                               ***
2060  REM
2070  REM *** ENTER FIRST TITLE. ***
2080  INPUT "ENTER TITLE";TITLE$
2090  REM
2100  REM *** LOOP TO GET DATA. ***
2110  WHILE TITLE$ <> "DONE"
2120      REM *** GET EACH BOOK'S AUTHOR AND RATING. ***
2130      INPUT "ENTER AUTHOR";AUTHR$
2140      INPUT "ENTER BOOK'S RATING (1-5)";RTG
2150      REM *** PRINT TITLE AND AUTHOR. ***
2160      LPRINT TAB(6);TITLE$;TAB(30);AUTHR$;TAB(42);
```

(figure continued on the next page)

FIGURE 7–19 Continued

```
2170    REM *** PRINT NUMBER OF STARS CORRESPONDING TO RATING. ***
2180    FOR POSITION = 1 TO RTG
2190       LPRINT "*";
2200    NEXT POSITION
2210    LPRINT
2220    REM *** GET THE NEXT TITLE. ***
2230    INPUT "ENTER TITLE";TITLE$
2240 WEND
2250 RETURN
```

```
RUN
ENTER TITLE? COMPETITIVE TANNING
ENTER AUTHOR? Z. HARRIS
ENTER BOOK'S RATING (1-5)  2
ENTER TITLE? BOMBAY
ENTER AUTHOR? C. GOODTIME
ENTER BOOK'S RATING (1-5)? 1
ENTER TITLE? DEATH IN CRETE
ENTER AUTHOR? M. KAY
ENTER BOOK'S RATING (1-5)? 4
ENTER TITLE? LEARNING TO LOVE C
ENTER AUTHOR? P. LORD
ENTER BOOK'S RATING (1-5)? 3
ENTER TITLE? DONE
```

```
              BOOK REVIEW RATINGS

   TITLE                 AUTHOR        RATING

   COMPETITIVE TANNING   Z. HARRIS     **
   BOMBAY                C. GOODTIME   *
   DEATH IN CRETE        M. KAY        ****
   LEARNING TO LOVE C    P. LORD       ***
```

New Statement Review

Statement Format	Explanation
line# WHILE expression [loop body] line# WEND	The boundaries of the loop are marked by the reserved words WHILE and WEND. The loop body executes as long as the expression in the WHILE statement is true.

line# FOR lcv = I TO J
  STEP K
  [loop body]
line# NEXT lcv
	The loop control variable (lcv) is initialized to I and incremented by the step value K each time the loop body is executed. When lcv is greater than the terminal value (J), the loop stops.

Summary Points

■ The basic elements of the loop structure follow:

1. The loop control variable is initialized to a particular value before loop execution begins.

2. The loop control variable is tested to determine whether the loop body should be executed or the loop exited.

3. The loop body, consisting of any number of statements, is executed.

4. At some point during loop execution, the value of the loop control variable must be modified to allow an exit from the loop.

5. The loop is exited when the stated condition determines that the right number of loop repetitions has been performed.

■ The FOR/NEXT loop executes the number of times specified in the FOR statement. The NEXT statement increments the loop control variable, tests it against the terminal value, and returns control to the statement immediately following the FOR statement if another loop execution is required.

■ Good programming practice dictates that all program structures have a single entry point and a single exit point.

■ The WHILE statement repeats execution of its loop body as long as the given condition in the WHILE statement is true.

■ The logical operators NOT, AND, and OR are used with conditions. NOT is a unary operator that negates a condition. An expression containing AND evaluates as true when both conditions joined by the AND are true. A condition containing OR is true if at least one of the joined conditions is true.

Vocabulary List

Counter

Counting loop

Infinite loop

Logical operator

Loop body

Loop control variable

Priming read

Sentinel value

Trailer value

Unary operator

Questions

Whenever appropriate, use complete sentences in answering the following questions.

1. When should a loop structure be used in a program?

2. What are the five elements of a controlled loop?

3. How many times will the following loop execute?

```
10 AMT = 10
20 WHILE AMT <= 20
30    AMT = AMT + 3
40 WEND
```

4. What type of value does the expression of a WHILE statement evaluate as?
   a. numeric
   b. character string
   c. true or false

5. Explain how trailer values can be used to control loops.

6. What is a counting loop? Which loop statements can be used to write counting loops?

7. Which of the following FOR statements will execute at least once?
   a. 20 FOR I = 8 TO 7
   b. 100 FOR K = 15 TO 20 STEP 6
   c. 500 FOR N = 3 TO 5 STEP 1
   d. 420 FOR X = -2 TO -1 STEP -1
   e. 160 FOR I = 1 TO 100 STEP 20

8. What is the output from the following statements?

```
50 X = 7
60 FOR X = 1 TO 4
70    PRINT X
80 NEXT
```

9. Can the WHILE loop in Figure 7–3 be rewritten using a FOR/NEXT loop? Why or why not?

10. Is the following FOR/NEXT loop valid?

```
10 FOR K = 10 TO 5 STEP -1
20    PRINT "K = ";K
30    INPUT N
40    K = N
50 NEXT K
```

11. How many times is the following inner loop executed? How many times is the outer loop executed?

```
10 Q = 10
20 W = 5
30 L1 = 4
40 FOR L1 = (Q - W) TO 1 STEP -1
50    FOR L2 = 1 TO W STEP 1
60       PRINT L1,L2
70    NEXT L2
80 NEXT L1
```

12. When is a WHILE loop a more appropriate choice than a FOR/NEXT loop?
13. Why is the use of the single-entry, single-exit point rule considered good structured programming?
14. List and explain the purpose of the three logical operators discussed in this chapter.
15. Evaluate the following expressions, assuming that $X = 4$, $Y = 3$, and $Z = 12$:

    a. `(Z - X ^ 3 > 12) AND (NOT (X > 3))`
    b. `(X ^ Y * 2 < 20) OR ((X <= 12) AND (Z - Y <> 9))`
    c. `NOT (Y - X > 0) AND (Y ^ Y >= 4)`
    d. `NOT ((Z - 6 > X + Y) OR (Y + X < Z / 2))`

Debugging Exercises

Identify the following programs or program segments that contain errors and debug them.

1.
```
10 *** GET NAMES OF FIVE COMPANIES. ***
20 WHILE CNT <= 5
30     INPUT "ENTER COMPANY";CMPNY
40     CNT = CNT + 1
50 WEND
```

2.
```
10   REM *** READ NAMES OF 5 ACCOUNTS.  IF THE ***
20   REM *** AMOUNT OWED IS $20 OR MORE, PRINT ***
30   REM *** THE NAME AND AMOUNT.            ***
40   K = 1
50   WHILE K <= 5
60     PRINT K
70     INPUT N$,AMT
80     IF AMT < 20 THEN 70
90     PRINT N$,AMT
100    K = K + 1
110 WEND
```

3.
```
10 REM *** LOOP TO DISPLAY EACH VALUE FROM HIGH TO LOW. ***
20 FOR H = HI TO LO STEP -1
30     PRINT H
40     INPUT AMT
50     IF AMT < LO THEN PRINT "--";AMT
           ELSE H = AMT - LO
60 NEXT H
```

4.
```
10 REM *** EXECUTE LOOP AS LONG AS  VALUE ENTERED ***
20 REM *** FOR MONTH IS NOT BETWEEN 1 AND 12.     ***
30 REM
40 INPUT "ENTER MONTH (1-12)";MONTH
50 WHILE (MONTH > 1) OR (MONTH < 12)
60     PRINT MONTH
70     INPUT "ENTER MONTH (1-12)";MONTH
80 WEND
```

Programming Problems

Level 1

1. Write a WHILE loop that displays the even integers between 1 and 21.

2. Write a WHILE loop that reads data until it encounters a negative number.

3. Write a WHILE loop to count by 5s until a given value is reached. For example, if the value read is 49, output should be similar to the following:

    5   10   15   20   25   30   35   40   45

4. Write a FOR/NEXT loop that displays the even integers between 1 and 21.

5. Write a nested FOR/NEXT loop that will read ten numbers. Each number should be added to itself twenty times.

6. Write a program segment that uses a FOR/NEXT loop to output the following pattern:

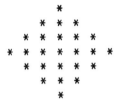

7. Write a program segment that uses FOR/NEXT loops to display the following design:

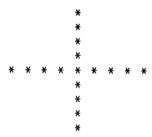

Level 2

1. Write a WHILE loop that reads the names, ages, and sexes of a group of voters. The loop should execute as long as "DONE" is not entered for a name and the age is greater than or equal to 21.

2. Write a program to display a multiplication table. The user should be allowed to enter the upper and lower limits of the table. Use the following format for the table:

X	1	2	3	4
1	1	2	3	4
2	2	4	6	8
3	3	6	9	12
4	4	8	12	16

3. Mr. Williams came up with a way of saving money to donate to his favorite charity. He wants to start with a penny on the first day and double the amount he gives for each subsequent day. Write a program to determine how much he will have donated after 15 days.

4. The computer science department needs a program that will display, in a horizontal bar graph, the number of students enrolled in each class section 300 through 309:

Section	Students
300	20
301	15
302	32
303	17
304	28
305	35
306	26
307	29
308	19
309	27

Use asterisks to create the bars, as was shown in Figure 7–19. The graph should have appropriate headings, and should be marked off in increments of 10.

5. The Happy Hedonist Health Club has opened a new branch in your town recently. The club is offering two types of membership: "weight-training" membership and "all facilities" membership. The manager has asked you to write a program to display a list of the new members of the club and the types of memberships they hold. A report with appropriate headings should be displayed. Use the following input data. An A indicates an all facilities membership, and W indicates a weight-training membership.

David Toth, A
Irene Bulas, A
John Drake, A
Bob Szymanski, W
Mike Costarella, W
Eileen Riley, A
Tom Neanderthal, W

6. The trustees of Bowling Green High School are considering a measure to give the ten full-time teachers a 4 percent, 4.5 percent, or 5 percent pay raise. To make their decision, they want to know how much additional money they would need in each of the three cases. Write a program to show sample salaries of $12,000 to $18,000 (by $1,000) and the three proposed increased salaries for each. Create a table like the following:

SALARY	+4%	+4.5%	+5%
12,000	XXXX	XXXX	XXXX
13,000	XXXX	XXXX	XXXX

7. Modify the program for Problem 6 so that an extra line of summary information is included at the bottom of the chart. This line should give the total of the seven sample salaries and the totals of each of the three increased salary columns. The chart should also display the difference between the sample salary total and each of the three increased totals. A sample summary follows:

<u>18,000</u>   <u>XXXXX</u>   <u>XXXXX</u>   <u>XXXXX</u>

XXXXXX   XXXXXX   XXXXXX   XXXXXX
+4% gross difference = XXXXX
+4.5% gross difference = XXXXXX
+5% gross difference = XXXXX

Projects

For each project, complete the following:

- Fill out a program specification chart.
- Develop a structure chart.
- Create a flowchart or pseudocode.
- Thoroughly document the final program.
- Test your program using a variety of data.

1. A local company has decided to sell three new products. The accounting department of the company has asked you to write a program to determine the break-even quantities of each of the products. The break-even formula is given as follows:

$$n = \frac{fc}{sp - vc}$$

where

sp = selling price/unit
fc = fixed costs
vc = variable costs/unit
n = break-even quantity

The following information will be necessary to write this program:

Product	Selling Price	Fixed Costs	Variable Costs
A	$25.00/unit	$ 650.00	$12.00
B	$15.00/unit	$ 275.00	$ 8.00
C	$38.00/unit	$1200.00	$15.00

The output should be formatted similar to the following:

PRODUCT	SELLING PRICE	FIXED COST	VARIABLE COSTS	BREAK-EVEN QUANTITY
X	$XX.XX/unit	$XXX.XX	$XXX.XX	XX.XX
.	.	.	.	.
.	.	.	.	.
.	.	.	.	.

2. Stewart and Sons Jewelers needs a program to accept its salespersons' sales for each of four months. Output the total sales and average monthly sales for each person, and the total sales for all four months. Use READ/DATA statements to read the following data:

Stewart Birsch	7,457.90	5,071.63	4,921.16	5,717.05
Monica Bulas	1,125.16	927.19	1,674.84	1,970.15
Carolyn Carstons	2,257.08	3,716.84	2,116.93	1,877.45
David Toth	871.69	1,199.72	1,299.60	941.38
Irene Drake	4,412.77	2,128.91	3,008.97	2,364.33
Anne Swetlick	2,740.08	3,165.75	2,981.39	1,886.40

The output should look similar to this:

SALESPERSON	TOTAL	AVERAGE
XXXXXXX	$XXXX	$XXXXX
.	.	.
.	.	.
.	.	.

TOTAL SALES = $XXXXXX

CHAPTER 8

Debugging and Testing Programs and Using Functions

Learning Objectives

After studying this chapter, you should be able to

1. Explain the difference between syntax and logic errors.
2. Use desk checking to locate errors.
3. Explain the difference between complete program testing and selective program testing.
4. Audit programs using correctly selected data.
5. Define library function.
6. Use the integer, sign, absolute value, and random number functions appropriately.
7. Use the LEN, LEFT$, RIGHT$, MID$, ASC, and CHR$ functions appropriately.
8. Use the VAL and STR$ functions to protect programs from invalid input.
9. Define user-friendly, and write user-friendly programs.

Introduction

We have discussed two basic characteristics of structured programming. The first is easy-to-follow logic. This means FOR/NEXT and WHILE loops are used whenever possible instead of the GOTO statement. The second basic characteristic is top-down design of the problem solution. A structure chart is developed to show how the solution is divided into subparts. When the program is actually coded, each module in the structure chart is implemented as a subroutine (except for those involving only a few lines of code, which may be left in the main program). This procedure results in a program that is divided into subroutines, each performing a specific task.

A program written using these techniques has a number of advantages over an unstructured program. Some of the major ones are

- The logic of the program is easy to follow.
- The programmer is able to use his or her time efficiently.
- The program is easy to modify and maintain (that is, to keep in working order). Programmers in business and industry must often make changes to programs that someone else wrote. It is much easier to make changes to a structured program than to an unstructured one.
- The program is more likely to be error-free than an unstructured program. If there are errors, they are generally easier to locate and correct.

Even with the many advantages of structured programming, programs rarely work correctly the first time they are executed. This chapter will introduce some proven methods for locating and correcting program errors. The techniques introduced here will help you correct your programs in an efficient, logical manner. At the end of the chapter, you will learn about *library functions*, which are special types of subprograms that are built into the BASIC system. They perform common tasks, such as combining a group of character strings to form a single new string.

Debugging and Testing

The Two Types of Program Errors

Program errors can be divided into two broad categories: syntax and logic. Each of these types will be discussed, along with techniques for avoiding and correcting them.

Syntax Errors   The most common type of error for beginning programmers is the syntax error. Fortunately, it is also the easiest type of error to locate and correct. Syntax errors are violations of the grammar rules of a programming language. Mistyping a word is the most frequent cause of syntax errors. Consider the following statement:

```
120 IS X >= 8 THEN PRINT X
```

The typing error in this statement can easily be spotted and can be corrected by reentering the line as follows:

```
120 IF X >= 8 THEN PRINT X
```

Most syntax errors can be caught by careful proofreading. All must be corrected before a program can be executed.

Logic Errors   Logic errors are flaws in the algorithm that has been developed to solve a programming problem. These errors can be divided into two categories: those that cause the program to stop executing prematurely (**run-time errors**), and those in which program execution terminates properly but the output is incorrect.

Run-time error

A logic error that causes program execution to stop prematurely.

There are many logic errors that can cause a program to stop executing prematurely. For example, the following statement will cause a run-time error because the computer will not allow division by zero:

```
230 AMT = 887.0 / 0
```

In the above example the error may seem obvious, but suppose this program segment were rewritten to look like this:

```
220 INPUT "ENTER THE DIVISOR";DIV
230 AMT = 887.0 / DIV
```

In this case, the program depends on the user to enter a number that can be used as a divisor. The programmer should rewrite this program segment so that if the user enters an unusable value, such as zero, he or she will be asked to reenter the divisor. It could be done like this:

```
20  INPUT "ENTER THE DIVISOR";DIV
30  WHILE DIV = 0
40      PRINT "DIVISION BY ZERO IS NOT ALLOWED."
50       INPUT "PLEASE ENTER A DIVISOR OTHER THAN ZERO";DIV
60  WEND
70  AMT = TTL / DIV
```

Error trapping

The technique of writing a program in such a way that it "traps" or catches input errors, such as invalid data.

This WHILE loop will be executed only if the user enters a zero. In that case, the user will be asked to reenter the number. This new number will then be checked to make certain it is not also a zero. This technique is referred to as **error trapping.** The program has been written in such a way that the error (which in this case is caused by invalid input) is trapped. Program execution cannot continue until the user enters a value for DIV that can be used by the program.

The most difficult aspect of run-time errors is that often they do not show up every time a program is executed. In the preceding example, the program will continue to execute correctly so long as a zero is not entered for the value of DIV. Table 8–1 lists some common run-time errors.

The program in Figure 8–1 contains the second type of logic error, which causes incorrect output. The loop in this program is supposed to execute five times, but because the controlling condition is incorrectly stated, it executes six times. This is referred to as an *off-by-one* error. Statement 50 should be rewritten:

```
50 WHILE DIGIT < 5
```

The WHILE loop executes until the expression in the WHILE statement is tested and found to be false. It does *not* stop executing the moment the loop control variable is modified in the loop body, making the expression false.

Program Testing Methods

It has been estimated that about 80 percent of professional programmers' time is spent in testing and modifying programs that have already been written. Even after the programmer thinks that a program is working correctly, it is difficult, if not impossible, to determine if it will always work properly with all types of data. The ability of a program to work properly

TABLE 8–1 Common Run-Time Errors

Division by zero.
Attempting to assign a character value to a numeric variable.
Attempting to transfer control to a nonexistent line number.
Running out of data when using READ/DATA statements.

FIGURE 8–1   Example of Incorrectly Written WHILE Loop

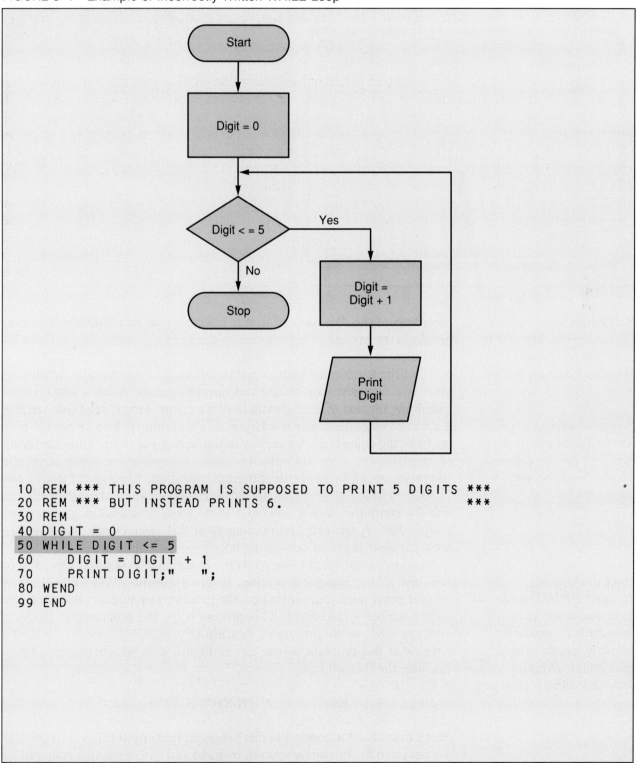

```
10 REM *** THIS PROGRAM IS SUPPOSED TO PRINT 5 DIGITS ***
20 REM *** BUT INSTEAD PRINTS 6.                      ***
30 REM
40 DIGIT = 0
50 WHILE DIGIT <= 5
60    DIGIT = DIGIT + 1
70    PRINT DIGIT;"   ";
80 WEND
99 END
```

(figure continued on the next page)

FIGURE 8–1 Continued

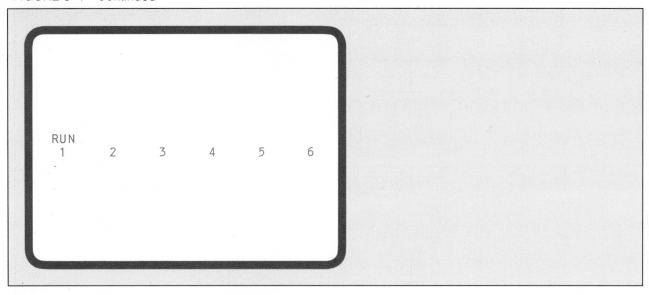

```
RUN
 1      2      3      4      5      6
```

Reliability
The ability of a program to work properly regardless of the type of data entered into it.

Program testing
Running a program with a variety of data to determine whether it always obtains correct results.

Program tracing
To insert PRINT statements at various points in a program to determine the values of specific variables at those points. Program tracing helps in locating logic errors.

regardless of the data entered to it is referred to as its **reliability. Program testing** is the process of systematically checking a program to determine its reliability.

All of the various methods of testing programs for errors can be divided into two categories: static testing and run-time testing. *Static testing* involves examining the text of the program itself for errors. One type of static testing is *desk checking*, discussed in Chapter 2. Programmers sometimes say they are "playing computer" when they desk-check a program. They are trying to mentally trace through the program, following the same steps the computer would follow during program execution. This type of testing can be used to locate both syntax and logic errors. Before entering a program into the computer, it is a good idea to do some desk checking with some sample data. A few extra minutes spent at this stage of program development can save hours of debugging later.

Run-time testing takes place while the program is executing. One type of run-time testing, **program tracing,** involves inserting PRINT statements into the program at locations where the programmer suspects that incorrect results are being calculated. This process helps the programmer pinpoint errors or flaws in the program's algorithm.

Look at the program at the top of Figure 8–2, which is supposed to calculate the following:

$$NMBR + (NMBR - 1) + (NMBR - 2) + \ldots$$

When the value 3 is entered to this program, the output value of SUM is 3. We can calculate the correct output by hand and determine that it should be

FIGURE 8–2   Locating an Error by Using Program Tracing

```
10   REM *** ADD THE NUMBERS 1 THROUGH N FOR ***
20   REM *** A GIVEN NUMBER N.                ***
30   REM
40   SUM = 0
50   INPUT "ENTER THE NUMBER ";NMBR
60   REM
70   WHILE NMBR > 0
80       NMBR = NMBR - 1
90       SUM = SUM + NMBR
100  WEND
110  REM
120  PRINT "THE SUM IS";SUM
999  END
```

```
RUN
ENTER THE NUMBER ? 3
THE SUM IS 3
```

```
10   REM *** ADD THE NUMBERS 1 THROUGH N FOR ***
20   REM *** A GIVEN NUMBER N.                ***
30   REM
40   SUM = 0
50   INPUT "ENTER THE NUMBER ";NMBR
60   REM
70   WHILE NMBR > 0
80       SUM = SUM + NMBR
90       NMBR = NMBR - 1
100  WEND
110  REM
120  PRINT "THE SUM IS";SUM
999  END
```

```
RUN
ENTER THE NUMBER ? 3
THE SUM IS 6
```

6. One way of determining what is wrong is to examine the values of NMBR and SUM each time through the loop. This is done by inserting the following statement right before the end of the loop:

```
95 PRINT "NMBR = ";NMBR,"SUM = ";SUM
```

Doing this will demonstrate that the value of SUM is 2 at the end of the first loop execution, when in fact it should be 3. This error occurs because the value of NMBR is decremented *before* it is added to SUM rather than afterward. The program at the bottom of Figure 8–2 shows how the program is correctly written. By using program tracing, we were able to pinpoint the logic error in this program.

Complete program testing
Testing all possible paths of program execution.

Selective program testing
Testing a program using data with specific characteristics.

Program testing falls into two basic categories: complete program testing and selective program testing. **Complete program testing** involves testing all possible paths of execution in the program. This approach is possible only with very small programs. The number of possible paths in moderate to large programs is so great that the complete testing approach is not practical. **Selective program testing,** which involves testing the program using data with specific characteristics, is therefore normally used to determine if a program obtains correct results. One method of selective testing is to make certain that a program works properly for boundary cases. *Boundary cases* are data that fall at the very extremes of the legal range of allowable data. Consider the following IF/THEN statement:

```
50 IF AGE > 21 THEN PRINT "THIS PERSON IS AN ADULT."
```

The purpose of this segment is to print the "adult" message if the person is 21 years of age or over. If we tested this segment by assigning a value of 21 to AGE (21 is at the boundary of the adult range), however, we would find that no message was printed. The problem is that the condition has been improperly stated. It is correctly written like this:

```
50 IF AGE >= 21 THEN PRINT "THIS PERSON IS AN ADULT."
```

This statement should also be run with AGE equal to 20 to determine that nothing is printed. Checking the boundary case helped us determine that the condition was not expressed properly. This procedure is more involved, however, for a more complex program segment such as the following:

```
70 IF OUNCES >= 12 THEN IF OUNCES >= 20 THEN SIZE$ = "A"
   ELSE SIZE$ = "B" ELSE SIZE$ = "C"
```

Drawing a flowchart to visualize all the possible paths of program execution can be helpful. Here is the flowchart for this example:

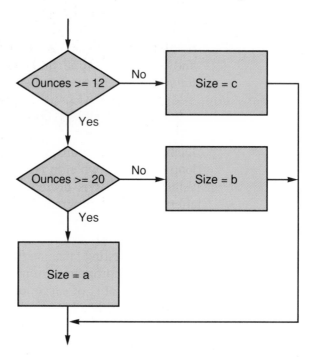

From this flowchart, we can determine that the following boundary values should be assigned to variable OUNCES for testing purposes: 12, 11, 19, and 20. If the program assigns the correct value to SIZE$ for each of these cases, we can be fairly certain that this IF/THEN/ELSE statement is working properly.

Auditing
Repeatedly executing a program with predetermined groups of data to determine whether results are correct.

Auditing Programs **Auditing** refers to executing a program with a number of data sets (groups of input data). The correct output should be determined by hand (or by using a calculator) before the program is run. The program results are then compared with the expected results. At the end of this chapter, we will show how an example program could be audited.

Using Functions

Library function
A subprogram that performs a specific task for the user such as joining together a group of character strings or determining the absolute value of a number.

BASIC has a variety of **library** (or **built-in**) **functions** that are designed to perform a specific task for the programmer. These functions are a part of the BASIC system. A function is a specific type of subprogram that determines a particular value. For example, the INT function determines the largest integer value that is less than the **argument.** This program segment,

```
20 INTGR = INT(35.67)
30 PRINT INTGR
```

Argument
A value used by a function to obtain its final result.

prints 35, which is the largest integer that is less than 35.67. The value 35.67 is referred to as the argument, which is the value that the function uses to determine its result. The argument of a function is always placed in parentheses following the name of the function and can be a constant, a variable, a mathematical expression, or another function. Functions can be divided into two categories: numeric and string.

Numeric Functions

The Integer Function As previously mentioned, the integer, or INT, function computes the largest integer less than or equal to the argument. For example:

X	INT(X)
8	8
5.34	5
16.9	16
−2.75	−3
−0.5	−1

Now Try This

Debug the following programs.

1.
```
10 REM *** READ THREE NUMBERS AND MULTIPLY THEM TOGETHER. ***
20 READ A,B,C
30 PRING A * B * C
99 END
```

2.
```
10 REM *** READ LIST OF VALUES UNTIL FIRST VALUE (C) IS ***
20 REM *** SMALLER THAN SECOND (D).                    ***
30 READ C,D
40 WHILE C > D
50    READ C,D
60 WEND
70 PRINT C;" IS LESS THAN ";D
80 DATA 5,5,5,4,8,5,5,6
```

3.
```
10 REM *** CONVERT A TEST SCORE   ***
20 REM *** INTO A PERCENTAGE.     ***
30 REM
40 PRINT "ENTER NUMBER OF QUESTIONS CORRECT"
50 INPUT "OUT OF 100";CRRT
60 REM *** CONVERT TO PERCENT CORRECT. ***
70 PRCT = CRRT * 100
80 PRINT "YOU GOT";PRCT;" % CORRECT."
99 END
```

If the argument is a positive value with a fractional part, the digits to the right of the decimal point are truncated (cut off). Notice from the preceding examples that truncation does not occur when the argument is negative. For instance, when the argument equals -2.75, the INT function returns -3, the largest integer *less than or equal to* that value. This fact can be seen on the number line, where the farther to the left a number lies, the less value it has:

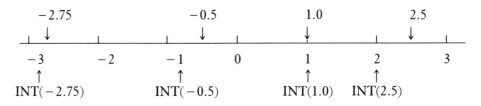

Although the INT function alone does not round its argument, it can be used in an expression that rounds to the nearest integer, nearest tenth, or nearest hundredth, or to any other degree of accuracy desired. The program in Figure 8–3 rounds a number to the nearest integer, as shown in line 50.

FIGURE 8–3   Rounding with the INT Function

```
10   REM *** ROUND A NUMBER TO THE NEAREST INTEGER, TENTH, ***
20   REM *** AND HUNDREDTH.                                 ***
30   REM
40   INPUT "PLEASE ENTER A NUMBER";NMBR
50   R1 = INT(NMBR + .5)
60   R2 = INT((NMBR + .05) * 10) / 10
70   R3 = INT((NMBR + .005) * 100) / 100
80   PRINT
90   PRINT "NEAREST";TAB(12);"NEAREST";TAB(23);"NEAREST"
100  PRINT "INTEGER";TAB(13);"TENTH";TAB(23);"HUNDREDTH"
110  PRINT R1;TAB(13);R2;TAB(24);R3
999  END
```

```
RUN
PLEASE ENTER A NUMBER? 10.378

NEAREST       NEAREST       NEAREST
INTEGER       TENTH         HUNDREDTH
 10            10.4          10.38
```

Line 60 rounds the same number to the nearest tenth by adding 0.05 to the number and multiplying the result by 10. Then the INT function is applied, and the result is divided by 10. The steps to round the number to the nearest hundredth follow the same pattern in line 70, but instead add 0.005 and multiply and divide by 100.

The Sign Function   The sign, or SGN, function determines the sign of a number. If $X > 0$, then $SGN(X) = 1$; if $X = 0$, then $SGN(X) = 0$; and if $X < 0$, then $SGN(X) = -1$. For example:

X	SGN(X)
8.5	1
0	0
−5.02	−1
−1005	−1

The Absolute Value Function The absolute value, or ABS, function returns the absolute value of its argument. Remember that the absolute value is always positive or zero; if the argument has a negative value, the ABS function removes the negative sign. For example:

X	ABS(X)
−2	2
0	0
3.54	3.54
−2.75	2.75

This function is often used to identify significant differences between given values. Suppose the Internal Revenue Service wants to know which individuals owe or are owed a substantial sum. The program in Figure 8–4 demonstrates how the absolute value function might be used to identify such individuals. Line 50 tests for people who either owe or are being refunded at least $1,000.00.

FIGURE 8–4   Program Demonstrating the ABS Function

```
10   REM *** IDENTIFY AUDIT CANDIDATES. ***
20   REM
30   READ NME$,AMT
40   WHILE NME$ <> "XXX"
50      IF ABS(AMT) >= 1000 THEN PRINT NME$;" TO BE AUDITED"
60      READ NME$,AMT
70   WEND
80   REM *** DATA STATEMENTS ***
90   DATA M.VOOTS,-1090,S.BAUMANN,4150,I.ROSTOV,-8070
100  DATA A.KURAGIN,999,XXX,0
999  END
```

```
RUN
M.VOOTS TO BE AUDITED
S.BAUMANN TO BE AUDITED
I.ROSTOV TO BE AUDITED
```

The Random Number Function   The random number, or RND, function produces a random number between 0 and 1. The term **random** means that any value in a given set of values is equally likely to occur. The function is useful for any situation requiring an input quantity of which the exact value is unpredictable. The RND function is particularly important in applications involving statistics, computer simulations, and games.

At first it might not seem hard to produce random values. The task is difficult for computers, however, because of their precise structure and logic. The numbers produced by a computer are not truly random, such as those resulting from a throw of dice, but are more accurately described as pseudo-random. In order to produce a sequence of seemingly unrelated numbers, the RND function uses a special algorithm. The particular sequence of numbers generated by this algorithm depends on a value known as a *seed*. When a new seed value is supplied to the algorithm, a new sequence of numbers is produced. If the seed is never changed, however, a program containing the RND function produces the same series of "random" numbers each time it is run. For example, each time this program segment,

```
10 X = RND
20 PRINT X
```

is executed, the same number is displayed.

The RANDOMIZE statement is needed to provide a new random number seed and therefore give a truly random result. Its format is

RANDOMIZE [integer]

or

RANDOMIZE TIMER

The integer, if used, must be changed each time the program runs to produce new numbers. If the integer is omitted, the prompt message

```
Random number seed (-32768 to 32767)?
```

asks the user to enter a number within this range.

If the function name TIMER is specified, a new number seed determined by the computer's clock is generated for each program run, and no prompt appears. For example, these statements

```
10 RANDOMIZE TIMER
20 PRINT RND
```

cause the computer to display a different number each time they are executed.

Random numbers greater than 1 can be produced by combining the RND function with other mathematical operations. The following formula generates a random number R between L (low limit) and H (high limit):

$$R = RND * (H - L) + L$$

A formula to generate a random integer I between L and H is

$$I = INT(RND * (H - L) + L)$$

If the range of the random integer should include L and H, the value 1 is added to H − L as follows:

$$I = INT(RND * (H - L + 1) + L)$$

The program in Figure 8–5 shows how these formulas can be used to generate random numbers in any given range. One common use of the RND function is for playing games. Figure 8–6 shows how it can be used to generate a number between 1 and 100. The user is then prompted to guess the number.

Now Try This

1. Write a program segment that generates a random number between 1 and 1000.

2. Write a program segment that displays the absolute value of a number and a plus or minus sign after the number, depending on whether the number is positive or negative. Use the ABS function to perform this task.

3. Rewrite Exercise 2 using the SGN function instead of the ABS function to determine the sign to be displayed after the number.

4. Write a statement that uses the INT function to display the integer portion of a positive real number. For example, if the number is 14.87, the integer 14 should be displayed.

5. Write a statement that uses the INT function to display the integer portion of a negative real number. For example, if the number is − 100.55, the integer − 100 should be displayed. Remember that ordinarily the INT function of − 100.55 would be − 101.

6. Use an IF statement to combine the statements written for Exercises 4 and 5 so that the integer portion of a real number is always displayed, regardless of whether the number is positive or negative. Use the SGN function to determine whether the number is positive.

FIGURE 8–5   Using the RND Function to Generate Numbers in a Specified Range

```
10    REM ***      GENERATE RANDOM NUMBERS FOR A GIVEN RANGE.    ***
20    REM
30    RANDOMIZE TIMER
40    READ LO,HI
50    R1 = RND *  (HI - LO) + LO
60    R2 = INT(R1)
70    PRINT "BETWEEN";LO;"AND";HI;":","REAL","INTEGER"
80    PRINT,,R1,R2
90    REM *** DATA STATEMENTS ***
100   DATA 10,20
999   END
```

```
RUN
BETWEEN 10 AND 20 :              REAL              INTEGER
                                 11.0343           11
```

String Functions

Up to this point, we have manipulated numbers but have done little with strings except to output them or compare them in IF/THEN statement tests. Many programming applications require more sophisticated manipulations of strings.

Concatenate
To join together.

BASIC string functions allow programmers to modify, **concatenate** (join together), compare, and analyze the composition of strings. These functions are useful for sorting lists of names, determining subject matter in text, printing mailing lists, and so forth. For example, the use of string functions can enable a program to determine that John J. Simmons is the same as

FIGURE 8–6   Using the RND Function to Play a Guessing Game

```
10   REM ***              PROGRAM GUESSING GAME              ***
20   REM
30   REM *** PROMPTS THE PLAYER TO GUESS AN INTEGER          ***
40   REM *** VALUE FROM 1 TO 100.  WHEN THE PLAYER           ***
50   REM *** ENTERS THE CORRECT VALUE, THE GAME STOPS.       ***
60   REM
70   RANDOMIZE TIMER
80   HI = 100
90   LO = 1
100  ANSWER = INT(RND * (HI - LO) + LO)
110  CLS
120  PRINT "THIS IS A GUESSING GAME"
130  PRINT
140  PRINT "TRY TO GUESS THE NUMBER BETWEEN 1 AND 100."
150  GUESS = -1
160  WHILE ANSWER <> GUESS
170     INPUT "ENTER YOUR GUESS ";GUESS
180     IF GUESS = ANSWER THEN PRINT "CORRECT!! YOU ARE A WINNER!"
           ELSE IF GUESS > ANSWER THEN PRINT "WRONG ANSWER -- TOO HIGH."
           ELSE PRINT "WRONG ANSWER -- TOO LOW."
190  WEND
999  END
```

```
RUN
THIS IS A GUESSING GAME

TRY TO GUESS THE NUMBER BETWEEN 1 AND 100.
ENTER YOUR GUESS ? 50
WRONG ANSWER -- TOO HIGH.
ENTER YOUR GUESS ? 25
WRONG ANSWER -- TOO LOW.
ENTER YOUR GUESS ? 36
CORRECT!! YOU ARE A WINNER!
```

Simmons, John J. The most common string functions are listed in Table 8–2.

Concatenation   Concatenation serves to join two strings end to end, forming a new string. It is not a library function, as are the other string functions discussed here; instead it is an operation performed on two string

TABLE 8–2 String Functions

Function	Operation	Example
string1 + string2	Concatenation; joins two strings.	"KUNG" + " FU" is "KUNG FU"
ASC(string)	Returns the ASCII code for the first character in the string.	If A$ = "DOG", then ASC(A$) is 68
CHR$(expression)	Returns the string representation of the ASCII code of the expression.	CHR$(68) is "D"
LEFT$(string, expression)	Returns the specified number of leftmost characters of a string specified by the expression.	LEFT$("ABCD",2) is "AB"
LEN(string)	Returns the length of a string.	If N$ = "HI THERE", then LEN(N$) is 8
MID$(string, expression1 [,expression2])	Starting with the character at expression1, returns the number of characters specified by expression2.	MID$("MARIE",2,3) is "ARI"
RIGHT$(string, expression)	Returns the number of rightmost characters specified by the expression.	RIGHT$("ABCDE",2) is "DE"
STR$(expression)	Converts a number to its string equivalent.	STR$(123) is "123"
VAL(string)	Returns the numeric value of a number string.	If N$ = "352 63" then VAL(N$) is 35263

operands, just as the arithmetic operators $+$, $-$, $*$, and $/$ act on two numeric values. The plus sign ($+$) serves as the concatenation operator. For example, the statement

```
20 A$ = "NIGHT" + "MARE"
```

assigns the string NIGHTMARE to the variable A$. Similarly, the following segment results in X$, containing the value SAN FRANCISCO:

```
20 A$ = "SAN "
30 B$ = "FRAN"
40 C$ = "CISCO"
50 X$ = A$ + B$ + C$
```

The program in Figure 8–7 demonstrates the use of concatenation.

The LEN Function   The length, or LEN, function returns the number of characters in the single string that is its argument. (Remember that blanks in quoted strings are counted as characters.) Its format is as follows:

```
LEN(string)
```

FIGURE 8–7   Program Demonstrating Concatenation

```
10   REM *** SEND A FORM LETTER. ***
20   REM
30   INPUT "ENTER LAST NAME";LNME$
40   INPUT "ENTER A 1 FOR MALE, 2 FOR FEMALE ";CODE
50   REM
60   REM *** DETERMINE FORM OF ADDRESS. ***
70   IF CODE = 1 THEN TITLE$ = "MR. " ELSE TITLE$ = "MS. "
80   PRINT
90   PRINT
100  PRINT "DEAR " + TITLE$ + LNME$ + ","
110  PRINT TAB(7);"WE ARE SORRY, BUT YOUR WORK DOES"
120  PRINT "NOT COINCIDE WITH OUR NEEDS AT THIS TIME. "
130  PRINT TAB(20);"THE HACK PUBLISHING HOUSE "
999  END
```

```
RUN
ENTER LAST NAME? CSONGAS
ENTER A 1 FOR MALE, 2 FOR FEMALE ? 2


DEAR MS. CSONGAS,
      WE ARE SORRY, BUT YOUR WORK DOES
NOT COINCIDE WITH OUR NEEDS AT THIS TIME.
                    THE HACK PUBLISHING HOUSE
```

An example of how the LEN function might be used is given in Figure 8–8. In this example, if the value of ALBM$ is less than fourteen characters long, this string and the associated price can be displayed within the predefined print zones. Otherwise, the TAB function is used to display the price.

The LEN function is useful when centering headings. For example, the following statements will center the specified heading on an 80-column line:

```
100 START = (80 - LEN("ACE RENTALS")) / 2
110 PRINT TAB(START) "ACE RENTALS"
```

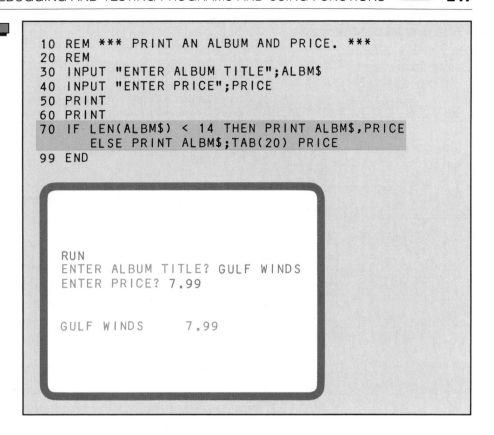

FIGURE 8–8 Program Demonstrating the LEN Function

```
10 REM *** PRINT AN ALBUM AND PRICE. ***
20 REM
30 INPUT "ENTER ALBUM TITLE";ALBM$
40 INPUT "ENTER PRICE";PRICE
50 PRINT
60 PRINT
70 IF LEN(ALBM$) < 14 THEN PRINT ALBM$,PRICE
      ELSE PRINT ALBM$;TAB(20) PRICE
99 END
```

```
RUN
ENTER ALBUM TITLE? GULF WINDS
ENTER PRICE? 7.99


GULF WINDS     7.99
```

The LEFT\$ and RIGHT\$ Functions The format of the LEFT\$ function is as follows:

LEFT$(string, expression)

The expression in parentheses has an integer value. The LEFT\$ function returns a string that consists of the leftmost portion of the string argument, from the first character to the character position specified by the expression. For instance, the following statement assigns to X\$ the value BE SEEING:

```
30 X$ = LEFT$("BE SEEING YOU!",9)
```

The LEFT\$ function is often useful when comparing character strings. Suppose a program asks the user to answer a yes or no question, but does not specify whether the question should be answered by typing the entire word YES or NO or just the first letter, Y or N. The LEFT\$ function can compare just the first character of the user's response, allowing the user to type either YES/NO or Y/N. The program in Figure 8–9 illustrates this.

The format of the RIGHT\$ function is similar to that of the LEFT\$ function:

RIGHT$(string, expression)

FIGURE 8–9 Program
Demonstrating the LEFT$
Function

```
10 REM *** MULTIPLY TWO NUMBERS. ***
20 REM
30 ANS$ = "Y"
40 WHILE ANS$ = "Y"
50    INPUT "ENTER TWO NUMBERS";N1,N2
60    PRINT "THE PRODUCT IS";N1 * N2
70    INPUT "WOULD YOU LIKE TO CONTINUE";ANS$
80    ANS$ = LEFT$(ANS$,1)
90 WEND
99 END
```

```
RUN
ENTER TWO NUMBERS? 14,3
THE PRODUCT IS 42
WOULD YOU LIKE TO CONTINUE? YES
ENTER TWO NUMBERS? 6,10
THE PRODUCT IS 60
WOULD YOU LIKE TO CONTINUE? NO
```

This function returns the *number of characters* specified by the expression from the right end of the string. The following instruction assigns the last nine characters of the string to X$, in this case the value EING YOU!:

```
30 X$ = RIGHT$("BE SEEING YOU!",9)
```

Figure 8–10 demonstrates the RIGHT$ function.

The MID$ Function The MID$ function has the following format, where the two expressions are integer expressions:

MID$(string,expression 1 [,expression 2])

The function returns the portion of the string beginning at the character position defined by *expression1* and extending for the number of characters given by *expression2*. *Expression2* can be omitted; in this case the characters from the starting position of *expression1* to the end of the string are returned. The following statement assigns to X$ a string four characters long, starting at the fifth character: PHAL.

```
20 X$ = MID$("ENCEPHALITIS",5,4)
```

FIGURE 8–10   Program Demonstrating the RIGHT$ Function

```
10 REM *** DISPLAY A PATTERN WITH THE RIGHT$ FUNCTION. ***
20 REM
30 INPUT "ENTER ANY STRING";BLURB$
40 PRINT
50 LNG = LEN(BLURB$)
60 FOR I = LNG TO 1 STEP -1
70    X$ = RIGHT$(BLURB$,I)
80     PRINT X$
90 NEXT I
99 END
```

```
RUN
ENTER ANY STRING? FETTERMAN

FETTERMAN
ETTERMAN
TTERMAN
TERMAN
ERMAN
RMAN
MAN
AN
N
```

The MID$ function is useful for examining some middle characters of a string. Assume you have a file of telephone numbers and you want to output only those with a prefix of 352. Here are the numbers:

491–354–1070
491–353–0011
491–352–3520
491–352–1910
491–352–7350
491–353–9822

The program in Figure 8–11 compares the exchange to 352 and prints the numbers that qualify.

The ASC and CHR$ Functions   The ASC function returns the ASCII value of the first character of its string argument. The format of the ASC function is as follows, where the argument is a string constant, variable, or expression.

ASC(string)

FIGURE 8–11   Program
Demonstrating the MID$
Function

```
10   REM *** PRINT NUMBERS WITH A 352 EXCHANGE. ***
20   REM
30   FOR I = 1 TO 6
40      READ TNUM$
50      IF MID$(TNUM$,5,3) = "352" THEN PRINT TNUM$
60   NEXT I
70   REM
80   REM *** DATA STATEMENTS ***
90   DATA 491-354-1070,491-353-0011,491-352-3520
100  DATA 491-352-1910,491-352-7350,491-353-9822
999  END


RUN
491-352-3520
491-352-1910
491-352-7350
```

Appendix C lists characters and their corresponding ASCII values. For example, the following statement examines the first character of the argument, R, and assigns its ASCII value of 82 to the variable RVALUE:

```
30 RVALUE = ASC("RETURN A VALUE")
```

The CHR$ function performs the reverse operation of the ASC function: it returns the single character that corresponds to a given ASCII value. The format of the function is as follows, where the expression evaluates as an integer in the range 0 through 255:

CHR$(expression)

The following statement assigns to MES$ the value HI!:

```
70 MES$ = CHR$(72) + CHR$(73) + CHR$(33)
```

The ASC and CHR$ functions are demonstrated in the program in Figure 8–12, which prints a listing of the alphabet with its corresponding ASCII values.

The ASC and CHR$ functions are helpful in allowing programs to respond to both lowercase and uppercase input. Using these functions, a program can allow the user to answer a yes or no question with y, Y, n, or N. Appendix C shows that the codes for the lowercase letters range from 97 through 122, and those for uppercase letters range from 65 through 90. An

FIGURE 8–12   Program to
Display ASCII Values

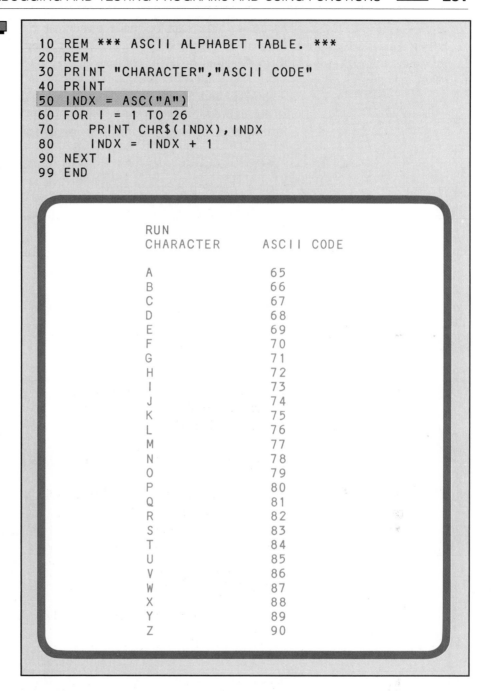

```
10 REM *** ASCII ALPHABET TABLE. ***
20 REM
30 PRINT "CHARACTER","ASCII CODE"
40 PRINT
50 INDX = ASC("A")
60 FOR I = 1 TO 26
70    PRINT CHR$(INDX),INDX
80    INDX = INDX + 1
90 NEXT I
99 END
```

```
RUN
CHARACTER          ASCII CODE

A                    65
B                    66
C                    67
D                    68
E                    69
F                    70
G                    71
H                    72
I                    73
J                    74
K                    75
L                    76
M                    77
N                    78
O                    79
P                    80
Q                    81
R                    82
S                    83
T                    84
U                    85
V                    86
W                    87
X                    88
Y                    89
Z                    90
```

IF/THEN statement can be used to compare the ASCII value of the user response to 96. If the value is greater than 96, a lowercase letter has been typed; if the value is less than 96, the letter is uppercase.

Once the program has determined the type of letter, it can convert the letter to either uppercase or lowercase for comparison. An uppercase letter can be changed to lowercase by adding 32 to the ASCII value, and a lowercase letter can be made uppercase by subtracting 32. The program segment in Figure 8–13 checks a user's reply and converts it to uppercase if necessary in order to compare it.

The VAL and STR$ Functions   The VAL function converts a numeric string expression (such as "12.34") to its equivalent numeric value. Its format is as follows, where the string consists of numeric characters:

VAL(string)

These characters can include the digits 0 through 9, the plus and minus signs, and the decimal point. Any leading blanks in the string are ignored. If the first non-blank character of the string is non-numeric, the function returns a value of zero. For example, the following statement would output 0:

```
70 PRINT VAL(" BG, OH 43402")
```

FIGURE 8–13   Converting Lowercase Letters to Uppercase

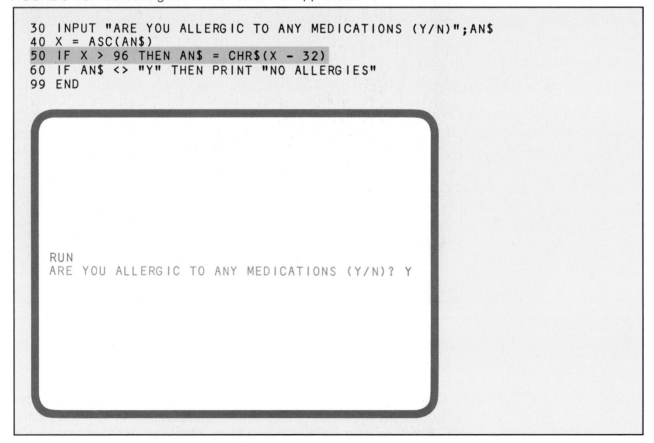

```
30 INPUT "ARE YOU ALLERGIC TO ANY MEDICATIONS (Y/N)";AN$
40 X = ASC(AN$)
50 IF X > 96 THEN AN$ = CHR$(X - 32)
60 IF AN$ <> "Y" THEN PRINT "NO ALLERGIES"
99 END
```

```
RUN
ARE YOU ALLERGIC TO ANY MEDICATIONS (Y/N)? Y
```

Otherwise, the function examines the string one character at a time until an unacceptable character is encountered. A blank is acceptable within a numeric string; it is simply ignored. The following statement would be valid and would assign to N1 the value 1084:

```
70 N1 = VAL(" 1084 WELSH VIEW DR.")
```

By using the VAL function, it is possible to change a number in a character string to a number that can be used in mathematical computations. The program in Figure 8–14 reads an integer value to a string variable and uses the VAL function to compute the sum of its digits.

FIGURE 8–14   Program Using the VAL Function

```
10   REM *** FIND THE SUM OF THE DIGITS OF AN INTEGER.  ***
20   REM *** MAJOR VARIABLES:                           ***
30   REM ***      NR$       NUMBER STRING               ***
40   REM ***      DIG$      SINGLE DIGIT CHARACTER       ***
50   REM ***      NDIG      NUMERIC VALUE OF DIGIT       ***
60   REM
70   SUM = 0
80   INPUT "ENTER A NON-NEGATIVE INTEGER";NR$
90   LNG = LEN(NR$)
100  FOR I = 1 TO LNG
110     DIG$ = MID$(NR$,I,1)
120     NDIG = VAL(DIG$)
130     SUM = SUM + NDIG
140  NEXT I
150  PRINT "SUM = ";SUM
999  END
```

```
RUN
ENTER A NON-NEGATIVE INTEGER? 7540
SUM =  16
```

The STR$ function performs the reverse of the VAL function operation: it converts a real number to a string. Its general format is as follows, where the expression evaluates as a numeric value:

STR$(expression)

The program in Figure 8–15 demonstrates the STR$ function. Remember that once a number has been converted to a string, it can no longer be used in mathematical computations unless it is converted back to a numeric value.

Writing User-Friendly Programs

User friendly
Describes a program that is
designed to be easy and
enjoyable for people to use.

A term commonly heard in the world of programming, **user friendly** refers to programs written to make them as easy and enjoyable as possible for people to use. Some characteristics of user-friendly programs are

■ The prompts are easy to understand, and the program is written to make it as easy as possible for the user to enter responses. For example, if the user

FIGURE 8–15   Program to Concatenate Dates

```
10   REM *** PRINT DATES WITH HYPHENS.   ***
20   REM *** MAJOR VARIABLES:            ***
30   REM ***      DT      NUMERIC DATE   ***
40   REM ***      DT$     STRING DATE    ***
50   REM ***      HDT$    HYPHENATED DATE ***
60   REM
70   FOR I = 1 TO 6
80      READ DT
90      DT$ = STR$(DT)
100     HDT$ = LEFT$(DT$,2) + "-" + MID$(DT$,3,2) + "-" + MID$(DT$,5,2)
110     PRINT HDT$
120  NEXT I
130  REM
140  REM *** DATA STATEMENTS ***
150  DATA 31585,21479,13162
160  DATA 10186,11463,32786
999  END
```

```
RUN
   3-15-85
   2-14-79
   1-31-62
   1-01-86
   1-14-63
   3-27-86
```

is directed to respond to a prompt with a y (for yes), a well-written program might also accept the following responses as the equivalent: Y, Yes, yeah, YES, and so forth.

- If the user has a number of options to choose from, a clearly stated menu should list all of these options and the codes necessary for choosing them.
- They should be able to handle invalid input and print a polite error message. If the program is interactive, the user should be prompted to reenter the necessary input.
- Any "bugs" that the programmer has discovered but not yet fixed, should be documented so that users can attempt to avoid them.

Programs written to handle a wide variety of invalid user input properly avoid many run-time and logic errors. For example, if the data to be entered should be within a given range, the program should make certain it meets the specified requirements before continuing. If it does not meet those requirements, an error message should be displayed, and the user should be prompted to reenter the data. Below is a program segment in which the user is supposed to enter a digit from 1 through 7 representing a day of the week:

```
100 INPUT "ENTER AN INTEGER REPRESENTING THE DAY (1-7)";DAY
110 WHILE (DAY < 1) OR (DAY > 7)
120    PRINT "THE NUMBER MUST BE BETWEEN 1 AND 7."
130    INPUT "PLEASE REENTER THE DAY";DAY
140 WEND
```

If the user enters a number outside the allowable range, he or she is prompted to reenter the number. However, if the user enters a character, the program stops executing. To protect this program segment from non-numeric input, it can be rewritten like this:

```
100 INPUT "ENTER AN INTEGER REPRESENTING THE DAY (1-7)";DAY$
110 WHILE (ASC(DAY$) < 49) OR (ASC(DAY$) > 55)
120    PRINT "THE NUMBER MUST BE BETWEEN 1 AND 7."
130    INPUT "PLEASE REENTER THE DAY";DAY$
140 WEND
```

The value that the user enters should be an integer. However, the value is read to the string variable DAY$, so that an error message will be avoided if a noninteger value is accidentally entered. The ASCII value of the character is checked to make certain that it falls within the 1 through 7 range. Programs that are user friendly should be able to handle any type of invalid data.

The program discussed in the following section ("A Programming Problem") illustrates the characteristics of a user-friendly program.

A Programming Problem

This section will be somewhat different from that in previous chapters. Rather than developing a new program, we will discuss how the program that was developed at the end of Chapter 6 might be tested to determine that

Now Try This

1. Write a statement that assigns the character corresponding to the ASCII value 100 to the variable C$.

2. Write a statement that uses the LEFT$ function to return the first four characters of the string variable ITEM$. Then rewrite the statement so that it uses the MID$ function instead of the LEFT$ function.

3. Write a statement that uses the RIGHT$ function to return the last four characters of the string variable ITEM$. Then rewrite the statement so that it uses the MID$ function instead of the RIGHT$ function. Hint: Use the LEN function to help in determining where to start the string.

4. Use the ASC function to display the ASCII values of each of the letters in your name.

---

it works properly. Figure 8–16 shows the program modified so that it is capable of handling invalid user input properly.

This program determines whether valid values have been entered for three types of data:

1. A valid price. Subroutine PRICE CHECK determines whether a valid real number has been entered for the price. The VAL function converts this value from a character string to a real number. If an invalid value has been entered, a zero is assigned to PRICE, causing the WHILE loop in lines 7080 through 7120 to prompt the user to reenter the price.
2. A valid type code. Subroutine CODE CHECK determines whether a 1, 2, or 3 has been entered as the type code. The WHILE loop in lines 5050 through 5080 is executed until a valid code is entered.
3. A valid response to a yes/no prompt. In lines 1190 and 3080, the user must enter a word beginning with an upper- or lowercase "Y" or "N" in response to these prompts. In subroutine DUPLICATE CHECK, the LEFT$ function is used to get the first letter of the response. If the user has entered a lowercase letter, line 6080 converts it to uppercase. If the answer does not equal "Y" or "N", line 6110 prompts the user to reenter it.

Let's now discuss how this program might be tested to determine its reliability. First, we can determine if the program works properly if non-numeric data are entered for the book price. For example, if the value $32.50 is entered as the price, the user should be prompted to reenter the price (the dollar sign is invalid input). Next, we can check to see if the program works properly when invalid data are entered for the type code. Because the type code should be a 1, 2, or 3, we might first check to

FIGURE 8–16   Program Protected from Invalid Input

```
10    REM ***                    PROGRAM BOOKCOST              ***
20    REM
30    REM ***   THIS PROGRAM CALCULATES THE TOTAL COST OF     ***
40    REM ***   A BOOK. THE TOTAL COST IS OBTAINED BY         ***
50    REM ***   ADDING THE PRICE OF THE BOOK TO THE PRO-      ***
60    REM ***   CESSING COST, WHICH IS BASED ON THE TYPE.     ***
70    REM ***        1.   REFERENCE BOOK                      ***
80    REM ***             NOT A DUPLICATE      $8.50          ***
90    REM ***             DUPLICATE            $7.40          ***
100   REM ***        2.   CIRCULATING BOOK                    ***
110   REM ***             NOT A DUPLICATE      $7.82          ***
120   REM ***             DUPLICATE            $6.60          ***
130   REM ***             BESTSELLER           $1.75 EXTRA    ***
140   REM ***        3.   PAPERBACK                           ***
150   REM ***             NOT A DUPLICATE      $4.60          ***
160   REM ***             DUPLICATE            $3.10          ***
170   REM
180   REM ***   MAJOR VARIABLES:                              ***
190   REM ***   PRICE          PRICE OF THE BOOK              ***
200   REM ***   CODE           TYPE OF BOOK AS ABOVE          ***
210   REM ***   DUP$           IS BOOK A DUPLICATE(Y/N)?      ***
220   REM ***   PRCST          PROCESSING COST                ***
230   REM ***   SELLER$        IS BOOK A BESTSELLER(Y/N)?     ***
240   REM ***   TTCST          TOTAL COST OF BOOK             ***
250   REM
260   REM *** CALL SUBROUTINE TO ENTER DATA. ***
270   GOSUB 1000
280   REM
290   REM *** CALL APPROPRIATE SUBROUTINE TO CALCULATE
300   REM *** THE PROCESSING COST.
310   ON CODE GOSUB 2000,3000,4000
320   REM
330   REM *** CALL SUBROUTINE TO ADD PROCESSING COST
340   REM *** TO BOOK PRICE AND DISPLAY TOTAL COST.
350   GOSUB 8000
999   END
1000  REM ***************************************************
1010  REM ***                SUBROUTINE INPUT               ***
1020  REM ***************************************************
1030  REM *** SUBROUTINE TO ALLOW USER TO ENTER DATA.       ***
1040  REM
1050  CLS
1060  INPUT "ENTER PRICE OF THE BOOK";PRICE$
1070  REM
1080  REM *** CHECK FOR INVALID PRICE. ***
1090  GOSUB 7000
1100  PRINT
1110  PRINT "1 - REFERENCE BOOK "
1120  PRINT "2 - CIRCULATING BOOK "
1130  PRINT "3 - PAPERBACK "
1140  INPUT "ENTER TYPE CODE FOR THE BOOK, USING THE CODES LISTED ABOVE";CODE$
1150  REM
1160  REM *** CHECK FOR INVALID CODE. ***
```

(figure continued on the next page)

FIGURE 8–16   Continued

```
1170 GOSUB 5000
1180 INPUT "IS BOOK A DUPLICATE (Y/N)";DUP$
1190 AN$ = DUP$
1200 REM
1210 REM *** CHECK FOR INVALID RESPONSE. ***
1220 GOSUB 6000
1230 DUP$ = AN$
1240 RETURN
2000 REM **************************************************
2010 REM ***                SUBROUTINE REFERENCE          ***
2020 REM **************************************************
2030 REM *** SUBROUTINE TO CALCULATE PROCESSING COST OF ***
2040 REM *** REFERENCE BOOK.                             ***
2050 REM
2060 IF DUP$ = "Y" THEN PRCST = 7.4 ELSE PRCST = 8.5
2070 RETURN
3000 REM **************************************************
3010 REM ***              SUBROUTINE CIRCULATING          ***
3020 REM **************************************************
3030 REM *** SUBROUTINE TO CALCULATE PROCESSING COST OF ***
3040 REM *** CIRCULATING BOOK.                           ***
3050 REM
3060 IF DUP$ = "Y" THEN PRCST = 6.6 ELSE PRCST = 7.82
3070 INPUT "IS THE BOOK A BESTSELLER (Y/N)";SELLER$
3080 AN$ = SELLER$
3090 REM
3100 REM *** CHECK FOR INVALID RESPONSE. ***
3110 GOSUB 6000
3120 SELLER$ = AN$
3130 IF SELLER$ = "Y" THEN PRCST = PRCST + 1.75
3140 RETURN
4000 REM **************************************************
4010 REM ***                SUBROUTINE PAPERBACK          ***
4020 REM **************************************************
4030 REM *** SUBROUTINE TO CALCULATE PROCESSING COST OF ***
4040 REM *** PAPERBACK BOOK.                             ***
4050 REM
4060 IF DUP$ = "Y" THEN PRCST = 3.1 ELSE PRCST = 4.6
4070 RETURN
5000 REM **************************************************
5010 REM ***                SUBROUTINE CODE CHECK         ***
5020 REM **************************************************
5030 REM ***   ALLOW CODE TO BE REENTERED IF INVALID.    ***
5040 REM
5050 WHILE (LEN(CODE$) > 1) OR ((CODE$ <> "1") AND (CODE$ <> "2")
        AND (CODE$ <> "3"))
5060   PRINT
5070   INPUT "TYPE CODE MUST BE 1, 2, OR 3. PLEASE REENTER CODE";CODE$
5080 WEND
5090 CODE = VAL(CODE$)
5100 RETURN
```

FIGURE 8-16   Continued

```
6000 REM ****************************************************
6010 REM ***              SUBROUTINE DUPLICATE CHECK        ***
6020 REM ****************************************************
6030 REM *** ALLOW USER RESPONSE TO BE REENTERED IF         ***
6040 REM *** INVALID.                                       ***
6050 REM
6060 AN$ = LEFT$(AN$,1)
6070 NUMDUP = ASC(AN$)
6080 IF NUMDUP > 96 THEN AN$ = CHR$(NUMDUP - 32)
6090 WHILE AN$ <> "Y" AND AN$ <> "N"
6100    PRINT
6110    INPUT "PLEASE ENTER A 'Y' OR 'N' ";AN$
6120    AN$ = LEFT$(AN$,1)
6130    NUMDUP = ASC(AN$)
6140    IF NUMDUP > 96 THEN AN$ = CHR$(NUMDUP - 32)
6150 WEND
6160 RETURN
7000 REM ****************************************************
7010 REM ***              SUBROUTINE PRICE CHECK            ***
7020 REM ****************************************************
7030 REM *** ALLOW PRICE TO BE REENTERED IF INVALID.        ***
7040 REM
7050 PRICE = VAL(PRICE$)
7060 REM
7070 REM *** REENTER PRICE UNTIL VALID. ***
7080 WHILE PRICE = 0
7090    PRINT
7100    INPUT "PLEASE ENTER ONLY DIGITS AND A DECIMAL POINT ";PRICE$
7110    PRICE = VAL(PRICE$)
7120 WEND
7130 RETURN
8000 REM ****************************************************
8010 REM ***                 SUBROUTINE PRINT               ***
8020 REM ****************************************************
8030 REM *** SUBROUTINE TO CALCULATE AND PRINT TOTAL        ***
8040 REM *** COST.                                          ***
8050 REM
8060 TTCST = PRCST + PRICE
8070 PRINT
8080 PRINT USING "\                         \ $$##.##";"*** TOTAL COST:",TTCST
8090 RETURN
```

(figure continued on the next page)

FIGURE 8–16 Continued

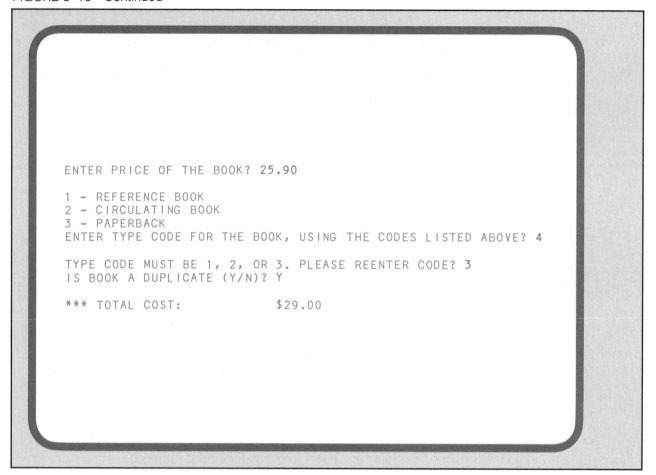

```
ENTER PRICE OF THE BOOK? 25.90

1 - REFERENCE BOOK
2 - CIRCULATING BOOK
3 - PAPERBACK
ENTER TYPE CODE FOR THE BOOK, USING THE CODES LISTED ABOVE? 4

TYPE CODE MUST BE 1, 2, OR 3. PLEASE REENTER CODE? 3
IS BOOK A DUPLICATE (Y/N)? Y

*** TOTAL COST:           $29.00
```

determine if the program works properly for values that are non-numeric, such as "a", "large", or "*". Then we can check to see if it works properly for integers outside the range 1 through 3, such as − 1 or 8. It is especially important to check the boundary cases 0 and 4. Another good idea is to see if it works properly for numbers that have a valid starting integer but are more than one digit in length, such as 15, 23, and 38.9.

In each of these cases, the program should prompt the user to reenter the type code until a valid code is entered. If the program is able to handle these situations properly, we can then check to make certain that the program does in fact execute correctly when a valid type code is entered. Because there are only three valid codes (1, 2, or 3), we can easily test each of them.

The prompts that require a response of Y or N in lines 1190 and 3080 should be checked to make certain that they work properly for both upper- and lowercase letters, and also for words starting with either a Y or an N.

Now we want to make certain that the program obtains the correct total for the book cost. Therefore, each of the following combinations needs to be checked:

Reference book	Circulating book	Paperback book
duplicate/nonduplicate	duplicate/nonduplicate bestseller/nonbestseller	duplicate/nonduplicate

As previously mentioned, auditing a program involves repeatedly running it with pre-established groups of data to determine if it obtains correct results. Table 8–3 contains eight sets of data to test for each of the combinations listed above. The correct results have already been calculated. When the program is run, the computer's results are compared with the correct results. If they match, we can be reasonably certain the program is working properly.

Programming Hints

- Double check the expression controlling loop execution to determine if it evaluates properly.
- The argument of a function must always be placed in parentheses.
- A function is evaluated as a single value immediately; it has a higher priority than arithmetic, relational, and logical operators.
- Remember that the INT function does not round to the nearest integer; instead, it returns the largest integer less than or equal to its argument.
- The RANDOMIZE statement must be used with the RND function to generate a new series of random numbers each time the program is run. (Otherwise, the same series of pseudo-random numbers will be generated each time.)

TABLE 8–3   Auditing a Program

Price	Book Type (1–3)	Duplicate (Y/N)	Bestseller (Y/N)	Correct Total	Total Obtained when Program Is Executed
14.55	1	Y	-----	21.95	
22.00	1	N	-----	30.50	
10.98	2	Y	Y	19.33	
50.24	2	N	Y	59.81	
18.70	2	Y	N	25.30	
13.49	2	N	N	21.31	
78.80	3	Y	-----	81.90	
31.95	3	N	-----	36.55	

Summary Points

- Structured programming uses loop structures such as the FOR/NEXT and WHILE/WEND rather than GOTO statements. Also, structured programs of any significant length are divided into subroutines that perform specific tasks. Some of the advantages of writing structured programs are that the logic of the finished program is easier to follow; the programmer's time is used efficiently; the resulting program is easier to modify and maintain; and the program is more likely to be error-free than an unstructured program.

- Syntax and logic errors are the two basic types of program errors.

- Syntax errors can often be avoided by careful typing and proofreading of the program before it is executed.

- Logic errors are caused by flaws in the program's algorithm. There are two types of logic errors: run-time errors, which cause execution to stop prematurely, and errors in which program execution terminates properly but the output is not always correct.

- Program testing is the process of systematically checking a program to determine its reliability, that is, its ability to work properly at all times.

- Complete program testing, which is generally impractical, involves testing all possible paths of execution of a program. Selective program testing involves testing programs using data with specific characteristics. When selective testing is used, programs are usually checked to determine if they work properly for boundary cases (that is, data at the very extremes of valid ranges).

- When a program is audited, it is executed with specific groups of data. The results are checked for accuracy.

- Library functions are built into the BASIC system and perform commonly needed tasks.

- The INT function computes the greatest integer less than or equal to the value specified as the argument.

- The SGN function produces a 1, 0, or −1, depending on whether the argument is positive, zero, or negative, respectively.

- The ABS function returns the absolute value of its argument.

- BASIC string functions permit modification, concatenation, comparison, and analysis of the composition of strings.

- The concatenation operation (+) joins two strings together.

- The LEN function is used to find the number of characters in a string.

- The LEFT$ function returns a specified number of leftmost characters of a string.

- The RIGHT$ function returns the specified rightmost characters of a string.

- The MID$ function enables the programmer to gain access to characters in the middle of a string.

- The ASC function returns the ASCII code for the first character in a string.

- The CHR$ function returns the string representation of the ASCII code of the expression.

- The VAL function is used to find the numeric equivalent of a string expression.

- The STR$ function acts as a reverse of the VAL function by converting a number to its string equivalent.

- User-friendly programs are pleasant to use and handle invalid input properly.

Vocabulary List

Argument

Auditing

Built-in function

Complete program testing

Concatenate

Error trapping

Library function

Program testing

Program tracing

Random

Reliability

Run-time error

Selective program testing

User friendly

Questions

Whenever appropriate, use complete sentences in answering the following questions.

1. What are the two categories of program errors?
2. How can syntax errors be avoided?
3. Explain how error trapping is used to protect a program from invalid data.
4. What is meant by auditing a program?
5. What are the boundary cases in the following statement?

```
50 IF SQ.YDS > 100 THEN RTE = 14.95
       ELSE RTE = 13.50
```

6. What are the values of the following expressions?
   a. INT ((2 - 4) / 4)
   b. ABS (INT (4.5))
   c. SGN (4 ^ 4 - 20)
7. What possible values can SGN (X) return?
8. The function ABS (X) always returns _____.
   a. a number greater than or equal to 0
   b. a number less than or equal to 0
   c. a whole number
   d. an even number
9. What is the purpose of the RANDOMIZE statement?
10. What is meant by string concatenation?
11. The _____ function returns the number of characters in a string.
12. Explain the use of the LEFT$, RIGHT$, and MID$ functions.
13. What is the restriction placed on an argument of the ASC function?
14. What function changes a number in character string format to a real number?
15. What does the STR$ function do?

Debugging Exercises

Identify the following programs or program segments that contain errors and debug them.

1.
```
10  REM *** PROMPT USER TO ENTER HIS OR HER ***
20  REM *** CLASS IN SCHOOL (1-4).          ***
30  INPUT "ENTER YOUR CLASS";CLASS$
40  WHILE (CLASS$ <> 1) OR (CLASS$ <> 2) OR (CLASS$  <> 3)
    OR (CLASS$ <> 4)
50     INPUT "INVALID VALUE. PLEASE REENTER CLASS (1-4)";CLASS$
60  WEND
```

2.
```
10  REM *** READ AND FIND THE SUM OF A GROUP OF POSITIVE NUMBERS. ***
20  READ N
30  WHILE N <> -1
40     TT = 0
50     TT = TT + N
60     READ N
70  WEND
80  DATA 18.49,6.53,8.71
90  DATA 21.47,4.93,5.22,-1
99  END
```

3.
```
10  REM *** PRINT ADDRESS IF IT IS ON AN AVENUE (AVE). ***
20  INPUT "ENTER ADDRESS";ST$
30  IF LEFT$(ST$,4) = "AVE." THEN PRINT ST$
99  END
```

4.
```
10  REM *** READ AND DISPLAY A PERSON'S NAME AND ADDRESS. ***
20  READ NME$,S$,CTY$,ST$,ZCDE
30  ADRS$ = CTY$ + " " + ST$ + " " + ZCDE
40  PRINT NME$
50  PRINT S$
60  PRINT ADRS$
70  DATA ELAINE JOHNSON,1704 CARBON ST.,TULSA, WYOMING,49023
99  END
```

Programming Problems

Level 1

1. Enter the following program into the computer and debug it.

```
10     REM *** THIS PROGRAM READS A LIST OF INTEGERS      ***
20     REM *** TYPED AT THE KEYBOARD ONE AT A TIME        ***
30     REM *** AND DETERMINES IF THEY ARE ODD OR EVEN.    ***
40     REM *** THEN ALL THE ODD NUMBERS ARE ADDED         ***
50     REM *** TOGETHER AND ALL THE EVEN NUMBERS ARE      ***
60     REM *** ADDED TOGETHER.  THESE TWO SUMS ARE        ***
70     REM *** PRINTED.                                   ***
80     REM *** MAJOR VARIABLES:                           ***
90     REM ***    ESUM       SUM OF EVEN NUMBERS          ***
```

```
100  REM ***      OSUM      SUM OF ODD NUMBERS       ***
110  REM ***      NMBR      INTEGER ENTERED          ***
120  REM ***      QUANT     NUMBER OF INTEGERS       ***
130  REM ***      EVEN$     IS INTEGER EVEN?         ***
140  ESUM = 0
150  OSUM = 0
160  INPUT "HOW MANY NUMBERS ARE THERE";QUANT
170  PRINT "ENTER THE NUMBERS"
180  REM
190  REM *** ENTER EACH NUMBER AND ASSIGN IT TO ***
200  REM *** THE APPROPRIATE SUM.              ***
210  FOR I = 1 TO QUANT
220     INPUT (NMBR)
230     GOSUB 1000
240     IF EVEN$ = Y THEN ESUM = ESUM + NMBR ELSE OSUM = OSUM + NMBR
250  NEXT I
260  PRINT
270  PRINT "THE SUM OF THE EVEN NUMBERS IS";ESUM
280  PRINT "THE SUM OF THE ODD NUMBERS IS";OSUM
1000 REM *********************************************
1010 REM ***              SUBROUTINE TEST          ***
1020 REM *********************************************
1030 REM *** DETERMINE IF INTEGER IS EVEN OR ODD.  ***
1040 REM
1050 X = NMBR / 2 - INT(NMBR / 2)
1060 IF X = 0 THEN EVEN$ = "Y" ELSE EVEN$ = "N"
1070 RETURN
```

2. Write a line of code that will transfer program execution to line 100, 200, or 300 depending on the sign of a value in the numeric variable A. If the value is negative, transfer control to line 100; if it is zero, to 200; and if it is positive, to 300.

3. Write a program that will read a positive integer as a character string and display it with commas inserted where appropriate if the number has four or more digits. (Hint: Concatenate digits with commas starting from the right end of the number.) Use the following data:

    45
    1345623
    100000
    0
    999
    3900

4. Write a program that displays the alphabet twice, in uppercase and in lowercase letters, with slashes (/) between the letters. Use the CHR$ function. A subroutine should be called by a GOSUB statement to concatenate the letter with the slash. The output should have the following format:

    ALPHABET
    A/B/C/. . ./Z

    alphabet
    a/b/c/d/e/. . ./z

5. Write a program to simulate the tossing of a coin ten times. After the ten tosses, it should display the total number of heads and tails. Generate random numbers to represent the tosses, where 1 = heads and 2 = tails.

6. Write a program that displays all social security numbers with the fourth and fifth digits of 64. Read each data line as a character string. Use the following data:

    316642789
    341425632
    278428909
    341648902
    316645430

The output should have the following format:

    XXX-XX-XXXX

7. Write a program that calculates the cost of a season pass to Fancher High School athletic events. The cost is as follows:

Children under 5	Free
Senior citizens and students	$24.00
Other adults	$32.00

Write the program so that it is protected from invalid user input. Prompt the user to enter the category of ticket and then display its price.

Level 2

1. The students of Bowsher High School each take six classes. Of these six classes, at least one must be from each of the following categories:

English	100 level classes
Math	200 level classes
Science	300 level classes

For example, the following selection of course numbers would meet this requirement: 102, 120, 204, 305, 306, 410. Write a program that prompts the student to enter the course numbers of the six classes being taken and displays a message stating whether the selection contains one class from each category.

2. Rewrite the last program in Chapter 5 (Figure 5–14) so that it is protected from invalid user input.

3. Write a program that prompts the user to enter a checking account balance. A message should be displayed stating whether the account is overdrawn.

4. A shoe store has devised a system to help detect errors in recording inventory. The last two digits of every stock number must be the sum of the preceding three digits. For example, the stock number QB412.07 is valid because 07 is the sum of 4 + 1 + 2. Write a program that reads in stock numbers and displays a list of any invalid numbers. Use the following data:

QB371.11	QA919.17
UT491.14	QB497.20
UT307.11	UT410.05
AT478.19	AT731.11
QB115.08	

5. Write a program that reads a sentence and switches all lowercase letters to capitals and all uppercase letters to lowercase. Display the original and converted sentences. Use the following data:

"Miss B. was seen Saturday at Serendipity with a British musician."
"Late Night with David Letterman is broadcast from the NBC studios."

6. The brightness of heavenly bodies can be represented by an apparent magnitude value. The brightest objects have negative magnitudes, and the faintest have positive magnitudes. Write a program that reads sample magnitudes and displays a chart classifying them according to brightness: negative values are bright, zeros are medium, and positive values are faint. Also, calculate the average magnitude rounded to the nearest tenth and display it. Use the SGN function and the following data:

Object	Magnitude
Sun	−26.5
Vega	0.0
Sirius	−1.4
Uranus	5.5
Neptune	7.8
Mars	−2.7
Jupiter	−2.6
Pluto	15.0

Projects

For each project, complete the following:

- Fill out a program specification chart.
- Develop a structure chart.
- Create a flowchart or pseudocode.
- Thoroughly document the final program.
- Test your program using a variety of data.

1. AAA wants you to write a program that will help the customers in the state of Ohio determine in which month their license plates need to be renewed and the amount due. The month is determined by the first character in the customer's last name. The following information should be used:

Membership in AAA $19.00
Non-membership $22.00

A–F   January
G–L   February
M–Q   March
R–Z   April

Subroutines should be called by a GOSUB statement to determine the amount due. Use the ASCII code to determine the month. The output should have the following format:

License Bureau

PLEASE ENTER YOUR LAST NAME: XXX
DO YOU BELONG TO AAA? X
AMOUNT DUE IS $XX.XX
RENEWAL MONTH IS XXXX

2. You have been hired to write a program to evaluate teachers. You have come up with a formula that will evaluate a teacher on the following scale:

negative number   bad teacher
zero   average teacher
positive number   good teacher

The formula operates on four variables, A, B, C, and X, which are evaluations of the teacher's performance. The rating is calculated as follows:

Rating $= 5 + Z * 0.85$

where $Z = X + A - (X * B) + (C/X)$. Write a program that will read the teacher's name and rating variables X, A, B, and C, and calculate the rating. Define a function to calculate the rating. Use the following data:

Teacher	X	A	B	C
Dixon	5	10	7	4
Meronk	10	1	1	6
Hastings	2	10	3	1
Mishler	10	9	3	7

Display each teacher and rating with appropriate headings.

CHAPTER 9

Tables

Learning Objectives

After studying this chapter, you should be able to
1. Explain the advantages of using tables.
2. Describe how tables are kept in storage.
3. Use the DIM statement to dimension tables.
4. Use subscripts to access table elements.
5. Read data to, print, and manipulate one- and two-dimensional tables.
6. Sort data items by using the bubble sort.
7. Use the merge sort to merge two sorted tables.
8. Search for specific data items using the sequential search.

Introduction

All of our programs thus far have used simple variables such as LBS, TITLE$, or HRS to represent single values. In programs required to handle many single values of the same type (such as 20 student scores), a loop has been used to allow one variable to represent these values one at a time. Now consider the problem of a television network poll. A program is needed to read and retain the daily viewing times of ten random viewers, calculate the average viewing time, and display the difference between each person's viewing time and the average in the following format:

NAME	HRS	DIFFERENCE FROM AVG
P. BUSCH	1	−3
C. CARSTENS	5	1
J. DRAKE	0	−4
H. POIROT	2	−2
M. BULAS	7	3
D. ZONGAS	3	−1
C. HASTINGS	4	0
T. ZEKLY	11	7
S. MCKINNIS	3	−1
G. BALDUCCI	4	0

AVERAGE VIEWING TIME = 4

Our past procedure for calculating averages has been to set up a loop to read and accumulate each value in a single variable. Each time a new value is read by this method, however, the previous value stored in the variable is lost. Thus, in the problem involving the television poll, we would not be able to compare each person's viewing time with the calculated average viewing time. To make the comparison, we must store each person's viewing time in a separate memory location. It is possible to use ten different variables to hold these values, but this is a cumbersome solution that would be even more impractical when dealing with a larger number of values.

Table
An ordered collection of related data items. A single variable name is used to refer to the entire collection of items.

There is an easier way: BASIC permits us to deal with many related data items as a group by means of a structure known as a **table.** Tables are also referred to as **arrays.** This chapter shows how tables can be used in a situation such as the television poll program, in which groups of data items must be stored and manipulated efficiently. Various methods of sorting and searching tables are also discussed.

One-Dimensional Tables

Using Subscripts

Element
An individual value stored in a table.

The individual data items within a table are called **elements.** A table consists of a group of consecutive storage locations in memory, each location containing a single element. The entire table is given one name, and the programmer indicates an individual element in the table by referring to its position. To illustrate, suppose that there are five test scores to be stored: 97, 85, 89, 95, 100. The scores could be put in a table called TESTS, which we might visualize like this:

97	85	89	95	100
TESTS(1)	TESTS(2)	TESTS(3)	TESTS(4)	TESTS(5)

Subscript
A value that is enclosed in parentheses and that identifies the position of a particular element in a table.

The table name TESTS now refers to all five storage locations containing the test scores. To gain access to a single test score within the table, a **subscript** (also called an **index**) is used. A subscript is a value enclosed in parentheses that identifies the position of a given element in the table. For example, the first element of table TESTS (containing the value 97) is referred to as TESTS(1). The second test score is in TESTS(2), the third test score is in TESTS(3), and so on. Therefore, the following statements are true:

TESTS(1) = 97
TESTS(2) = 85
TESTS(3) = 89
TESTS(4) = 95
TESTS(5) = 100

The subscript enclosed in parentheses does not have to be an integer constant; it can consist of any valid numeric expression. When a table element subscript is indicated by an expression, the BASIC system carries out the following steps:

- It evaluates the expression within the parentheses.
- If the subscript is a real number, it is rounded to the nearest integer.

■ It accesses the indicated element in the table. Keep in mind that the subscript value of a table element is entirely different from the contents of that element. In the previous example, the value of TESTS(4) is 95; the subscript 4 tells where the value 95 is located in the table.

Subscripted variable

A variable that refers to a specific element of a table.

Unsubscripted variable

A simple variable; one that does not refer to a table element.

Variables that refer to specific elements of tables, such as TESTS(4), are called **subscripted variables.** In contrast, simple variables such as we have used in previous chapters are called **unsubscripted variables.** Both kinds of variables store a single value, numeric or string, and both can be used in BASIC statements in the same manner. The important difference between the two is that a subscripted variable refers to one value in a table of related values; it is possible to access a different value in the group simply by changing the subscript. An unsubscripted variable, on the other hand, does not necessarily have any special relationship to the values stored before or after it in memory.

The same rules that apply to naming simple variables also apply to naming tables. Remember that only numeric values can be stored in tables with numeric variable names, and that character string tables can contain only string values.

Assume that the table X and the variables A and B have the following values:

$$X(1) = 2 \qquad A = 3$$
$$X(2) = 15 \qquad B = 5$$
$$X(3) = 16$$
$$X(4) = 17$$
$$X(5) = 32$$

The following examples show how the various forms of subscripts are used.

Example	Reference
X(3)	Third element of X, or 16.
X(B)	B = 5; thus the fifth element of X, or 32.
X(X(1))	X(1) = 2; thus the second element of X, or 15.
X(A − 2)	A − 2 = 1; thus the first element of X, or 2.

Dimensioning a Table

When a subscripted variable is found in a program, the BASIC system recognizes it as part of a table and automatically reserves 11 storage locations for the table. These elements have the subscripts 0 through 10. The programmer does not have to fill all of the reserved table storage spaces with values; it is illegal, however, to refer to a table element for which space has not been reserved.

The DIM, or dimension, statement enables the programmer to override this standard table space reservation and reserve space for a table of any desired size. A DIM statement is not required for tables of 11 or fewer elements, but it is good programming practice to use DIM statements for all tables to help document the arrays used by a program.

The general format of the DIM statement follows:

line# DIM variable1(limit1)[,variable2(limit2)] . . .

The variables are the names of tables. Each limit is an integer constant that specifies the maximum subscript value possible for that particular table. For example, if space is needed to store twenty-five elements in a table ITEM$, the following statement reserves the necessary storage locations:

```
10 DIM ITEM$(24)
```

Although it may seem that this statement sets aside only 24 positions, remember that table positions 0 through 24 are actually equal to 25 locations. For the sake of clarity and program logic, programmers often ignore the zero element. If you have a table with 20 items, the program's logic is easier to follow if the table subscripts are 1 through 20 rather than 0 through 19. Therefore, we will follow the practice of ignoring the zero position. If we choose not to use the zero position, we would dimension the array ITEM$ as follows in order to have 25 positions:

```
10 DIM ITEM$(25)
```

There is no problem if fewer than 25 values are read into table ITEM$. Table subscripts can vary in the program from 0 to the limit declared in the DIM statement, but no subscript can exceed that limit.

As indicated in the statement format, more than one table can be declared in a DIM statement. For example, the following statement declares ACCNT, NAM$, and OVERDRAWN as arrays:

```
10 DIM ACCNT(100),NAM$(150),OVERDRAWN(50)
```

Table ACCNT may contain up to 101 elements, NAM$ up to 151 elements, and OVERDRAWN up to 51 elements. Or, ignoring the zero position, 100, 150, and 50.

DIM statements must appear in a program before the first references to the tables they describe; a good practice is to place them at the beginning of the program. The following standard preparation symbol is often used to flowchart the DIM statement:

Storing Data in a Table

A major advantage of using tables is the ability to use a variable rather than a constant as a subscript. Because a single name such as TESTS(I) can refer to any element in the table TESTS, depending on the value of I, this subscripted variable name can be used in a loop that varies the value of the subscript I. A FOR/NEXT loop can be an efficient method of reading data to a table if the exact number of items to be read is known in advance. The following program segment reads a list of five numbers into the table TESTS:

```
10 FOR I = 1 TO 5
20     READ TEST(I)
30 NEXT I
40 DATA 85,71,63,51,99
```

The first time this loop is executed, the loop variable I equals 1. Therefore, when line 20 is executed, the computer reads the first number from the data list (which is 85) and stores it in TESTS(I), which evaluates as TESTS(1) during this loop execution. The second time through the loop, I equals 2. The second number is read to TESTS(I), which now refers to TESTS(2)—the second location in the table. The loop processing continues until all five numbers have been read and stored. This process is outlined as follows:

For I =	Action	Table TESTS
1	READ TESTS(1)	85
2	READ TESTS(2)	85 71
3	READ TESTS(3)	85 71 63
4	READ TESTS(4)	85 71 63 51
5	READ TESTS(5)	85 71 63 51 99

A table can also be filled with values using an INPUT statement or an assignment statement within a loop. To initialize an array of ten elements to zero, the following statements could be used:

```
50 FOR I = 1 TO 10
60     SCORES(I) = 0
70 NEXT I
```

It is often possible to read data to several tables within a single loop. In the following segment, each data line contains data for one element of each of three tables:

```
10 DIM NAM$(5),AGE(5),SSN$(5)
20 FOR I = 1 TO 5
30    READ NAM$(I),AGE(I),SSN$(I)
40 NEXT I
50 DATA "TOM BAKER",41,"268-66-1071"
60 DATA "LALLA WARD",28,"353-65-2861"
70 DATA "MASADA WILMOT",33,"269-59-9064"
80 DATA "PATRICK JONES",52,"379-44-8184"
90 DATA "BERYLE JONES",49,"271-55-1773"
```

When the exact number of items to be read to a table is unknown, a WHILE loop and a trailer value can be used. This method is demonstrated in the following segment, where the data contain a trailer value of -1. Care must be taken, however, that the number of items read does not exceed the size of the table.

```
10 DIM X(50)
20 I = 1
30 INPUT X(I)
40 WHILE (I < 50) AND (X(I) <> -1)
50    I = I + 1
60    INPUT X(I)
70 WEND
```

Notice that the condition in the WHILE loop checks both for the trailer value and to make certain that the subscript is not too large.

Displaying the Contents of a Table

A FOR/NEXT loop can be used to display the contents of the table TESTS, as shown in the following segment.

```
70 FOR T = 1 TO 5
80    PRINT TEST(T)
90 NEXT T
```

```
RUN
 85
 71
 63
 51
 99
```

Because there is no punctuation at the end of the PRINT statement in line 80, each value will be displayed on a separate line. The values could be displayed on the same line instead by placing a semicolon at the end of the line:

```
70 FOR T = 1 TO 5
80     PRINT TEST(T);
90 NEXT T
```

```
RUN
85  71  63  51  99
```

As the loop control variable T varies from 1 to 5, so does the value of the table subscript, and the computer displays elements 1 through 5 of array TESTS.

Performing Calculations on Table Elements

Now consider again the problem of the television network viewing poll presented earlier in this chapter. The output format required that each line contain the viewer's name, number of viewing hours, and the difference between those hours and the average hours of all the viewers. This problem is solved in the program in Figure 9–1. The solution can be broken into the following steps:

1. Read the data to two tables: a character string table for the names and a numeric table for the hours.
2. Calculate the average viewing hours.
3. Calculate for each viewer the difference between his or her hours and the average; these differences can be stored in a third table.
4. Display the required information from the three tables.

The viewers' names and hours are read to their appropriate tables in line 200 as part of a FOR/NEXT loop. Line 210 performs an accumulation of all the elements of the table HRS. As I varies from 1 to 10, the elements 1 through 10 of HRS are added to the total hours (THRS). Therefore, when this loop is exited, the tables NME\$ and HRS are filled with values, and the unsubscripted variable THRS contains the sum of all the values contained in HRS. The average number of viewing hours is then calculated in line 230.

The FOR/NEXT loop starting in line 260 calculates the difference from the average viewing time for each viewer and stores the results in the table DAVG. Thus the first element of each table contains information about the first viewer, the second element about the second viewer, and so on. All of the information can then be displayed in the required format by the FOR/NEXT loop of lines 320 through 340.

Sometimes not every element of a table needs to be manipulated in the same way. If we wanted to find the product of only the odd-numbered entries in a table, K, containing 25 numbers, we could use the following statements:

```
90  PROD = 1
100 FOR I = 1 TO 25 STEP 2
110 PROD = PROD * K(I)
120 NEXT I
```

FIGURE 9–1   Program Using a One-Dimensional Table

```
10   REM ***            NETWORK VIEWING TIME SURVEY          ***
20   REM
30   REM *** THIS PROGRAM DETERMINES THE AVERAGE VIEWING ***
40   REM *** TIME BY A GROUP OF VIEWERS. IT THEN DETER-   ***
50   REM *** MINES THE DIFFERENCE FOR EACH VIEWER FROM    ***
60   REM *** THE AVERAGE AND THEIR ACTUAL VIEWING TIME.   ***
70   REM *** MAJOR VARIABLES:                             ***
80   REM ***      NME$     TABLE OF VIEWERS               ***
90   REM ***      HRS      TABLE OF HOURS                 ***
100  REM ***      DAVG     TABLE OF DIFFERENCES FROM AVG  ***
110  REM ***      AVG      AVERAGE VIEWING HRS            ***
120  REM ***      THRS     TOTAL VIEWING HRS              ***
130  REM
140  REM *** DIMENSION THE TABLE SIZES. ***
150  DIM NME$(10),HRS(10),DAVG(10)
160  THRS = 0
170  REM
180  REM *** READ DATA AND CALCULATE TOTAL HOURS. ***
190  FOR I = 1 TO 10
200     READ NME$(I),HRS(I)
210     THRS = THRS + HRS(I)
220  NEXT I
230  AVG = THRS / 10
240  REM
250  REM *** CALCULATE DIFFERENCES. ***
260  FOR I = 1 TO 10
270     DAVG(I) = HRS(I) - AVG
280  NEXT I
290  REM
300  REM *** DISPLAY RESULTS. ***
310  PRINT "NAME","HRS";TAB(22);"DIFFERENCE FROM AVG"
320  FOR I = 1 TO 10
330     PRINT NME$(I),HRS(I),DAVG(I)
340  NEXT I
350  PRINT
360  PRINT "AVERAGE VIEWING TIME = ";AVG
370  REM
380  REM *** DATA STATEMENTS ***
390  DATA P. BUSCH, 1, C. CARSTENS, 5, J. DRAKE, 0, H. POIROT, 2
400  DATA M. BULAS, 7, D. CSONGAS, 3, C. HASTINGS, 4, T. ZEKLY, 11
410  DATA S. MCKINNIS, 3, G. BALDUCCI, 4
999  END
```

(figure continued on the next page)

FIGURE 9–1 Continued

```
RUN
NAME            HRS     DIFFERENCE FROM AVG
P. BUSCH         1              -3
C. CARSTENS      5               1
J. DRAKE         0              -4
H. POIROT        2              -2
M. BULAS         7               3
D. CSONGAS       3              -1
C. HASTINGS      4               0
T. ZEKLY        11               7
S. MCKINNIS      3              -1
G. BALDUCCI      4               0

AVERAGE VIEWING TIME =   4
```

Two-Dimensional Tables

The tables shown so far in this chapter have all been one-dimensional—that is, tables that store values in the form of a single list. Two-dimensional tables enable a programmer to represent more complex groups of data. For example, suppose that a fast-food restaurant chain is running a four-day promotional T-shirt sale at its three store locations. It might keep the following table of data concerning the number of shirts sold by each of the three restaurants.

		Store		
		1	2	3
	1	12	14	15
Day	2	10	16	12
	3	11	18	13
	4	9	9	10

Each row of the data refers to a specific day of the sale, and each column contains the sales data for one store. Thus, the number of shirts sold by the second store on the third day of the sale (18) can be found in the third row, second column.

Data items that can be grouped into rows and columns such as this can be stored easily in a two-dimensional table. A two-dimensional table named SHIRTS containing the preceding data can be pictured like this:

Table SHIRTS

12	14	15
10	16	12
11	18	13
9	9	10

The table SHIRTS consists of 12 elements arranged as four rows and three columns. In order to reference a single element of a two-dimensional table such as this, two subscripts are needed: one to indicate the row and a second to indicate the column. For instance, the subscripted variable SHIRTS(4,1) contains the number of shirts sold on the fourth day by the first store (9). In BASIC, the first subscript gives the row number and the second subscript gives the column number.

The rules regarding one-dimensional tables also apply to two-dimensional tables. Two-dimensional tables are named in the same way as other variables and cannot use the same name as another table (of any dimensions) in the same program. A two-dimensional table can contain only one type of data; numeric and character string values cannot be mixed.

As with one-dimensional tables, subscripts of two-dimensional tables can be indicated by any valid numeric expression:

```
SHIRTS(3,3)
SHIRTS(1,2)
SHIRTS(I,J)
SHIRTS(1,I+J)
```

Assume that I = 4 and J = 2, and that the table X contains the following 16 elements:

Table X

10	15	20	25
50	55	60	65
90	95	100	105
130	135	140	145

The following examples show how the various forms of subscripts are used:

Example	**Refers to**
X(4,I)	X(4,4)—The element in the fourth row, fourth column of X, which is 145.
X(J,I)	X(2,4)—The element in the second row, fourth column of X, which is 65.
X(3,J + 1)	X(3,3)—The element in the third row, third column, which is 100.
X(I − 1,J − 1)	X(3,1)—The element in the third row, first column, which is 90.

Now Try This

1. Write a DIM statement for a table to store the names of up to 150 inventory items. The table should be named ITEMS$.

2. Write a program segment to sum the 10 values in a numeric table named QUANTITY.

3. Table SALARIES has 30 elements. Write a program segment that displays elements 20 through 30.

4. Rewrite Exercise 3 so that elements 20 through 30 of table SALARIES are displayed in reverse order (element 30, element 29, and so forth). Use a FOR/NEXT loop with a negative step value.

If a two-dimensional table is not dimensioned, the BASIC system automatically sets aside space for a table with 11 rows and 11 columns. Thus, the "default" space for a two-dimensional table is $11 \times 11 = 121$ elements. If the zero positions of both the rows and the columns are ignored (as we have been doing in this book), the table can store a maximum of 100 elements (10×10). However, as previously mentioned, it is always better to use the DIM statement to dimension a table, regardless of its size. The format for the DIM statement for a two-dimensional table is

> line# DIM variable(limit1,limit2)

where the variable is the table name, and the limits are the highest possible values of the subscripts for each dimension. For example, the following statement reserves space for the two-dimensional string table STDNT$, with up to sixteen rows and six columns, for a total of $16 \times 6 = 96$ elements (or $15 \times 5 = 75$ elements if the subscripts begin at 1):

```
30 DIM STDNT$(15,5)
```

Manipulating Two-Dimensional Tables

Recall from the previous sections of this chapter that a FOR/NEXT loop is a convenient means of accessing all the elements of a one-dimensional table. The loop control variable of the FOR statement is used as the table subscript, and as the loop control variable changes value, so does the table subscript:

```
30 DIM X(5)
40 FOR I = 1 TO 5
50     INPUT "ENTER VALUE";X(I)
60 NEXT I
```

FOR/NEXT loops can also be used to read data to and display information from a two-dimensional table. It may be helpful to think of a two-dimensional table as a group of one-dimensional tables, with each row making up a single one-dimensional table. A single FOR/NEXT loop can read values to one row. This process is repeated for as many rows as the table contains; therefore, the FOR/NEXT loop that reads a single row is nested within a second FOR/NEXT loop controlling the number of rows being accessed.

The table SHIRTS of the previous example can be filled from the sales data table one row at a time, moving from left to right across the columns. The following segment shows the nested FOR/NEXT loops that do this:

```
130 FOR I = 1 TO 4
140     FOR J = 1 TO 3
150         READ SHIRTS(I,J)
160     NEXT J
170 NEXT I
```

Notice that each time line 150 is executed, one value is placed in a single element of the table; the element is determined by the current values of I and J. This statement is executed $4 \times 3 = 12$ times, which is the number of elements in the table.

The outer loop (loop I) controls the rows, and loop J controls the columns. Each time the outer loop is executed once, the inner loop is executed three times. While I = 1, J becomes 1, 2, and finally 3 as the inner loop is executed. Therefore, line 150 reads values to SHIRTS(1,1), SHIRTS(1,2), and SHIRTS(1,3), and the first row is filled:

	J = 1	J = 2	J = 3
I = 1	12	14	15

While I equals 2, J again varies from 1 to 3, and line 150 reads values to SHIRTS(2,1), SHIRTS(2,2), and SHIRTS(2,3) to fill the second row:

	J = 1	J = 2	J = 3
	12	14	15
I = 2	10	16	12

I is incremented to 3 and then to 4, and the third and fourth rows are filled in the same manner.

To display the contents of the entire table, the programmer can substitute a PRINT statement for the READ statement in the nested FOR/NEXT loops. The following segment prints the contents of the table SHIRTS, one row at a time:

```
220 FOR I = 1 TO 4
230     PRINT I;
240     FOR J = 1 TO 3
250         PRINT TAB(J*10) SHIRTS(I,J);
260     NEXT J
270     PRINT
280 NEXT I
```

The semicolon at the end of line 250 tells the BASIC system to display the three values on the same line. After the inner loop is executed, the blank PRINT statement in line 270 causes a carriage return so that the next row is displayed on the next line. The program in Figure 9–2 shows how the data table for the T-shirt sales results can be read to a two-dimensional table and displayed in table form with appropriate headings.

Adding Row Elements

Once data have been stored in a table, it is often necessary to manipulate certain table elements. For instance, the sales manager in charge of the T-shirt promotional sale might want to know how many shirts were sold on the last day of the sale.

Because the data for each day are contained in a row of the table, it is necessary to total the elements in one row of the table (the fourth row) to find the number of shirts sold on the fourth day. The fourth row can be thought of by itself as a one-dimensional table. One loop is therefore required to access all the elements of this row:

```
30 D4SALES = 0
40 FOR J = 1 TO 3
50     D4SALES = D4SALES + SHIRTS(4,J)
60 NEXT J
```

Notice that the first subscript of SHIRTS(4,J) restricts the computations to the elements in row 4, while the column J varies from 1 to 3. The process performed in line 50 is pictured in the following diagram:

FIGURE 9–2   Program Using a Two-Dimensional Table

```
10    REM ***                    T-SHIRT SALES REPORT              ***
20    REM
30    REM *** THIS PROGRAM PRINTS A REPORT ON THE NUMBER OF        ***
40    REM *** T-SHIRTS SOLD PER STORE FOR 4 DIFFERENT DAYS.        ***
50    REM *** MAJOR VARIABLES:                                     ***
60    REM ***      SHIRTS         TABLE OF T-SHIRTS SOLD           ***
70    REM ***      I,J            LOOP CONTROL VARIABLES           ***
80    REM
90    REM *** DIMENSION ARRAY. ***
100   DIM SHIRTS(4,3)
110   REM
120   REM *** READ THE DATA. ***
130   FOR I = 1 TO 4
140       FOR J = 1 TO 3
150           READ SHIRTS(I,J)
160       NEXT J
170   NEXT I
180   REM *** DISPLAY TABLE OF QUANTITIES SOLD. ***
190   REM
200   PRINT "DAY #";TAB(10);"STORE 1";TAB(20);"STORE 2";TAB(30);"STORE 3"
210   FOR I = 1 TO 4
220       PRINT I;
230       FOR J = 1 TO 3
240           PRINT TAB(J*10);SHIRTS(I,J);
250       NEXT J
260       PRINT
270   NEXT I
280   REM
290   REM *** DATA STATEMENTS ***
300   DATA 12,4,15,10,6,12,11,8,13,9,9,10
999   END
```

```
RUN
DAY #       STORE 1     STORE 2     STORE 3
 1           12          4           15
 2           10          6           12
 3           11          8           13
 4            9          9           10
```

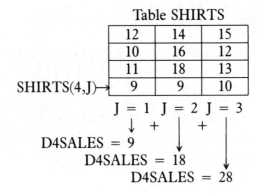

Table SHIRTS

Adding Column Elements

To find the total number of T-shirts sold by the third store, it is necessary to total the elements in the third column of the table. This time we can think of the column by itself as a one-dimensional table of four elements. This operation calls for a FOR/NEXT loop, as shown here:

```
40 S3SHOP = 0
50 FOR I = 1 TO 4
60    S3SHOP = S3SHOP + SHIRTS(I,3)
70 NEXT I
```

In line 60, the second subscript (3) restricts the computations to the elements in the third column, while the row I varies from 1 to 4. This process is pictured in the following diagram:

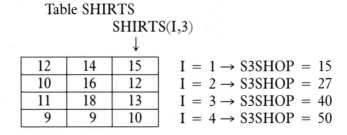

Table SHIRTS

Totaling Two-Dimensional Table Elements

Consider now the problem of finding the grand total of all T-shirts sold during the entire four-day special offer. The program must access all the elements of the table one at a time and add them to the grand total. Remember that nested FOR/NEXT loops were used to display or read values to a two-dimensional table. This same method can be used to total the elements of a table by substituting an addition operation for the INPUT or PRINT statement:

```
50   TOTAL.SHIRTS = 0
60   FOR I = 1 TO 4
70      FOR J = 1 TO 3
80         TOTAL.SHIRTS = TOTAL.SHIRTS + SHIRTS(I,J)
90      NEXT J
100 NEXT I
```

This segment adds the elements in a row-by-row sequence. While I equals 1, the inner loop causes J to vary from 1 to 3, thus adding the contents of the first row elements to the total accumulated in TOTAL .SHIRTS. When the outer loop terminates, the contents of all four rows will have been added to the total.

This totaling of all the elements of the table can also be performed in a column-by-column sequence:

```
50   TOTAL.SHIRTS = 0
60   FOR J = 1 TO 3
70      FOR I = 1 TO 4
80         TOTAL.SHIRTS = TOTAL.SHIRTS + SHIRTS(I,J)
90      NEXT I
100 NEXT J
```

Note that the two loops have been interchanged from the first example. Now the outer loop, loop J, controls the columns, and the inner loop, loop I, controls the rows. While J equals 1, I varies from 1 to 4, and the elements of the first column are added to the total: SHIRTS(1,1), SHIRTS(2,1), SHIRTS(3,1), and SHIRTS(4,1). J is then incremented to 2, the second column is added, and so on.

Sorting

Many programming applications require data items stored in tables to be sorted or ordered in some way. For example, names must be alphabetized, social security numbers must be arranged from lowest to highest, sports statistics must be arranged by numeric value, and so on.

Of course, when dealing with short lists of data, it is no problem to arrange the items mentally in their proper order. In the following example, it is fairly simple to arrange the scores from lowest to highest:

Table 1 (unsorted)	Table 2 (sorted)
75	55
92	66
66	75
100	92
55	100

If there were 100 test scores to sort, however, the operation would be quite tedious and time-consuming. Fortunately, the computer is well suited to this task. There are various methods the programmer can use to sort data items, some more efficient than others. In the next section, you will learn the bubble sort, as it is relatively easy to understand.

The Bubble Sort

Bubble sort

A sort that progressively arranges the elements of a table in ascending or descending order by making a series of comparisons of the adjacent table values and exchanging values that are out of order.

The basic idea behind the **bubble sort** is to arrange the elements of a table progressively in ascending or descending order by making a series of comparisons of the adjacent values in the table. If the adjacent values are out of sequence, they are exchanged.

When arranging a table in ascending order, the bubble sort "bubbles" the largest values to the end. The values of adjacent table elements are compared and are switched if the value of the first element is larger than the value of the second. Then the next pair of adjacent elements is compared and switched if necessary.

This sequence of comparisons (called a *pass*) is then repeated, starting from the beginning. After each complete pass through the table, however, the element moved to the end of the table need not be included in the comparisons of the next pass, because it is now in its proper position. Successive passes are continued through the table until no elements are switched, indicating that the entire table is sorted.

To illustrate this bubbling procedure, a table consisting of five integers is sorted into ascending order in Figure 9–3. Notice that after each pass is completed, the largest of the numbers compared in that pass is moved to the end of those numbers. After one pass through the table, some of the numbers are closer to their proper positions, but the table is not yet completely ordered. The largest value, 7, has been successfully positioned at the end of the table and is therefore not included in the comparisons of the following passes.

After each pass is made through the table, the program checks a "flag" that indicates whether the table is in its final order. After a fourth pass through, the table is completely arranged in ascending order, but another pass is required to set the flag value to indicate this fact.

From this illustration, we get an idea of the steady "bubbling" process involved in this sorting routine. Now let's take a look at the actual code for a bubble sort, as illustrated in Figure 9–4.

This program sorts ten astronaut names into alphabetical order. Because the computer automatically assigns a collating sequence (or ASCII) value to every character it is capable of representing, it compares the ASCII values for each letter to determine that the letter A is less than the letter B, B is less than C, and so on. The subroutine starting at line 1000 simply reads the astronauts' names into a table ASTRO$ and displays them. The subroutine starting at line 2000 performs the bubble sort. Let us examine it carefully to see what happens.

FIGURE 9–3   The Bubble
Sort Process

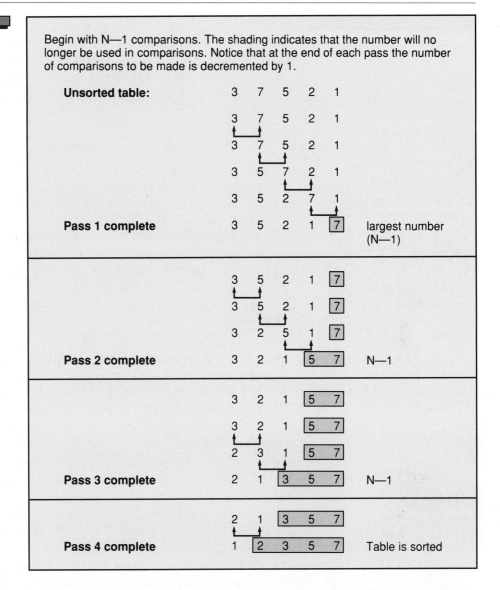

Begin with N—1 comparisons. The shading indicates that the number will no longer be used in comparisons. Notice that at the end of each pass the number of comparisons to be made is decremented by 1.

Line 2060 refers to the variable FLAG. It is initialized to 1; its value is later checked by the computer to determine if the entire table has been sorted.

Notice that FINL is set to one less than the number of items to be sorted. This is because two items at a time are compared. J varies from 1 to 9, which means that the computer eventually will compare item 9 with item 9 + 1. If the terminal value were 10 (the number of names), the computer would try to compare item 10 with item 11, which does not exist in the table.

The IF/THEN statement in line 2100 tells the computer whether to interchange two compared values. For example, when J = 1, the computer compares JETSON, G. with SOLONG, H. Because J is less than S, there is no need to switch these two items:

FIGURE 9–4   Bubble Sort Program

```
10    REM ***                    ASTRONAUT'S MIX-UP               ***
20    REM
30    REM *** THIS PROGRAM SORTS THE ASTRONAUTS OF THE    ***
40    REM *** ASTRO AIR STATION INTO ALPHABETICAL ORDER. ***
50    REM *** MAJOR VARIABLES:                            ***
60    REM ***    ASTRO$          NAMES OF THE ASTRONAUTS  ***
70    REM ***    FLAG            EXCHANGES MADE?           ***
80    REM
90    REM *** DIMENSION NAME TABLE.  ***
100   DIM ASTRO$(10)
110   REM
120   REM *** READ UNSORTED NAMES TO TABLE AND DISPLAY THEM. ***
130   GOSUB 1000
140   REM
150   REM *** BUBBLE SORT. ***
160   GOSUB 2000
170   REM
180   REM *** DISPLAY SORTED LIST. ***
190   GOSUB 3000
999   END
1000  REM *********************************************************
1010  REM ***             SUBROUTINE ORIGINAL LIST          ***
1020  REM *********************************************************
1030  REM ***   READ NAMES INTO TABLE AND DISPLAY THEM.     ***
1040  REM
1050  PRINT "ASTRO AIR STATION--UNSORTED"
1060  PRINT
1070  FOR I = 1 TO 10
1080     READ ASTRO$(I)
1090     PRINT ASTRO$(I)
1100  NEXT I
1110  PRINT
1120  PRINT
1130  REM *** DATA STATEMENTS ***
1140  DATA "JETSON, G.", "SOLONG, H.", "QUIRK, J."
1150  DATA "SKYWALTZER, L.", "MADER, D.", "MCSOY, DR."
1160  DATA "KANOBI, B.", "SPECK, MR.", "OHORROR, LT."
1170  DATA "CHECKUP, V."
1180  RETURN
2000  REM *********************************************************
2010  REM ***               SUBROUTINE BUBBLE SORT           ***
2020  REM *********************************************************
2030  REM *** SORT LIST OF NAMES IN ASCENDING ORDER.         ***
2040  REM
2050  FINL = 9
2060  FLAG = 1
2070  WHILE FLAG = 1
2080     FLAG = 0
2090     FOR J = 1 TO FINL
```

FIGURE 9–4 Continued

```
2100       IF ASTRO$(J) > ASTRO$(J+1) THEN SWAP ASTRO$(J), ASTRO$(J+1)
           : FLAG = 1
2110    NEXT J
2120    FINL = FINL - 1
2130 WEND
2140 RETURN
3000 REM ***********************************************************
3010 REM ***          SUBROUTINE DISPLAY SORTED LIST          ***
3020 REM ***********************************************************
3030 REM ***    DISPLAY HEADING AND SORTED NAMES.             ***
3040 REM
3050 PRINT "ASTRO AIR STATION -- SORTED"
3060 PRINT
3070 FOR I = 1 TO 10
3080    PRINT ASTRO$(I)
3090 NEXT I
3100 RETURN
```

```
RUN
ASTRO AIR STATION--UNSORTED

JETSON, G.
SOLONG, H.
QUIRK, J.
SKYWALTZER, L.
MADER, D.
MCSOY, DR.
KANOBI, B.
SPECK, MR.
OHORROR, LT.
CHECKUP, V.


ASTRO AIR STATION -- SORTED

CHECKUP, V.
JETSON, G.
KANOBI, B.
MADER, D.
MCSOY, DR.
OHORROR, LT.
QUIRK, J.
SKYWALTZER, L.
SOLONG, H.
SPECK, MR.
```

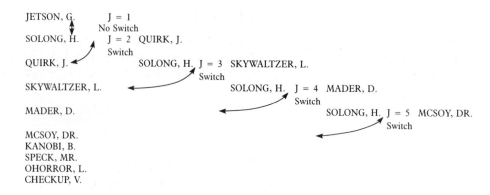

Then J is incremented to 2, and SOLONG, H. is compared with QUIRK, J. Because QUIRK comes before SOLONG, these two names must be exchanged. Microsoft BASIC contains a special statement, called the SWAP statement, that allows the values in two variables to be exchanged. After the following program segment is executed, X will equal 10 and Y will equal 20:

```
10 X = 20
20 Y = 10
30 SWAP X,Y
```

Line 2100 in Figure 9–4 uses the SWAP statement to exchange the out-of-order names. In addition, FLAG is set to 1, indicating an exchange has taken place.

The FOR/NEXT loop in lines 2090–2110 continues until every item in the table has been examined. After one pass through the FOR/NEXT loop, the table ASTRO$ looks like this:

JETSON, G.
QUIRK J.
SKYWALTZER, L.
MADER, D.
KANOBI, B.
SOLONG, H.
OHORROR, L.
CHECKUP, V.
SPECK, MR.

Although several switches have been made, the list is not sorted completely. That is why we need the WHILE loop. As long as FLAG equals 1, the computer knows that switches have been made, and the sorting process must continue. When the loop is completed without setting FLAG equal to 1—that is, when no switches are made—the computer finds FLAG equal to 0 and knows that the list is ordered. Numbers can also be sorted by this same method.

The Merge Sort

Merge sort

A sort that combines two sorted tables into a single sorted table.

The **merge sort** is yet another type of sort. It merges, or combines, two sorted lists into one larger sorted list. Suppose that two sorted integer tables, table A and table B, need to be merged into table C:

Table A
2	4

Table B
1	2	3

To begin, the first elements in each table are compared to each other and the smaller integer is placed in table C. Because 1 is less than 2, table C looks like this:

Table C
1				

The integer placed into table C is not considered again. Next, the integer 2 in table A is compared to the integer 2 in table B. They are of equal value, so table B is chosen arbitrarily to supply the next element of table C. The 2 in table B is no longer considered. Table C now appears this way:

Table C
1	2			

The integers 2 (of table A) and 3 (of table B) are now compared. Because 2 is less than 3, 2 is moved into table C:

Table C
1	2	2		

The 2 in table A is no longer considered. Now 3 and 4 are compared, and 3 is moved into table C:

Table C
1	2	2	3	

At this point, all of table B has been transferred into table C. The remaining element of table A is now moved to table C; if table A were larger, many integers would need to be moved. Table C finally contains all the elements of both A and B, in sorted order:

Table C
1	2	2	3	4

Figure 9–5 presents a subroutine that performs a merge sort. It is assumed that the sizes of tables A and B have been established in the main program, and that table C is large enough to hold the elements of both tables. The loop of lines 1110 through 1140 places values into C until either A or B has no more elements left to be considered.

As indicated in the preceding traced example, if two compared integers are equal, the integer from table B is placed in table C. This comparison and the appropriate move into C are made in line 1120. The WHILE loop of lines 1170 through 1210 adds the remaining elements of table A (if any) to the end of C. If values of A run out before those of B, the loop of lines 1230 through 1270 adds the remaining values of B to table C.

Searching

A table search consists of examining the contents of a table until a desired value or values are found. For example, you may want to know the number of scores greater than 89 in an array QUIZ containing 40 test scores. The following segment performs this task:

```
50 CNT = 0
60 FOR I = 1 TO 40
70 IF QUIZ(I) > 89 THEN CNT = CNT + 1
80 NEXT I
```

The variable CNT holds a count of the scores greater than 89. The loop is set up to check the value of each table element in numeric order, and the count is incremented only if the score being checked is greater than 89.

Another type of search might involve locating a single value. Suppose you wanted information regarding the August 19th concert at the local concert hall. The computer might prompt you to enter the data of the concert in which you are interested. It then would search a table of concert dates until it matched the given date. Finally, the computer would access the corresponding values from the tables containing the rest of the concert information and display those values on the monitor screen.

Note that if more than one table holds corresponding (related) data, the data must be contained in the same relative position in each table. In other words, if the desired date matches the third element of the date table, the third elements of the other tables are also accessed. This process is shown in Figure 9–6.

Sequential search

A search that examines table elements in order until the desired element or elements are found.

Both the searches just described are **sequential searches,** which examine the first element, then the second element, then the third, and so on in numeric sequence until the desired element is found or the end of the table is reached.

FIGURE 9–5   Merge Sort Subroutine

```
1000 REM **************************************************
1010 REM ***            SUBROUTINE MERGE SORT           ***
1020 REM **************************************************
1030 REM ***  MERGE SORTED TABLES A AND B INTO C.  ***
1040 REM
1050 REM ***          INITIALIZE TABLE INDEXES.          ***
1060 AINDX = 1
1070 BINDX = 1
1080 CINDX = 1
1090 REM
1100 REM *** MERGE UNTIL END OF A TABLE IS REACHED. ***
1110 WHILE (AINDX <= ASIZE) AND (BINDX <= BSIZE)
1120     IF A(AINDX) < B(BINDX) THEN C(CINDX) = A(AINDX) : AINDX = AINDX + 1
             ELSE C(CINDX) = B(BINDX) : BINDX = BINDX + 1
1130     CINDX = CINDX + 1
1140 WEND
1150 REM
1160 REM *** ADD REMAINING ITEMS TO END OF NEW TABLE. ***
1170 WHILE AINDX <= ASIZE
1180     C(CINDX) = A(AINDX)
1190     AINDX = AINDX + 1
1200     CINDX = CINDX + 1
1210 WEND
1220 REM
1230 WHILE BINDX <= BSIZE
1240     C(CINDX) = B(BINDX)
1250     BINDX = BINDX + 1
1260     CINDX = CINDX + 1
1270 WEND
1280 RETURN
```

FIGURE 9–6   Concert
Information Example

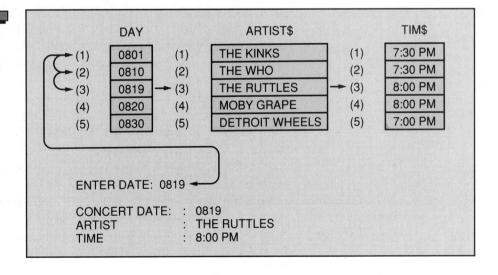

Now Try This

1. Write a DIM statement for a two-dimensional table PRODUCTS that has 40 rows and 12 columns.

2. Write a program segment that totals the columns of a table whose DIM statement follows, putting the sums of the columns in a one-dimensional table SUMS:

   `10 DIM X(15,20)`

3. Rewrite Exercise 2 so that SUMS contains the sums of the rows rather than the sums of the columns.

4. Write a program segment that uses a WHILE loop to search a table GRADES for a value of 17. When this value is located, the loop should stop executing. GRADES has 20 elements.

A Programming Problem

Problem Definition

The scorekeepers of the Centrovian Open Ice Skating Championships need a program to determine the winner of the final round. Each competitor is given six scores, of which the highest and lowest are discarded. The remaining four scores are then averaged to obtain the final score. The maximum score for each event is 6.0. Write a program that allows the user to enter the names and scores of ten finalists and produces a printed listing of the skaters' names and final scores in order of finish. The program specification chart is shown in Figure 9–7. The listing should be printed on paper using the format given in Figure 9–8.

Solution Design

The problem provides us with seven items of data for each skater—a name and six scores—and asks for a list of names and averages, sorted by average. Once the data items have been entered (the first step), there are two basic operations that must be performed in order to produce the listing: the averages must be calculated, and these averages with their associated names must be sorted. Thus, the problem can be broken into four major tasks: (1) enter the data, (2) calculate the averages, (3) sort the names and averages, and (4) print the sorted information. The structure chart is shown in Figure 9–9.

FIGURE 9–7 Program
Specification Chart for
Skating Competition Problem

PROGRAM SPECIFICATION CHART

PROGRAM NAME:	PROGRAMMER'S NAME:	DATE:
Skating Final Results	S. Baumann	2/7/92

INPUT:
Each skater's name and 6
judges' scores for that skater.

OUTPUT:
Printed listing of skating
competition results, see figure 9-8

SOURCE OF INPUT:
Stored in program

DESTINATION OF OUTPUT:
Paper

PURPOSE: This program reads the name of each skater
in the skating competition and the 6 judges' scores. Each
skater's high and low score is disregarded and the remaining
scores are averaged. The scores are then sorted in descending order.

The input for this problem consists of two types of data, alphabetic and numeric, so two tables must be used to store them. The output calls for the names already stored plus a new set of values, the averages, so another table can be used to store these averages. In calculating the averages, variables will also be needed to keep track of the high and low scores. The main variables needed can be summarized as follows.

Input variables

| table of names | (SKNM$) |
| table of scores | (PTS) |

Program variables

high score for a competitor	(HI)
low score for a competitor	(LO)
total of four scores	(TPTS)

Output variables

| table of averages | (AVG) |

In order to calculate the averages, a search must be done on the six scores of each skater to find the high and low scores.

FIGURE 9–8   Printer Spacing Chart for Skating Competition Problem

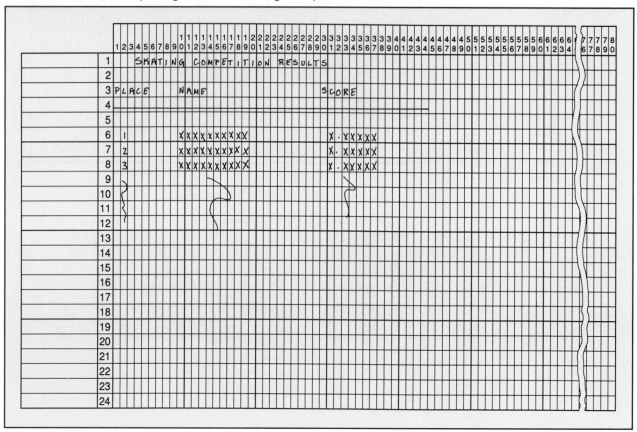

FIGURE 9–9   Structure Chart for Skating Competition Problem

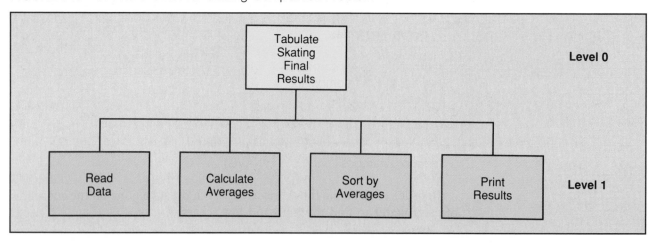

A sort is required in the third step of our algorithm. A descending-order bubble sort will be used here. A crucial point is that, as the averages are rearranged, the corresponding skater's name must be carried with each average. This means, for example, that the average for the fourth skater (SKNM$(4)) must be stored in AVG(4). The flowchart and pseudocode in Figure 9–10 illustrate the logic of the solution.

The Program

The program of Figure 9–11 shows the solution to the problem. Line 140 of the main program reserves space for a two-dimensional table for the scores. Each row of table PTS contains the scores for one skater, so ten rows with six columns each are needed.

The first subroutine called by the main program reads the names and scores to their respective tables. The second subroutine finds the average score of each skater. It does this by performing a sequential search on each row of the scores table (table PTS) in lines 2080 through 2110. When the low and high scores for the row have been found, lines 2150 through 2170 add all the scores for that row. Then the high and low scores are subtracted and the average for that row is calculated.

The sorting of the final averages is performed in the bubble sort of the third subroutine. The condition AVG(COUNT)<AVG(COUNT+1) in line 3100 causes the averages to be sorted from highest to lowest. Every time an average is moved, its corresponding name from the array SKNM$ is also moved. The sorted results are printed by the fourth subroutine in lines 4000 through 4130.

Programming Hints

When programming with tables, keep the following points in mind.

■ Remember that only numbers can be stored in numeric variable tables, and only character strings can be stored in string variable tables.
■ The BASIC system automatically reserves room for only 11 elements if a one-dimensional table is not declared in a DIM statement, and 11 rows and columns for a two-dimensional table. It is good programming practice to dimension all tables, regardless of their size.
■ A DIM statement must appear before the table that it dimensions is used in the program.
■ Remember that the first subscript refers to the rows of a table, and the second subscript refers to its columns.
■ Table subscripts can vary in the program from 0 to the limit declared in the DIM statement, but no subscript can exceed that limit.
■ A name used for a two-dimensional table cannot be used for a one-dimensional table in the same program.
■ A merge sort can be performed only on two lists that are sorted in ascending or descending order.

FIGURE 9–10 Flowchart and Pseudocode for Skating Competition Problem

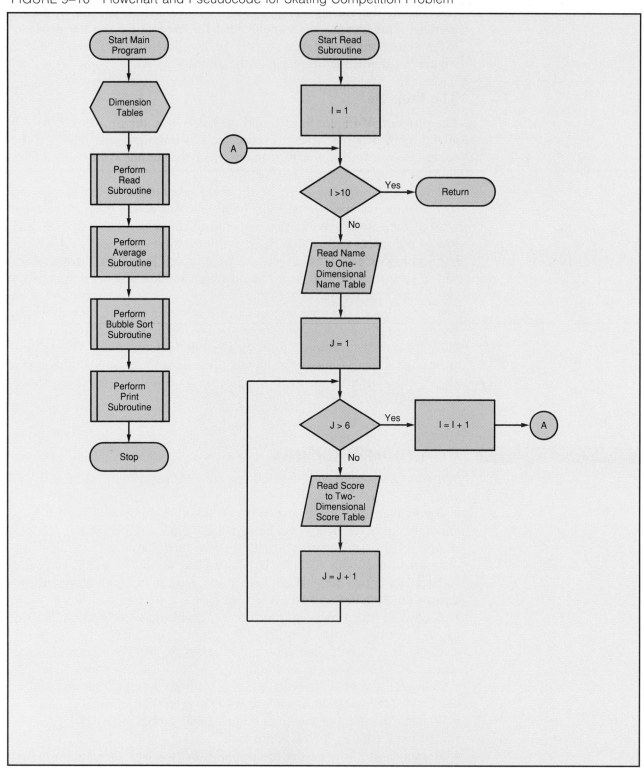

FIGURE 9–10 Continued

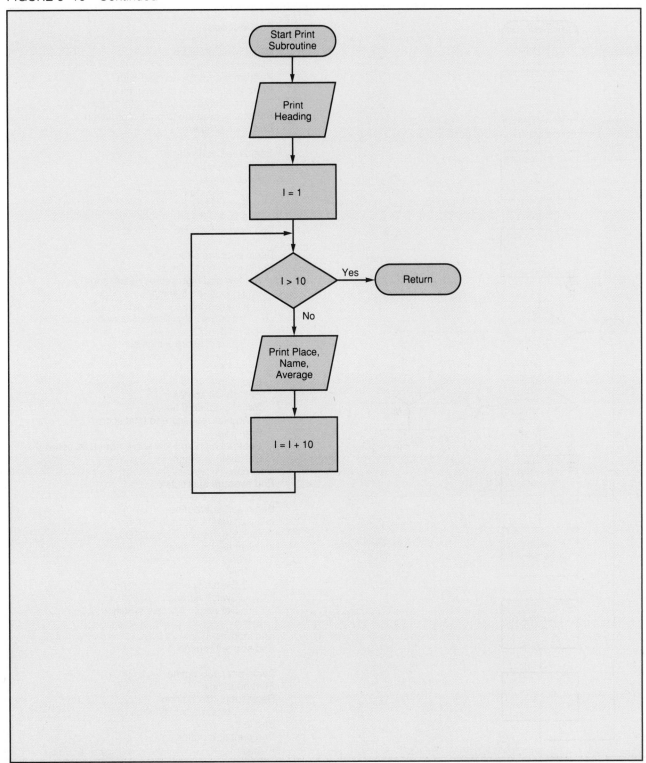

(figure continued on the next page)

FIGURE 9–10   Continued

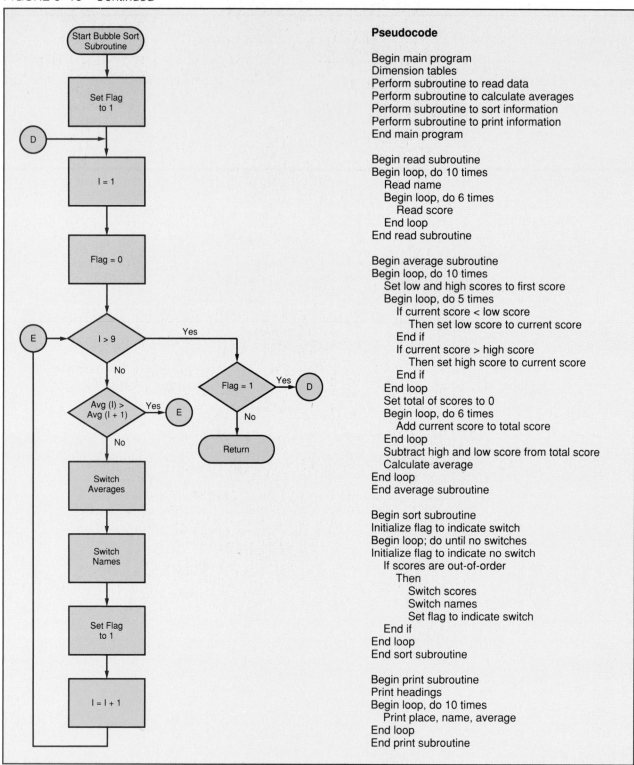

Pseudocode

Begin main program
Dimension tables
Perform subroutine to read data
Perform subroutine to calculate averages
Perform subroutine to sort information
Perform subroutine to print information
End main program

Begin read subroutine
Begin loop, do 10 times
   Read name
     Begin loop, do 6 times
       Read score
     End loop
End read subroutine

Begin average subroutine
Begin loop, do 10 times
   Set low and high scores to first score
   Begin loop, do 5 times
     If current score < low score
       Then set low score to current score
     End if
     If current score > high score
       Then set high score to current score
     End if
   End loop
   Set total of scores to 0
   Begin loop, do 6 times
     Add current score to total score
   End loop
   Subtract high and low score from total score
   Calculate average
End loop
End average subroutine

Begin sort subroutine
Initialize flag to indicate switch
Begin loop; do until no switches
Initialize flag to indicate no switch
   If scores are out-of-order
     Then
       Switch scores
       Switch names
       Set flag to indicate switch
   End if
End loop
End sort subroutine

Begin print subroutine
Print headings
Begin loop, do 10 times
   Print place, name, average
End loop
End print subroutine

FIGURE 9–10 Continued

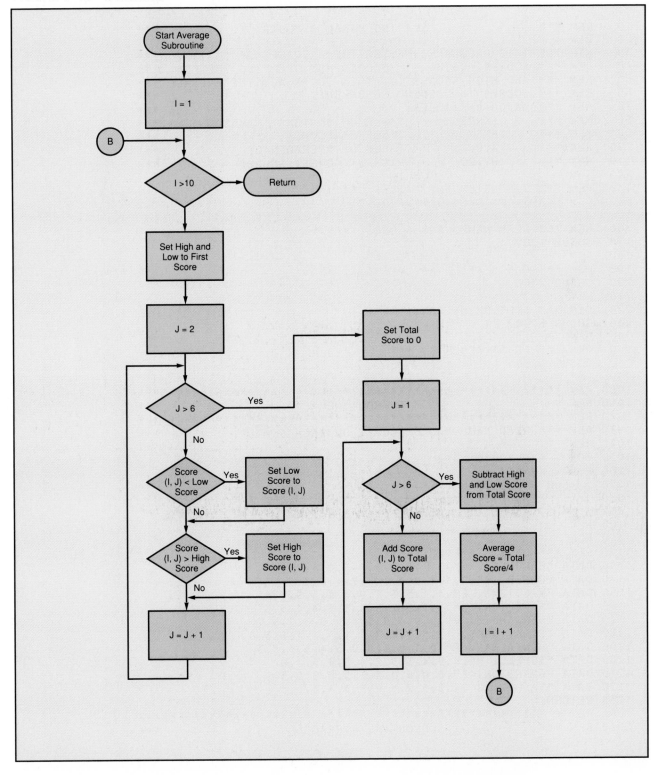

FIGURE 9–11   Skating Competition Program

```
10    REM ***                    SKATING FINAL RESULTS              ***
20    REM
30    REM *** THIS PROGRAM COMPUTES THE AVERAGES OF SKATING          ***
40    REM *** SCORES, USING SIX SCORES AND DROPPING THE LOW          ***
50    REM *** AND HIGH SCORES. IT THEN SORTS ALL THE AVERAGE         ***
60    REM *** SCORES IN DESCENDING ORDER.                            ***
70    REM *** MAJOR VARIABLES:                                       ***
80    REM ***        SKNM$           TABLE OF SKATERS' NAMES         ***
90    REM ***        PTS             TABLE OF SCORES                 ***
100   REM ***        AVG             TABLE OF AVERAGES               ***
110   REM ***        HI,LO           HIGHEST/LOWEST SCORES           ***
120   REM
130   REM *** DIMENSION THE TABLES. ***
140   DIM SKNM$(10),PTS(10,6),AVG(10)
150   REM
160   REM *** READ NAMES AND SCORES. ***
170   GOSUB 1000
180   REM
190   REM *** CALCULATE FINAL AVERAGE. ***
200   GOSUB 2000
210   REM
220   REM *** SORT BY AVERAGE. ***
230   GOSUB 3000
240   REM
250   REM *** PRINT RESULTS. ***
260   GOSUB 4000
999   END
1000  REM ***********************************************************
1010  REM ***                    SUBROUTINE READ                   ***
1020  REM ***********************************************************
1030  REM *** READ NAME AND 6 SCORES OF EACH SKATER.               ***
1040  REM
1050  FOR I = 1 TO 10
1060  READ SKNM$(I)
1070     FOR J = 1 TO 6
1080        READ PTS(I,J)
1090     NEXT J
1100  NEXT I
1110  REM
1120  REM *** DATA STATEMENTS ***
1130  DATA "BALDUCCI, G",5.7,5.3,5.1,5.0,4.7,4.8
1140  DATA "CREED, A",3.1,4.9,4.1,3.7,4.6,3.9
1150  DATA "WILLIAMS, E",4.1,5.3,4.9,4.4,3.9,5.4
1160  DATA "HAMILTON, S",5.1,5.7,5.6,5.5,4.4,5.3
1170  DATA "HERNANDEZ, P",5.9,4.8,5.5,5.0,5.7,5.7
1180  DATA "STRAVINSKY, I",5.1,4.7,4.1,3.1,4.6,5.0
1190  DATA "MONTALBAN, R",5.1,5.1,4.9,3.4,5.5,5.3
1200  DATA "SCHELL, M",4.9,4.3,5.2,4.5,4.6,4.9
1210  DATA "CRANSTON, T",6.0,6.0,5.7,5.8,5.9,5.9
1220  DATA "VALDEZ, S",4.3,5.2,5.9,5.3,4.3,6.0
1230  RETURN
2000  REM ***********************************************************
2010  REM ***                    SUBROUTINE AVERAGE                 ***
```

FIGURE 9–11   Continued

```
2020 REM ************************************************************
2030 REM ***     DROP HIGH/LOW SCORES, THEN AVERAGE SCORE.     ***
2040 REM
2050 FOR I = 1 TO 10
2060    HI = PTS(I,1)
2070    LO = PTS(I,1)
2080    FOR J = 2 TO 6
2090       IF PTS(I,J) < LO THEN LO = PTS(I,J)
2100       IF PTS(I,J) > HI THEN HI = PTS(I,J)
2110    NEXT J
2120    REM
2130    REM *** TOTAL SCORES. ***
2140    TPTS = 0
2150    FOR J = 1 TO 6
2160       TPTS = TPTS + PTS(I,J)
2170    NEXT J
2180    REM *** SUBTRACT HIGH AND LOW SCORE FROM TOTAL. ***
2190    TPTS = TPTS - LO - HI
2200    REM *** DIVIDE REMAINING TOTAL BY FOUR. ***
2210    AVG(I) = TPTS / 4
2220 NEXT I
2230 RETURN
3000 REM ************************************************************
3010 REM ***                SUBROUTINE BUBBLE SORT              ***
3020 REM ************************************************************
3030 REM ***          SORT AVERAGES IN DESCENDING ORDER.        ***
3040 REM
3050 FLAG = 1
3060 FINAL = 9
3070 WHILE FLAG = 1
3080    FLAG = 0
3090    FOR COUNT = 1 TO FINAL
3100       IF AVG(COUNT) < AVG(COUNT+1) THEN SWAP AVG(COUNT), AVG(COUNT+1)
               : SWAP SKNM$(COUNT), SKNM$(COUNT+1) : FLAG = 1
3110    NEXT COUNT
3120    FINAL = FINAL - 1
3130 WEND
3140 RETURN
4000 REM ************************************************************
4010 REM ***                SUBROUTINE PRINT RESULTS            ***
4020 REM ************************************************************
4030 REM ***          PRINT THE HEADINGS AND THE RESULTS.       ***
4040 REM
4050 LPRINT TAB(4);"SKATING COMPETITION RESULTS"
4060 LPRINT
4070 LPRINT "PLACE";TAB(10);"NAME";TAB(30);"SCORE"
4080 LPRINT "------------------------------------------"
4090 LPRINT
4100 FOR I = 1 TO 10
4110    LPRINT I;TAB(10);SKNM$(I);TAB(30);AVG(I)
4120 NEXT I
4130 RETURN
```

(figure continued on the next page)

FIGURE 9–11 Continued

```
          SKATING COMPETITION RESULTS

     PLACE       NAME                    SCORE
     ---------------------------------------------

       1          CRANSTON, T            5.9
       2          HERNANDEZ, P           5.475001
       3          HAMILTON, S            5.375
       4          VALDEZ, S              5.175
       5          MONTALBAN, R           5.1
       6          BALDUCCI, G            5.049999
       7          SCHELL, M              4.725001
       8          WILLIAMS, E            4.675
       9          STRAVINSKY, I          4.6
      10          CREED, A               4.075
```

New Statement Review

Statement Format	Explanation
line# DIM table-name(limit)	Dimensions a one-dimensional table. Subscripts can range from 0 through *limit*.
line# DIM table-name(limit1,limit2)	Dimensions a two-dimensional table. Row subscripts can range from 0 through *limit1*, and column subscripts can range from 0 through *limit2*.
line# SWAP variable1,variable2	Interchanges the values of two variables.

Summary Points

- A table is a collection of related values stored under a single variable name.
- Individual table elements can be accessed by using subscripts.
- A subscript of a table element can be any legal numeric expression.
- The DIM statement sets up storage for arrays and must appear before the first reference to the table it describes.
- Table manipulation is carried out through the use of loops.
- A two-dimensional table stores values as a table, grouped into rows and columns.

- The first subscript of a two-dimensional table refers to the element's row and the second subscript to the column.
- The bubble sort places elements of a table in ascending or descending order by comparing adjacent elements.
- The merge sort combines two sorted lists into one larger, sorted list.
- A sequential search of a table consists of examining each element in the table until the desired value is located.

Vocabulary List

Array	Sequential search
Bubble sort	Subscript
Element	Subscripted variable
Index	Table
Merge sort	Unsubscripted variable

Questions

Whenever appropriate, use complete sentences in answering the following questions.

1. What is a table?

2. Variables that refer to specific elements in a table are called _____variables, whereas simple variables are called _____ variables.

3. Give two advantages of using tables.

4. What is a subscript?

5. Given the following program segment, create a diagram showing how table AMOUNT will appear in storage.

```
10 DIM AMOUNT(6)
20 X = 4
30 AMOUNT(X-1) = 14.35
40 AMOUNT(2^2) = 80.42
50 AMOUNT(14-13) = 19.8
60 AMOUNT(2*3) = 45.79
```

6. Assume $X = 1$, $Y = 2$, and $Z = 3$. What are the values of the variables $A(X)$, $A(Y - X)$, and $A(X * Z)$ if table A contains the following values?

Table A

1	11
2	42
3	37
4	90
5	17

7. In a two-dimensional table, the first subscript refers to the _____, and the second subscript refers to the _____.

8. Explain the difference between a two-dimensional and a one-dimensional table.

9. What is the maximum number of elements that can be contained in each of the following two-dimensional tables (ignoring the zero subscript positions)?

a. `120 DIM POSITION(35,17)`
b. `10 DIM CLASS(6,3)`
c. `40 DIM TAX(100,85)`

10. Use the following program segment, create a diagram like the one below and show how table GROSS.PAY will appear in storage.

```
10 DIM GROSS.PAY(3,5)
20 X = 7
30 Y = 3
40 GROSS.PAY(Y-1,4) = 1715.75
50 GROSS.PAY(Y/3,3) = 1203.01
60 GROSS.PAY(X-4,2*2) = 1593.09
70 GROSS.PAY(3,10-9) = 2080.52
```

	1	2	3	4	5
1					
2					
3					

11. How are nested loop statements used to display the contents of a two-dimensional table?

12. Explain how the bubble sort works.

13. The _____ sort combines two sorted lists into a single sorted list.

14. How is a sequential search performed?

15. How does searching a two-dimensional table differ from searching a one-dimensional table?

Debugging Exercises

Identify the following programs or program segments that contain errors, and debug them.

```
1. 10 REM *** ENTERS DATA TO TABLE A. ***
   20 FOR I = 1 TO 20
   30     INPUT "ENTER VALUE";A(I)
   40 NEXT I
   99 END
```

```
2. 10 REM *** TOTAL ELEMENTS OF TABLE. ***
   20 DIM X(10)
   30 T = 0
   40 FOR I = 1 TO 10
   50    T = T + X(1)
   60 NEXT I
```

```
3. 10 REM *** READ THE CONTENTS OF THE 2-DIMENSIONAL TABLE X. ***
   20 DIM X(5,4)
   30 FOR I = 1 TO 4
   40    FOR J = 1 TO 5
   50       READ X(I,J)
   60    NEXT J
   70 NEXT I
```

```
4.10    DIM VALUES(26)
                .
                .
                .
 50 REM *** BUBBLE SORT NUMBERS IN ***
 60 REM *** ASCENDING ORDER.        ***
 70 FLAG = 1
 80 FINAL = 26
 90 WHILE FLAG = 1
100     FLAG = 0
110     FOR COUNT = 1 TO FINAL
120        IF VALUES(COUNT) > VALUES(COUNT+1)
              THEN SWAP VALUES(COUNT),VALUES(COUNT+1) : FLAG = 1
130     NEXT COUNT
140     FINAL = FINAL - 1
150 WEND
```

Programming Problems

Level 1

1. Write a program segment that reads the following data to a one-dimensional table and then displays the results.

20, 22, 45, 60, 24, 16

2. Write a FOR/NEXT loop that displays every other element in a table of 30 elements.

3. The Adams Restaurant Supply Company wants a program that will keep track of the inventory of five items for its three outlet locations. These items and their starting quantities are given below:

	Outlet		
	1	2	3
Chef's Knife	133	107	90
Food Processor	69	53	42
Mixer	83	68	21
Chopping Block	140	121	94
Soup Kettle	85	71	50

Create two tables, a one-dimensional table to store the name of each item and a corresponding two-dimensional table to store the inventory. Then enter the above data to the tables.

4. Create a 4 × 5 two-dimensional table. Assign a random number between 1 and 100 to each of the table's elements.

5. The table X contains 50 numbers. Write a FOR/NEXT loop that will display all the numbers that are greater than 20 and less than 40, using a sequential search.

6. The planet Uranus has five named satellites. You are to write a program that will read the satellite names to two tables and merge them so that the output looks like this:

SATELLITES

MIRANDA
ARIEL
UMBRIEL
TITANIA
OBERON

Use the READ/DATA statements to enter data for the following tables:

Table 1	Table 2
Miranda	Ariel
Umbriel	Titania
Oberon	

Level 2

1. Write a program that reads the numbers 1 through 20, assigning the even numbers to the table EVEN and the odd numbers to the table ODD. Use a FOR/NEXT loop that will assign an even number and odd number each time it executes, and total the values in each table.

Your output should look something like this:

EVEN NUMBERS	ODD NUMBERS
X	X
X	X
X	X
XXX	XXX

2. Read 12 numbers to table A and 12 numbers to table B. Compute the product of the corresponding elements of the two tables, and place the results in table C. Display a table similar to the following at the end of your program:

A	B	C
2	3	6
7	2	14
.	.	.
.	.	.
.	.	.

3. A department store is having a close-out sale on all its merchandise. Write a program that will store all its prices and discounts in one table, then calculate the corresponding sale prices and store them in a second table. Print the original prices, the discount rates, and the corresponding sale prices.

PRICE	DISCOUNT	SALE PRICE
3.50	.25	X.XX
4.00	.50	X.XX
5.25	.25	X.XX
6.00	.30	X.XX

4. The computer department has asked you to produce a computer dictionary from a list of words and definitions. The department has not specified a format for the output, so you can use whatever format you wish. The list of words and definitions follows:

> BASIC—A programming language for beginners.
> Byte—A unit of storage made up of bits.
> Microcomputer—A very small computer.
> Secondary storage—External storage such as disks.
> Field—A meaningful item of data.

5. The *New York Times* needs to determine the standings for the Patrick Division of the NHL. Six teams are included in the division. Their names, wins, and losses are as follows:

> | | | |
> |---|---|---|
> | Pittsburg Penguins | 2 | 13 |
> | Washington Capitals | 8 | 7 |
> | Philadelphia Flyers | 7 | 8 |
> | New York Rangers | 8 | 7 |
> | New York Islanders | 10 | 5 |
> | New Jersey Devils | 0 | 15 |

Sort the data in descending order by wins, and display the results.

6. Iowa State University set up two sections of advanced Latin, both scheduled to meet at 8 A.M. Many of the students found this class too early to attend, so they dropped out. Seven students were left in one class and nine in the other, so the university decided to combine the two classes. Now it needs a program to merge the two lists of remaining students, keeping them in alphabetical order. Use the following data:

Class A	Class B
Baez	Andrews
Christoph	Cohn
Guthrie	Farina
Miller	Garcia
Mooser	Kim
Smothers	Pontello
Travers	Seeger
	Perez
	Wahl

Projects

For each project, complete the following:

- Fill out a program specification chart.
- Develop a structure chart.
- Create a flowchart or pseudocode.

- Thoroughly document the final program.
- Test your program using a variety of data.

1. Connor Video, Inc. operates three video games in four different arcades. Mr. Connor has received the following table of data concerning the number of games played at each of the four arcades:

Arcade	Krystal Kastles	Off Road	Copter Race
Video Madness	100	250	200
Sappy Sam's	500	600	700
Krazy Kevin	200	225	230
City Arcade	120	520	500

Mr. Connor would like to know how many games were played at each arcade, how many games per video were played, and the total number of games played together. The output should include the preceding table.

2. Junior Johnson wants a program that will keep track of all his baseball cards. He is tired of looking through all his cards whenever he wants to know something about a certain player. He would like to be able to enter the player's name and have the computer display the player's team, the number of games he has played, the number of at bats, the number of RBIs, and the player's batting average. The output should look like this:

NAME: Last name, first initial
CLUB: Club name
GAMES: XX
AT BATS: XXX
RBI'S: XX
AVERAGE: 0.XXX

Use this data:

Player	Club	Games	At Bats	RBIs	Average
Ramos	Expos	26	41	3	0.195
Hisle	Brewers	27	87	11	0.230
Driessen	Reds	82	233	33	0.236
Bonnel	Blue Jays	66	227	28	0.220
Murcer	Yankees	50	117	24	0.260
Ayala	Orioles	44	86	13	0.279

The players, clubs, games, at bats, RBIs, and averages should be in separate tables. The data items for each player should be in the same positions in their respective tables as the position of the corresponding player.

CHAPTER

10

Business Software Development and Report Writing

Learning Objectives

After studying this chapter, you should be able to
1. Define the term information system.
2. Explain how input, processing, output, and feedback are related to one another.
3. Give the four components of an information system.
4. List the five categories of processing functions.
5. Discuss several reasons why structured programming techniques are widely used in business.
6. Describe different methods of implementing a new program and some advantages of each.
7. Discuss the importance of evaluating a program.
8. Name and describe several computer-related careers.
9. Write programs that output well-formatted reports.
10. Identify the different parts of a report.
11. Write reports with detail lines, grand totals, and control totals.

Introduction

Throughout this textbook, we have emphasized writing well-designed structured programs. This chapter reinforces these principles and also presents additional structured programming techniques that are used in business. Computer programs are often written to create business reports. At the end of this chapter you will learn to create well-formatted reports.

Developing Software in Business

System
A group of related elements that work together toward a common goal.

Information system
A system designed to turn data into useful information.

Data-processing department
A department composed of computer professionals who are responsible for the development of new programs and the maintenance of the company's information system.

People in business often talk about **systems.** This is a general term that simply means a group of related elements that work together toward a common goal. There are many different kinds of systems. For example, the human body is a system whose parts work together to keep us alive and healthy.

All systems have input, processing, output, and feedback. Consider a newspaper. The input consists of the news items that are collected by reporters. The writing, editing, typesetting, and printing of the stories are the processing steps that turn the news items into output (the final printed paper). Feedback may come from internal or external sources. The opinions of the publisher and others on the newspaper's staff are examples of internal feedback. Letters to the editor from readers and people dropping their newspaper subscriptions are examples of external feedback.

In this chapter we are concerned with **information systems,** which are systems designed to turn data into useful information. The **data-processing department** of a company is responsible for maintaining its information system. Figure 10–1 shows the flow of data in an information system. Input enters the system by means of an input device such as the keyboard. It is then transformed by a series of processes (the program instructions) and is outputted in a useful manner, such as being displayed on a monitor screen

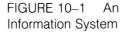

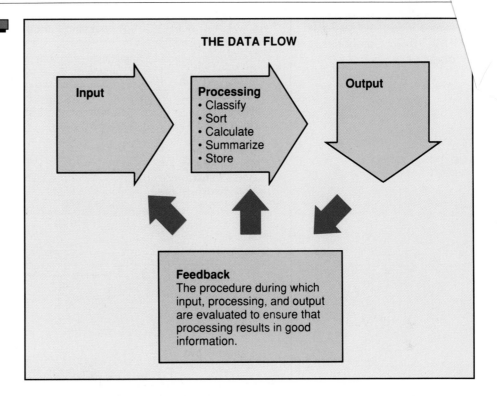

FIGURE 10–1 An Information System

THE DATA FLOW

Input

Processing
• Classify
• Sort
• Calculate
• Summarize
• Store

Output

Feedback
The procedure during which input, processing, and output are evaluated to ensure that processing results in good information.

Feedback

Information that tells a system how well it is working.

or printed on paper. **Feedback** tells the information system how it is working. One type of feedback is the self-testing functions that determine whether the computer's circuits are working properly. If they are malfunctioning, an error message is displayed. This is an example of *internal* feedback because it comes from within the system itself. In addition, the programmer offers feedback when he or she audits the program to determine whether its output is accurate. This is *external* feedback.

The processing done by an information system can be divided into five broad categories:

1. *Classifying*—Organizing data into groups, such as grouping employees by department.
2. *Sorting*—Arranging a list in numerical or alphabetical order.
3. *Calculating*—Performing arithmetic operations.
4. *Summarizing*—Totaling numeric data.
5. *Storing*—Saving program results in a file so that they can be used again.

Figure 10–2 illustrates these five categories.

The Components of an Information System

An information system consists of many components. The four major ones are

FIGURE 10–2   Categories of Processing

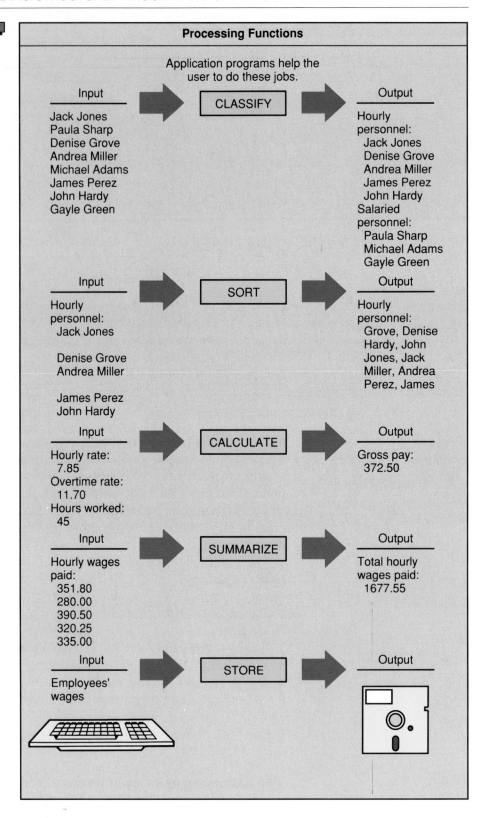

1. Hardware
2. Software
3. Data
4. People

Hardware The most visible part of an information system is the hardware. In large information systems there are dozens and even hundreds of pieces of hardware. They are often joined together in a **network** so that their resources can be shared. Networks use special cables or telephone lines that allow users to share peripheral devices (such as printers), software, and so forth. In addition, they can send messages, called **electronic mail,** to one another.

Software Software instructs the hardware in the tasks it is to perform. Large information systems have enormous libraries of software. Today, virtually all data-processing departments use structured programming techniques in writing their programs. Programs are divided into modules according to task. Most companies have strict rules concerning program documentation and the manner in which programs must be coded. As we've previously discussed, using structured programming techniques decreases the number of programming errors. In addition, following these rules becomes critical when many programmers are developing a single software package.

Network
A group of computers and peripheral devices joined together by special cables or telephone lines so that information and resources can be shared.

Electronic mail
Messages sent by cable or telephone lines between computer systems.

FIGURE 10–3 People Are an Important Part of an Information System

FIGURE 10–4 Businesses Often Network Computers to Share Software and Hardware

Garbage in–garbage out (GIGO)

A popular expression indicating that if input data is incorrect, the output of a program will also be incorrect.

Data As we discussed in Chapter 1, information is data that has been processed to make it meaningful. The votes in an election are an example of data. The election results are information because they have a definite meaning to people. Yet not all information is equally valuable. The value of information varies depending on how it was gathered and processed and how new it is. A business manager cannot use outdated or incomplete information. The term **GIGO**, or **garbage in–garbage out**, summarizes the idea that the quality of output of a program can only be as good as the quality of the input data. This is one reason that it is vitally important that the programmer check all data to determine whether it falls within the allowable range. For example, if a company assigns each employee a four-digit identification number from 1000 through 9999, the payroll program should make certain that the number falls within the allowable range. Not only must the information be accurate, it must be timely. If a manager wants to know how well a company's sales are going, he or she is interested in the most recent sales information possible, not information from a year ago.

People People are an extremely important part of any information system. The final value of the system depends on the desire of the data-processing employees to make it as well-designed as possible. Later in this chapter, you will learn about the various careers available in computer-related fields.

The Software Development Life Cycle

Developing software in business can be a long, tedious process. Before writing a new program, one should make sure that there are no similar

Now Try This

1. What department in a company is responsible for developing and maintaining the software?

2. What are the four components of an information system?

3. What does the term GIGO stand for? What is its significance in data processing?

4. Why is feedback so important in a system?

5. Give an example of internal and external feedback.

---

commercial software packages already available. If there is one, it is generally cheaper and quicker to use it than to write new software. However, if a new program needs to be developed, the steps in the programming process, originally introduced in Chapter 2, can serve as a partial guideline:

1. Define and document the problem.
2. Design and document a solution.
3. Write and document the program.
4. Test and debug the program, revising the documentation if necessary.

In business, the details of each of these steps are expanded. In addition, three more steps must be added:

5. Implement the program.
6. Evaluate the program.
7. Maintain the program.

Software development life cycle
The steps in the development and maintenance of programs.

In business, these steps are commonly called the **software development life cycle,** which is illustrated in Figure 10–5. We will review the first four steps first and then discuss the three new ones.

Defining the Problem The task of defining the problem in business is generally given to a computer professional called a **systems analyst** who is highly trained to understand the needs of the program user and the overall needs of the company. The "user" may be an entire department. For example, a program may need to be developed that the purchasing department can use to keep track of orders. As discussed in Chapter 2, it is important that the user of the program be consulted when developing the program specifications. If the user group is an entire department, an individual (or small group) within that department is chosen to develop the

Systems analyst
A computer professional who, along with the program user, develops the specifications for new programs.

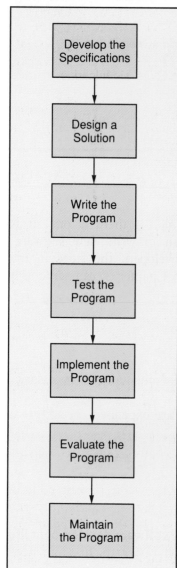

FIGURE 10–5 The Software Development Life Cycle

specifications with the systems analyst. At this point, the systems analyst and user representative thoroughly document the specifications so that they have a common understanding of what the program will be like. Often the systems analyst interviews a number of potential users to get ideas of their expectations of the new program. Questionnaires can also be useful, particularly if there are a large number of users.

Designing the Solution Once the specifications are documented, a programmer is assigned to code the program. If the program is large, a team of programmers will be assigned, each working on one or more modules. The systems analyst meets with the programmer or programmers, and together they discuss the program specifications. The systems analyst must make certain that the programmer has a clear idea of how the program should work.

At this point the programmer begins to design the solution, documenting it throughout the process. Many companies have strict guidelines that the programmer must adhere to when documenting the solution. For example, flowcharts may have to be written in a very precise manner with only certain types of symbols being allowed. Top-down design is used to improve the logic of the solution. By dealing with the major problems first and leaving the details until later, the programmer is more likely to determine early in the programming process whether a particular solution will actually work.

After the solution is designed, many data-processing departments conduct a **structured walkthrough,** in which the programmer arranges for a meeting with a group of programmers to evaluate the logic of the solution. Usually, every attempt is made to keep these meetings informal so that programmers will feel free to share ideas concerning improving the proposed program. The purpose of this meeting is to make the program better, not to judge the programmer. Structured walkthroughs are often conducted at several points in the programming process: first, when a solution has been documented, and later, when the program is actually being written in a programming language.

Coding the Program Once the design has been approved, the programmer codes the program. The language used for the program depends upon the standards of the company. In many companies, certain types of programs must be written in certain languages. Therefore, the programmer usually has little choice concerning the programming language. Usually, the programmer will use a structure chart in determining which modules to write first. When writing large programs, stubs should be inserted for those modules not yet written. This allows the modules to be tested in a structured manner.

Testing and Debugging the Program The programmers usually test their modules separately before placing them into the program. Individual modules can be tested by writing a simple driver program that calls them

Structured walkthrough
An evaluation of the design of a program by a group of computer professionals.

and assigns various test data to the variables. The results are checked for accuracy. Thoroughly testing modules individually and in small groups before combining them with the entire program is an important concept of structured programming. In fact, it is necessary if a large program is to be written in an orderly manner. Test data must be carefully developed to test the various control structures in the program. This test data is used to audit the program, and written records of the results obtained are checked against the pre-calculated correct results.

Implementing the Program When writing a small program for a programming class, implementing it involves simply loading it into the computer and running it. However, implementing a program in a business, particularly a large one, can be a long, drawn-out process.

Programs are implemented only after they have been thoroughly audited and debugged. Implementing a program before thorough testing can cause many problems. A program that stops working unexpectedly (*crashes*), obtains incorrect results, or is difficult to use can cause a great deal of extra work for the user group and damage the reputation of the data-processing department.

Before the actual implementation begins, *user's manuals* must be developed to explain everything the user will need to know. It is important that they use language that the user can understand. In addition, training sessions are often held so that data-processing personnel can be on hand while the users are first learning the program.

There are a variety of ways in which a new program can be implemented. One is a *crash implementation* in which all processing is switched over to the new program. Sometimes this is necessary because it is not feasible to continue the old method of processing after the new method is being used.

A second method is a *pilot conversion*, in which a small portion of the processing is switched to the new program while the majority of processing continues under the old method.

A third method is a *parallel conversion*, in which both the new program and the old processing method are used on all data. Parallel conversion allows the users to compare the processing results of both systems for accuracy. Eventually, after the users feel comfortable with the new program, the old processing method is discontinued. The parallel conversion method is the most expensive and tends to drag out the time needed for implementation of a new program. However, it is also the safest method.

Evaluating the Program Once a program is successfully implemented, the data-processing department's job is by no means over. It is important that the program be evaluated periodically. While the program is still fairly new, periodic meetings should be held between the systems analyst and a representative of the users group. This feedback allows the users to express any concerns they may have about the program. The users may want the program to perform additional tasks, make entering data simpler, have output formatted differently, and so forth. By listening carefully, the systems analyst shows the users that the data-processing department wants them to be happy with their new program. Obviously, it may not be possible to make all of the changes the users would like. Both parties must agree on which modifications are feasible.

Maintaining the Program Beginning programmers rarely realize the importance of program maintenance in business. In a typical data-processing department, approximately 80 percent of programmers' time is spent on maintaining programs that already exist. This maintenance includes fixing minor bugs that users have discovered, modifying a program so that it is more user-friendly, or adding new modules to an existing program so that it can perform additional tasks or alter the way in which it performs an old task. For example, a department may want to alter the format of a report or create a bar chart or line graph illustrating a program's output.

Frequently, the data processing department will become aware of "bugs" in a program that it cannot immediately correct. Either the time is not available or the bug would be very difficult to eliminate. The users should be made aware of the problem so they can attempt to avoid it. At least they will understand what is happening if the software behaves erratically or crashes because of the problem. When you (or others) are using programs you have written, be sure to document any bugs. This helps the program user and also helps you in improving the program when you have time for program maintenance.

The real benefits of structured programming become evident in program maintenance. Often, the person performing the modification is not the original programmer. It is much simpler for a programmer to modify a structured program than an unstructured one. Because the program is divided into modules, the programmer need only locate those modules that perform the task being modified. When modifying a program, the programmer must also remember to modify any corresponding program documentation such as remarks in the program, design flowcharts, or user's manuals that accompany the program.

Computer-Related Careers

Today, practically every working person has some contact with computers on his or her job. However, some careers are more computer-oriented than others. We'll discuss some of the more common computer-related careers in this chapter. First, the *systems analyst*, discussed previously, is a professional who knows the capabilities and limitations of the computer systems being used in his or her company. In addition, systems analysts must have some knowledge of the business in which they are working so that they can determine user needs. Often they are required to have advanced college degrees. Finally, many of them specialize in an area called *management information systems* (MIS), in which they learn how business information systems function.

Most data-processing departments are headed by a professional with the title *computer systems director* or something similar. This person has extensive knowledge of information systems and also of the particular company for which he or she works. The position is commonly held by a systems analyst with many years of experience. The overall quality of a company's information system is highly dependent on the capabilities of this person.

Computer programmers are the people who actually write the programs. You became a computer programmer when you wrote BASIC programs in this class. Because programming has become very complex, programmers often specialize in writing certain types of programs in specific languages. Programmers typically have either a two-year technical degree or a four-year bachelor's degree in computer science.

Computer operators take care of the hardware and make certain the computer itself and the peripheral devices are functioning properly. They often are called on to make minor repairs. In addition, it is generally their responsibility to call in a computer repair technician if a problem arises that they cannot handle. Computer operators may attend a technical school to learn the needed skills or be trained on the job.

Data-entry clerks enter data into the computer system, usually by means of the keyboard. Many companies have enormous quantities of data that must be "keyed in." This job can be tedious and requires a great deal of attention to detail. Errors made at this point will probably lead to incorrect output.

Computer repair technicians fix problems involving computer hardware. They usually work for a particular computer company such as IBM or Digital Equipment Corporation. They often take a two-year course to learn basic electronic skills and then are sent to technical schools operated by their company for further intensive training.

Report Writing

In business, computer programs often are written to generate reports. For example, a company might need a report showing expenses and profits for the past year for each department. Or it might need to itemize the amount owed by each of a company's customers, referred to as an *accounts receivable* report, or list the bills owed by a company, referred to as an *accounts payable* report. All of these reports involve summarizing information in order to give the reader an overall analysis of large quantities of data. So far in this textbook, you have written many programs that created simple business reports. In this chapter, you will learn a number of additional techniques for writing programs that generate reports. We will begin by discussing the parts of a simple report.

The Parts of a Report

Most reports have a number of different parts. Figure 10–6 contains a printer spacing chart for an accounts receivable report that will be printed on paper (rather than displayed on the screen). If a report is displayed on the screen, the CLS command should be used to clear the screen before outputting the report. In addition, make certain that the report does not have more than 24 lines, which is the maximum that most monitor screens can display at a time. If there are more than 24 lines, some lines will scroll off the top of the screen and the reader will not be able to see them.

The major parts of the report in Figure 10–6 are labeled. The **report headings** identify the entire report. This report has three headings: the company name, the type of report (accounts receivable), and the date on which it was created. The headings are usually centered at the top of the page. Remember that the typical page has 80 columns across.

The individual lines of the report in Figure 10–6 contain information on bills owed to R. W. Horton Advertising Agency—the account number of the company owing the bill, the company's name, and the amount of the bill. Each of these report lines is referred to as a **detail line,** since it contains the "details" concerning a specific bill. The bottom line of the report is the total amount owed by all companies and is referred to as the **grand total.** The line of hyphens following the headings and at the end of the report are called **rulings;** they separate the different sections of the report.

The program that creates the report in Figure 10–6 is shown in Figure 10–7. The data concerning each bill is entered at the keyboard. Notice that if a company has several bills (for example, BERK INSURANCE has two bills outstanding), these bills must be entered one after another. In addition, the bills are entered in ascending order by account number. They must be typed in that order into the computer.

Control Breaks

The report in Figure 10–6 could be made more useful in several ways. One improvement would be to add a subtotal listing the amount owed on each account. This type of subtotal is referred to as a **control total,** a subtotal that is printed when the value of a specified variable changes. In this example, a control total will be printed each time the account number changes. Examine the printer spacing chart in Figure 10–8 in which control totals have been added to the accounts receivable report. When this program is written, a variable will be added to keep track of the total bills for the company currently being processed. When a new account number is entered, a **control break** occurs, signaling the program that a control total should be printed. Consider the following input data:

Report heading
The title of a report; it is usually centered at the top.

Detail line
An individual data line in a report.

Grand total
The total value of all items of a specific type.

Ruling
A line used to separate two different parts of a report.

Control total
A subtotal that is calculated until the value of a specified data item changes (that is, until a control break occurs).

Control break
The situation in which there is a change in the value of a specified data item.

FIGURE 10–6 Printer Spacing Chart for Accounts Receivable Report

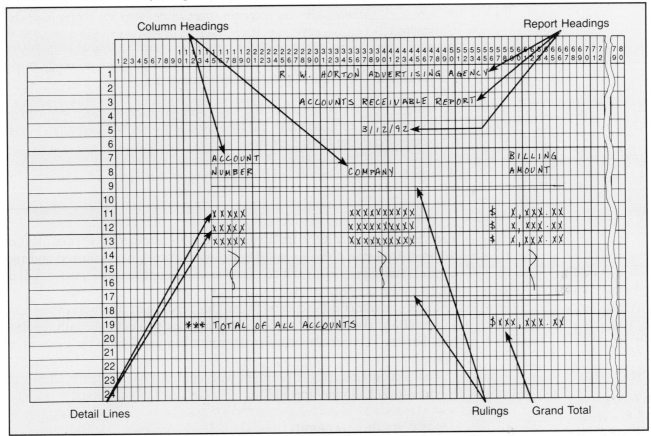

Column Headings

Report Headings

Detail Lines

Rulings   Grand Total

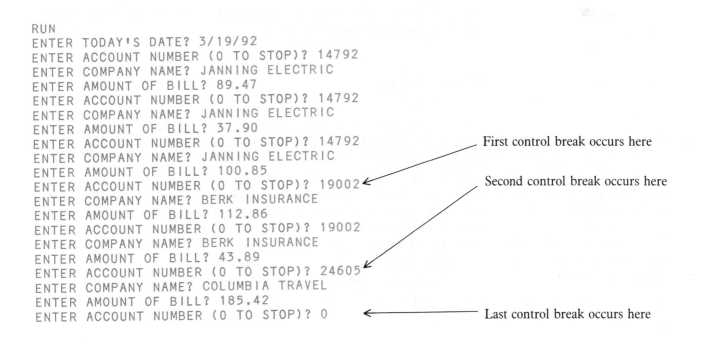

```
RUN
ENTER TODAY'S DATE? 3/19/92
ENTER ACCOUNT NUMBER (0 TO STOP)? 14792
ENTER COMPANY NAME? JANNING ELECTRIC
ENTER AMOUNT OF BILL? 89.47
ENTER ACCOUNT NUMBER (0 TO STOP)? 14792
ENTER COMPANY NAME? JANNING ELECTRIC
ENTER AMOUNT OF BILL? 37.90
ENTER ACCOUNT NUMBER (0 TO STOP)? 14792
ENTER COMPANY NAME? JANNING ELECTRIC
ENTER AMOUNT OF BILL? 100.85
ENTER ACCOUNT NUMBER (0 TO STOP)? 19002
ENTER COMPANY NAME? BERK INSURANCE
ENTER AMOUNT OF BILL? 112.86
ENTER ACCOUNT NUMBER (0 TO STOP)? 19002
ENTER COMPANY NAME? BERK INSURANCE
ENTER AMOUNT OF BILL? 43.89
ENTER ACCOUNT NUMBER (0 TO STOP)? 24605
ENTER COMPANY NAME? COLUMBIA TRAVEL
ENTER AMOUNT OF BILL? 185.42
ENTER ACCOUNT NUMBER (0 TO STOP)? 0
```

First control break occurs here

Second control break occurs here

Last control break occurs here

Now Try This

1. A(n)_____ meets with the program users to develop the program specifications.

2. In a(n)_____, programmers meet to discuss a program currently being developed and share suggestions for improving it.

3. A(n) _____ implementation of a new program involves switching a small portion of the processing to the new program while still performing most processing under the old method.

4. Approximately 80 percent of programmers' time is spent on _____.

Each time data for a bill is entered, the account number is checked. If it is different from the previous number, a control break has occurred and the control total is printed. If the account number is unchanged, the new bill is added to the previous total.

There is another difference between this report and the report shown in Figure 10–6. The account number and name are printed only with the first bill. For the subsequent bills for the same company, only the amount is printed.

The accounts receivable program with control totals added is shown in Figure 10–9. Examine line 2070:

```
2070 TEMP = ATNMBR
```

Variable ATNMBR is used to keep track of the account number. The first account number is read before the WHILE loop is entered, because ATNMBR is also used to control the loop's repetition; the user enters a zero to signal when there is no more data to be entered. The current account number is assigned to variable TEMP so that when the next account number is read, it can be compared to the previous one:

```
2170     INPUT "ENTER ACCOUNT NUMBER (0 TO STOP)";ATNMBR
2180     IF ATNMBR <> TEMP THEN GOSUB 3000
```

If the current account number is different from the old one, a control break has occurred and subroutine 3000 is called to print the control total. After the control total is printed in lines 3050–3130, the variable TACCT is reset to zero so that the control total for the next account can be calculated. In addition, TEMP is set equal to the new account number.

As previously discussed, this program has also been altered so that an account's number and name are printed only the first time a bill is printed; only the amount owed is printed for subsequent bills. The variable FIRST$

FIGURE 10–7   Program to Create an Accounts Receivable Report

```
10    REM ***              ACCOUNTS RECEIVABLE REPORT           ***
20    REM
30    REM ***   THIS PROGRAM PREPARES AN ACCOUNTS RECEIVABLE    ***
40    REM ***   REPORT FOR THE R. W. HORTON ADVERTISING AGENCY. ***
50    REM ***   CUSTOMER BILLS ARE ARRANGED BY ACCOUNT NUM-     ***
60    REM ***   BER AND ENTERED AT THE KEYBOARD.  A BILLING     ***
70    REM ***   REPORT IS THEN PRINTED ON PAPER.  A GRAND TOTAL ***
80    REM ***   IS CALCULATED AND PRINTED AT THE BOTTOM OF THE  ***
90    REM ***   REPORT.                                         ***
100   REM
110   REM ***   MAJOR VARIABLES:                                ***
120   REM ***      ATNMBR             ACCOUNT NUMBER            ***
130   REM ***      ANME$              NAME OF THE COMPANY       ***
140   REM ***      AMT                AMOUNT OF THE BILL        ***
150   REM ***      TTL                TOTAL OF ALL ACCOUNTS     ***
160   REM
170   REM *** PERFORM INITIALIZATION OPERATIONS.
180   GOSUB 1000
190   REM
200   REM *** PERFORM PROCESS BILLS SUBROUTINE. ***
210   GOSUB 2000
220   REM
230   REM *** PERFORM PRINT GRAND TOTAL SUBROUTINE ***.
240   GOSUB 3000
999   END
1000  REM *******************************************************
1010  REM ***                INITIALIZATION OPERATIONS          ***
1020  REM *******************************************************
1030  REM *** INITIALIZE TOTAL AND PRINT HEADINGS.             ***
1040  REM
1050  TTL = 0
1060  REM *** PRINT HEADINGS.  ***
1070  LPRINT TAB(25) "R. W. HORTON ADVERTISING AGENCY"
1080  LPRINT
1090  LPRINT TAB(28) "ACCOUNTS RECEIVABLE REPORT"
1100  LPRINT
1110  INPUT "ENTER TODAY'S DATE";DTE$
1120  LPRINT TAB(37) DTE$
1130  LPRINT
1140  LPRINT TAB(15) "ACCOUNT";TAB(60) "BILLING"
1150  LPRINT TAB(15) "NUMBER";TAB(35) "COMPANY";TAB(60) "AMOUNT"
1160  LPRINT TAB(15);
1170  FOR I = 1 TO 53
1180     LPRINT  "-";
1190  NEXT I
1200  LPRINT
1210  LPRINT
1220  RETURN
2000  REM *******************************************************
2010  REM ***                   PROCESS RECORDS                 ***
2020  REM *******************************************************
2030  REM *** GET INFORMATION FOR EACH BILL AND UPDATE         ***
2040  REM *** GRAND TOTAL.                                     ***
2050  REM
2060  INPUT "ENTER ACCOUNT NUMBER (0 TO STOP)";ATNMBR
```

(figure continued on the next page)

FIGURE 10–7   Continued

```
2070 WHILE ATNMBR <> O
2080     INPUT "ENTER COMPANY NAME";ANME$
2090     INPUT "ENTER AMOUNT OF BILL";AMT
2100     TTL = TTL + AMT
2110     L1$ = "               #####                    \          \ $  #,###.
##"
2120     LPRINT USING L1$;ATNMBR,ANME$,AMT
2130     INPUT "ENTER ACCOUNT NUMBER (0 TO STOP)";ATNMBR
2140 WEND
2150 RETURN
3000 REM ***********************************************************
3010 REM ***                 PRINT FINAL TOTAL               ***
3020 REM ***********************************************************
3030 REM *** PRINT TOTAL AMOUNT OWED ON ALL ACCOUNTS.        ***
3040 REM
3050 LPRINT
3060 LPRINT TAB(15);
3070 FOR I = 1 TO 53
3080     LPRINT "-";
3090 NEXT I
3100 LPRINT
3110 LPRINT
3120 L2$ = "            \                              \ $###,###.##"
3130 LPRINT USING L2$;"*** TOTAL OF ALL ACCOUNTS",TTL
3140 RETURN
```

```
RUN
ENTER TODAY'S DATE? 3/12/92
ENTER ACCOUNT NUMBER (0 TO STOP)? 14792
ENTER COMPANY NAME? JANNING ELECTRIC
ENTER AMOUNT OF BILL? 89.47
ENTER ACCOUNT NUMBER (0 TO STOP)? 14792
ENTER COMPANY NAME? JANNING ELECTRIC
ENTER AMOUNT OF BILL? 37.90
ENTER ACCOUNT NUMBER (0 TO STOP)? 14792
ENTER COMPANY NAME? JANNING ELECTRIC
ENTER AMOUNT OF BILL? 100.85
ENTER ACCOUNT NUMBER (0 TO STOP)? 19002
ENTER COMPANY NAME? BERK INSURANCE
ENTER AMOUNT OF BILL? 112.86
ENTER ACCOUNT NUMBER (0 TO STOP)? 19002
ENTER COMPANY NAME? BERK INSURANCE
ENTER AMOUNT OF BILL? 43.89
ENTER ACCOUNT NUMBER (0 TO STOP)? 24605
ENTER COMPANY NAME? COLUMBIA TRAVEL
ENTER AMOUNT OF BILL? 185.42
ENTER ACCOUNT NUMBER (0 TO STOP)? 0
```

FIGURE 10–7 Continued

```
              R. W. HORTON ADVERTISING AGENCY

              ACCOUNTS RECEIVABLE REPORT

                      3/12/92

     ACCOUNT                                    BILLING
     NUMBER              COMPANY                 AMOUNT
     ------------------------------------------------------

     14792           JANNING ELECTRIC        $       89.47
     14792           JANNING ELECTRIC        $       37.90
     14792           JANNING ELECTRIC        $      100.85
     19002           BERK INSURANCE          $      112.86
     19002           BERK INSURANCE          $       43.89
     24605           COLUMBIA TRAVEL         $      185.42

     ------------------------------------------------------

 *** TOTAL OF ALL ACCOUNTS                   $      570.39
```

acts as a flag to determine what information is printed. It is set to YES in line 2080. If FIRST\$ equals YES in line 2160, everything is printed, and FIRST\$ is set to NO; otherwise only the amount of the bill is printed. FIRST\$ continues to be NO as long as bills for the same account are being entered. When a control break occurs, FIRST\$ is reset to YES in line 3160. It will again be changed to NO after the first bill of the new account is printed. This process continues until all the data are entered.

To summarize, each time a control break occurs, subroutine PRINT ACCOUNT TOTALS is called and the following tasks are performed:

1. The total amount owed on that account is printed.
2. The variable used to keep track of account totals is reset to zero.
3. A flag (FIRST\$) is set to indicate that a new account is being started. This flag is necessary so that all of the information on the new account will be printed.

A Programming Problem

Problem Definition

The sales manager of Martinez Medical Supply Company would like a program to create a report on the salespeoples' sales and commissions. The program should prompt the user to enter each salesperson's name, com-

FIGURE 10–8 Printer Spacing Chart for Accounts Receivable Report with Control Breaks

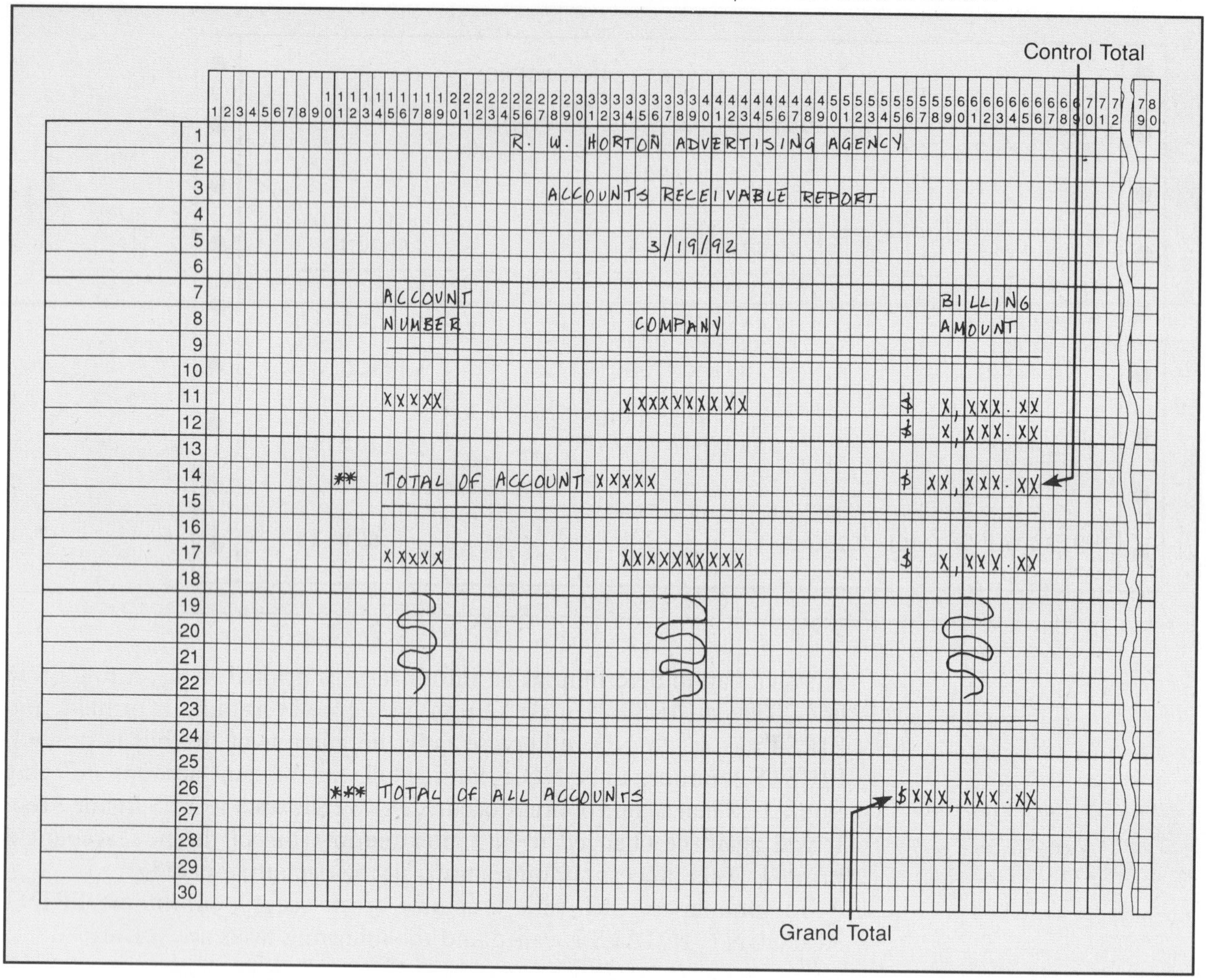

mission rate, and the amount of each sale made by that salesperson. The commission rates vary, depending on the salesperson, from 20 through 30 percent of the sale price of the item. The input data is similar to the following:

Salesperson's Name	Commission Rate	Price of Item
Frederickson	0.30	4050.00
Ling	0.25	1500.00
Ling		280.00

All of the data for one salesperson must be entered before data is entered for the next salesperson. A salesperson's commission rate is entered only with

FIGURE 10–9   Accounts Receivable Report with Control Breaks

```
10    REM ***                 ACCOUNTS RECEIVABLE REPORT            ***
20    REM
30    REM ***  THIS PROGRAM PREPARES AN ACCOUNTS RECEIVABLE       ***
40    REM ***  REPORT FOR THE R. W. HORTON ADVERTISING AGENCY.    ***
50    REM ***  CUSTOMER BILLS ARE ARRANGED BY ACCOUNT             ***
60    REM ***  NUMBER AND ENTERED AT THE KEYBOARD.  A BILLING     ***
70    REM ***  REPORT IS THEN PRINTED ON PAPER. BOTH THE TOTAL    ***
80    REM ***  OWED ON EACH ACCOUNT AND THE GRAND TOTAL ARE       ***
90    REM ***  PRINTED.                                           ***
100   REM
110   REM ***  MAJOR VARIABLES:                                   ***
120   REM ***     ATNMBR            ACCOUNT NUMBER                ***
130   REM ***     ANME$             NAME OF THE COMPANY           ***
140   REM ***     AMT               AMOUNT OF THE BILL            ***
150   REM ***     TACCT             TOTAL OF EACH ACCOUNT         ***
160   REM ***     TTL               TOTAL OF ALL ACCOUNTS         ***
170   REM
180   REM *** PERFORM INITIALIZATION OPERATIONS.
190   GOSUB 1000
200   REM *** PERFORM PROCESS BILLS SUBROUTINE. ***
210   GOSUB 2000
220   REM *** PERFORM PRINT GRAND TOTAL SUBROUTINE ***.
230   GOSUB 4000
999   END
1000  REM ************************************************************
1010  REM ***                  INITIALIZATION OPERATIONS            ***
1020  REM ************************************************************
1030  REM *** INITIALIZE TOTAL AND PRINT HEADINGS.                 ***
1040  REM
1050  TACCT = 0
1060  TTL = 0
1070  REM *** PRINT HEADINGS.  ***
1080  LPRINT TAB(25) "R. W. HORTON ADVERTISING AGENCY"
1090  LPRINT
1100  LPRINT TAB(28) "ACCOUNTS RECEIVABLE REPORT"
1110  LPRINT
1120  INPUT "ENTER TODAY'S DATE";DTE$
1130  LPRINT TAB(37) DTE$
1140  LPRINT
1150  LPRINT TAB(15) "ACCOUNT";TAB(60) "BILLING"
1160  LPRINT TAB(15) "NUMBER";TAB(35) "COMPANY";TAB(60) "AMOUNT"
1170  LPRINT TAB(15);
1180  FOR I = 1 TO 53
1190      LPRINT  "-";
1200  NEXT I
1210  LPRINT
1220  LPRINT
1230  RETURN
2000  REM ************************************************************
2010  REM ***                    PROCESS RECORDS                    ***
2020  REM ************************************************************
2030  REM *** GET INFORMATION FOR EACH BILL AND UPDATE ACCOUNT ***
2040  REM *** TOTAL AND GRAND TOTAL.                            ***
2050  REM
2060  INPUT "ENTER ACCOUNT NUMBER (0 TO STOP)";ATNMBR
2070  TEMP = ATNMBR
```

(figure continued on the next page)

FIGURE 10–9   Continued

```
2080 FIRST$ = "YES"
2090 WHILE ATNMBR <> 0
2100    INPUT "ENTER COMPANY NAME";ANME$
2110    INPUT "ENTER AMOUNT OF BILL";AMT
2120    TTL = TTL + AMT
2130    TACCT = TACCT + AMT
2140    L1$ = "               #####             \            \ $  #,###.
##"
2150    L2$ = "                                             $  #,###.
##"
2160    IF FIRST$ = "YES" THEN LPRINT USING L1$;ATNMBR,ANME$,AMT : FIRST$ = "NO"
           ELSE LPRINT USING L2$;AMT
2170    INPUT "ENTER ACCOUNT NUMBER (0 TO STOP)";ATNMBR
2180    IF ATNMBR <> TEMP THEN GOSUB 3000
2190 WEND
2200 RETURN
3000 REM ***********************************************************
3010 REM ***              PRINT ACCOUNT TOTALS             ***
3020 REM ***********************************************************
3030 REM *** PRINT TOTAL AMOUNT OWED ON CURRENT ACCOUNT.   ***
3040 REM
3050 LPRINT
3060 L3$ = "          \                \ #####            $ ##,###.##"
3070 LPRINT USING L3$;"** TOTAL OF ACCOUNT",TEMP,TACCT
3080 LPRINT TAB(15);
3090 FOR I = 1 TO 53
3100    LPRINT "-";
3110 NEXT I
3120 LPRINT
3130 LPRINT
3140 TACCT = 0
3150 TEMP = ATNMBR
3160 FIRST$ = "YES"
3170 RETURN
4000 REM ***********************************************************
4010 REM ***                PRINT FINAL TOTAL              ***
4020 REM ***********************************************************
4030 REM *** PRINT TOTAL AMOUNT OWED ON ALL ACCOUNTS.      ***
4040 REM
4050 LPRINT
4060 LPRINT
4070 L3$ = "          \             \ $###,###.##"
4080 LPRINT USING L3$;"*** TOTAL OF ALL ACCOUNTS",TTL
4090 RETURN
```

FIGURE 10–9   Continued

```
ENTER TODAY'S DATE? 3/19/92
ENTER ACCOUNT NUMBER (0 TO STOP)? 14792
ENTER COMPANY NAME? JANNING ELECTRIC
ENTER AMOUNT OF BILL? 89.47
ENTER ACCOUNT NUMBER (0 TO STOP)? 14792
ENTER COMPANY NAME? JANNING ELECTRIC
ENTER AMOUNT OF BILL? 37.90
ENTER ACCOUNT NUMBER (0 TO STOP)? 14792
ENTER COMPANY NAME? JANNING ELECTRIC
ENTER AMOUNT OF BILL? 100.85
ENTER ACCOUNT NUMBER (0 TO STOP)? 19002
ENTER COMPANY NAME? BERK INSURANCE
ENTER AMOUNT OF BILL? 112.86
ENTER ACCOUNT NUMBER (0 TO STOP)? 19002
ENTER COMPANY NAME? BERK INSURANCE
ENTER AMOUNT OF BILL? 43.89
ENTER ACCOUNT NUMBER (0 TO STOP)? 24605
ENTER COMPANY NAME? COLUMBIA TRAVEL
ENTER AMOUNT OF BILL? 185.42
ENTER ACCOUNT NUMBER (0 TO STOP)? 0
```

(figure continued on the next page)

FIGURE 10–9 Continued

```
            R. W. HORTON ADVERTISING AGENCY

              ACCOUNTS RECEIVABLE REPORT

                       3/19/92

    ACCOUNT                                 BILLING
    NUMBER           COMPANY                AMOUNT
    ---------------------------------------------------

    14792           JANNING ELECTRIC     $     89.47
                                         $     37.90
                                         $    100.85

 ** TOTAL OF ACCOUNT  14792              $    228.22
    ---------------------------------------------------

    19002           BERK INSURANCE       $    112.86
                                         $     43.89

 ** TOTAL OF ACCOUNT  19002              $    156.75
    ---------------------------------------------------

    24605           COLUMBIA TRAVEL      $    185.42

 ** TOTAL OF ACCOUNT  24605              $    185.42
    ---------------------------------------------------


*** TOTAL OF ALL ACCOUNTS                $    570.39
```

with the first sale. The program should then calculate the commission on each item and print (on paper) the following:

1. Each salesperson's name (only the first time data on a salesperson is output).
2. Each salesperson's commission rate (also only the first time).
3. Cost of each item sold.
4. Commission on each item sold.
5. Each salesperson's total sales.
6. Each salesperson's total commissions.
7. Total sales on all items.
8. Total commissions on all items.

The program specification chart is shown in Figure 10–10. The final printed report should be formatted as shown in Figure 10–11.

Now Try This

1. Write the statements needed to center the following report heading on an 80-column line.

Galena Paint and Paper

Employee Payroll

2. Center the following column headings below the report headings in Exercise 1:

Employee Name   Hours Worked   Gross Pay

3. Create a loop that reads the data needed to calculate the payroll for the Galena Paint and Paper Store. The loop should read each employee's name and gross pay. The grand total of all employees' gross pay should be displayed at the bottom of the report. Be sure to properly label the total.

4. Alter Exercise 3 so that the net pay is also calculated and printed. To calculate the net pay, taxes must be deducted as follows:

Pay range	Taxes
Less than 200.00	None
From 200.00 through 400.00	60.00
Over 400.00	100.00

Both the total net pay and total gross pay should be displayed at the bottom of the report.

Solution Design

There are only a few input variables needed for this report: the salesperson's name, commission rate, and amount of each sale. The commission is calculated by multiplying the commission rate by the amount of the sale. Two control totals, individual sales and individual commissions, must be calculated and printed. Total sales and commissions also must be printed.

The operations to be performed are

1. Perform initial tasks.
    1.A. Initialize variables to keep track of totals.
    1.B. Print headings.
2. Process data for each sale.
    2.A. Get each name, commission rate, and amount of each sale.
    2.B. Calculate commission.

FIGURE 10–10   Program Specification Chart for Sales Commissions Report

PROGRAM SPECIFICATION CHART

PROGRAM NAME:	PROGRAMMER'S NAME:	DATE:
Sales Commissions Report	S. Baumann	3/26/92

INPUT: Each salesperson's name, commission rate, and amount of each sale.

OUTPUT: See printer spacing chart (Figure 10-11)

SOURCE OF INPUT: Keyboard

DESTINATION OF OUTPUT: Printer

PURPOSE: Prompts user to enter sales data and calculates and prints each salesperson's name, commission rate, individual sales and total sales and commissions earned. At the end of the report, the overall sales and commissions are printed.

    2.C. Total individual sales and commissions.
    2.D. Total overall sales and commissions.
    2.E. Print sales data.
  3. Print control totals.
    3.A. Print individual total sales.
    3.B. Print individual total commissions.
  4. Print grand totals.
    4.A. Print total sales.
    4.B. Print total commissions.

The structure chart for this problem is illustrated in Figure 10–12. The module that processes the data will be fairly complex. First, it needs to check for a control break. This involves comparing the current salesperson's name with the previous one. If they are different, the control totals must be outputted. In addition, if the current data is the first data on a salesperson, his or her name and commission rate must be printed. Otherwise, only the amount of the sale is printed. A WHILE loop is a logical choice for entering this data. The loop can execute until a trailer value is entered.

When a control break occurs, not only must the individual totals be printed, but the variables that store these totals must be reset to zero.

The flowchart and pseudocode for the solution are shown in Figure 10–13.

FIGURE 10–11   Printer Spacing Chart for Sales Commissions Report

```
                              MARTINEZ MEDICAL SUPPLIES

                              SALES COMMISSION REPORT

                              FOR MONTH OF APRIL


                                        COMMISSION        AMOUNT          COMMISSION
              NAME                      RATE              OF SALE         EARNINGS


              XXXXXXXXXXXXXXY           X.XX        $  XX,XXX.XX     $   X,XXX.XX
                                                    $  XX,XXX.XX     $   X,XXX.XX




TOTAL SALES:                                                        $  XX,XXX.XX
TOTAL COMMISSIONS:                                                  $  XX,XXX.XX




TOTAL SALES FOR ALL SALESPEOPLE                                     $ XXX,XXX.XX
TOTAL COMMISSIONS FOR ALL SALESPEOPLE                               $ XXX,XXX.XX
```

The Program

Figure 10–14 contains the final program. It is divided into five subroutines. Not only is there a subroutine for each module at Level 1 in the structure chart, but there is also a module to output a dividing line (or ruling). Each time a dividing line is needed, this subroutine is called; therefore, these statements need to be written only one time.

Subroutine PROCESS DATA performs a number of steps. The salesperson's name is entered first; it is used to determine whether a control break has occurred. If it is different from the previous name, subroutine PRINT SALESPERSON'S TOTALS is called to print the control totals. In addition, lines 3110 and 3120 reset the control totals to zero, and line 3130 resets the control break flag FIRST$ to "YES". TEMP$ is set to the current salesperson's name so that it can be compared with the next name.

FIGURE 10–12   Structure Chart for Sales Commissions Report

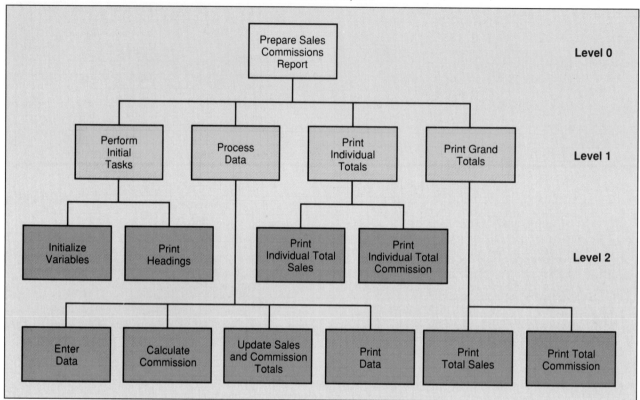

Examine line 2200. If FIRST$ equals "YES", all of the data on the current salesperson is printed; otherwise, only the amount of the sale is printed. The next salesperson's name is entered at the bottom of the loop, control branches back to line 2100, and processing continues. When all the data has been entered, subroutine PRINT GRAND TOTALS is called to print the final total sales and commissions, and program execution terminates.

Programming Hints

■ Printer spacing charts can be very useful, especially when creating reports that have control breaks. Fill them out carefully and refer to them as you write the program.

■ Blank lines and rulings between sections of a report make the report easier to understand.

■ Each time data is entered to the program, be certain to check for a control break.

■ When a control break occurs, remember to reset the variable used for the control totals to zero. If this is not done, a grand total will be accumulated, rather than a control total.

FIGURE 10–13   Pseudocode and Flowchart for Sales Commissions Report

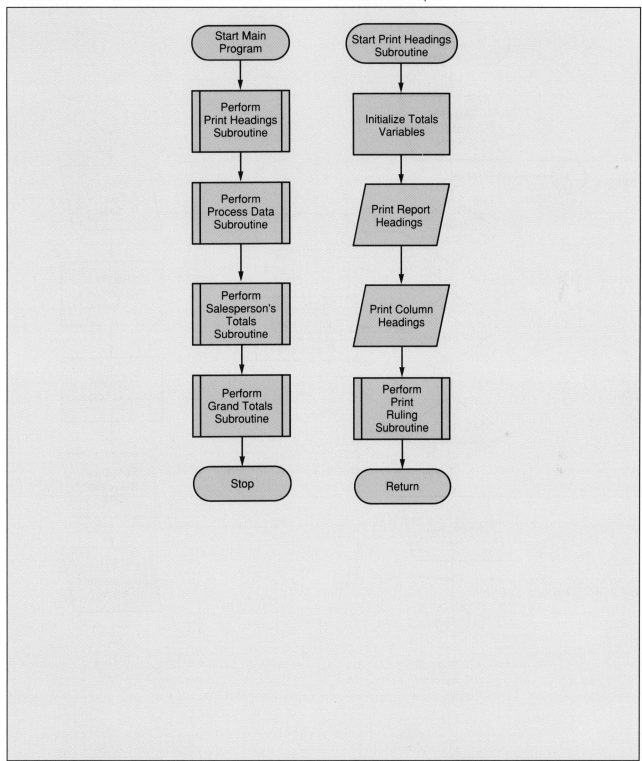

(figure continued on the next page)

FIGURE 10–13   Continued

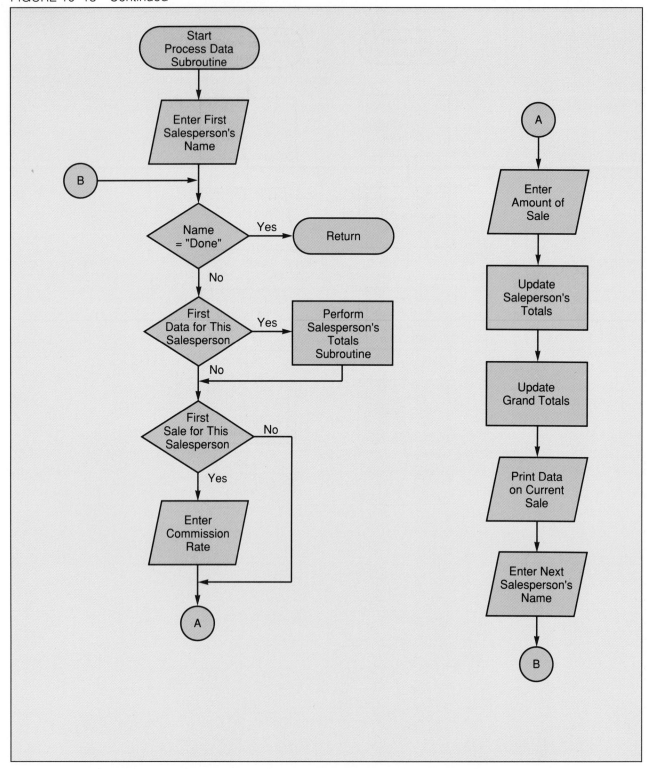

FIGURE 10–13   Continued

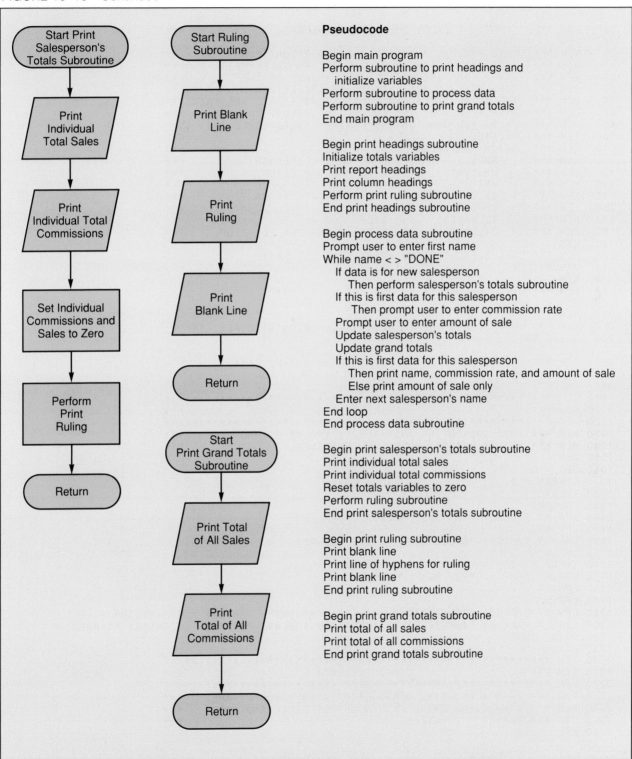

Pseudocode

Begin main program
Perform subroutine to print headings and
  initialize variables
Perform subroutine to process data
Perform subroutine to print grand totals
End main program

Begin print headings subroutine
Initialize totals variables
Print report headings
Print column headings
Perform print ruling subroutine
End print headings subroutine

Begin process data subroutine
Prompt user to enter first name
While name < > "DONE"
  If data is for new salesperson
    Then perform salesperson's totals subroutine
  If this is first data for this salesperson
    Then prompt user to enter commission rate
  Prompt user to enter amount of sale
  Update salesperson's totals
  Update grand totals
  If this is first data for this salesperson
    Then print name, commission rate, and amount of sale
    Else print amount of sale only
  Enter next salesperson's name
End loop
End process data subroutine

Begin print salesperson's totals subroutine
Print individual total sales
Print individual total commissions
Reset totals variables to zero
Perform ruling subroutine
End print salesperson's totals subroutine

Begin print ruling subroutine
Print blank line
Print line of hyphens for ruling
Print blank line
End print ruling subroutine

Begin print grand totals subroutine
Print total of all sales
Print total of all commissions
End print grand totals subroutine

FIGURE 10–14   Program for Sales Commissions Report

```
10    REM ***               SALES COMMISSIONS REPORT            ***
20    REM
30    REM ***   THIS PROGRAM PREPARES A SALES REPORT FOR        ***
40    REM ***   MARTINEZ MEDICAL SUPPLIES.   EACH SALESPERSON'S ***
50    REM ***   NAME, COMMISSION RATE, AND AMOUNT OF THE        ***
60    REM ***   CURRENT SALE ARE ENTERED AT THE KEYBOARD.       ***
70    REM ***   THE TOTAL SALES AND COMMISSIONS EARNED ARE THEN ***
80    REM ***   DISPLAYED.  AT THE END OF THE REPORT THE TOTAL  ***
90    REM ***   SALES AND COMMISSIONS FOR ALL SALESPEOPLE ARE   ***
100   REM ***   PRINTED.                                        ***
110   REM ***   MAJOR VARIABLES:                                ***
120   REM ***      NME$                NAME OF SALESPERSON       ***
130   REM ***      CMSSNRTE            RATE OF COMMISSION        ***
140   REM ***      AMT                 AMOUNT OF EACH SALE       ***
150   REM ***      SALES               INDIVIDUAL TOTAL SALES    ***
160   REM ***      CMMSSN              INDIVIDUAL TOTAL COMMISSION ***
170   REM ***      TTLSALES            SALES FOR ALL SALESPEOPLE ***
180   REM ***      TTLCMMSSN           COMMISSIONS FOR ALL PEOPLE ***
190   REM
200   REM *** CALL SUBROUTINE TO PRINT HEADINGS. ***
210   GOSUB 1000
220   REM
230   REM *** CALL SUBROUTINE TO PROCESS DATA. ***
240   GOSUB 2000
250   REM
260   REM *** CALL SUBROUTINE TO PRINT SALEPERSON'S TOTALS. ***
270   GOSUB 3000
280   REM
290   REM *** CALL SUBROUTINE TO PRINT GRAND TOTALS. ***
300   GOSUB 4000
999   END
1000  REM ************************************************************
1010  REM ***                    PRINT HEADINGS               ***
1020  REM ************************************************************
1030  REM *** THIS SUBROUTINE INITIALIZES VARIABLES AND       ***
1040  REM *** PRINTS REPORT AND COLUMN HEADINGS.              ***
1050  REM
1060  SLS = 0
1070  CMMSSN = 0
1080  TTLSALES = 0
1090  TTLCMMSSN = 0
1100  LPRINT TAB(28) "MARTINEZ MEDICAL SUPPLIES"
1110  LPRINT
1120  LPRINT TAB(29) "SALES COMMISSIONS REPORT"
1130  LPRINT
1140  INPUT "ENTER MONTH OF REPORT";MNTH$
1150  LPRINT TAB(31) "FOR MONTH OF ";MNTH$
1160  LPRINT
1170  LPRINT
1180  LPRINT TAB(33) "COMMISSION"; TAB(49) "AMOUNT"; TAB(62) "COMMISSION"
1190  LPRINT TAB(10) "NAME"; TAB(33) "RATE"; TAB(49) "OF SALE"; TAB(62) "EARNED"
1200  GOSUB 5000
1210  RETURN
2000  REM ************************************************************
2010  REM ***                    PROCESS DATA                 ***
2020  REM ************************************************************
2030  REM *** THIS SUBROUTINE READS EACH SALESPERSON'S NAME,  ***
2040  REM *** COMMISSION RATE, AND AMOUNT OF SALES AND CALC-  ***
2050  REM *** ULATES THE TOTALS.                              ***
2060  REM
```

FIGURE 10–14 Continued

```
2070 FIRST$ = "YES"
2080 INPUT "ENTER SALESPERSON'S NAME (DONE TO STOP)";NME$
2090 TEMP$ = NME$
2100 WHILE NME$ <> "DONE"
2110    IF TEMP$ <> NME$ THEN GOSUB 3000
2120    IF FIRST$ = "YES" THEN INPUT "ENTER SALESPERSON'S COMMISSION RATE";
          CMSSNRTE
2130    INPUT "ENTER AMOUNT OF SALE";AMT
2140    SALES = SALES + AMT
2150    TTLSALES = TTLSALES + AMT
2160    CMMSSN = CMMSSN + AMT * CMSSNRTE
2170    TTLCMMSSN = TTLCMMSSN + CMMSSN
2180    F1$ = "         \                      \        #.##     $  ##,###.##    $  #
#,###.##"
2190    F2$ = "                                          $  ##,###.##    $  #
#,###.##"
2200    IF FIRST$ = "YES" THEN LPRINT USING F1$;NME$,CMSSNRTE,
          AMT,CMSSNRTE * AMT : FIRST$ = "NO"
          ELSE LPRINT USING F2$;AMT,CMSSNRTE * AMT
2210    INPUT "ENTER SALESPERSON'S NAME (DONE TO STOP)";NME$
2220 WEND
2230 RETURN
3000 REM ************************************************************
3010 REM ***              PRINT SALESPERSON'S TOTALS           ***
3020 REM ************************************************************
3030 REM   PRINTS EACH SALESPERSON'S TOTAL SALES AND TOTAL    ***
3040 REM *** COMMISSIONS EARNED.                               ***
3050 REM
3060 L3$ =      "\                            \              $  #
#,###.##"
3070 LPRINT
3080 LPRINT USING L3$;"TOTAL SALES:",SALES
3090 LPRINT USING L3$;"TOTAL COMMISSIONS:";CMMSSN
3100 GOSUB 5000
3110 SALES = 0
3120 CMMSSN = 0
3130 FIRST$ = "YES"
3140 TEMP$ = NME$
3150 RETURN
4000 REM ************************************************************
4010 REM ***                 PRINT GRAND TOTALS               ***
4020 REM ************************************************************
4030 REM *** PRINTS THE TOTAL SALES AND COMMISSIONS FOR ALL   ***
4040 REM *** SALESPEOPLE.                                      ***
4050 REM
4060 F4$ = "\                                \         $ ###,#
##.##"
4070 LPRINT USING F4$;"TOTAL SALES FOR ALL SALESPEOPLE";TTLSALES
4080 LPRINT USING F4$;"TOTAL COMMISSIONS FOR ALL SALESPEOPLE";TTLCMMSSN
4090 RETURN
5000 REM ************************************************************
5010 REM ***                  PRINT RULING                    ***
5020 REM ************************************************************
5030 REM
5040 LPRINT
5050 FOR I = 1  TO 80
5060    LPRINT "-";
5070 NEXT I
5080 LPRINT
5090 RETURN
```

(figure continued on the next page)

FIGURE 10–14 Continued

```
RUN
ENTER MONTH OF REPORT? APRIL
ENTER SALESPERSON'S NAME (DONE TO STOP)? FREDERICKSON
ENTER SALESPERSON'S COMMISSION RATE? 0.30
ENTER AMOUNT OF SALE? 4050.00
ENTER SALESPERSON'S NAME (DONE TO STOP)? LING
ENTER SALESPERSON'S COMMISSION RATE? 0.25
ENTER AMOUNT OF SALE? 1500.00
ENTER SALESPERSON'S NAME (DONE TO STOP)? LING
ENTER AMOUNT OF SALE? 280.00
ENTER SALESPERSON'S NAME (DONE TO STOP)? LING
ENTER AMOUNT OF SALE? 2200.00
ENTER SALESPERSON'S NAME (DONE TO STOP)? GARCIA
ENTER SALESPERSON'S COMMISSION RATE? 0.30
ENTER AMOUNT OF SALE? 2905.00
ENTER SALESPERSON'S NAME (DONE TO STOP)? DONE
```

```
                        MARTINEZ MEDICAL SUPPLIES

                        SALES COMMISSIONS REPORT

                        FOR MONTH OF APRIL


                        COMMISSION          AMOUNT          COMMISSION
        NAME            RATE                OF SALE         EARNED
        ------------------------------------------------------------------

        FREDERICKSON    0.30          $     4,050.00    $     1,215.00

TOTAL SALES:                                            $     4,050.00
TOTAL COMMISSIONS:                                      $     1,215.00

        ------------------------------------------------------------------

        LING            0.25          $     1,500.00    $       375.00
                                      $       280.00    $        70.00
                                      $     2,200.00    $       550.00

TOTAL SALES:                                            $     3,980.00
TOTAL COMMISSIONS:                                      $       995.00

        ------------------------------------------------------------------

        GARCIA          0.30          $     2,905.00    $       871.50

TOTAL SALES:                                            $     2,905.00
TOTAL COMMISSIONS:                                      $       871.50

        ------------------------------------------------------------------

TOTAL SALES FOR ALL SALESPEOPLE                         $    10,935.00
TOTAL COMMISSIONS FOR ALL SALESPEOPLE                   $     3,901.50
```

Summary Points

- A system is a group of related elements that work together toward a common goal. Systems must have input, processing, output, and feedback.
- An information system is designed to turn data into useful information. To be useful, the information must be accurate and timely.
- Large companies have data-processing departments that are responsible for developing software and maintaining the information system.
- Processing can be divided into five categories: Classifying, sorting, calculating, summarizing, and storing.
- The major components of an information system are the hardware, software, data, and people.
- The steps in the software-development life cycle are

  1. Define and document the problem.
  2. Design and document a solution.
  3. Write and document the program.
  4. Test and debug the program, revising the documentation if necessary.
  5. Implement the program.
  6. Evaluate the program.
  7. Maintain the program.

- The systems analyst and the user (or a representative of the user group) develop the specifications, which are then presented to the programmer to design and code a solution. One or more structured walkthroughs are held to allow programmers to share ideas for writing the program.
- After the program is thoroughly tested, it is implemented. In a crash implementation, all processing is immediately transferred to the new program. A pilot conversion involves switching over a small portion of the processing. In a parallel conversion, the safest and most expensive type of conversion, both methods continue to be used until it is certain the new program works properly.
- After the program is implemented, it is periodically evaluated to determine whether any changes need to be made.
- Program maintenance takes up about 80 percent of programmers' time and can involve correcting bugs, adding new modules so the program can perform more tasks, or making the program more user-friendly. Structured programs are much easier to maintain.

- In business, computers are often hooked together by special cables or telephone lines to form a network so that users can share hardware, software, and data files. Also, they can send messages to one another.
- Some computer-related careers are systems analyst, computer systems director, programmer, computer operator, data-entry clerk, and computer repair technician.
- Report writing is used in business to output tables of information, such as financial reports. The information is lined up in columns.
- Each individual line of data is called a detail line. A report can have any number of detail lines.
- The total of all values of a particular type (such as wages of all employees) is called the grand total. A control total is a total that is outputted when a specified value (such as a department number) changes. This is referred to as a control break.

Vocabulary List

Control break   Information system
Control total   Network
Data-processing department   Report heading
Detail line   Ruling
Electronic mail   Software development life cycle
Feedback   Structured walkthrough
Garbage in–garbage out (GIGO)   System
Grand total   Systems analyst

Questions

Whenever appropriate, use complete sentences in answering the following questions.

1. What is a system?

2. Give an example of a system. What is the input, processing, output, and feedback of this system?

3. Into what five categories can processing be divided?

4. List several reasons why most data-processing departments use structured programming techniques.

5. Why are structured walkthroughs helpful in developing well-designed programs?

6. Describe three methods of implementing a new program.

7. Why is it important that the performance of a program be evaluated periodically after it has been implemented?

8. Why is it very important that a program be thoroughly tested before it is implemented?

9. What is a detail line?

10. What is the purpose of using rulings?

11. Explain the term control break. Why are control breaks useful?

12. How is a control total related to a control break?

13. Explain the difference between a control total and a grand total.

14. What determines whether or not a control break occurs in the program in Figure 10–9?

15. What is the purpose of the variable FIRST$ in Figure 10–14?

Debugging Exercises

Identify the following programs or program segments that contain errors, and debug them.

```
1. 10   REM *** CENTER THE HEADING IN AN 80 COLUMN LINE. ***
   20   REM
   30   PRINT TAB (80 - LEN("CHARLES CITY POLICE DEPARTMENT"))
```

```
2. 100 REM *** GET LIST OF INVENTORY ITEMS AND QUANTITIES. ***
   110 REM *** AND CALCULATE TOTAL QUANTITY OF ALL ITEMS.  ***
   120 TTL = 0
   130 INPUT "ENTER NAME OF FIRST ITEM";ITEM$
   140 WHILE ITEM$ <> "FINISHED"
   150    INPUT "ENTER QUANTITY";QUANTITY
   160    TTL = QUANTITY
   170    INPUT "ENTER NAME OF NEXT ITEM";ITEM$
   180 WEND
```

```
3. 10 REM *** PRINT REPORT HEADING AND DIVIDING LINE. ***
   20 REM
   30 LPRINT TAB(30) "BAUMANN'S HOME BAKERY"
   40 FOR I = 1 TO 80
   50    LPRINT "-"
   60 NEXT I
```

```
4. 200 REM *** LOOP TO READ AND CALCULATE TOTAL BILL. ***
   210 REM
   220 INPUT "ENTER HOURS WORKED";HRS
   230 WHILE HRS <> 0
   240    INPUT "ENTER HOURLY RATE";RTE
   250    COST = HRS * RTE
   260    REM *** PRINT TOTAL COST. ***
   270    PRINT "TOTAL COST IS:   $";COST
   280 WEND
```

Programming Problems

Level 1

1. Write the statements necessary to center the following headings on an 80-column line:

BEAUMONT JUNIOR COLLEGE

FRESHMEN   SOPHOMORES   JUNIORS   SENIORS

2. Write the statements necessary to center the following headings on a 60-column line:

State Historical Society

Annual Budget Report

3. Write a report listing the following cities and their high temperatures for the day.

City	Temperature
Detroit	50
Phoenix	82
San Francisco	65
Iowa City	54

Allow the user to enter the data to tables. Then display the contents of the tables in report format with appropriate headings.

4. Alter Problem 3 so that the cities are listed in alphabetical order. Use a bubble sort to alphabetize the list.

5. Write a report listing the identification numbers and names of the following employees.

2840	Michael Mailice
1008	Jennifer Jenkins
4775	Jon Baumann
3090	Larry Eash
9846	Jeremiah Garcia

Allow the user to enter the needed data at the keyboard. The data should be sorted by employee identification number and then displayed in report format with appropriate headings.

6. Alter the program in Figure 10–7 so that the data does not have to be entered in order by account number. The data will have to be entered into three tables: one for the account number, one for the company name, and one for the amount of the bill. It must then be sorted by account number and processed.

Level 2

1. The Subterranean Art Gallery is preparing for its annual auction held in Washington Square. The *Village Voice* is preparing a printed listing containing information on the paintings to be auctioned. Write a program that allows the user to enter the name of each painting, the artist, and the painting's estimated value at the keyboard. A report, with appropriate headings, then should be printed on paper. The report should be formatted similar to the following:

Painting	Artist	Value
Alton, M.	Starry Night	5000.00
Alton, M.	Self Portrait	3095.00
Perez, J.	The Wheat Field	1090.00
Perez, J.	Beige Tones	2450.00
Remington, H.	Sunday Afternoon	504.00

Create your own data to test the program.

2. Rewrite Problem 1 so that a control break occurs each time a new artist is entered (you can assume that the paintings will be entered in alphabetical order by artist's last name). When the name of a new artist is entered, the total value of paintings by the previous artist should be printed.

3. Gary Mueller has hired you to keep track of his band's payroll. Write a program that will read the following information:

Section	Number of Musicians	Hourly Pay Rate per Musician
Bongos	3	$10.00
Horns	10	$ 5.50
Guitars	4	$ 9.50
Strings	6	$ 7.50
Maracas	20	$ 3.65

A report should be displayed containing this information plus the following totals:

Total number of musicians.
Total hourly rate.

4. Rewrite Problem 3 so that the user is prompted to enter the number of hours the band played. In addition to the output specified in Problem 3, a final total bill should be displayed.

5. The Movie Maniacs' Association is conducting a survey of 150 moviegoers to see which movie they would pick as their all-time favorite. The association would like you to write a program to show the results of the survey. The program should use INPUT statements to enter the data. Also, the program should display a report of the survey, giving the name of the movie, the percentage of votes it received, and the number of votes it received. At the end of the report, print the total number of votes. Use the following data:

Star Wars	58
The Wizard of Oz	21
E.T.	12
Casa Blanca	17
The Sound of Music	29
Nightmare on Elm Street	8

6. A university would like a program that will generate a report regarding enrollment in three of its colleges. The program should use the following data:

	College		
Year	Business	Education	Music
1986	548	426	321
1987	593	447	203
1988	641	430	346
1989	650	398	401

The report should indicate what percentage of each year's total enrollment is enrolled in each college. The total enrollment for each year should also be indicated. The format for the report is as follows:

ENROLLMENT PERCENTAGE FOR EACH YEAR

YEAR	BUSINESS	MUSIC	EDUCATION	TOTAL
1986	XX.XX%	XXXX%	XX.XX%	XXXX
1987				
1988				
1989				

Projects

For each project, complete the following:

- Fill out a program specification chart.
- Develop a structure chart.
- Create a flowchart or pseudocode.
- Thoroughly document the final program.
- Test your program using a variety of data.

1. Cedar Valley High School's marching band is having its annual magazine sale and would like you to write a program to keep track of each member's sales. The program should allow the user to enter each member's name and sales at the keyboard. Then a sales report should be printed on paper. Each person's total sales and the overall total sales should be printed. Make up your own input data to test the program. The input data should be similar to the following:

Name	Sales
Jeremy Anderson	25.90, 16.39
Paula Rodriguez	14.50, 20.00, 13.85
Kathy Shieh	32.40

The final report should list only the total sales for each student (not individual sales) and the grand total. In addition, determine which student had the most sales, and print his or her name at the bottom of the report.

2. Pulschen's Furniture Manufacturing Company makes two items: an end table and a coffee table. The company needs a program that will keep track of each employee's performance for a given week. Write a program that will allow the user to enter the following data on each employee at the keyboard:

ID number
Number of hours worked
Number of end tables made
Number of coffee tables made

Calculate the wages for each employee, assuming all employees are paid $7.40 an hour. Also assume that the company sells the end tables for $87.50 of which $48.74 is the cost of materials, overhead, and so on. The coffee tables sell for $129.90, with cost of materials and overhead averaging $70.65. Figure out the amount of money the company has made from the products made by each of its employees.

CHAPTER

11

Using Data Files

Learning Objectives

After studying this chapter, you should be able to
1. List several advantages of using data files.
2. Explain the difference between a program file and a data file.
3. Discuss the relationship between files, records, and fields.
4. Explain the difference between sequential organization and relative organization.
5. Describe the different secondary storage media commonly used to store files.
6. Create a sequential file.
7. Write data to a sequential file.
8. Append data to the end of an existing sequential file.
9. Read the contents of a sequential file.
10. Explain the advantages of using random files.
11. Create random files and declare the fields in them.
12. Write records to a random file.
13. Update and delete records in a random file.
14. Compare random and sequential files.

Introduction

Up to this point, you have been entering data into programs in one of three ways:

1. Using an assignment statement (such as "QUANTITY = 10") to assign a value to a variable.
2. Prompting the user to enter data during program execution with the INPUT statement.
3. Placing the data in DATA statements within the program and then assigning these values to variables with READ statements.

In all three of these cases the data is then kept in the computer's primary storage unit while the program is executing. The contents of the storage locations can be displayed on the screen or printed on paper. However, there are a number of disadvantages to each of these methods. First, using assignment statements involves actually altering program statements to enter new data. Therefore, it is not useful for entering large amounts of input or input that will change frequently. The READ statement has similar problems; each time data changes, someone must edit the DATA statements. In addition, what if a very large quantity of data needs to be entered? This happens often in business—for example, a department store may have large numbers of charge account customers to bill each month. Using the assignment and READ/DATA statements would be virtually impossible in these situations.

The INPUT statement is simple to use, but the data must be entered each time the program is run. Also, if the user makes a mistake in entering one value, the entire program must be run again.

These problems can be solved by using **files.** A file is a collection of related data kept in secondary storage. In this chapter you will learn to

File

A collection of related data items, organized in a meaningful way and kept in secondary storage.

Program file
A file that stores a program.

Data file
A file used to store data to be used by one or more programs.

create data files that your programs can access. As you may know, you have been creating files all along in this class. Your programs are stored in files. The name under which you save a program is a file name. When you type in the directory (DIR) command, you get a list of the names of all of the files on the disk currently being accessed. Files containing programs are referred to as **program files,** whereas the files you will be creating in this chapter are **data files;** they store the data your program accesses.

What Is a File?

Data files provide an alternative means of organizing and storing related data. A major advantage of data files is that they are kept in secondary storage, which is virtually unlimited. On personal computers, expanding secondary storage is usually as simple as buying another floppy disk. In addition, these floppy disks can be moved from one computer to another. On larger computers, such as minicomputers and mainframes, magnetic tapes and disks are commonly used storage devices.

Many users can access the same data file, and the file can be created and then accessed by the same program at a later time. Files allow easy updating of data, too.

Record
One or more fields that together describe a single unit. Records group together to form files.

Field
The smallest division within a file, consisting of a single data item. Fields group together to form records.

There are two major divisions within a file. Figure 11–1 shows a file that a high school might use to contain data on its students. Each collection of data on a single student is a **record.** Files are made up of a group of records. The individual data items in the record are **fields.** In Figure 11–1, each record has three fields:

1. Student's name
2. Student's address
3. Student's grade (9 through 12)

FIGURE 11–1   File Containing Student Records

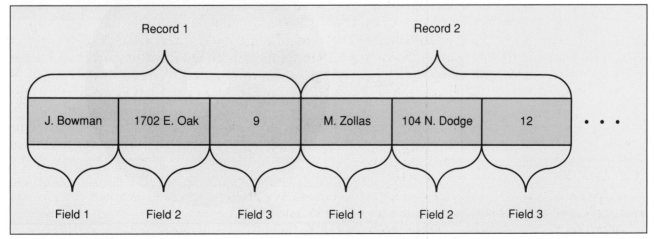

A computer file can be compared with a filing cabinet. A particular filing cabinet often contains information on one general topic, such as the records of students. Each student record is kept in a separate folder. The individual pieces of information in each folder are similar to the record fields.

File Organization

The method used to organize records in a file determines how these records can be used by BASIC programs. Microsoft BASIC provides two types of file organization: sequential and relative.

Sequential organization stores records in a sequence, one record immediately following another, from the beginning of the file to the end. The records are stored on the disk in the order in which they are entered into the computer. In other words, the second record written to a file is stored physically next to the first record, the third record is physically adjacent to the second, and so on. Figure 11–2 demonstrates this idea.

Relative organization stores each record in a numbered location in secondary storage. Location 1 contains the first record in the file, location 2 contains the second record, and so forth.

File Access Methods

An **access method** is the way the computer transmits data between secondary storage and the primary storage unit. Just as there are two types of file organization in Microsoft BASIC, there are two methods of file access: sequential and random.

Sequential organization
A method of organizing records within a file whereby the records are stored in the same order in which they are written to the file.

Relative organization
A method of organizing records in a file in which each record is stored in a numbered location.

Access method
The way in which the computer transmits data between secondary storage and the primary storage unit.

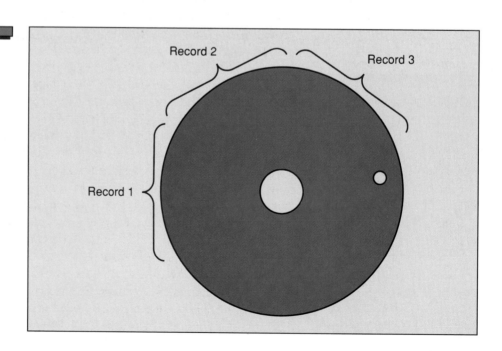

FIGURE 11–2 Sequential Organization on Disk

Sequential access

Accessing a record by accessing all records, starting at the beginning of the file, until the needed record is reached.

Sequential access retrieves a record based on its sequential position within the file. When a programmer uses sequential access to retrieve a record, all records that precede the needed record must be accessed first. For example, before the fifth record of a file can be accessed, the first four records must be accessed.

Sequential files allow only sequential access. Records are accessed in the order in which they are stored in the file. If you have accessed the tenth record and then wish to access the fifth one, you must go back to the beginning of the file and start over with the first record. Sequential files can be thought of as being one-way streets. If you visit the tenth house on the block and then wish to go back to the second house, you must drive around the block to the first house and then go on to the second house. Remember that a sequential *file* is not the same as sequential *access*. The term *sequential file* refers to the organization of the file, whereas *sequential access* refers to the manner in which the individual records within the file are retrieved.

Random access

Accessing a record directly, often by using a record number.

Random access allows a record to be accessed directly, usually by using its numbered location in the file. Random access can be compared with dialing a telephone number. The number allows the system to connect you with a single telephone line out of many thousands of lines.

Secondary Storage

As previously mentioned, secondary storage refers to storage media separate from the primary storage unit. Files can be permanently kept in secondary storage. Some forms of secondary storage media are magnetic tapes, magnetic disks, floppy disks, and hard disks. These last two are commonly used on microcomputers. Larger computers, such as mainframes, commonly use magnetic tape and disks.

A reel of *magnetic tape* looks similar to a reel of video tape. Magnetic tape is usually 2,400 feet long and is spun by a tape drive, as shown in Figure 11–3. Because of the design of the tape drive, records must be read sequentially. The read/write head, which performs the actual reading and writing of data, cannot skip to a particular record on the tape; the tape must spin until the read/write head locates the needed records. Figure 11–1 illustrates how records are stored on magnetic tape.

Magnetic disks, which are commonly used on mainframe and minicomputers, look like record albums. Data is stored on the disk in *tracks*, which are series of concentric circles on the surface of the disk. A collection of concentric disk tracks with the same radius is called a *cylinder*. Both cylinders and tracks are numbered. A group of disks is a *disk pack* (shown in Figure 11–4), which looks like a stack of record albums with a spindle passing through the middle. Figure 11–5 shows the inside of a disk pack. Read/write heads retrieve and store data on the disks. Notice that there are two read/write heads for each disk, one for the upper surface and one for the lower surface. (The top and bottom disks in the disk pack each have only

FIGURE 11–3   A Tape Drive

one read/write head for control purposes.) The read/write arm, which holds the read/write heads, can move backward and forward, and the disk pack can rotate on the spindle as well. By using the numbered tracks and cylinders and the movement of the disk pack, the computer can find a record either randomly or sequentially.

A *floppy disk* looks like a small record album in its cover. To locate a record, the computer uses *tracks* that are located on the disk. Each track is divided into *sectors*. The disk contains an *index hole*, which the computer

FIGURE 11–4   Disk Packs

FIGURE 11–5   The Inside of a Disk Pack

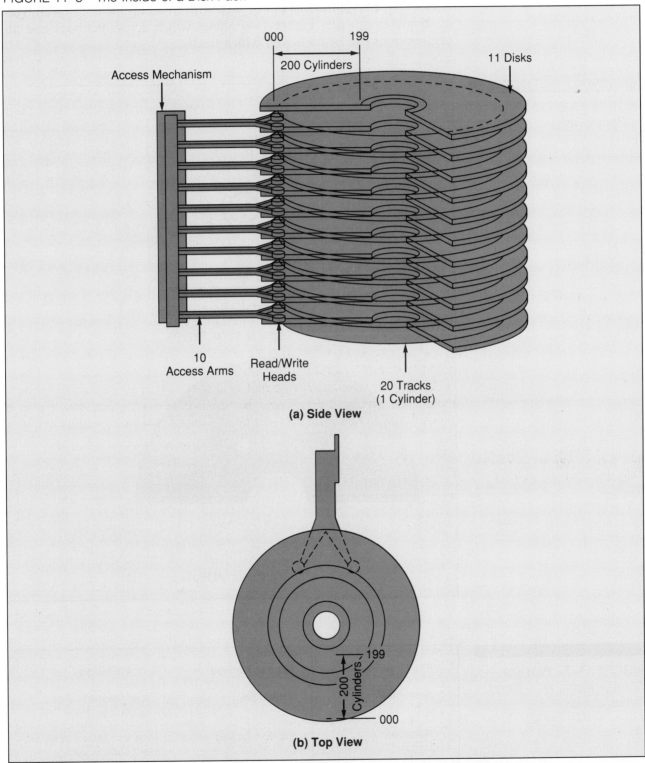

(a) Side View

(b) Top View

uses to calculate the location of a particular sector by timing the disk's rotation. Figure 11–6 shows the parts of a 5¼-inch floppy disk.

Not all file organizations can be used with all access methods on all types of secondary storage. Figure 11–7 shows which access methods and file organizations can be used with which media.

FIGURE 11–6   The Parts of a Floppy Disk

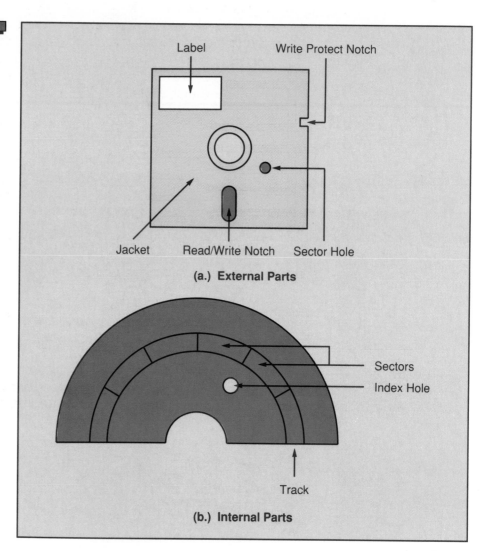

FIGURE 11–7   Possible Storage Media for Different Types of Files

File Organization	Access Method	Storage Media
Sequential	Sequential	Tape, Magnetic Disk, Floppy Disk, Hard Disk
Relative	Random or Sequential	Magnetic Disk, Floppy Disk, Hard Disk

File Position Pointers

File position pointer
An imaginary pointer indicating the next record to be processed.

Associated with each file is an imaginary **file position pointer** that "points to" the next record to be processed. This imaginary pointer can be thought of as a window that "looks ahead" to the next record. The computer adjusts this pointer when a file statement is executed in a program. For instance, when you first access a file to read its records, the pointer is set to the beginning of the file so that the first record in the file is available for processing. After the program reads this first record, the file pointer automatically advances to the next record. In the following diagram of a file called NAMES, the file pointer is set at the location of the record Mike when the file is first accessed:

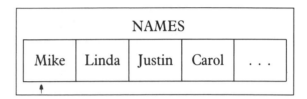

After the first record is read, the pointer advances to the next record, Linda:

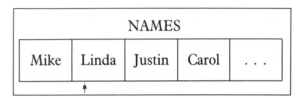

The file position pointer has no effect on the data contained in the file; it simply indicates the position of the next record to be processed.

Now Try This

1. Name four different methods that can be used to place data into variables in a program.

2. Files are divided into _____, which are further subdivided into _____.

3. _____ organization stores records in the order in which they are written to the file, whereas _____ organization stores records in numbered locations.

4. Files stored on tape can be accessed either sequentially or randomly (true or false).

5. A(n) _____ is a collection of concentric disk tracks.

Using Sequential Files

A number of operations can be performed on sequential files, including creating and accessing files, adding records, and displaying the contents of records.

Creating and Accessing a File

To use data files, you must be able to create new files and access existing ones. Both operations are performed by the OPEN statement, which provides the BASIC system with the following information:

1. *The name of the file.* The same rules apply to naming data files that apply to naming program files: the name may have from one to eight characters and an optional extension having from one to three characters. You may wish to assign the same name to both the program file and its data file and use extensions to differentiate them. For example, if INVEN.BAS is an inventory program, the file storing the inventory data might be named INVEN.DAT.

2. *The mode, or way, in which the file is to be used.* The mode can be OUTPUT, INPUT, or APPEND. OUTPUT indicates that data is written to the file from the program. In INPUT mode, the contents of the file are being read into the program. APPEND mode allows new records to be added (appended) to an existing file.

Buffer

A temporary storage location used for data being written to or read from a file.

3. *The number of the buffer to be associated with the file.* A **buffer** is a reserved part of the primary storage unit used as a temporary storage area for data that is being written to or read from a file. When data is being written to a file, it is first copied from the variable to the buffer and then copied from the buffer into the correct location in the file. Each file is assigned a numbered buffer. A maximum of three buffers can be used at a time. This means that you can access three different files at once.

The following statement creates a file named PAYROLL.DAT:

```
70 OPEN "PAYROLL.DAT" FOR OUTPUT AS #1
```

This statement instructs the system to

1. Create a new file named PAYROLL.DAT. If a file with this name already exists, it is destroyed, and a new, empty file is created.
2. Prepare the file to receive data (the word OUTPUT indicates that this file will have data written to it).
3. Associate the file PAYROLL.DAT with buffer #1 as long as this file is open. Buffer #1 will be used to temporarily hold data before it is written to the file on disk. Other statements in the program use this number to identify the file.

Closing a File

When a program is through using a file, the CLOSE statement closes the file. Closing the file causes its contents to be stored permanently on disk. If the file is opened for output, the CLOSE statement moves any data remaining in the buffer to the file (this is often referred to as "dumping the buffer"). No input or output can be performed on a closed file. The following statement closes the file that was previously opened:

```
250 CLOSE #1
```

Notice that the CLOSE statement does not use the name of the file (which is PAYROLL.DAT) but rather uses its buffer number (#1). Any number of files can be closed in a single statement:

```
280 CLOSE #1,#3
```

Using the CLOSE statement alone closes all files that have been opened in a program:

```
90 CLOSE
```

If you wish to change the mode of an open file, you must first close that file and then reopen it in another mode. The file can be reopened with the same or a different file number.

Now Try This

1. Write an OPEN statement that creates a new file CUSTLIST.DAT with a file number 3. The file should be prepared to have records written to it.

2. Write an OPEN statement that creates a new file named ADDRESS.DAT that will have records written to it.

3. Write a statement to close file #3 and file #1.

4. Write a statement that closes all of the files opened in a program.

Writing to a File

When a file will have new data written to it, it must be opened for output. The new file is created, but it is empty. To store records in a new file, perform the following steps:

1. Open the file for output.
2. Write data to the file.
3. Close the file to protect its contents.

The WRITE# statement places records in the file. It operates much like the PRINT statement, except that it sends values to a file in secondary storage rather than displaying them on the monitor screen. For example, the following statement sends the values of the variables NAM$ and SALARY to the file PAYROLL.DAT:

```
100 WRITE #1,NAM$,SALARY
```

The BASIC system places the values of NAM$ and SALARY in the file at the storage location indicated by the file position pointer and advances the pointer to the next record position. The file now contains the data on one employee.

The program in Figure 11–8 creates a sequential file PAYROLL.DAT and allows the user to write employee records to it. Each record contains an employee's identification number, name, and salary. Figure 11–9 illustrates how the file will look after the program is executed.

Appending Records to a File

If it is necessary to add records to an existing file, the OPEN statement must contain the APPEND clause. For example:

```
130 OPEN "PAYROLL.DAT" FOR APPEND AS #1
```

When a file is opened for input or output, the file position pointer is placed at the first record in the file; however, new records can be written only at the *end* of a sequential file. The APPEND clause sets the file position pointer to the end of the specified file and thus permits the user to add new records without losing any of the old ones. The three basic steps for appending data to an existing sequential file are

1. Open the file for APPEND.
2. Write the new data to the end of the file.
3. Close the file.

Figure 11–10 shows a program that adds records to the PAYROLL.DAT file, which was created by the program in Figure 11–8. The only change is in the OPEN statement. When adding records to an existing file, be careful to open the file for APPEND rather than OUTPUT. The OUTPUT clause destroys the contents of the existing file.

FIGURE 11–8   Program to Create a Sequential File

```
10   REM ***                    PAYROLL PROGRAM                    ***
20   REM ***                                                       ***
30   REM ***    THIS PROGRAM CREATES A SEQUENTIAL FILE.  THE       ***
40   REM ***    USER IS PROMPTED TO ENTER THE DATA WHICH IS THEN   ***
50   REM ***    WRITTEN TO THE FILE.                               ***
60   REM ***    FILE USED:                                         ***
70   REM ***       PAYROLL.DATA    SEQUENTIAL PAYROLL FILE         ***
80   REM ***    MAJOR VARIABLES USED:                              ***
90   REM ***       IDNUM    EMPLOYEE'S IDENTIFICATION NUMBER       ***
100  REM ***       NAM$     EMPLOYEE'S NAME                        ***
110  REM ***       SALARY   EMPLOYEE'S YEARLY SALARY               ***
120  REM
130  OPEN "PAYROLL.DAT" FOR OUTPUT AS #1
140  INPUT "ENTER EMPLOYEE'S IDENTIFICATION NUMBER (0 TO STOP)";IDNUM
150  WHILE IDNUM <> 0
160     INPUT "ENTER EMPLOYEE'S NAME";NAM$
170     INPUT "ENTER EMPLOYEE'S SALARY";SALARY
180     WRITE #1,IDNUM,NAM$,SALARY
190     INPUT "ENTER EMPLOYEE'S IDENTIFICATION NUMBER (0 TO STOP)";IDNUM
200  WEND
210  CLOSE #1
999  END
```

```
RUN
ENTER EMPLOYEE'S IDENTIFICATION NUMBER (0 TO STOP)? 100
ENTER EMPLOYEE'S NAME? M. STILES
ENTER EMPLOYEE'S SALARY? 15000
ENTER EMPLOYEE'S IDENTIFICATION NUMBER (0 TO STOP)? 101
ENTER EMPLOYEE'S NAME? I. MARTINEZ
ENTER EMPLOYEE'S SALARY? 17500
ENTER EMPLOYEE'S IDENTIFICATION NUMBER (0 TO STOP)? 102
ENTER EMPLOYEE'S NAME? S. JONES
ENTER EMPLOYEE'S SALARY? 16500
ENTER EMPLOYEE'S IDENTIFICATION NUMBER (0 TO STOP)? 103
ENTER EMPLOYEE'S NAME? E. MATHEY
ENTER EMPLOYEE'S SALARY? 19000
ENTER EMPLOYEE'S IDENTIFICATION NUMBER (0 TO STOP)? 0
```

FIGURE 11–9 Contents of
Payroll File

```
100,"M. STILES",15000
101,"I. MARTINEZ",17500
102,"S. JONES",16500
103,"E. MATHEY",19000
```

The file PAYROLL.DAT contains the following values after the program in Figure 11–10 is executed:

```
100 ,"M. STILES",15000
101 ,"I. MARTINEZ",17500
102 ,"S. JONES",16500
103 ,"E. MATHEY",19000
104 ,"P. WASHINGTON",21400
105 ,"M. MICHAELS",18000
```

Reading from a Sequential File

Writing records to a file is useful only if you are able to use those records at a later time. The transfer of data from a file to the computer's primary storage is referred to as *reading a file*. The three steps involved in reading from a sequential file are as follows:

1. Open the file for input.
2. Read the data from the file.
3. Close the file.

The INPUT# statement reads data from a file. The INPUT# statement is similar to the INPUT statement. Whereas the INPUT statement accepts data from the keyboard, the INPUT# statement takes values from a file and assigns them to the listed variables on a one-to-one basis. The following example reads three data items (the first record) from the PAYROLL.DAT file and assigns them to the variables IDNUM, NAM$, and SALARY:

```
100 OPEN "PAYROLL.DAT" FOR INPUT AS #2
110 INPUT #2,IDNUM,NAM$,SALARY
```

These statements would cause variables IDNUM, NAM$, and SALARY to be assigned the values 100, M. STILES, and 15000 respectively.

The INPUT# statement reads the record to which the file position pointer is currently pointing, and places its contents in the variables of the variable list. After the INPUT# statement is executed, the file position pointer advances automatically to the next record. In a sequential file, an INPUT# operation begins with the first record in the file (where the OPEN statement sets the pointer). Each successive INPUT# statement retrieves the next values in the file and places them in the listed variables.

FIGURE 11–10   Program to Append Records to a Sequential File

```
10   REM ***                      PAYROLL PROGRAM                      ***
20   REM ***                                                           ***
30   REM ***   THIS PROGRAM APPENDS NEW DATA TO THE END OF AN          ***
40   REM ***   EXISTING SEQUENTIAL FILE.  THE USER ENTERS THE          ***
50   REM ***   NEW DATA WHICH IS THEN APPENDED TO THE FILE.            ***
60   REM ***   FILE USED:                                              ***
70   REM ***      PAYROLL.DATA    SEQUENTIAL PAYROLL FILE              ***
80   REM ***   MAJOR VARIABLES USED:                                   ***
90   REM ***      IDNUM    EMPLOYEE'S IDENTIFICATION NUMBER            ***
100  REM ***      NAM$     EMPLOYEE'S NAME                             ***
110  REM ***      SALARY   EMPLOYEE'S YEARLY SALARY                    ***
120  REM
130  OPEN "PAYROLL.DAT" FOR APPEND AS #1
140  INPUT "ENTER EMPLOYEE'S IDENTIFICATION NUMBER (0 TO STOP)";IDNUM
150  WHILE IDNUM <> 0
160     INPUT "ENTER EMPLOYEE'S NAME";NAM$
170     INPUT "ENTER EMPLOYEE'S SALARY";SALARY
180     WRITE #1,IDNUM,NAM$,SALARY
190     INPUT "ENTER EMPLOYEE'S IDENTIFICATION NUMBER (0 TO STOP)";IDNUM
200  WEND
210  CLOSE #1
999  END
```

```
RUN
ENTER EMPLOYEE'S IDENTIFICATION NUMBER (0 TO STOP)? 104
ENTER EMPLOYEE'S NAME? P. WASHINGTON
ENTER EMPLOYEE'S SALARY? 21400
ENTER EMPLOYEE'S IDENTIFICATION NUMBER (0 TO STOP)? 105
ENTER EMPLOYEE'S NAME? M. MICHAELS
ENTER EMPLOYEE'S SALARY? 18000
ENTER EMPLOYEE'S IDENTIFICATION NUMBER (0 TO STOP)? 0
```

If you attempt to read more records than exist in a file, an error occurs. The computer places a special character, called an *end-of-file marker*, after the last data item in a file. An attempt to read past this marker results in an error message and termination of program execution.

The end-of-file marker acts as a trailer value that is useful when reading the contents of a file. A special function, called the *EOF (end-of-file) function*, is used to check for the end-of-file marker. For example, the following expression determines whether the end of file number 1 has been reached:

```
EOF(1)
```

If there are more records to be read, EOF is false; when the end-of-file marker is reached, EOF becomes true. Because the EOF function results in a value of true or false, it can be used to control the execution of a WHILE loop. A loop that reads records from a file should execute until the end of the file has been reached.

The program in Figure 11–11 reads and prints the data records stored in the file PAYROLL.DAT, which was created in Figure 11–8 and added to in Figure 11–10. Notice the condition controlling the WHILE loop:

```
200 WHILE NOT EOF(1)
```

As long as the end of PAYROLL.DAT is not reached, each record will be read from the file and displayed on the screen. In Figure 11–11, each record in the file is accessed and used. Consider a situation where just one record from a file is needed. Suppose you want to display the third record of the file PAYROLL.DAT. The rules of sequential access dictate that all preceding records must be accessed first, starting at the beginning of the file. You do this by reading, but not printing, the first two records of the file PAYROLL.DAT. Remember that an INPUT# statement automatically advances the file position pointer to the next record in the file. After the second record is read, the pointer is set to the third record, which you can then read and display. The following segment reads three records from the PAYROLL.DAT file, but displays only the third record.

```
30 OPEN "PAYROLL.DAT" FOR INPUT AS #1
40 INPUT #1,IDNUM,NAM$,SALARY
50 INPUT #1,IDNUM,NAM$,SALARY
60 INPUT #1,IDNUM,NAM$,SALARY
70 PRINT IDNUM,NAM$,SALARY
80 CLOSE #1
```

Using Random Files

The previous section discussed sequential files. That method of storing data is adequate for some applications, but not for others.

Suppose you need to get only one record from a sequential file. If the record is at the end of a large file, then sequential access is both inefficient

▬▬▬▬▬▬

FIGURE 11–11   Program to Read the Contents of a Sequential File

```
10   REM ***                    PAYROLL PROGRAM                    ***
20   REM ***                                                       ***
30   REM ***   THIS PROGRAM READS A SEQUENTIAL FILE NAMED          ***
40   REM ***   PAYROLL.DAT.  A LOOP IS USED TO READ EACH RECORD    ***
50   REM ***   UNTIL THE END OF THE FILE IS REACHED.               ***
60   REM ***   FILE USED:                                          ***
70   REM ***      PAYROLL.DATA   SEQUENTIAL PAYROLL FILE           ***
80   REM ***   MAJOR VARIABLES USED:                               ***
90   REM ***      IDNUM    EMPLOYEE'S IDENTIFICATION NUMBER        ***
100  REM ***      NAM$     EMPLOYEE'S NAME                         ***
110  REM ***      SALARY   EMPLOYEE'S YEARLY SALARY                ***
120  REM
130  OPEN "PAYROLL.DAT" FOR INPUT AS #1
140  CLS
150  PRINT TAB(30) "PAYROLL REPORT"
160  PRINT
170  PRINT TAB(10) "IDENTIFICATION"
180  PRINT TAB(10) "NUMBER"; TAB(30) "NAME"; TAB(50) "SALARY"
190  PRINT "--------------------------------------------------------"
200  WHILE NOT EOF(1)
210     INPUT #1,IDNUM,NAM$,SALARY
220     PRINT TAB(10) IDNUM; TAB(30) NAM$; TAB(50) SALARY
230  WEND
240  CLOSE #1
999  END
```

```
RUN                              PAYROLL REPORT

          IDENTIFICATION
          NUMBER                 NAME                   SALARY
---------------------------------------------------------------
          100                    M. STILES              15000
          101                    I. MARTINEZ            17500
          102                    S. JONES               16500
          103                    E. MATHEY              19000
          104                    P. WASHINGTON          21400
          105                    M. MICHAELS            18000
```

Now Try This

1. The file BILLING.DAT consists of records containing two character string fields—a name and an address. Write a segment that will add one record to the file, which is associated with file #3.

2. Write a program segment that will read and display the first record of the file BILLING.DAT in Exercise 1.

3. Which of the following statements causes a record described in Exercise 1 to be transmitted from a file on disk to the computer's primary storage?

    a. `90  WRITE #3,NAM$,ADDRESS$`
    b. `90  INPUT BILLING,NAM$,ADDRESS$`
    c. `90  PRINT #3,NAM$,ADDRESS$`
    d. `90  INPUT #3,NAM$,ADDRESS$`

4. Write a program segment that will access the file BILLING.DAT in Exercise 1 and (a) display the second record, then (b) display the first record.

---

and slow. For example, a personnel administrator might need to change the salary data for an employee named Rose Zenith. If the records are stored alphabetically by last name, then Ms. Zenith's record will be near the end of the file. Before the personnel administrator can update the record, all preceding records must be read. If there are 20,000 records in the file, imagine how long it would take to get Ms. Zenith's record!

We can use relative files with random access, or, as they are commonly called, *random files*, to solve these problems. In a relative file records are stored in numbered locations: location 1 contains the first record relative to the start of the file, location 2 contains the second record relative to the start of the file, and so on. By using random access with relative files, you can retrieve any record in the file by specifying the number of the record needed. You do not have to read all preceding records in a file.

Creating a Random File

As with sequential files, a random file must first be created or accessed before it can be used. This is accomplished by using the OPEN statement. Its format is as follows:

> line# OPEN "filename" AS #filenumber LEN = buffer-size

The first part of the statement is the same as for sequential files. *Filename* is a character string that names the file. *Filenumber* is an integer value that identifies the buffer associated with the file. Other program statements will then use this number to identify the file. *Buffer-size* specifies the length of each record within the file. For example, if each record will have 30 characters, buffer-size is set to 30. Since the commands for reading from and writing to random files are different than for sequential files, no mode needs to be specified.

As with sequential files, only three files (sequential, random, or a combination of both) can be opened at any given time. The following is an example of the OPEN statement:

```
10 OPEN "CUSTOMER.DAT" AS #2 LEN=48
```

This line instructs the computer to do the following:

1. Access the file named CUSTOMER.DAT. If no file by that name exists, a new file named CUSTOMER.DAT is created.
2. Associate buffer number 2 with the CUSTOMER.DAT file as long as this file is open.
3. Give each record in the CUSTOMER.DAT file a record length of 48 characters.

It is important to note here that, as with sequential files, the CLOSE statement should be used when you are through using a random file. By closing files, you prevent data from being lost.

Once the file is opened and the record length is specified, the length of each field within the record must be declared. The FIELD statement accomplishes this by specifying the field length of every field within the record.

The following is an example of the FIELD statement and its associated OPEN statement:

```
10 OPEN "CUSTOMER.DAT" AS #2 LEN=48
20 FIELD #2,10 AS ACCT$,30 AS NAM$,8 AS BAL$
```

These lines tell the computer that file #2, or CUSTOMER.DAT, will contain three fields. The first field, accessed by the string variable name ACCT$, is 10 characters long. The second field, accessed by the string variable name NAM$, is 30 characters long. The last field, accessed by the string variable name BAL$, is 8 characters long. The total length of the three fields must add up to the buffer-size in the OPEN statement, in this case 48. The format for the FIELD statement is as follows:

```
line# FIELD #filenumber,fieldwidth AS fieldname[,fieldwidth AS fieldname] . . .
```

The *filenumber* is the same file number that was specified by the OPEN statement. The *fieldwidth* gives the length of the field called *fieldname*. Every *fieldname* within the record must be given a string variable name.

Storing Numeric Data in Random Files

In order for data to be stored in a random file, each field must contain character data. This becomes a problem when storing integers and real numbers. To accommodate numeric data, Microsoft BASIC has three standard functions used to translate numbers to character values for storage in random files. These functions do not convert the numeric values to character string values; they simply help the computer interpret numbers as characters. The three functions are

1. MKI$(integer expression)
2. MKS$(single-precision expression)
3. MKD$(double-precision expression)

Notice that a different function is used for each type of number. MKI$ translates integer values (whole numbers between -32768 and 32767) to a character string value. MKS$ translates single-precision numbers (real numbers with seven or fewer digits) to a character string value. MKD$ translates double-precision numbers (real numbers with eight or more digits) to a character string. Examples of these functions follow:

MKI$	MKS$	MKD$
70 N% = 24	70 N = 300.99	70 N# = 44090.999
80 C$ = MKI$(N%)	80 C$ = MKS$(N)	80 C$ = MKD$(N#)

In this textbook, we have been using single-precision variables to store numeric data. (Remember that an integer value can be stored as a real number.) Therefore, we will continue that practice.

Updating a Random File

So far in this chapter, you have learned how to create and access a random file. You have also learned how to translate numeric values into character values so the computer can store them in a random file. Now you will learn how to update a random file, by both inserting and deleting records.

Inserting Records into a Random File In order for records to be inserted into a random file, data must be assigned to the file buffer by assigning data to each field name specified in the FIELD statement. This is done with the LSET or RSET statements. Besides moving data into the file buffer, the LSET statement adds blanks to the end of the data if the data is shorter in length than the field. Conversely, the RSET statement adds blanks to the beginning of the data. For example, if NAM$ is a field with a length of 20 characters, when these statements are executed—

```
80 N$ = "CARL COUCH"
90 LSET NAM$ = N$
```

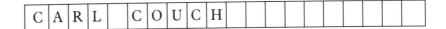

—the field will be stored like this:

| C | A | R | L | | C | O | U | C | H | | | | | | | | | | |

If RSET is used instead—

```
80 N$ = "CARL COUCH"
90 RSET NAM$ = N$
```

—the last character of the name will be in the rightmost position:

| | | | | | | | | | C | A | R | L | | C | O | U | C | H |

Some more examples follow:

```
70 LSET BAL$ = MKS$(300)
80 LSET NAM$ = "STRONG"
```

```
70 RSET BAL$ = MKS$(BAL)
80 RSET NAM$ = N$
```

Notice that numeric data is stored by first using MKS$ to prepare it to be stored, and the value is then placed in the specified field.

Once the data is stored in the correct fields, the PUT statement is used to store the data in the random file. For example, the following statement places the value of the fields in the third record position in file #2:

```
200 LSET ACCT$ = A$
210 LET NAM$ = N$
220 LSET BAL$ = MKS$(B)
230 PUT #2,3
```

The general format of the PUT statement is

line# PUT filenumber[,recordnumber]

The *filenumber* is the file number specified in the OPEN statement for the file you wish to store the record in. The *recordnumber* is an integer between 1 and 32,767 (the number of records allowed in a random file). The *recordnumber* specifies the relative record position where the record will be stored in the file. For example, a *recordnumber* of 1 specifies that the record will be stored as the first record in the file. A *recordnumber* of 10 specifies that the record will be stored as the tenth record in the file. If a *recordnumber* is not given, the record is stored in the position immediately following the position of the last record that was stored. If a *recordnumber* is not given and a record has not been stored in the program, the record will be stored as the first record in the file. If you have a file with data in it, make sure you specify a record number in the PUT statement, otherwise you could accidentally write over some important data.

Examine the program in Figure 11–12. This program uses a FOR/NEXT loop to write records to a random file named CUSTOMER.DAT. The user is prompted to enter the three values for the fields of each record. Then the LSET function stores the values in the appropriate field. Because the balance (B) is a numeric value, the MKS$ function is used to convert it to a string and assign it to BAL$. Examine line 230:

```
230    PUT #1, I
```

Because the value of I varies from 1 through 5, these records are written in the first five positions in the file. However, the following statement would have accomplished the same purpose:

```
230    PUT #1
```

If no relative position is specified, the system begins storing records in the first position and continues on from there.

Deleting Records from a Random File   Deleting records is not as easy as inserting records in a random file. Although Microsoft BASIC has standard commands to delete a file from a disk, it does not have any standard features to delete a record. To delete a record from a file, we suggest that you simply write another record on top of the one you wish to delete. Another way to delete a record is to write blank characters or asterisks over the existing record as shown in the following program. This is not the best method, though, because it wastes space.

```
10 OPEN "CUSTOMER.DAT" AS #1 LEN=48
20 FIELD #1,10 AS ACCT$,30 AS NAM$,8 AS BAL$
30 LSET ACCT$ = "**********"
40 LSET NAM$ = " "
50 LSET BAL$ = MKI$(0)
60 PUT #1,10
70 CLOSE #1
99 END
```

Reading a Random File

In order for a record to be read from a random file, it must be moved from secondary storage to the file buffer. The GET statement performs this operation, causing all of the data to be temporarily stored in the string variable names found in the FIELD statement. The following examples illustrate the GET statement.

```
30 GET #1,18
```

FIGURE 11–12   Creating a Random File

```
10   REM ***                    CREATE CUSTOMER FILE            ***
20   REM ***                                                    ***
30   REM *** THIS PROGRAM CREATES A RANDOM FILE.                ***
40   REM *** FILE USED:                                         ***
50   REM ***     CUSTOMER.DAT                                   ***
60   REM *** RECORD FIELDS:                                     ***
70   REM ***     ACCT$   ACCOUNT NUMBER FIELD                   ***
80   REM ***     NAM$    ACCOUNT NAME FIELD                     ***
90   REM ***     BAL$    ACCOUNT BALANCE FIELD                  ***
100  REM *** MAJOR VARIABLES:                                   ***
110  REM ***     A$      ACCOUNT NUMBER                         ***
120  REM ***     N$      ACCOUNT NAME                           ***
130  REM ***     B$      ACCOUNT BALANCE                        ***
140  REM
150  OPEN "CUSTOMER.DAT" AS #1 LEN = 48
160  FIELD #1,10 AS ACCT$,30 AS NAM$,8 AS BAL$
170  CLS
180  FOR I = 1 TO 5
190      INPUT "ENTER ACCOUNT NUMBER, NAME, AND BALANCE";A$,N$,B
200      LSET ACCT$ = A$
210      LSET NAM$ = N$
220      LSET BAL$ = MKS$(B)
230      PUT #1,I
240  NEXT I
250  CLOSE #1
999  END
```

```
ENTER ACCOUNT NUMBER, NAME, AND BALANCE? 1048,M & B BUILDING SERVICES,408.55
ENTER ACCOUNT NUMBER, NAME, AND BALANCE? 4057,FREEMAN SECURITY SYSTEMS,882.09
ENTER ACCOUNT NUMBER, NAME, AND BALANCE? 2940,GATEWAY PLUMBING,702.12
ENTER ACCOUNT NUMBER, NAME, AND BALANCE? 2412,ACE TRANSMISSIONS,1090.75
ENTER ACCOUNT NUMBER, NAME, AND BALANCE? 4839,MIDWEST ADVERTISING,256.8
```

This line instructs the computer to get the eighteenth record of the file associated with buffer 1.

```
30 GET #3
```

This line instructs the computer to get the first record of the file associated with buffer 3, unless there was a previous GET statement in the program. If there was another GET statement, the computer would get the record that follows the last record accessed.

The format of the GET statement is

```
line# GET #filenumber[,recordnumber]
```

The *filenumber* is the number of the file, as specified in the OPEN statement. The *recordnumber* is the number, or record position, of the record to be retrieved. If the *recordnumber* is omitted, the next record in the sequence will be retrieved.

All of the data retrieved with a GET statement is still interpreted as character data by the computer. Thus, any numbers stored in character format must be translated back into numeric values. The three functions used to do this are

CVI(character string)
CVS(character string)
CVD(character string)

CVI translates a character string back to an integer. CVS translates a character string back to a single-precision number. CVD translates a character string back to a double-precision number. As previously mentioned, for the types of programs used in this textbook, we have only used single-precision numbers. Below are some examples of converting character strings to real numbers:

```
CVS(AMT$)
CVS(BALANCE$)
CVS(NUM.ITEMS$)
```

The following program segment retrieves and displays the first two records of CUSTOMER.DAT:

```
10 OPEN "CUSTOMER.DAT" AS #1 LEN=48
20 FIELD #1, 10 AS ACCT$,30 AS NAM$,8 AS BAL$
30 GET #1
40 PRINT ACCT$,NAM$,CVS(BAL$)
50 GET #1
60 PRINT ACCT$,NAM$,CVS(BAL$)
```

Figure 11–13 contains a program that uses the GET statement to access and display any record in the file CUSTOMER.DAT. The user enters the relative number of the record, and the program accesses it in line 220. The record's fields are then displayed by the following statement:

```
260      PRINT ACCT$;TAB(20) NAM$;TAB(50) CVS(BAL$)
```

The CVS function translates the character string BAL$ to a numeric value before displaying it. The WHILE loop continues executing as long as the user wishes to locate more records.

Comparison of Random and Sequential Files

The following is a comparison of random and sequential files:

- Records in sequential files are written to the disk one after the other, starting with record 1.
- Records in random files may be written in any order desired.
- Records in sequential files are read from the disk one after the other, starting with record 1.
- Records in random files may be read in any order desired.
- Records in sequential files can be different lengths.
- Records in random files must all be the same length.
- For updates on the majority of records in a file, sequential files are more efficient.
- For small updates on large files, random files are faster and more efficient.
- Both sequential and random files must be opened before they can be accessed and closed when processing is completed.

A Programming Problem

Problem Definition

Anytown Bank, a rapidly growing bank, would like to make more efficient use of its computer. Currently, every time a customer makes a deposit or a withdrawal on a savings or checking account, the entire sequential file containing customer balances must be read. Customer bank statement processing is consequently slow. The manager would like to use a random file to keep track of customer accounts. The user should be able to enter new records or update old records in the file by entering the data at the keyboard. Two programs need to be written. The first will create a random file containing all of the customer information, and the second will access the data in this file so that savings and checking account balances can be updated. The program specification charts are shown in Figures 11–14 and 11–15.

FIGURE 11–13   Locating a Record

```
10   REM ***              LOCATE RECORD IN CUSTOMER FILE              ***
20   REM ***                                                          ***
30   REM ***   THIS PROGRAM ACCESSES A SPECIFIC RECORD IN            ***
40   REM ***   THE CUSTOMER FILE AND DISPLAYS ITS CONTENTS.          ***
50   REM ***   FILE USED:                                            ***
60   REM ***      CUSTOMER.DAT                                       ***
70   REM ***   RECORD FIELDS:                                        ***
80   REM ***      ACCT$    ACCOUNT NUMBER FIELD                      ***
90   REM ***      NAM$     ACCOUNT NAME FIELD                        ***
100  REM ***      BAL$     ACCOUNT BALANCE FIELD                     ***
110  REM ***   MAJOR VARIABLES:                                      ***
120  REM ***      NUM      RELATIVE NUMBER OF THE RECORD TO BE       ***
130  REM ***                   PRINTED                               ***
140  REM ***      ANS$     MORE RECORDS TO PRINT?                    ***
150  REM
160  OPEN "CUSTOMER.DAT" AS #1 LEN=48
170  FIELD #1,10 AS ACCT$,30 AS NAM$,8 AS BAL$
180  ANS$ = "Y"
190  CLS
200  WHILE ANS$ = "Y"
210      INPUT "ENTER NUMBER OF RECORD TO BE ACCESSED";NUM
220      GET #1,NUM
230      PRINT
240      PRINT "ACCOUNT NUMBER";TAB(20);"ACCOUNT NAME";TAB(50);"BALANCE"
250      PRINT "------------------------------------------------------------"
260      PRINT ACCT$;TAB(20) NAM$;TAB(50) CVS(BAL$)
270      PRINT
280      INPUT "ARE THERE MORE RECORDS TO LOCATE (Y/N)";ANS$
290  WEND
300  CLOSE #1
999  END
```

```
ENTER NUMBER OF RECORD TO BE ACCESSED? 3

ACCOUNT NUMBER        ACCOUNT NAME                    BALANCE
------------------------------------------------------------
2940                  GATEWAY PLUMBING                702.12

ARE THERE MORE RECORDS TO LOCATE (Y/N)? Y
ENTER NUMBER OF RECORD TO BE ACCESSED? 1

ACCOUNT NUMBER        ACCOUNT NAME                    BALANCE
------------------------------------------------------------
1048                  M & B BUILDING SERVICES         408.55

ARE THERE MORE RECORDS TO LOCATE (Y/N)? N
```

FIGURE 11–14   Program Specification Chart for Creating Bank Account Data File

PROGRAM SPECIFICATION CHART

PROGRAM NAME:	PROGRAMMER'S NAME:	DATE:
Create Bank Account File	S. Baumann	5/1/92

INPUT: Account number, customer's name, address, city, state, zip code, checking account, balance, and savings account balance.

OUTPUT: Random file containing records, with the following fields: name, address, city, state, zip code, checking balance, savings balance.

SOURCE OF INPUT:
Keyboard

DESTINATION OF OUTPUT:
Random File ACCOUNTS. DAT

PURPOSE: This program prompts the user to enter data for bank account records. The records are stored in a random file.

FIGURE 11–15   Program Specification Chart for Updating Bank Account Data File

PROGRAM SPECIFICATION CHART

PROGRAM NAME:	PROGRAMMER'S NAME:	DATE:
Update Bank Account File	S. Baumann	5/4/92

INPUT: File ACCOUNTS. DAT Number of accounts to be updated, type of transaction (checking or savings), amount of deposit or withdrawal.

OUTPUT: Updated bank customer file

SOURCE OF INPUT:
Keyboard and File

DESTINATION OF OUTPUT:
Random File ACCOUNTS. DAT

PURPOSE: This program allows the user to update records in a bank account file. The user enters the account number and the transaction data. The updated record is then displayed.

Now Try This

1. Write an OPEN statement to create a new file called VENDOR, which is file #1 and has a record length of 80 characters.

2. Write a FIELD statement to match the file opened in Exercise 1. Use the following fields and lengths. Supply your own variable names.

FIELD	LENGTH
VENDOR.ID	4
NAME	30
ADDRESS	20
CITY	14
STATE	2
ZIP	10

3. Name two ways to delete a record from a random file.

4. Write a GET statement to retrieve record 70 from the VENDOR file, which was opened as file #3.

Solution Design

We will first discuss the program used to create the file. The program needs to perform three main tasks: (1) the file has to be opened, with the necessary fields specified; (2) the records must be written to the file; and (3) the file has to be closed.

The input needed for this program will be the necessary data for each customer. This data will be written to a relative file, of which each record will contain the following seven fields:

customer's name	(NAM$)
customer's street address	(ADR$)
city	(CITY$)
state	(STATE$)
zip code	(ZIP$)
checking account balance	(CHECK$)
savings account balance	(SAVINGS$)

This program can be written using prompts to ask the user to enter the appropriate data to each field until the desired number of records has been inserted. The structure chart is shown in Figure 11–16 and the flowchart and pseudocode in Figure 11–17.

The second program is more complicated. The record that needs to be updated must be directly accessed and then correctly modified. Therefore,

FIGURE 11–16   Structure Chart for Creating Bank Account Data File

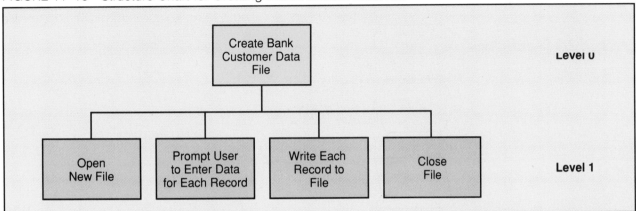

the major steps in this program are (1) opening the file, (2) accessing the correct record and updating it, (3) displaying it, and (4) closing the file.

Updating the file involves one of two actions: either the checking account balance is modified, or the savings account balance is modified. Because each of these actions requires a number of steps, they will be listed as separate substeps under Step 2. Refer to the structure chart in Figure 11–18 and the flowchart and pseudocode in Figure 11–19.

The Programs

The program to create random file ACCOUNTS.DAT appears in Figure 11–20. Line 190 opens the file. Each of the seven fields is listed in the FIELD statement in line 200. The program contains two subroutines: one to prompt the user to enter the data for each record and the second to write this record to the file. Notice that in lines 2120 and 2130 the balances of the checking and savings accounts (CH and SAV) are converted to the character strings CHECK$ and SAVINGS$. Using a random file allows the user to access the needed record directly in the second program, which will update any specified record in the file.

The purpose of the program in Figure 11–21 is to access and update as many records as desired in CUSTOMERS.DAT. The WHILE loop in lines 290 through 370 continues to execute as long as the user wants to update more records. It first prompts the user to enter the account number, the type of transaction (checking or savings) and whether the transaction is a deposit or a withdrawal. If a checking transaction is being made, program control branches to subroutine UPDATE CHECKING ACCOUNT at line 1000; otherwise, control transfers to UPDATE SAVINGS ACCOUNT at line 2000. In each subroutine, the user enters the amount of the transaction and, depending on whether a deposit or withdrawal is taking place, this amount (AMT) is added to or subtracted from the account. Notice that the

FIGURE 11–17   Flowchart and Pseudocode for Creating Bank Account Data File

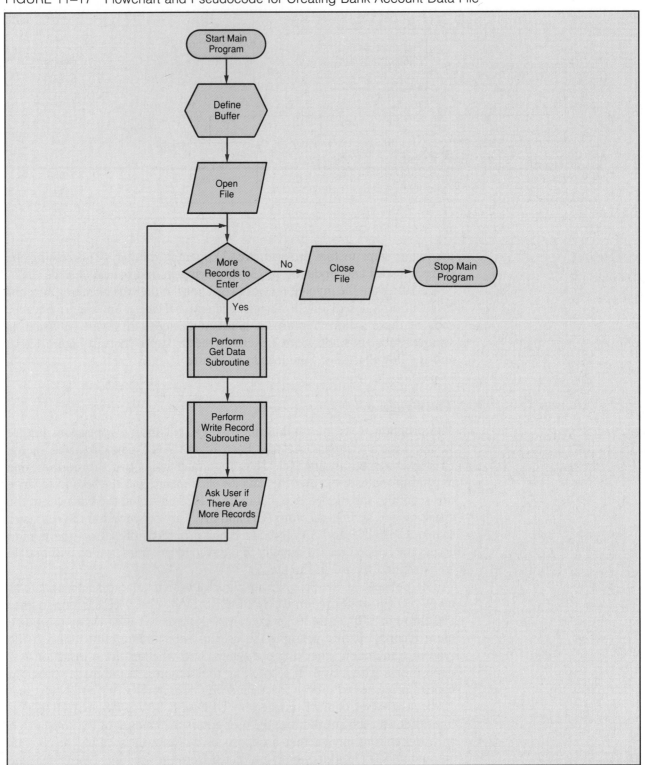

FIGURE 11–17 Continued

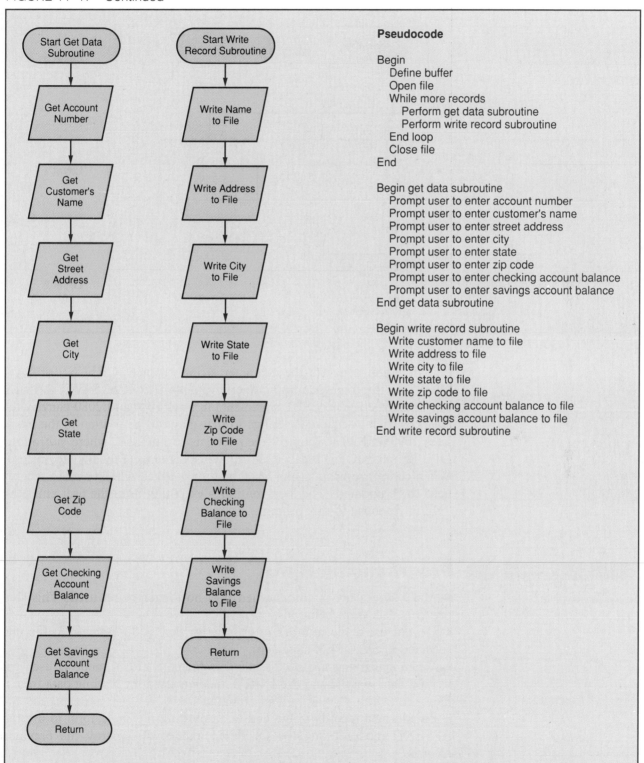

Pseudocode

Begin
    Define buffer
    Open file
    While more records
        Perform get data subroutine
        Perform write record subroutine
    End loop
    Close file
End

Begin get data subroutine
    Prompt user to enter account number
    Prompt user to enter customer's name
    Prompt user to enter street address
    Prompt user to enter city
    Prompt user to enter state
    Prompt user to enter zip code
    Prompt user to enter checking account balance
    Prompt user to enter savings account balance
End get data subroutine

Begin write record subroutine
    Write customer name to file
    Write address to file
    Write city to file
    Write state to file
    Write zip code to file
    Write checking account balance to file
    Write savings account balance to file
End write record subroutine

FIGURE 11–18   Structure Chart for Updating Bank Account Data File

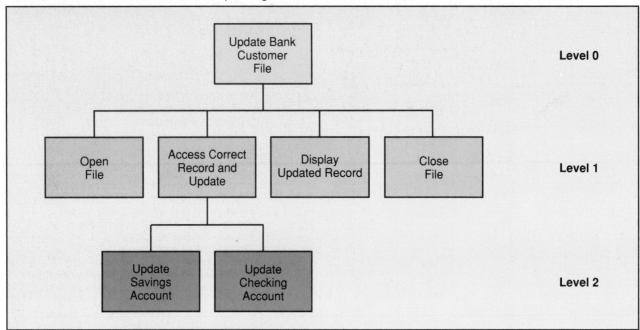

CVS function converts the character string balance (CHECK$ or SAV-INGS$) to the corresponding numeric value (CHECK or SAVE) so that it can be updated. The LSET statements in lines 1080 and 2080 convert the balances back to character strings so that they can be written to the file in lines 1090 and 2090. Control then returns to line 350, where subroutine DISPLAY RECORD is called to display the contents of the updated record. When control returns to line 360, the user is asked whether more records need to be updated. The loop continues executing until the user enters an "N" in response to this prompt.

Programming Hints

- Make sure a file is closed when it is no longer being used. This step prevents data from being lost.
- Do not use a file number in a program that is different from the one specified in the OPEN statement.
- When specifying a mode, remember that OUTPUT mode is used for writing data to a file and the INPUT mode is used for reading data from a file.
- To add new records to the end of an existing file, be careful to use the APPEND mode. Using the OUTPUT mode will destroy the previous records.

FIGURE 11–19   Flowchart and Pseudocode for Updating Bank Account Data File

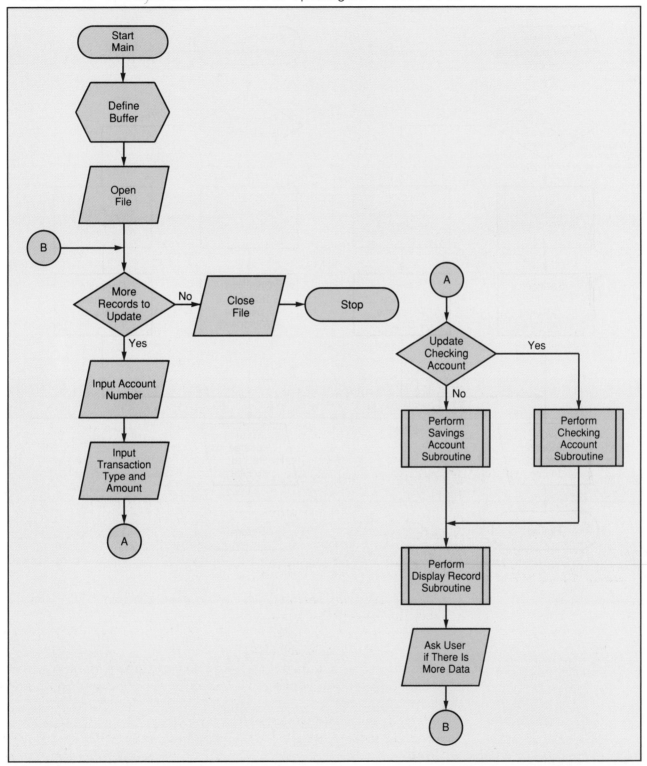

(figure continued on the next page)

FIGURE 11–19 Continued

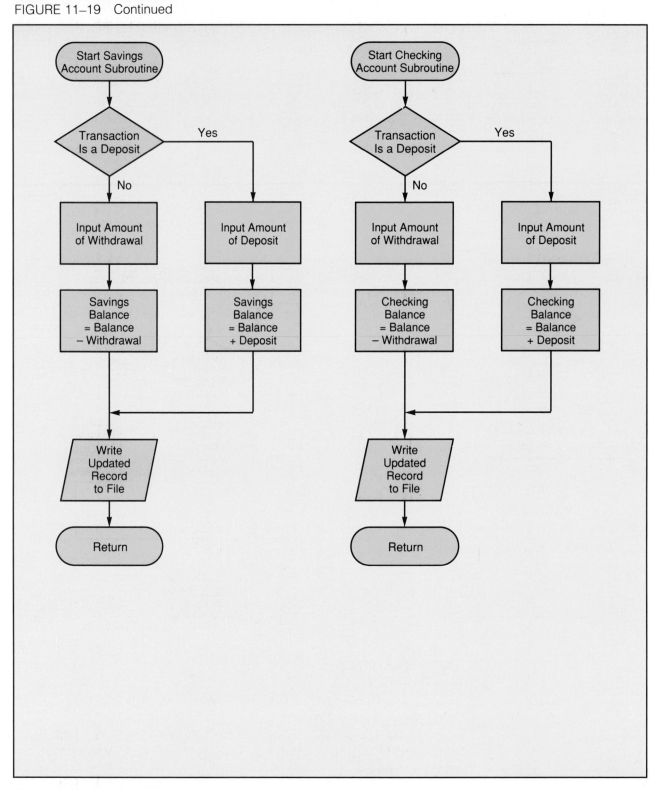

FIGURE 11–19   Continued

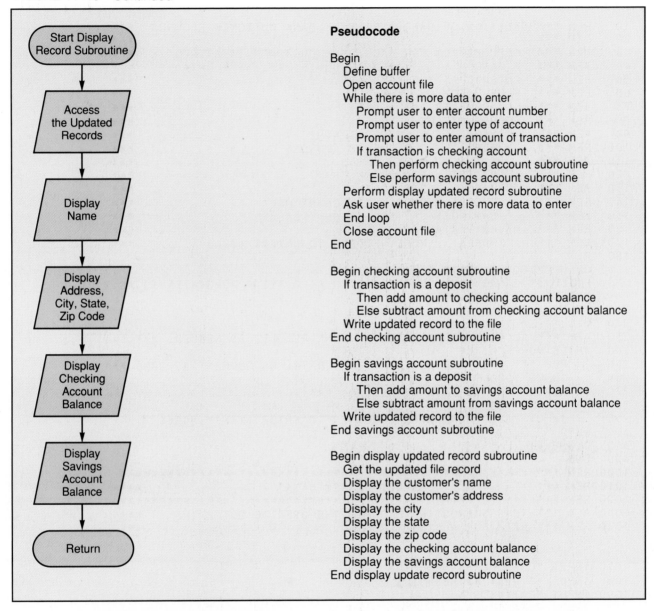

Pseudocode

Begin
   Define buffer
   Open account file
   While there is more data to enter
      Prompt user to enter account number
      Prompt user to enter type of account
      Prompt user to enter amount of transaction
      If transaction is checking account
         Then perform checking account subroutine
         Else perform savings account subroutine
   Perform display updated record subroutine
   Ask user whether there is more data to enter
   End loop
   Close account file
End

Begin checking account subroutine
   If transaction is a deposit
      Then add amount to checking account balance
      Else subtract amount from checking account balance
   Write updated record to the file
End checking account subroutine

Begin savings account subroutine
   If transaction is a deposit
      Then add amount to savings account balance
      Else subtract amount from savings account balance
   Write updated record to the file
End savings account subroutine

Begin display updated record subroutine
   Get the updated file record
   Display the customer's name
   Display the customer's address
   Display the city
   Display the state
   Display the zip code
   Display the checking account balance
   Display the savings account balance
End display update record subroutine

- Make sure you use the LSET and RSET statements before you write to a random file.
- Make sure you specify the length of the record in the OPEN statement and the lengths of the fields in the FIELD statement.
- Use PUT to write to a random file; GET to read from a random file.
- Specify the record number in the PUT statement to avoid writing over an important record.

FIGURE 11–20   Program to Create Bank Account Data File

```
10    REM *** CREATION OF RANDOM FILE OF BANK CUSTOMER RECORDS   ***
20    REM ***                                                     ***
30    REM ***   INFORMATION FOR EACH BANK CUSTOMER IS STORED IN   ***
40    REM ***   A RANDOM FILE NAMED ACCOUNTS.DAT.   THE DATA IS   ***
50    REM ***   ENTERED AT THE KEYBOARD.                          ***
60    REM ***   FILE USED:                                        ***
70    REM ***       ACCOUNTS.DAT                                  ***
80    REM ***   RECORD FIELDS:                                    ***
90    REM ***       NAM$      CUSTOMER'S NAME                     ***
100   REM ***       ADR$      CUSTOMER'S ADDRESS                  ***
110   REM ***       CITY$     CITY                                ***
120   REM ***       STATE$    STATE                               ***
130   REM ***       ZIP$      ZIP CODE                            ***
140   REM ***       CHECK$    CHECKING ACCOUNT BALANCE            ***
150   REM ***       SAVINGS$ SAVINGS ACCOUNT BALANCE             ***
160   REM ***   MAJOR VARIABLES:                                 ***
170   REM ***       MORE$     MORE RECORDS TO ENTER? (Y/N)       ***
180   REM
190   OPEN "ACCOUNTS.DAT" AS #1 LEN=80
200   FIELD #1,20 AS NAM$,20 AS ADR$,10 AS CITY$,2 AS STATE$,10 AS ZIP$,9 AS
      CHECK$,9 AS SAVINGS$
210   MORE$ = "Y"
220   CLS
230   REM *** ALLOW USER TO ENTER AS MANY RECORDS AS NEEDED. ***
240   WHILE MORE$ = "Y"
250     REM *** CALL SUBROUTINE TO GET DATA FOR CURRENT RECORD. ***
260     GOSUB 1000
270     REM *** WRITE DATA TO RECORD. ***
280     GOSUB 2000
290     INPUT "ARE THERE MORE ACCOUNTS TO ENTER (Y/N)";MORE$
300   WEND
310   CLOSE #1
999   END
1000  REM ****************************************************************
1010  REM ***                   SUBROUTINE GET DATA                   ***
1020  REM ****************************************************************
1030  REM *** THIS SUBROUTINE PROMPTS THE USER TO ENTER THE   ***
1040  REM *** DATA FOR A SINGLE RECORD.                       ***
1050  REM
1060  INPUT "ACCOUNT NUMBER";ACCT
1070  INPUT "CUSTOMER'S NAME";N$
1080  INPUT "STREET ADDRESS";A$
1090  INPUT "CITY";C$
1100  INPUT "STATE";S$
1110  INPUT "ZIP CODE";Z$
1120  INPUT "CHECKING ACCOUNT BALANCE";CH
1130  INPUT "SAVINGS ACCOUNT BALANCE";SAV
1140  RETURN
2000  REM ****************************************************************
2010  REM ***                 SUBROUTINE WRITE RECORD                 ***
2020  REM ****************************************************************
2030  REM *** THIS SUBROUTINE WRITES DATA TO THE FIELDS OF    ***
2040  REM *** THE RECORD WHOSE POSITION IS SPECIFIED BY THE   ***
```

FIGURE 11–20   Continued

```
2050 REM *** VALUE OF ACCT.                        ***
2060 REM
2070 LSET NAM$ = N$
2080 LSET ADR$ = A$
2090 LSET CITY$ = C$
2100 LSET STATE$ = S$
2110 LSET ZIP$ = Z$
2120 LSET CHECK$ = MKS$(CH)
2130 LSET SAVINGS$ = MKS$(SAV)
2140 PUT #1,ACCT
2150 RETURN
```

```
            ACCOUNT NUMBER? 1
            CUSTOMER'S NAME? JOANNE KOHNE
            STREET ADDRESS? 1791 PRESTON AVE
            CITY? AKRON
            STATE? OH
            ZIP CODE? 44313
            CHECKING ACCOUNT BALANCE? 300.45
            SAVINGS ACCOUNT BALANCE? 100.34
            ARE THERE MORE ACCOUNTS TO ENTER (Y/N)? Y
            ACCOUNT NUMBER? 2
            CUSTOMER'S NAME? KATIE MANSON
            STREET ADDRESS? 4683 QUICK RD
            CITY? PENINSULA
            STATE? OH
            ZIP CODE? 44264
            CHECKING ACCOUNT BALANCE? 250.58
            SAVINGS ACCOUNT BALANCE? 100.46
            ARE THERE MORE ACCOUNTS TO ENTER (Y/N)? Y
            ACCOUNT NUMBER? 3
            CUSTOMER'S NAME? MARTIN OFSTEAD
            STREET ADDRESS? 1135 BROOKPARK DR
            CITY? CUYAHOGA FALLS
            STATE? OH
            ZIP CODE? 44313
            CHECKING ACCOUNT BALANCE? 170.98
            SAVINGS ACCOUNT BALANCE? 4000.03
            ARE THERE MORE ACCOUNTS TO ENTER (Y/N)? N
```

FIGURE 11–21   Program to Update Bank Account Data File

```
10     REM ***                    UPDATE BANK CUSTOMERS FILE                ***
20     REM ***                                                             ***
30     REM ***    THIS PROGRAM ALLOWS THE USER TO ENTER THE                ***
40     REM ***    ACCOUNT NUMBER OF THE RECORD TO BE UPDATED.              ***
50     REM ***    THE CHECKING ACCOUNT OR SAVINGS ACCOUNT FIELD            ***
60     REM ***    CAN THEN BE UPDATED.   THE PROGRAM THEN ASKS FOR         ***
70     REM ***    THE TYPE OF TRANSACTION, DEPOSIT OR WITHDRAWAL,          ***
80     REM ***    THAT NEEDS TO BE PERFORMED.   THE ACCOUNT IS             ***
90     REM ***    THEN UPDATED.                                            ***
100    REM ***    FILE USED:                                               ***
110    REM ***  ·    ACCOUNTS.DAT                                          ***
120    REM ***    RECORD FIELDS:                                           ***
130    REM ***        NAM$              CUSTOMER'S NAME                    ***
140    REM ***        ADR$              ADDRESS                            ***
150    REM ***        CITY$             CITY                               ***
160    REM ***        STATE$            STATE                              ***
170    REM ***        ZIP$              ZIP CODE                           ***
180    REM ***        CHECK$            CHECKING ACCOUNT BALANCE           ***
190    REM ***        SAVINGS$          SAVINGS ACCOUNT BALANCE            ***
200    REM ***    MAJOR VARIABLES:                                         ***
210    REM ***        TYPE$             TYPE OF ACCOUNT (C/S)              ***
220    REM ***        MORE$             MORE ACCOUNTS TO UPDATE?           ***
230    REM
240    OPEN "ACCOUNTS.DAT" AS #1 LEN=80
250    FIELD #1,20 AS NAM$,20 AS ADR$,10 AS CITY$,2 AS STATE$,10 AS ZIP$,
           9 AS CHECK$,9 AS SAVINGS$
260    MORE$ = "Y"
270    CLS
280    REM *** ALLOW USER TO UPDATE AS MANY RECORDS AS NEEDED. ***
290    WHILE MORE$ = "Y"
300        INPUT "ENTER ACCOUNT NUMBER TO BE UPDATED";NUM
310        GET #1,NUM
320        INPUT "ENTER TYPE OF ACCOUNT TO BE UPDATED (C/S)";TYPE$
330        INPUT "ENTER TRANSACTION TYPE (D/W)";TRANS$
340        IF TYPE$ = "C" THEN GOSUB 1000
               ELSE GOSUB 2000
350        GOSUB 3000
360        INPUT "MORE ACCOUNTS TO UPDATE (Y/N)";MORE$
370    WEND
380    CLOSE #1
999    END
1000   REM ******************************************************************
1010   REM ***                   UPDATE CHECKING ACCOUNT              ***
1020   REM ******************************************************************
1030   REM *** THIS SUBROUTINE ALLOWS THE USER TO ENTER A             ***
1040   REM ***    CHECKING ACCOUNT TRANSACTION.                       ***
1050   REM
1060   IF TRANS$ = "D" THEN INPUT "ENTER AMOUNT OF DEPOSIT";AMT
           : CHECK = CVS(CHECK$) : CHECK = CHECK + AMT
1070   IF TRANS$ = "W" THEN INPUT "ENTER AMOUNT OF WITHDRAWAL";AMT
```

FIGURE 11–21   Continued

```
           : CHECK = CVS(CHECK$) : CHECK = CHECK - AMT
1080 LSET CHECK$ = MKS$(CHECK)
1090 PUT #1,NUM
1100 RETURN
2000 REM ***********************************************************
2010 REM ***                 UPDATE SAVINGS ACCOUNT            ***
2020 REM ***********************************************************
2030 REM *** THIS SUBROUTINE ALLOWS THE USER TO ENTER A        ***
2040 REM ***   SAVINGS ACCOUNT TRANSACTION.                    ***
2050 REM
2060 IF TRANS$ = "D" THEN INPUT "ENTER AMOUNT OF DEPOSIT";AMT
        : SAVE = CVS(SAVINGS$) : SAVE = SAVE + AMT
2070 IF TRANS$ = "W" THEN INPUT "ENTER AMOUNT OF WITHDRAWAL";AMT
        : SAVE = CVS(SAVINGS$) : SAVE = SAVE - AMT
2080 LSET NAM$ = NAM$
2090 PUT #1,NUM
2100 LSET SAVINGS$ = MKS$(SAVE)
2110 RETURN
3000 REM ***********************************************************
3010 REM ***                   DISPLAY RECORD                  ***
3020 REM ***********************************************************
3030 REM ***   THIS SUBROUTINE DISPLAYS THE FIELDS OF THE      ***
3040 REM ***   UPDATED RECORD.                                 ***
3050 REM
3060 CLS
3070 GET #1,NUM
3080 PRINT "CUSTOMER'S NAME:         ";NAM$
3090 PRINT "CUSTOMER'S ADDRESS:      ";ADR$
3100 PRINT "CUSTOMER'S CITY:         ";CITY$
3110 PRINT "CUSTOMER'S STATE:        ";STATE$
3120 PRINT "CUSTOMER'S ZIP CODE:     ";ZIP$
3130 PRINT "CHECKING ACCOUNT BALANCE ";CVS(CHECK$)
3140 PRINT "SAVINGS ACCOUNT BALANCE ";CVS(SAVINGS$)
3150 RETURN
```

(figure continued on the next page)

FIGURE 11–21　Continued

```
ENTER ACCOUNT NUMBER TO BE UPDATED? 2
ENTER TYPE OF ACCOUNT TO BE UPDATED (C/S)? C
ENTER TRANSACTION TYPE (D/W)? D
ENTER AMOUNT OF DEPOSIT? 100
```

```
CUSTOMER'S NAME:          KATIE MANSON
CUSTOMER'S ADDRESS:       4683 QUICK RD
CUSTOMER'S CITY:          PENINSULA
CUSTOMER'S STATE:         OH
CUSTOMER'S ZIP CODE:      44264
CHECKING ACCOUNT BALANCE  450.58
SAVINGS ACCOUNT BALANCE   100.46
MORE ACCOUNTS TO UPDATE (Y/N)? N
```

New Statement Review

Statement Format	Explanation
Sequential Files	
line# OPEN "filename" FOR mode AS [#]filenumber	Opens a sequential file for access in one of three modes: OUTPUT (to be written to), INPUT (to be read), or APPEND (to have new records added to the end of it).
line# CLOSE [list of filenumbers]	Permanently saves a file on disk. If no *filenumber* is specified, all opened files are closed.
line# WRITE #filenumber, value-list	The *filenumber* is the number under which the sequential file was opened. The values are written to this file.
line# INPUT #filenumber, variable-list	The *filenumber* is the number under which the sequential file was opened. Values are read from the file to the listed variables.
Random Files	
line# OPEN "filename" AS #filenumber LEN = buffer-size	Opens a random file. The *buffer-size* is the total number of characters in each record.
line# FIELD #filenumber, fieldwidth AS fieldname [,fieldwidth AS field-name] . . .	Declares the length and name of each field in a random file's records. The total lengths of all fields must equal the *buffer-size* stated in the OPEN statement. The fields must be string variables.
line# LSET string-variable-name = string-expression	Stores a string expression in the field with the specified string variable name. The first character in the expression is placed in the first position in the field.
line# RSET string-variable-name = string-expression	Stores a string expression in the field with the specified string variable name. The last character in the expression is placed in the last position in the field.
line# PUT filenumber [,recordnumber]	A record is written to the random file specified by *filenumber* at the relative position specified by the *recordnumber*. If no *recordnumber* is specified, the record is written to the next file position.

(New Statement Review continued on the next page)

New Statement Review Continued

Statement Format	Explanation
Random Files	
line# GET filenumber [,recordnumber]	A record is read from the file specified by *filenumber* into the computer's main memory. If a *recordnumber* is specified, the record in that relative position is read; otherwise, the next record in the random file is read.

Summary Points

- Files organize large amounts of data. Because they are kept in secondary storage, they solve the problem of limited space in the computer's primary storage unit.
- A given file can be accessed by many different programs.
- Files are divided into records, which in turn are divided into fields.
- In sequential organization, records are stored one after another, in the order in which they are sent to the file.
- Sequential access retrieves a record based on the record's sequential order within the file. If it is necessary to access the fifth record, for example, the first four records must be accessed first.
- The following statements are used with sequential files:
  1. The OPEN statement accesses an existing file or creates a new one.
  2. When processing is completed on a file, the CLOSE statement must be used to close it so that its contents are not lost.
  3. The WRITE# statement places data items in a file.
  4. The INPUT# statement reads data items from a file.
- The following statements are used with random files:
  1. The OPEN statement accesses an existing file or creates a new one; it also specifies the record length.
  2. The FIELD statement declares the fields, their lengths, and their positions within a record and assigns each field a string variable name.
  3. The LSET and RSET statements are used to place data into a file buffer under the field names specified in the FIELD statement so the data can be stored in a random file.
  4. The PUT statement stores data items in a file.
  5. There are two ways to delete records from a random file: write a new record over the old one, or write asterisks or blanks over the record.
  6. The GET statement accesses data items in a file.
  7. The MKI$, MKS$, and MKD$ functions translate numeric values into character string values for storage; the CVI, CVS, and CVD functions translate the character string values back to numeric values for processing.

Vocabulary List

Access method
Buffer
Data file
Field
File position pointer
File

Program file
Random access
Record
Relative organization
Sequential access
Sequential organization

Questions

Whenever appropriate, use complete sentences in answering the following questions.

1. What is a data file?
2. What are the advantages and disadvantages of using a data file?
3. Name the divisions of a file, explain how they are related to each other, and give an example of each.
4. Explain sequential file organization.
5. What is a buffer, and how is it used?
6. In using sequential files, what are the three modes of the OPEN statement, and how is each used?
7. What are the general steps in writing to a newly created sequential file?
8. What are the general steps in reading from a sequential file?
9. Why must a file be closed?
10. To what is the file position pointer set when the OPEN statement is executed using the APPEND clause?
11. Explain how the OPEN statement for a random file is different than for a sequential file.
12. How are records inserted into a random file?
13. What is the difference between the LSET statement and the RSET statement?
14. Can random files be accessed sequentially?
15. List some differences between random and sequential files.

Debugging Exercises

Identify the following programs or program segments that contain errors, and debug them.

1.
```
190 REM *** APPEND DATA TO END OF FILE RECIPE.***
200 OPEN "RECIPE" FOR APPEND AS #1
210 INPUT INGREDIENT,QUANT
220 WRITE #1 INGREDIENT,QUANT
230 INPUT INGREDIENT,QUANT
240 WRITE #1 INGREDIENT,QUANT
250 CLOSE #1
999 END
```

```
2.  50   REM *** READ FILE BOARD AND PRINT DATA. ***
    60   OPEN "BOARD" FOR INPUT AS #3
    70   INPUT #3,MEMBER$,ADDRESS$
    80   PRINT MEMBER$,ADDRESS$
    90   INPUT #3,MEMBER$,ADDRESS$
    100  PRINT MEMBER$,ADDRESS$
    110  REM *** REOPEN FILE TO APEND NEW DATA. ***
    120  OPEN "BOARD" FOR APPEND AS #2
    130  INPUT "NAME, ADDRESS: ",MEMBER$,ADDRESS$
    140  WRITE #2,MEMBER$,ADDRESS$
    150  CLOSE
    999  END
```

```
3.  10   REM *** WRITE RECORD TO FILE TUITION. ***
    20   OPEN "TUITION" AS #2 LEN=40
    30   FIELD 2,30 AS SCHOOL$,10 AS BAL$
    40   LSET SCHOOL$ = "LEXINGTON COMMUNITY COLLEGE"
    50   RSET BAL$ = 342
    60   PUT #2,3
    70   CLOSE #2
```

```
4.  10   REM *** WRITE RECORD TO FILE EXAMPLE. ***
    20   FIELD #1,40 AS PART$,20 AS QTY$
    30   LSET PART$ = "LED SUBASSEMBLY"
    40   RSET QTY$ = MKS$(600)
    50   PUT #1,88
    60   CLOSE #1
```

Programmming Problems

Level 1

1. A new mail-order company, Horizons, needs a program to create and maintain its mailing list. You are to write a program that allows the user to enter customer records to a sequential file (the records need not be alphabetized at that time). The sample data used to test the program is as follows:

Browning, M.	223 State St.	Toledo OH
Reed, R.	78 Eighth St.	Lansing MI
Crosby, D.	1098 Walnut Ave.	Richmond VA
Bell, G.	298 29th St.	New York NY

The list displayed should resemble the following:

NAME	ADDRESS
Browning, M.	223 State St., Toledo, OH

2. The company now needs a program that allows the user to add records to the existing mailing list (from Problem 1) and to display the newly updated list. The records to be added are as follows:

McKinniss, S.	167 Cambell Rd.	Raleigh NC
Keeler, J.	97 Forest St.	Atlanta GA

3. Create a sequential file for the Weston Retail Warehouse's inventory using the following data:

Stock No.	Unit Price	On Hand	On Order
AK123	$4.82	50	30
BB423	$9.73	79	20
JZ887	$5.00	20	10

4. Using the file created in Problem 3, determine the value of inventory on hand for each item and the total inventory value. Display these values, using appropriate headings.

5. Write a program that creates a random file named PEOPLE.DAT with the following fields: each person's account number (4 characters), last name (10 characters), first name (10 characters), sex (1 character), city (10 characters), and state (2 characters). Allow the user to enter the data at the keyboard.

6. Write a program that accesses PEOPLE.DAT in Problem 5 and displays a particular record when the number of that record is entered.

7. Write a program that accesses the file PEOPLE.DAT from Problem 5 and counts the number of males, the number of females, and the number of people who live in Ohio. At the end of the program, display these totals.

Level 2

1. Write a program to create a sequential file containing employee payroll data. Use the following sample data:

Name	Hours	Hourly Wage
Greenbill	30	4.00
Henderson	42	5.50

2. Use the file created in Problem 1 to create a second file containing the name, hours worked, gross pay, and net pay for each employee. The net pay is calculated by subtracting taxes withheld, using a tax rate of 25 percent. The total gross pay of all employees should also be calculated as each record is processed and added to the end of the second file. Then print a report of the contents of the second file.

3. Write a program to create a file of the customer credit-account data for Monique's Boutique. In the given sample data, a negative balance indicates the amount a customer owes, and a positive balance means the customer has overpaid and has credit in the account.

Account #	August Balance
1090	−67.31
4750	13.50
5108	−79.99

4. One month later, Monique needs a program to update the credit-account file. For each account, display the account number and the amount due or the credit.

Then input account activity for September. Finally, write the new balances to a September disk file, and also display them on the screen.

Account #	September Activity Amount
1090	− 13.88
4750	− 24.99
5108	79.99

5. The school library needs a program to create a random file that is named LIBRARY.DAT to keep track of student fines. Each record should contain the following fields:

1. Student's name (15)
2. Title of book (25)
3. Type of book (1)
4. Days overdue (2)

The user should be prompted to enter the data at the keyboard.

6. Now the school library needs a program to access the file created in Problem 5, display the contents of each record, and calculate and display the amount of each fine. There are two types of books. If the type of book is "1," the fine rate is 25 cents a day and if the type is "2," the rate is 40 cents a day.

Projects

For each project, complete the following:

- Fill out a program specification chart.
- Develop a structure chart.
- Create a flowchart or pseudocode.
- Thoroughly document the final program.
- Test your program using a variety of data.

1. The Hoytville Citizens' Bank is holding an employee election to determine a proposed employee insurance-policy change. The bank has a main office and two branches. You have been asked to write a program that will create a sequential file containing the following election data:

Location	Total Employees	In Favor	Opposed
Hoytville	53	37	14
Rudolph	20	15	5
Custar	12	4	6

Use this file to generate a report listing the office locations, the number of votes in favor, the number of votes opposed, and the percentage of employees who voted (print these to two decimal places). Also display the total number of votes for both decisions. The output should appear as follows:

LOCATION	% VOTED	IN FAVOR	OPPOSED
XXXX	XX.XX	XX	XX
.	.	.	.
.	.	.	.
.	.	.	.
TOTALS:		XXX	XXX

2. The Sleazy Room Hotel has rooms numbered from 1 through 200. The manager wants to use a random file to record the status of each room. Each record in the file should have two fields. The first one indicates whether the room is full, and the second one contains the name of the guest. When a guest checks in, FULL is written to the record in the position of the room number, and the guest's name is entered. For example, if room number 140 is occupied, record 140 should have FULL in its first field and the guest's name in its second field. If a room is empty, EMPTY is written to the corresponding record's first field, and its second field is filled with blanks. The manager should be able to display the status of any room and update it if necessary.

CHAPTER 12

Graphics and Sound

Learning Objectives

After studying this chapter, you should be able to

1. Define text mode, medium-resolution graphics mode, and high-resolution graphics mode.
2. Describe how text and graphics can be used together on the screen.
3. Create graphics images using the SCREEN, LOCATE, LINE, CIRCLE, COLOR, PSET, PRESET, and DRAW statements.
4. Create sound using the BEEP, SOUND, and PLAY statements.

Introduction

Text mode

The mode in which text characters are displayed on the screen.

Graphics mode

A mode in which illustrations can be displayed on the screen. The screen is divided into small dots called pixels that can be turned off and on.

Pixel

A dot of light that can be turned on or off to create images. In graphics mode the entire screen is divided into a grid of pixels.

The monitor screen accepts two types of images: text and graphics images. So far in this book, only programs displaying output in **text mode** have been written. In text mode, characters (letters, numbers, and special symbols) are displayed on the screen. When **graphics mode** is used, the entire screen is divided into tiny dots, called **pixels.** These dots can be turned on and off to create images. Many types of illustrations can be created using graphics. However, in business programming, the most common use is creating charts and graphs to illustrate program output.

Sound is used sparingly in most programming applications. It is ordinarily used to alert the user that he or she has entered invalid data. However, the IBM PC can produce more music than the single, rude beep most users hear. In this chapter you will learn to use both graphics and sound in your programs.

Display Modes

The IBM PC displays information on the screen in one of three modes: text; medium-resolution graphics; and high-resolution graphics. Most graphics programming is done in medium-resolution mode. If you plan to use either of the graphics modes, your IBM PC must have a graphics card.

Text Display Mode

The overwhelming majority of programs are written in text mode. In text mode, the screen display consists of an 80-column by 25-row grid. Figure 12–1 demonstrates how you can display up to 2,000 (80 × 25) characters on the screen in text mode. The twenty-fifth line is normally used to explain how the function keys can be used to perform commands. Using the KEY OFF command erases this line so that you can use it for program output.

There are 256 characters that can be displayed on the screen. The first 128 are the *standard ASCII character set.* Appendix C shows the characters

FIGURE 12–1   Text-Mode Display Grid

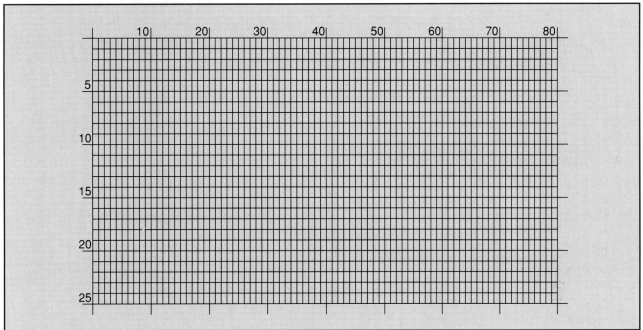

for ASCII codes 32 through 127. The second 128 characters are defined as the *IBM extended character set* (see Figure 12–2). You can display these characters on the monitor screen in text mode any time from a BASIC program; however, to display the extended character set, you must use the CHR$ function. The CHR$ function returns the character assigned to the argument. For example, to display the character assigned to the ASCII value 90, you would use the statement PRINT CHR$(90), which would display the letter Z. Similarly, to display the character assigned to the extended ASCII value 192, you would use the statement PRINT CHR$(192), which would display the lower left corner of a text-style box (⌞).

Figure 12–3 contains a simple BASIC program that displays 254 of the 256 text-mode characters. Notice that characters 11 and 12 are omitted from the output; that's because displaying them will cause the program to overwrite what was already printed. ASCII 11 is a carriage return, which moves the cursor to the beginning of the line it is currently on. ASCII 12 is a form feed, which clears the screen. ASCII 7 is "displayed" but does not appear on the screen; its "character" is a beep.

Medium- and High-Resolution Graphics Display Modes

If your computer has a graphics card that can switch from text to graphics mode, you can display all sorts of interesting pictures. In medium-resolution graphics mode, you can consider the display a 320-column by

FIGURE 12–2 Additional Characters Defined for the IBM PC

ASCII value	Character displayed	ASCII value	Character displayed	ASCII value	Character displayed	ASCII value	Character displayed
128	Ç	160	á	192	└	224	α
129	ü	161	í	193	┴	225	β
130	é	162	ó	194	┬	226	Γ
131	â	163	ú	195	├	227	π
132	ä	164	ñ	196	─	228	Σ
133	à	165	Ñ	197	┼	229	σ
134	å	166	ª	198	╞	230	μ
135	ç	167	º	199	╟	231	τ
136	è	168	¿	200	╚	232	Φ
137	ë	169	⌐	201	╔	233	θ
138	è	170	¬	202	╩	234	Ω
139	ï	171	½	203	╦	235	δ
140	î	172	¼	204	╠	236	∞
141	ì	173	¡	205	═	237	∅
142	Ä	174	«	206	╬	238	∈
143	Å	175	»	207	╧	239	∩
144	É	176	░	208	╨	240	≡
145	æ	177	▒	209	╤	241	±
146	Æ	178	▓	210	╥	242	≥
147	ô	179	│	211	╙	243	≤
148	ö	180	┤	212	╘	244	⌠
149	ò	181	╡	213	╒	245	⌡
150	û	182	╢	214	╓	246	÷
151	ù	183	╖	215	╫	247	≈
152	ÿ	184	╕	216	╪	248	°
153	Ö	185	╣	217	┘	249	●
154	Ü	186	║	218	┌	250	·
155	¢	187	╗	219	█	251	√
156	£	188	╝	220	▄	252	ⁿ
157	¥	189	╜	221	▌	253	²
158	Pts	190	╛	222	▐	254	■
159	ƒ	191	┐	223	▀	255	(blank 'FF')

FIGURE 12–3   BASIC Program to Display 254 of the 256 Characters of the IBM PC Character Set

```
10    REM  **************************************************
20    REM  ***           ADDITIONAL IBM PC CHARACTERS           ***
30    REM  **************************************************
40    REM
50    CLS
60    FOR I = 0 TO 255
70       IF (I = 11) OR (I = 12) GOTO 100
80          PRINT CHR$ (I);
90          PRINT " ";
100      NEXT I
999   END
```

200-row grid of dots; in high-resolution mode, the matrix is 640 columns by 200 rows. Each dot is known as a *picture element*, or *pixel*.

Two coordinate systems, similar to that in mathematics, are used to reference a particular location on the display screen. The coordinate systems for both text and graphics modes start in the upper left corner of the display; however, there the similarities end. In text mode, the coordinate system references *character cells*, or simply characters. Eight-row by 8-column squares of pixels define each character. These characters are referenced in the order (row, column), and numbering starts at (1, 1). To write to the fourth character in the third row, you would reference text-mode coordinate (3, 4). In graphics mode, however, the coordinate system defines pixels; the pixels are referenced in the order (column, row); and numbering starts at (0, 0). Therefore, the pixel in row 10, column 50 is (50, 10). You will need to practice referencing characters and pixels to become comfortable with the coordinate systems.

Mixing Text and Graphics

An unlabeled graph is useless. For that reason, the PRINT and PRINT USING statements are often used to clarify graphics. These statements behave the same in both text and graphics modes. Printing text can be tricky during program development, because the cursor is turned off while the screen is in graphics mode.

Graphics Commands

The following section describes the four most commonly used graphics statements: LOCATE, SCREEN, LINE, and CIRCLE. Three more statements are added for flexibility: PSET, PRESET, and DRAW.

The LOCATE Statement

The LOCATE statement performs three functions:

- It moves the cursor to the specified location on the display.
- It tells the cursor to blink.
- It allows you to determine the size of the cursor.

The format for the LOCATE statement is as follows:

line# LOCATE [row][,[column][,[cursor][,[start][,stop]]]]

where

- *row* is the row number on which to place the cursor and must be from 1 through 25.
- *column* is the column number in which to place the cursor and must be from 1 through 80.
- *cursor* specifies whether to display the cursor or not. Zero turns it off; all other values turn it on.
- *start* is the line to start building the cursor and must be from 1 through 31.
- *stop* is the line to stop building the cursor and must be from 1 through 31.

Notice that all parameters in the LOCATE statement are optional. If you do not wish to change the current setting of the parameter, omit it, but leave a comma in its place.

Here are some examples of the LOCATE statement:

```
100 LOCATE 14,40
110 PRINT "!"
```

The preceding program segment moves the cursor to row 14, column 40, and prints an exclamation point.

```
100 LOCATE,,1
```

The preceding statement turns on the cursor.

```
100 LOCATE ,,1,0,14
```

The preceding statement turns on the cursor and changes it into a big fat box.

```
100 LOCATE ,,,13,13
```

The preceding statement changes the cursor into a narrow line.

You will need to experiment with the start and stop values to learn how they affect the size of the cursor. The greater the difference between the two values, the larger the cursor.

The SCREEN Statement

The SCREEN statement defines the desired mode for the display screen. It specifies either text mode or one of the graphics modes. The hardware configuration of your particular computer defines the legal parameters for the SCREEN statement.

The format for the SCREEN statement is as follows:

```
line#      SCREEN [mode][,[colorswitch]]
```

where

■ *mode* is the predefined mode number required and must be one of the following values: 0, 1, 2, 7, 8, 9, 10; the three modes that concern us are
  —Mode 0: text mode; 80×25 characters
  —Mode 1: medium-resolution graphics; 320×200 pixels
  —Mode 2: high-resolution graphics; 640×200 pixels
■ *colorswitch* is used primarily when the monitor screen is a composite or TV screen. It is a numeric expression that is either true (a nonzero integer) or false (zero); a value of zero turns color off and permits the display of black and white only.

When you first turn the computer on, you are automatically in text mode. If you are in graphics mode and want to get back to text mode, use the following statement:

```
100 SCREEN 0
```

The following statement puts the screen into medium-resolution graphics mode.

```
100 SCREEN 1
```

The LINE Statement

The LINE statement draws a line or a box on the screen. LINE works only in graphics mode. The format for the LINE statement is as follows:

```
line#      LINE [(c1, r1)] – (c2, r2)[,[attribute][,B[F]][,style]]
```

where

- *(c1, r1)* is the starting coordinate of a line, or one corner of a box. The starting coordinate is optional; if it is omitted, the last point referenced is used instead. After a LINE statement is executed, the ending coordinate becomes the last point referenced.
- *(c2, r2)* is the ending coordinate of a line, or the corner opposite *(cl, rl)* when drawing a box.
- attribute defines the color and intensity of the line. For more information, see the section on the COLOR statement.
- *B* specifies that a box is to be drawn.
- *F* specifies that the box is to be filled in.
- *style* is a four-digit hexadecimal number specifying the desired pixel pattern, or line style, to display. For a summary of various line styles, see Table 12–1.

Here are some examples of the LINE statement:

```
100 SCREEN 1
110 LINE (0,0) - (319,199)
```

The preceding program segment draws a diagonal line from the upper left corner of the screen to the lower right corner in medium-resolution graphics mode.

```
100 SCREEN 2
200 LINE (40,60) - (60,120),,B
```

The preceding program segment draws an empty box on the display in high-resolution graphics mode.

```
100 SCREEN 1
110 LINE (0,90)-(319,110),,BF
130 LINE (0,100)-(319,100),,,&H8FF
```

In the preceding program segment, line 110 draws a filled-in box. Line 130 draws a horizontal line across the middle of the display in a dot-dash-dot-dash pattern.

The CIRCLE Statement

The CIRCLE statement is used to draw circles, ellipses, and angles on the screen. It works only in graphics mode. The format for the CIRCLE statement is as follows:

```
line#    CIRCLE (c,r),radius[,[color][,[start],[end][,aspect]]]
```

TABLE 12–1   Line Styles for the LINE Statement

```
10   REM ***   LINESTYLE EXAMPLES FOR THE LINE STATEMENT ***
20   REM ***
30   CLS
40   SCREEN 1
50   KEY OFF
60   LOCATE  1,1: PRINT "&H1   ": LINE (60, 4)-(319,  4),,,&H1
70   LOCATE  2,1: PRINT "&H1010": LINE (60,12)-(319, 12),,,&H1010
80   LOCATE  3,1: PRINT "&H1111": LINE (60,20)-(319, 20),,,&H1111
90   LOCATE  4,1: PRINT "&HAAAA": LINE (60,28)-(319, 28),,,&HAAAA
100  LOCATE  5,1: PRINT "&HFF08": LINE (60,36)-(319, 36),,,&HFF08
110  LOCATE  6,1: PRINT "&HFF24": LINE (60,44)-(319, 44),,,&HFF24
120  LOCATE  7,1: PRINT "&HF248": LINE (60,52)-(319, 52),,,&HF248
130  LOCATE  8,1: PRINT "&HF8F8": LINE (60,60)-(319, 60),,,&HF8F8
140  LOCATE  9,1: PRINT "&HFF00": LINE (60,68)-(319, 68),,,&HFF00
150  LOCATE 10,1: PRINT "&HFCFC": LINE (60,76)-(319, 76),,,&HFCFC
160  LOCATE 11,1: PRINT "&HFEFE": LINE (60,84)-(319, 84),,,&HFEFE
170  LOCATE 12,1: PRINT "&HFFFF": LINE (60,92)-(319, 92),,,&HFFFF
180  LOCATE 21,1
999 END
```

Line Style   **Pattern Produced**

&H1
&H1010
&H1111
&HAAAA
&HFF08
&HFF24
&HF248
&HF8F8
&HFF00
&HFCFC
&HFEFE
&HFFFF

where

- *(c,r)* are the column, row coordinates of the center of the circle.
- *radius* denotes the radius of the circle in pixels.
- *color* specifies the color of the circle. For more information, see the section on the COLOR statement.
- *start* and *end* are angles in radians defining where the arcs of the circle are to begin and end. You can simplify this process by entering these values in degrees and converting to radians as follows: Radians = Degrees × 3.1416.

The values of *start* and *end* must be in the range of $-2 \times$ Pi . . $2 \times$ Pi. If the value is negative, the ellipse is connected to the center point with a line, and the angles are treated as if they are positive.

■ *aspect* defines the aspect ratio of the *x* radius to the *y* radius. The default ratio is 4:3. The value of the aspect ratio determines if the drawing is a true circle or an ellipse. You will want to experiment with this to determine how it works.

Here are some examples of the CIRCLE statement:

```
100  SCREEN 1
110  CIRCLE(160,100),10
```

The preceding program segment draws a circle 10 pixels in radius in the middle of the screen.

```
100  DEGREESTORADIANS = 3.16 / 180
110  SCREEN 1
120  CIRCLE (130,130),30,,0,270 * DEGREESTORADIANS
130  CIRCLE(130,130),30,,,,5/3
```

Line 120 in the above program segment draws a 270-degree arc at location (130, 130) with a radius of 30 pixels. Line 130 draws an ellipse with the same center and radius.

The PRESET and PSET Statements

The PRESET and PSET statements turn off or on a single pixel on the screen. The coordinates can be either in absolute or relative form.

The absolute forms of these statements are as follows:

line#	PRESET (c,r)[,color]
line#	PSET (c,r)[,color]

The relative forms of these statements are as follows:

line#	PRESET STEP (c-increment,r-increment)[,color]
line#	PSET STEP (c-increment,r-increment)[,color]

where

■ *(c,r)* are the column, row coordinates of the desired pixel.
■ *color* is the color of the pixel.
■ *(c-increment,r-increment)* are the column and row offsets to add to the previous PSET or PRESET statement's coordinates.

Here are some examples of the PSET and PRESET statements:

```
100 PRESET (10,10)
```

The preceding statement turns off the pixel at (10,10).

```
100 PSET STEP (0,9)
```

The preceding statement turns on the pixel 9 rows directly beneath the last pixel referenced.

```
100 PSET STEP (-3,-50)
```

The preceding statement turns on the pixel 3 columns left of and 50 rows above the last pixel referenced.

The DRAW Statement

The DRAW statement is used to draw a figure. The format for the DRAW statement is as follows:

```
line#      DRAW string
```

where *string* is a string expression containing the commands to draw the figure. See Table 12–2 for a list of the DRAW commands.

Here are some examples of the DRAW statement:

```
90    SCREEN 1
100   DRAW "U10;L10;D10;R10"
110   DRAW "BM50,50 M+10,+0 M+0,+10 M-10,+0 M+0,-10"
120   DRAW "BM160,150M170,150M170,160M160,160M160,150"
```

All three of the above DRAW statements draw identical boxes on the screen, but notice how differently the statements are constructed. Line 100 starts at the last defined pixel coordinate; if this is the first one referenced, the default will be the center of the display. This statement uses the predefined "up-left-down-right" commands, which move the specified relative distance in a right angle from the current position. Line 110 first moves to coordinates (50,50) using the M command, without drawing a line (as instructed by preceding the M with a B). Then it makes *relative* movements across the display, using the M command and inserting a "+" or a "−" before the x coordinate. Last, statement 120 draws a box using the M command and *absolute* coordinates.

In addition to the above observations, notice how the commands are separated from one another. In statement 100 the commands are separated

TABLE 12–2   DRAW Statement Command Summary

Movement Commands

The following are *relative* movement commands; they begin movement from the current graphics position. Movement distance depends on the scale factor multiplied by *n*, where the default for *n* is 1.

Command	Description
U *n*	up
D *n*	down
L *n*	left
R *n*	right
E *n*	diagonally up and right
F *n*	diagonally down and right
G *n*	diagonally down and left
H *n*	diagonally up and left
M *x,y*	Move absolute or relative and draw a line. To write this command in relative form, insert a "+" or "−" before the *x*.

Prefix Commands

The following prefixes may be added to the above movement commands.

Command	Description
B	Move, but don't plot any points.
N	Move, but return here when done.
A *n*	Set angle *n*, where *n* is in the range [0 . . 3]. This command is used to rotate figures, and *n* represents the multiple of 90 degrees to turn (0 = 0 degrees, 1 = 90 degrees, and so on).
TA *n*	Turn angle *n*, where *n* is in the range [− 360 . . 360].
C *n*	Set color *n*.
S *n*	Set scale factor *n*, where *n* is in the range [1 . . 255]. *n* is divided by 4 to derive the scale factor. The scale factor is multiplied by the distances given in the U, D, L, R, E, F, G, H, and the relative M commands to travel the correct distance. The default is 4.
x *string;variable*	Execute a substring. *string* contains movement commands.
P *paint, boundary*	Defines the desired color and filled-in pattern for a figure. *paint* is the desired color, and *boundary* defines the border color.

by semicolons; in statement 110 they are separated by blanks; and in 120 they are concatenated together. All three forms of separation are legal.

```
90   SCREEN 1
100 DRAW "BM100,20,F50 E50 L99"
```

The above program segment draws a triangle starting at pixel (100,20). This statement demonstrates how the different commands—*M*, the right-angle, and the 45-degree statements (*E, F, G,* and *H*)—can be combined in one DRAW statement.

Using Loops in Graphics

Graphics statements can be used in loops the same way ordinary statements may be used. Loops are a simple method of providing animation to your graphics. Figure 12–4 shows a simple example of animation in which a

FIGURE 12–4   Example Animation Program: "Falling Ball"

```
10   REM ***                   FALLING BALL                    ***
20   REM ***                                                   ***
30   REM ***   THIS PROGRAM USES ANIMATION TO ILLUSTRATE       ***
40   REM ***   A FALLING BALL.                                 ***
50   REM
60   CLS
70   SCREEN 2
80   KEY OFF
90   BALLRADIUS   =   50
100  DUSTRADIUS   =    3
110  FRAME        =    2
120  GROUND       = 133
130  VERTLINE     = 320
140  REM
150  REM  *** THE BALL IS FALLING...
160  REM
170  LINE (0,GROUND)-(639,GROUND)
180  FOR HEIGHT = BALLRADIUS TO (GROUND - (BALLRADIUS * 3/7)) STEP FRAME
190     CIRCLE (VERTLINE,HEIGHT),BALLRADIUS,1
200     CIRCLE (VERTLINE,HEIGHT - FRAME),BALLRADIUS,0
210  NEXT HEIGHT
220  CIRCLE (VERTLINE, HEIGHT - FRAME),BALLRADIUS,0
230  REM
240  REM *** SPLAT!
250  FOR PIECE = 1 TO 25
260     DUSTX = VERTLINE - BALLRADIUS + INT (RND * BALLRADIUS * 2)
270     DUSTY = GROUND - INT (RND * BALLRADIUS)
280     CIRCLE (DUSTX, DUSTY),DUSTRADIUS
290  NEXT PIECE
999  END
```

FOR/NEXT loop controls a ball's height. Each time the loop executes, the ball moves closer to the ground.

Color Graphics

Although three modes are available on the screen, only the medium-resolution graphics mode permits color. If you want to use color in your graphics, your SCREEN statement must define the *colorswitch* parameter as zero. The statement would then be SCREEN 1,0. SCREEN 1,1 would activate monochrome, or black-and-white, medium-resolution graphics.

There are two main colors you need to define before you start drawing your graphics: the background color and the foreground color. (The foreground color is the color of the box, line, circle, or other image you wish to draw.) In ordinary text mode, the background color of the screen is black, or off; the pixels are not lit. The colors available for the foreground and background are shown in Table 12–3.

The COLOR Statement

The COLOR statement defines the current background and foreground colors. The format for the COLOR statement is as follows:

line#	COLOR [background color][,[palette]]

where

- *background color* is a color selected from the background color list in Table 12–3. Background color must be in the range of 0 . . 15.
- *palette* defines the foreground colors available from one of the two palettes in Table 12–3. Palette must be in the range of 0 . . 1.

Here is an example of the COLOR statement:

```
100 SCREEN 1
110 COLOR 2,0
```

The preceding statement turns the background green (2) and selects palette 0, which permits foreground colors of green, red, or brown. If you draw a green object with a green background color, the object will be drawn but will be invisible.

Sound

Three statements produce sounds on the IBM PC: BEEP, SOUND, and PLAY. BEEP is the one most often used.

TABLE 12–3 Colors Used in Medium-Resolution Graphics

Background Colors

Color	Number	Color	Number
Black	0	Gray	8
Blue	1	Light blue	9
Green	2	Light green	10
Cyan	3	Light cyan	11
Red	4	Light red	12
Magenta	5	Light magenta	13
Brown	6	Yellow	14
White	7	Bright white	15

Foreground Colors

Palette 0		Palette 1	
Color	Number	Color	Number
Green	1	Cyan	1
Red	2	Magenta	2
Brown	3	White	3

Now Try This

1. Write a statement that will draw a horizontal line 100 pixels long starting at (160,100).

2. Write a statement that will draw a filled-in box. Two of its corners are at (0,70) and (319,130).

3. Write a statement that draws a circle 25 pixels in radius in the center of the screen.

4. Write a statement that will draw an octagon whose sides are all 25 units long.

The BEEP Statement

BEEP causes the computer to make a short, steady beeping noise. It is used most often to announce an error. The format of the BEEP statement is as follows.

Here is an example of the BEEP statement:

```
80 BEEP
90 PRINT "Invalid input.  Try again."
```

The SOUND Statement

The SOUND statement allows you to generate your own sound through the speaker. The format of the SOUND statement is as follows:

> line#   SOUND frequency,duration

where

- *frequency* is the desired frequency in Hertz (Hz). *frequency* must be in the range of 37 . . 32767. The larger this number, the higher pitched the sound will be.
- *duration* is the duration of the sound in clock ticks. The computer has an internal clock that ticks 18.2 times a second. *duration* must be in the range of 0 . . 65535. Therefore, the following statement generates a sound at 800 Hz for two seconds:

120 SOUND 800,18.2 * 2

Figure 12–5 shows several examples of the SOUND statement.

The PLAY Statement

The PLAY statement allows you to create a sequence of notes or tones—in short, to play music. Figure 12–6 gives two examples of coded music strings. Although they look difficult to play, they are simple to code.

The format for the PLAY statement is as follows:

> line#   PLAY string

where *string* is a character string composed of the special music commands. Figure 12–7 shows four octaves of notes. Table 12–4 summarizes the music commands.

Creating Business Charts and Graphics

The greatest business use for graphics is to display numerical data in pictorial form. These pictures usually take one of three forms: the line graph, the bar chart, or the pie diagram. Each has its best use; it is up to you to decide which graph is suited to your need.

FIGURE 12–5   Using the SOUND Statement

```
10    REM  ***************************************************
20    REM  ***           EXAMPLES OF SOUND STATEMENT           ***
30    REM  ***************************************************
40    REM
50    REM    *** SIMPLE TONES ***
60    REM
70    FOR I = 300 TO 1200 STEP 100
80        SOUND I,8
90        FOR J = 1 TO 500        ' PAUSE FOR EFFECT
100       NEXT J
110   NEXT I
120   REM
130   FOR J = 1 TO 600            ' PAUSE BETWEEN EXAMPLES
140   NEXT J
150   REM
160   REM    *** SIREN ***
170   REM
180   FOR I = 1 TO 3
190       FOR J = 450 TO 1200
200           SOUND J, .1
210       NEXT J
220       FOR J = 1200 TO 450 STEP -1
230           SOUND J, .1
240       NEXT J
250   NEXT I
999   END
```

FIGURE 12–6   Coded Music

10 PLAY "O3L4CEL2G"   20 PLAY "O3L8GABGL4AL8GB"

Now Try This

1. Write a statement that will play a 1200-Hz tone for two seconds.

2. Write a statement that will play the music shown in Figure 12–8.

3. Write a statement that will cause the computer to beep if a value greater than 200 is entered for variable N.

FIGURE 12–7   Octaves 1 through 4

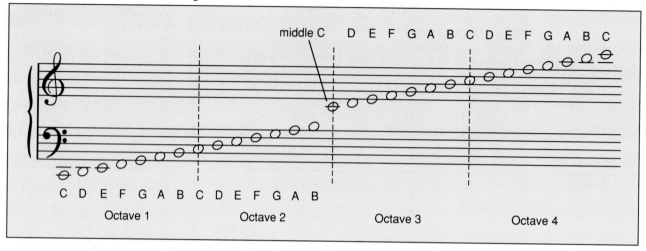

FIGURE 12–8   Sheet Music Excerpt: "So Long (It's Been Good to Know Ya)"

Line Graph

The line graph shows the relationships between sets of numbers plotted on a pair of axes. The vertical axis usually represents amounts, and the horizontal axis usually represents time. A line graph is commonly used to illustrate business-related topics such as profits over a fiscal year, or sales per month.

An example of a line graph is shown in Figure 12–9. Note that the trickiest part of creating a line graph for the programmer is selecting the correct horizontal and vertical scales. For example, each point on the graph might be represented by 20 pixels. The location of the graph on the display will be fixed between pre-specified pixels but the range of values on the axes will likely change from graph to graph. Then, once the scale factor for each axis is found, it is a simple matter to plot the points (draw the lines) within the graph.

Bar Chart

The bar chart is composed of horizontal or vertical bars of the same width but scaled in length to represent some quantity. The vertical axis usually represents quantity. The horizontal axis shows either (1) different items at

TABLE 12–4 PLAY Statement Command Summary

Command	Description
A–G [#, +, −]	A through G are notes. The optional #, +, and − signs follow the note. The # and + signs both denote a sharp; the − denotes a flat.

L*n*	L defines the length of each note. *n* must be in the range [1 . . 64]. This statement affects all the notes following it until the next L statement is encountered. Alternatively, for one note only, the length of the note may follow the note.
	    Example 1: "L2CD" denotes a half-note played at notes C and D.
	    Example 2: "L4CCC8D8C" denotes the first two Cs as quarter notes, the next C and D as eighth notes, and the last C as a quarter note.

ML	Music Legato. Each note plays the full period specified by L, so that the notes flow smoothly together.
MN	Music Normal. After this command, each note plays seven-eighths of the time determined by the last L (length command).
MS	Music Staccato. Each note plays three-quarters of the time specified by L. When playing staccato, the notes sound abrupt and quite distinct from each other.
O*n*	Set the current octave. *n* must be in the range [0 . . 6]; middle C is at the beginning of octave 3.
P*n*	Pause. *n* must be in the range [1 . . 64], and indicates the length of each pause; for more details, see the L command.
T*n*	Tempo. *n* specifies the number of quarter notes (L4s) per minute, and must be in the range [32 . . 255]. The default is 120.
.	A period following a note changes the duration the note is played (L) to 3/2 the original duration.
X*string*;	Play the substring *string*, where *string* is a variable assigned to a string of PLAY commands. This command is useful when a section of music must be repeated.

the same time, (2) the same item at different times, or (3) the different parts that make up some whole.

Figure 12–10 shows an example of a bar chart. The bar chart has the same tricky characteristic of the line diagram: selecting the correct horizontal and vertical scale factor. Note, too, that when more than one bar is

FIGURE 12–9   Example of a Line Diagram

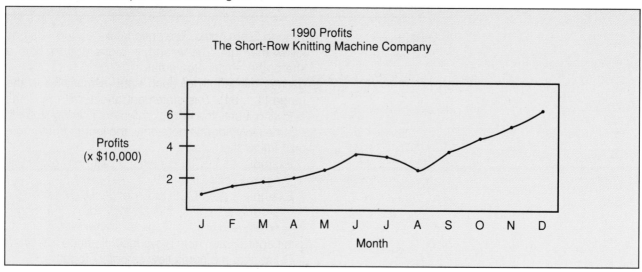

FIGURE 12–10   Example of a Bar Chart

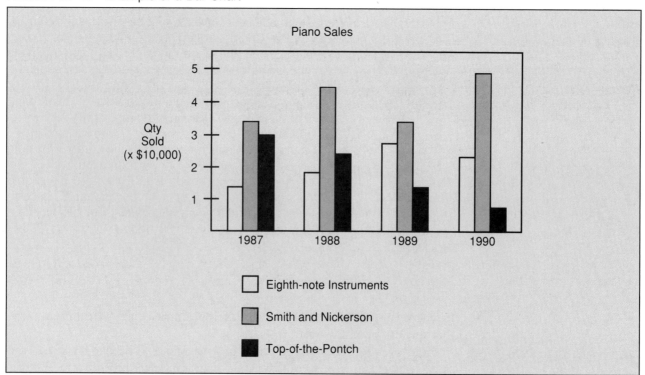

displayed on the graph per entry, a legend appears beneath the chart defining the different-colored bars.

Pie Diagram

A pie diagram looks like its name: it is a circle divided into wedges. The entire circle represents 100 percent, and the wedges show the various ways the circle is divided. A common use for a pie diagram is a budget; there is only so much money in the budget, to be spent in various ways. See Figure 12–11 for an example of a pie diagram.

The most difficult part about drawing the slices in a pie diagram is figuring out where the dividing lines go. Suppose the center of the pie is at coordinates (160, 100), and the radius of the circle is 75. Furthermore, suppose you want to divide the pie into sections representing 49%, 5% , and 22%, plus whatever is left over—24%.

Origin line

In a pie diagram, the origin line is a horizontal line extending from the center of the circle to the 3:00 position. All later angular measurements start from this line.

Start by drawing a horizontal line from the center of the circle to the 3:00 position. We can call this line the **origin line.** For each of the lines to draw, you will need to do the following:

1. Find the angle between the origin line and the new line in radians.
2. Find the coordinates of the endpoints of the new line.
3. Draw the line.

So for the first line, the one at 49%, the angle is 0.49 × 360, or 176.4 degrees (because we want 49% of a full circle). We multiply 176.4 by a constant conversion factor of Pi/180, or 0.017, and get the angle in radians as 2.999.

The next step is to find the coordinates of the endpoints of the line. You will need the following equations for this:

edge x = center x + r × cos (angle)
edge y = center y + r × sin (angle) × aspect ratio

These equations use the trigonometric functions sine (sin) and cosine (cos). Do not worry if you have not had trigonometry. Simply be careful to follow the instructions exactly.

Notice that the y-coordinate must be multiplied by an aspect ratio to end at the edge of the circle. For high-resolution graphics mode (SCREEN 2), this constant is 0.42.

Using the above equations, the coordinates become

edge x = 160 + 75 × cos (2.999) = 86
edge y = 100 + 75 × sin (2.999) × 0.42 = 104

FIGURE 12–11   Example of a Pie Diagram

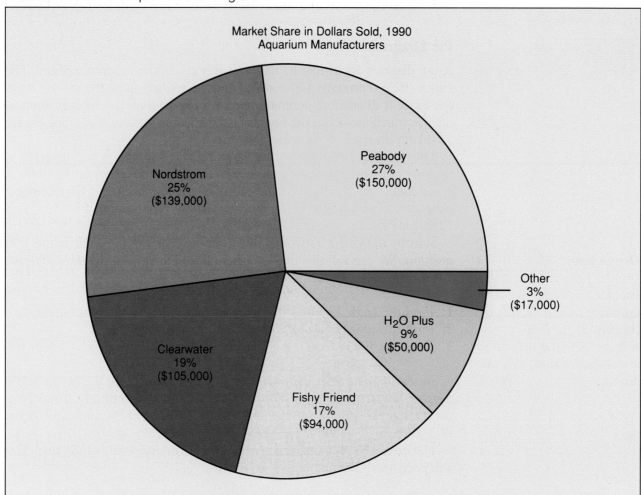

Market Share in Dollars Sold, 1990
Aquarium Manufacturers

Peabody
27%
($150,000)

Nordstrom
25%
($139,000)

Other
3%
($17,000)

H₂O Plus
9%
($50,000)

Clearwater
19%
($105,000)

Fishy Friend
17%
($94,000)

Fortunately, BASIC contains library functions to determine the sine and cosine of angles. The following statements return the cosine and sine of angle X (X must be stated in radians):

```
20 COSINE = COS(X)
30 SINE = SIN(X)
```

Finally, to draw the line we use the LINE statement:

```
110 SCREEN 1
120 LINE (CENTER.X, CENTER.Y) - (EDGE.X, EDGE.Y)
```

or

LINE (160, 100) − (86, 104)

To draw the rest of the lines, the steps are the same *except* that the sum of the previous percentages must always be added to the current percentage. For the second line, for example, you would work with a percentage of 49 + 5; for the third, it will be 49 + 5 + 22.

A Programming Problem

Problem Definition

You are the owner of a rent-a-programmer business. One morning, the owner of a pet store arrives to employ your services. She says, "I want a program that will ask me how many pets we sold each month for an entire year. We never sell more than, oh, five hundred pets per month. Then I want the program to display this information in a bar chart for me."

"Piece of cake," you assure her. You write up the program specification chart shown in Figure 12–12 to verify that you understand the program requirements. Then, together, you decide on the format of the report, shown in Figure 12–13. Notice that the chart has horizontal and vertical "tick marks" to make the graph more readable.

FIGURE 12–12   Pet Store Program Specification Chart

PROGRAM SPECIFICATION CHART		
PROGRAM NAME: Pet Store	PROGRAMMER'S NAME: S. Baumann	DATE: 5/27/92
INPUT: Pets sold per month. Title of Bar Chart.	OUTPUT: Bar Chart displaying pets sold per month.	
SOURCE OF INPUT: Keyboard	DESTINATION OF OUTPUT: Monitor screen	
PURPOSE: Prompts for quantity of pets sold from January through December, inclusive. Then prints a bar chart on the monitor screen.		

FIGURE 12–13   Format for Pet Store Bar Chart

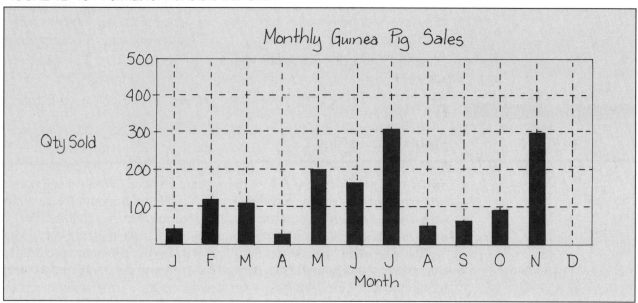

Solution Design

There are three basic tasks to be performed here:

1. Assign names to the constants used in creating the chart.
2. Prompt the user for the input.
3. Draw the graph.

In graphics programs, it is usually easiest to name constants that are used repeatedly in the program. If a value needs to be changed later on, it needs to be changed in only one place, rather than everywhere it appears. Therefore, when this program is written, the first step will be to assign variable names to the constants used in the program. The values contained in these variables will not be altered during execution.

Step 2 can be divided into three substeps:

2.A. Prompt the user to enter the bar chart's title.
2.B. Prompt the user to enter the sales for each month.
2.C. Verify that each sales value is within the allowable range.

Step 3 can be broken down as follows:

3.A. Draw the bar chart title.
3.B. Draw the axes and labels.
3.C. Draw the bars for each month.

The structure chart for this problem is shown in Figure 12–14. The flowchart and pseudocode are shown in Figure 12–15.

The Program

Examine the program shown in Figure 12–16. Subroutine INITIALIZE is called first so that constants can be established. As previously mentioned, using constants simplifies altering the chart at a later time. A good example of this is AXISROWMAX, which is the bottom horizontal line of the graph. Suppose you decide to make this graph taller; with a *constant* AXISROWMAX, you only need to change line 1170 instead of lines 1190, 3210, 3300, 3460, 3530, and 3630.

Notice that in lines 1260 through 1370 the names of the months are assigned to array MONTH$. Later, when the name of a month needs to be printed, the corresponding array element can be accessed.

Subroutine GET DATA prompts the user to enter the graph title and the quantity of pets sold each month. If the value is outside the allowable range (the maximum value, 500, was established in line 1220), the WHILE loop prompts the user to reenter it.

FIGURE 12–14   Structure Chart for Pet Store Problem

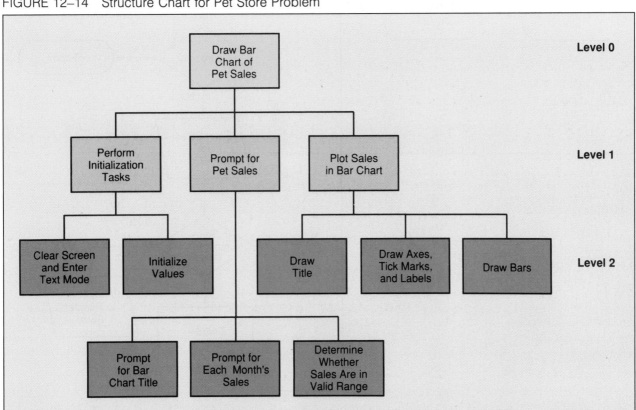

FIGURE 12–15   Flowchart and Pseudocode for Pet Store Problem

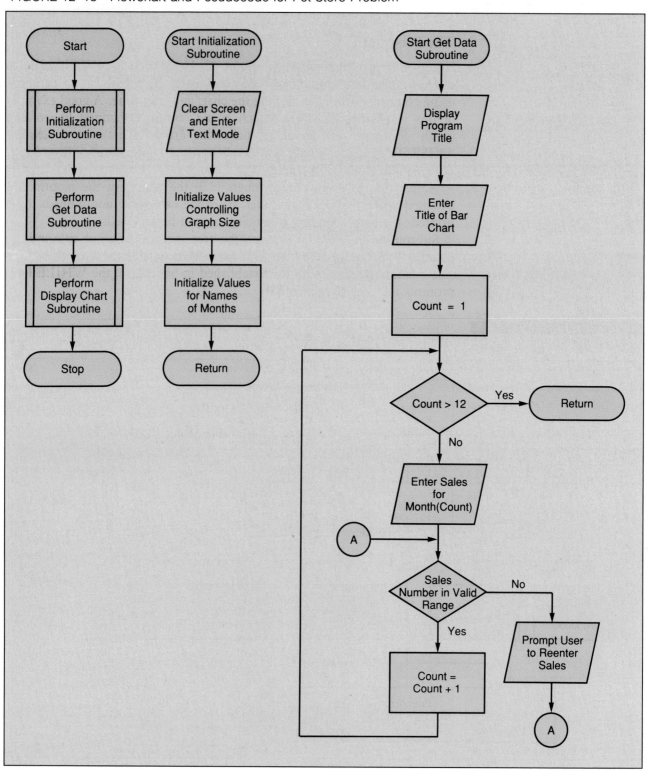

FIGURE 12–15 Continued

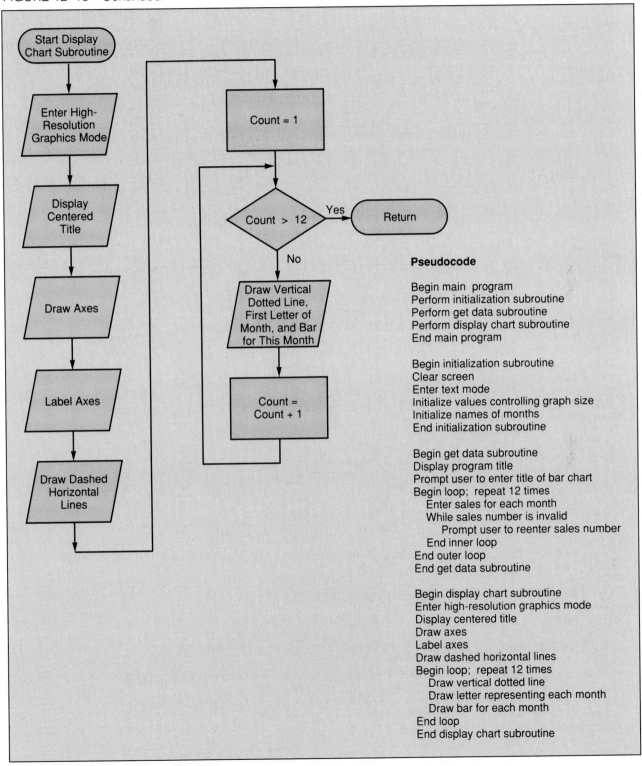

Pseudocode

Begin main program
Perform initialization subroutine
Perform get data subroutine
Perform display chart subroutine
End main program

Begin initialization subroutine
Clear screen
Enter text mode
Initialize values controlling graph size
Initialize names of months
End initialization subroutine

Begin get data subroutine
Display program title
Prompt user to enter title of bar chart
Begin loop; repeat 12 times
    Enter sales for each month
    While sales number is invalid
        Prompt user to reenter sales number
    End inner loop
End outer loop
End get data subroutine

Begin display chart subroutine
Enter high-resolution graphics mode
Display centered title
Draw axes
Label axes
Draw dashed horizontal lines
Begin loop; repeat 12 times
    Draw vertical dotted line
    Draw letter representing each month
    Draw bar for each month
End loop
End display chart subroutine

FIGURE 12–16   Pet Store Program

```
 10  REM ***                    PET SHOP SALES PROGRAM            ***
 20  REM ***                                                      ***
 30  REM *** THIS PROGRAM CREATES A BAR CHART ILLUSTRATING        ***
 40  REM *** MONTHLY PET SALES FOR A PET STORE.  THE USER         ***
 50  REM *** IS PROMPTED TO ENTER THE DATA DURING PROGRAM         ***
 60  REM *** EXECUTION.  THE CHART IS THEN DISPLAYED ON THE       ***
 70  REM *** MONITOR.                                             ***
 80  REM ***                                                      ***
 90  REM *** MAJOR CONSTANTS: (don't change during execution)***
100  REM ***                                                      ***
110  REM *** AXISCOLMAX  : the maximum column, in pixels,         ***
120  REM ***                of the axis                           ***
130  REM *** AXISCOLMIN  : the minimum column, in pixels,         ***
140  REM ***                of the axis                           ***
150  REM *** AXISCOLINC  : distance between horizontal axis       ***
160  REM ***                tick marks, in pixels                 ***
170  REM *** AXISROWMAX  : the maximum row, in pixels, of         ***
180  REM ***                the axis                              ***
190  REM *** AXISROWMIN  : the minimum row, in pixels, of         ***
200  REM ***                the axis                              ***
210  REM *** AXISROWINC  : distance between vertical axis         ***
220  REM ***                tick marks, in pixels                 ***
230  REM *** BARWIDTH    : horizontal width of the bars, in       ***
240  REM ***                pixels                                ***
250  REM *** MONTH$      : a 12-element array containing          ***
260  REM ***                the spelled-out months of the        ***
270  REM ***                year.                                 ***
280  REM ***                                                      ***
290  REM *** MAJOR VARIABLES: (change during execution)           ***
300  REM ***                                                      ***
310  REM *** COLUMN      : temporary column variable              ***
320  REM *** ROW         : temporary row variable                 ***
330  REM *** SOLD        : a 12-element array containing          ***
340  REM ***                the quantity of pets sold per         ***
350  REM ***                month                                 ***
360  REM *** TITLE$      : character string containing the        ***
370  REM ***                title of the graph                    ***
380  REM ***                                                      ***
390  REM
400  REM  *** CALL SUBROUTINE TO PERFORM INITIALIZATION TASKS.
410  GOSUB 1000
420  REM
430  REM *** CALL SUBROUTINE TO GET MONTHLY SALES DATA.
440  GOSUB 2000
450  REM
460  REM *** CALL SUBROUTINE TO DISPLAY BAR CHART.
470  GOSUB 3000
999  END
1000 REM ****************************************************************
1010 REM ***               SUBROUTINE INITIALIZE              ***
1020 REM ****************************************************************
1030 REM ***   THIS SUBROUTINE INITIALIZES CONSTANTS USED     ***
1040 REM ***   BY THE PROGRAM.                                ***
```

FIGURE 12–16   Continued

```
1050 REM
1060 CLS
1070 SCREEN 0
1080 KEY OFF
1090 REM *** THE FOLLOWING COLUMN VALUES GIVE A BORDER OF 14
1100 REM *** CHARACTERS.
1110 AXISCOLMAX = 527
1120 AXISCOLMIN = 112
1130 REM *** THERE ARE 13 COLUMNS. ***
1140 AXISCOLINC  = (AXISCOLMAX - AXISCOLMIN) / 13
1150 REM
1160 REM *** THE FOLLOWING ROW VALUES GIVE A BORDER OF 5 ROWS.
1170 AXISROWMAX  = 160
1180 AXISROWMIN  =  40
1190 AXISROWINC  = (AXISROWMAX - AXISROWMIN) /  5  ' 5 rows
1200 REM
1210 BARWIDTH    = INT (AXISCOLINC * 2 / 3)
1220 MAXSOLD     = 500
1230 REM
1240 DIM SOLD(12)
1250 DIM MONTH$ (12)
1260 MONTH$ ( 1) = "January   :"
1270 MONTH$ ( 2) = "February  :"
1280 MONTH$ ( 3) = "March     :"
1290 MONTH$ ( 4) = "April     :"
1300 MONTH$ ( 5) = "May       :"
1310 MONTH$ ( 6) = "June      :"
1320 MONTH$ ( 7) = "July      :"
1330 MONTH$ ( 8) = "August    :"
1340 MONTH$ ( 9) = "September :"
1350 MONTH$ (10) = "October   :"
1360 MONTH$ (11) = "November  :"
1370 MONTH$ (12) = "December  :"
1380 RETURN
2000 REM ********************************************************
2010 REM ***                   SUBROUTINE GET DATA          ***
2020 REM ********************************************************
2030 REM ***   THIS SUBROUTINE PROMPTS THE USER TO ENTER THE  ***
2040 REM ***   QUANTITY OF PETS SOLD EACH MONTH.              ***
2050 REM
2060 PRINT TAB(29) "Pet Store Sales Program"
2070 PRINT TAB(29) "-----------------------"
2080 PRINT
2090 INPUT "Title of bar chart";TITLE$
2100 PRINT
2110 FOR I = 1 TO 12
2120    PRINT "Pets sold in ";MONTH$ (I);
2130    INPUT " ";TEMP
2140    REM *** DETERMINE WHETHER QUANTITY IS WITHIN VALID RANGE.
2150    WHILE (0 > TEMP) OR (TEMP > MAXSOLD)
2160       PRINT "*** Error: ";TEMP;
2170       PRINT " is outside the legal range [0.."; MAXSOLD;"].  Try again."
2180       INPUT " ";TEMP
```

(figure continued on the next page)

FIGURE 12–16 Continued

```
2190    WEND
2200    SOLD (I) = TEMP
2210 NEXT I
2220 RETURN
3000 REM ***************************************************
3010 REM ***             SUBROUTINE DISPLAY CHART          ***
3020 REM ***************************************************
3030 REM ***   THIS SUBROUTINE DISPLAYS THE AXIS AND THE BARS ***
3040 REM ***   CORRESPONDING TO THE PET SALES FOR EACH OF THE ***
3050 REM ***   12 MONTHS.                                  ***
3060 REM
3070 PRINT
3080 INPUT "Press any key to draw the bar chart ";TEMP$
3090 REM
3100 REM *** PUT DISPLAY IN HIGH-RESOLUTION GRAPHICS MODE.
3110 CLS
3120 SCREEN 2
3130 REM
3140 REM *** WRITE THE TITLE AT THE TOP OF THE DISPLAY.
3150 COLUMN = (80 - LEN (TITLE$)) / 2
3160 ROW = 3
3170 LOCATE ROW, COLUMN
3180 PRINT TITLE$
3190 REM
3200 REM *** DRAW THE AXES.
3210 LINE (AXISCOLMIN,AXISROWMIN) - (AXISCOLMAX,AXISROWMAX),,B
3220 REM
3230 REM *** LABEL AND DRAW TICK MARKS ON THE VERTICAL AXIS, WHICH
3240 REM *** WILL SHOW THE QUANTITY OF PETS SOLD.
3250 LOCATE 12, 1
3260 PRINT "Qty Sold"
3270 REM
3280 COLUMN   = 10
3290 TICKMARK = MAXSOLD
3300 FOR ROW = AXISROWMIN TO (AXISROWMAX-AXISROWINC) STEP AXISROWINC
3310    LINE (AXISCOLMIN,ROW) - (AXISCOLMAX,ROW),,,&H101
3320    LOCATE INT (ROW/8), COLUMN        ' Label the lines.
3330    PRINT TICKMARK
3340    TICKMARK = TICKMARK - MAXSOLD / 5
3350 NEXT ROW
3360 REM
3370 REM *** LABEL AND DRAW TICK MARKS ON THE HORIZONTAL AXIS,
3380 REM *** WHICH WILL SHOW THE MONTHS.  AT THE SAME TIME, DRAW
3390 REM *** THE BARS.
3400 LOCATE 23, 37
3410 PRINT "Month"
3420 REM
3430 BARSTART = AXISCOLMIN + AXISCOLINC
3440 BAREND   = AXISCOLMAX - AXISCOLINC
3450 I        = 1
3460 ROW      = (AXISROWMAX / 8) + 1
3470 REM
3480 REM *** FOR EACH OF THE HORIZONTAL TICKS, DO THE FOLLOWING:
```

FIGURE 12–16   Continued

```
3490 REM *** (1) DRAW ITS VERTICAL DOTTED LINE; (2) LABEL IT WITH
3500 REM *** THE FIRST LETTER OF THE MONTH; AND (3) DRAW ITS BAR.
3510 FOR COLUMN = BARSTART TO BAREND STEP AXISCOLINC
3520    REM *** DRAW THE VERTICAL DOTTED LINE.
3530    LINE (COLUMN,AXISROWMAX) - (COLUMN,AXISROWMIN),,,&H101
3540    REM *** LABEL THE LINE WITH THE FIRST LETTER OF THE MONTH.
3550    LOCATE ROW + 1, INT ((COLUMN + 8) / 8)
3560    PRINT  (LEFT$ (MONTH$ (I), 1))
3570    REM *** DRAW THE BAR, CONNECTING THE LOWER LEFT CORNER
3580    REM *** WITH THE UPPER RIGHT CORNER.
3590    LLCOL      = COLUMN - (BARWIDTH / 2)
3600    LLROW      = AXISROWMAX
3610    URCOL      = COLUMN + (BARWIDTH / 2)
3620    PERCENTMAX = 1 - (SOLD (I) / MAXSOLD)
3630    URROW = PERCENTMAX * (AXISROWMAX - AXISROWMIN) + AXISROWMIN
3640    LINE (LLCOL, LLROW) - (URCOL, URROW),,BF
3650    I = I + 1
3660 NEXT COLUMN
3670 LOCATE 1,1
3680 RETURN
```

```
                 Pet Store Sales Program
                 ------------------------

    Title of bar chart? Monthly Guinea Pig Sales

    Pets sold in January    ? 48
    Pets sold in February   ? 24
    Pets sold in March      ? 15
    Pets sold in April      ? 88
    Pets sold in May        ? 117
    Pets sold in June       ? 322
    Pets sold in July       ? 310
    Pets sold in August     ? 296
    Pets sold in September  ? 208
    Pets sold in October    ? 8
    Pets sold in November   ? 0
    Pets sold in December   ? 16

    Press any key to draw the bar chart? x
```

(figure continued on the next page)

FIGURE 12–16   Continued

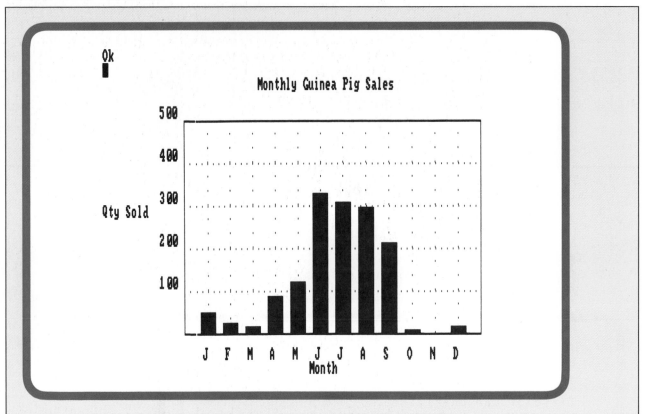

Finally, the chart is drawn in subroutine DISPLAY CHART. The title is centered at the top. Lines 3230 through 3350 draw and label the vertical axis and draw the tick marks. Carefully examine lines 3480 through 3680. The documentation included in these statements explains the action of this program segment.

Programming Hints

- Use constants in the appropriate way to keep future edits to a minimum.
- Do not overdo your use of color. Keep the quantity of colors down to two or three.
- Center your titles and graphs on the display; they will look more professional.
- If your graph includes a circle, use high-resolution graphics mode. It will produce fewer jagged edges than medium-resolution mode.

- During the debugging stage of your drawing, concentrate on one small part of the picture and program at a time. Finish one T-intersection, for example, before worrying about the lines angling off in the wrong direction on the other side of the screen.
- When you draw multiple objects on the screen, be consistent about how they are drawn. For example, start with the topmost point of the picture and draw in a counterclockwise direction. Or draw in a clockwise direction starting with the lowest point. Always list the upper-left, then lower-right coordinates in a LINE statement, or perhaps the lower-left then the upper-right coordinates. The technique is not terribly important, but being consistent will make debugging and comprehension easier.

Summary Points

- The PC has three display modes: text, medium-resolution graphics, and high-resolution graphics.
- The text mode divides the screen into 80 columns and 25 rows of characters, for a total of 2,000 characters starting at (1,1). Each character is referenced in the form (row, column).
- The medium-resolution graphics mode divides the screen into 320 columns and 200 rows, for a total of 64,000 pixels starting at (0,0). Each pixel is referenced in the form (column, row). In this mode, 40 characters are displayed per line.
- The high-resolution graphics mode divides the screen into 640 columns and 200 rows, for a total of 128,000 pixels starting at (0,0). Each pixel is referenced in the form (column, row). In this mode, 80 characters are displayed per line.
- Only the medium-resolution mode supports color. There are sixteen possible background colors (0 through 15) and two palettes (0 and 1). Both palettes support three foreground colors (0 through 2).

Vocabulary List

Graphics mode
Pixel

Origin line
Text mode

New Statement Review

Statement Format	Explanation
line# BEEP	Causes a short "beep" on the PC's speaker.
line# CIRCLE (c,r),radius [,[color][,[start],[end] [,aspect]]]	Draws a circle of the specified radius.
line# COLOR [background color][,[palette]]	Defines the foreground and background colors.
line# DRAW string	Draws figures on the monitor screen.
KEY OFF	Turns off the soft key display at the bottom of the screen.
line# LINE [(c1, r1)] − (c2, r2)[,[attribute][,B[F]][,style]]	Draws a line, an empty box, or a filled-in box.
line# LOCATE [row] [,[column][,[cursor][,[start] [,stop]]]]	Puts the cursor in the desired character position on the monitor screen.
line# PLAY string	Causes a sequence of specified notes to be played on the PC's speaker.
line# PRESET (c,r)[,color]	Turns off an individual pixel on the monitor screen. This is the absolute form of the command.
line# PRESET STEP (c-increment,r-increment) [,color]	Turns off an individual pixel on the monitor screen. This is the relative form of the command.
line# PSET (c,r)[,color]	Turns on an individual pixel on the monitor screen. This is the absolute form of the command.
line# PSET STEP (c-increment,r-increment) [,color]	Turns on an individual pixel on the monitor screen. This is the relative form of the command.
line# SCREEN [mode][,[colorswitch]]	Sets the desired monitor screen mode.
line# SOUND frequency,duration	Causes one tone to be played for the specified frequency and duration.

Questions

Whenever appropriate, use complete sentences in answering the following questions.

1. What display modes are available on the PC?

2. What type of equipment is required if you are going to use medium- and high-resolution graphics modes?

3. What is the display format of the PC when it is in text mode?

4. How are the character positions referenced when using text mode?

5. The characters displayed on the text-mode screen can be selected from a set of _____ characters numbered _____ through _____.

6. Give two examples of how the ampersand character (&) can be displayed on the text-mode screen.

7. What is a pixel?

8. The medium-resolution graphics mode divides the display screen into _____ pixels across and _____ pixels down, for a total of _____ pixels.

9. The high-resolution graphics mode divides the display screen into _____ pixels across and _____ pixels down, for a total of _____ pixels.

10. Write a statement that will draw a line from pixel (10, 20) to pixel (40, 80).

11. Write a statement that will draw a diamond whose vertices are at (160,0); (200,100); (160,200); and (120,100).

12. On a PC, an octave runs from note _____ to note _____.

13. The PC can play notes in _____ octaves, and they are numbered _____ through _____.

14. You need to show pictorially the quantity of each type of part, for all the parts of an assembly. What type of diagram is most appropriate: a line graph, bar chart, or pie diagram?

15. You need to show pictorially the changing cost of producing an assembly over the last ten years. What type of diagram is most appropriate: a line graph, bar chart, or pie diagram?

Debugging Exercises

Identify the following programs and program segments that contain errors, and debug them.

1.
```
10 REM *** PRINT A TITLE AT THE TOP OF THE SCREEN.
20 CLS
30 KEY OFF
40 SCREEN 1
50 LOCATE 1,50
60 PRINT "Medium-resolution Graphics"
99 END
```

2.
```
10 REM *** DRAW TWO CIRCLES. ***
20 CLS
30 KEY OFF
40 SCREEN 2,0
50 COLOR 11,1
60 CIRCLE (100,100),110,2
70 CIRCLE (200,20),10,1
99 END
```

```
3.  10 REM *** DRAW A DASHED LINE. ***
    20 CLS
    30 KEY OFF
    40 SCREEN 1,0
    50 COLOR 2,0
    60 LINE (50,50) - (100,100),B,1
    99 END


4.  10 REM *** PLAY A LITTLE MUSIC. ***
    20 PAY "O3L4CEL2G"
    30 PLAY "O3L8GABGL4AL8GB"
    99 END
```

Programming Problems

Level 1

1. Write a program that draws a border around the screen.
2. Write a program that draws a box within a circle.
3. Write a program that draws eight concentric circles, all of different diameters.
4. Write a program in medium-resolution graphics mode that draws the picture in Figure 12–17.
5. Write a program in high-resolution graphics mode that draws the picture in Figure 12–18.
6. Write a program that clears the screen, displays the word "Done!" in the center of the screen, beeps, and then erases the word.
7. Write a program that plays the music in Figure 12–19.

Level 2

1.–4. You are the lead programmer for Various Videos, a company specializing in computer graphics. Your boss asks you to develop a four-frame animated advertisement for an advertising agency. It should look like a cartoon and be similar to the pictures shown in Figures 12–20 through 12–23.

Write a separate program for each frame, and save each in a different file. The name of each program should correspond to the title of each of the frames. Link the four programs together by including the statement 9999 RUN"program-name" as the last line in the first three programs. For example, the last line of program SCREEN1.BAS should be 9999 RUN "SCREEN2.BAS", and the last line of the next program should be 9999 RUN "SCREEN3.BAS", and so on until the last file. At the end of the last program, you should produce an infinite loop with the statement 9999 GOTO 9999. You may want to write a caption for each cartoon frame. If you wish to display one screen longer than another, create a pause by using an empty FOR/NEXT loop, such as 9900 FOR I = 1 to 500:NEXT I.

Write the required four-frame cartoon.

5. Write a program in medium-resolution graphics mode that draws the picture in Figure 12–24.
6. Write a program that plays the music in Figure 12–25.

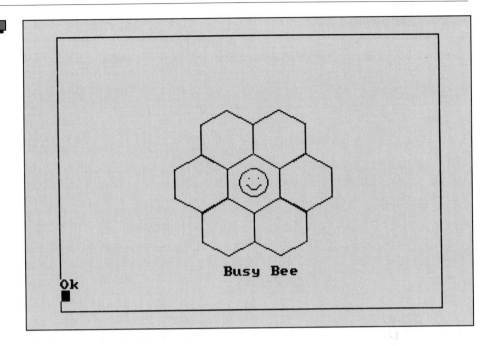

FIGURE 12–17 Busy Bee Honey Company Logo

Projects

For each project, complete the following:

- Fill out a program specification chart.
- Develop a structure chart.
- Create a flowchart or pseudocode.

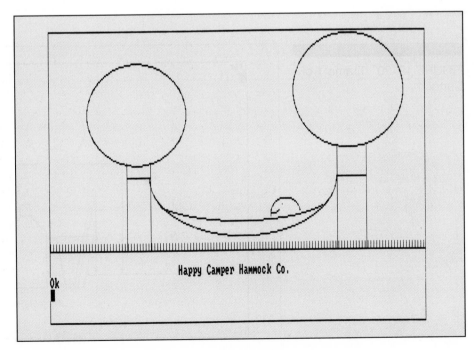

FIGURE 12–18 Happy Camper Hammock Company Logo

FIGURE 12–19   Sheet Music Excerpt: "Jingle Bells"

FIGURE 12–20   Frame 1 of Cartoon

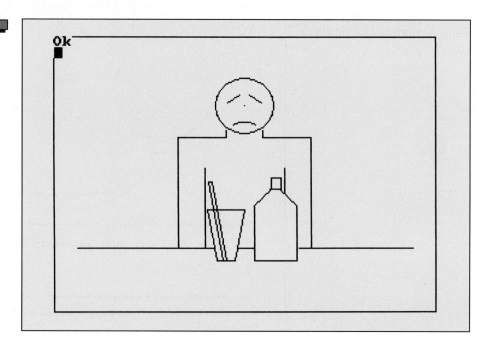

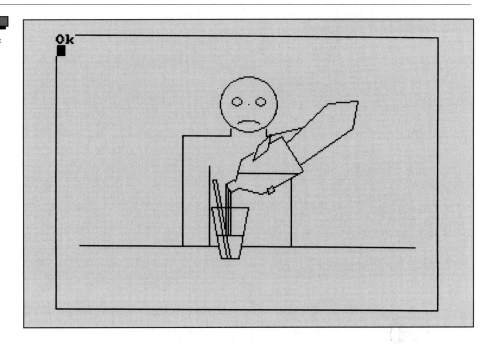

FIGURE 12–21   Frame 2 of
Cartoon

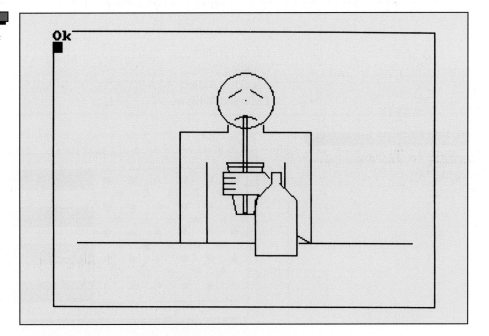

FIGURE 12–22   Frame 3 of
Cartoon

- Thoroughly document the final program.
- Test your program using a variety of data.

1. You are writing a term paper on the lumber business in Michigan's Upper Peninsula. You would like to illustrate your paper with a pie diagram containing the following information:

FIGURE 12–23 Frame 4 of
Cartoon

TITLE: Distribution of Trees: City Park Area
DATA:

Silver Birch: 56
Quaking Aspen: 44
Speckled Alder: 25
Diamond Willow: 21

FIGURE 12–24 American
Flag

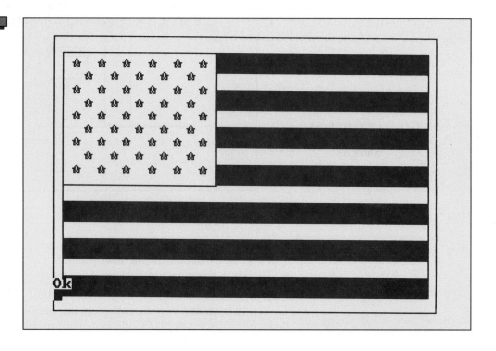

FIGURE 12–25   Sheet Music Excerpt: "Menuet," by J. S. Bach

Eastern Hophornbeam: 14
Northern Red Oak: 10
Paper Birch: 6

Write a program to produce the pie diagram. Center the title at the top of the page, and label each slice appropriately.

2. You are the owner of a rent-a-programmer business. One day a stockbroker comes in and asks you to write a program that will ask the user for a data file name, read in the data stored in that data file, ask what kind of diagram to draw, and then draw it. The stockbroker removes several sheets of paper from an inner jacket pocket and shoves them at you. "Here, I've got some notes for you. I want this stuff stored in a data file like this, on the first page." Page 1 is shown in Figure 12–26. "On this second page, I had my secretary write an example list of data." Page 2 is shown in Figure 12–27. "This last sheet here, it's the kind of graph I want to see except not hand-drawn. I want it neat, and professional-looking." Page 3 is shown in Figure 12–28.

FIGURE 12–26   Sample
Data File Format

> Data File Format
>
> line 1: title of graph
> line 2: horizontal axis label
> line 3: vertical axis label
> line 4: horizontal axis minimum, maximum, and increment value
> line 5: vertical axis minimum, maximum, and increment value
> lines 6 through last line of file: coordinates of data
>   points in format <u>x-axis</u>, <u>y-axis</u>

FIGURE 12–27 Sample
Data File

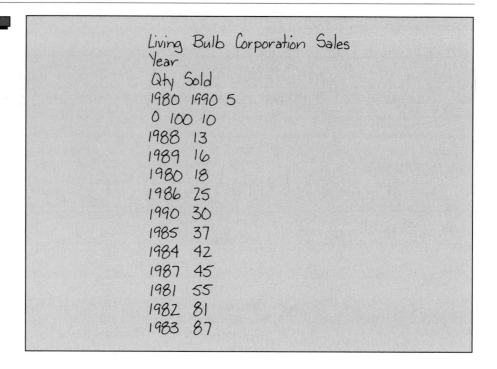

FIGURE 12–28 Sample Line Graph

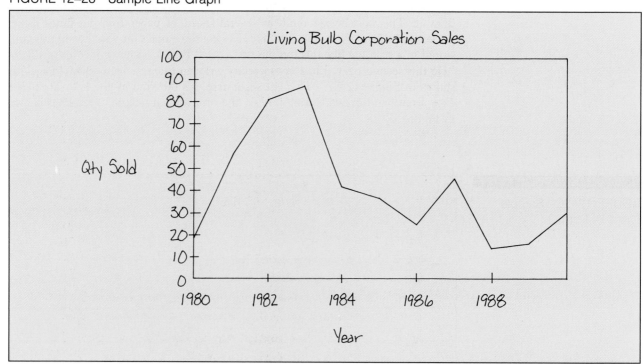

Reserved Words

ABS
AND
ASC
ATN
AUTO
BEEP
BLOAD
BSAVE
CALL
CDBL
CHAIN
CHDIR
CHR$
CINT
CIRCLE
CLEAR
CLOSE
CLS
COLOR
COM
COMMON
CONT
COS
CSNG
CSRLIN
CVD
CVI
CVS
DATA
DATE$
DEF
DEFDBL
DEFINT
DEFSNG
DEFSTR
DELETE

DIM
DRAW
EDIT
ELSE
END
ENVIRON
ENVIRON$
EOF
EQV
ERASE
ERDEV
ERDEV$
ERL
ERR
ERROR
EXP
FIELD
FILES
FIX
FN*xxxxxxxx*
FOR
FRE
GET
GOSUB
GOTO
HEX$
IF
IMP
INKEY$
INP
INPUT
INPUT#
INPUT$
INSTR
INT
IOCTL

IOCTL$
KEY
KILL
LEFT$
LEN
LET
LINE
LIST
LLIST
LOAD
LOC
LOCATE
LOCK
LOF
LOG
LPOS
LPRINT
LSET
MERGE
MID$
MKDIR
MKD$
MKI$
MKS$
MOD
MOTOR
NAME
NEW
NEXT
NOT
OCT$
OFF
ON
OPEN
OPTION
OR

OUT	RETURN	SYSTEM
PAINT	RIGHT$	TAB(
PALETTE	RMDIR	TAN
PALETTE USING	RND	THEN
PCOPY	RSET	TIME$
PEEK	RUN	TIMER
PEN	SAVE	TO
PLAY	SCREEN	TROFF
PMAP	SGN	TRON
POINT	SHARED	USING
POKE	SHELL	USR
POS	SIN	VAL
PRESET	SOUND	VARPTR
PRINT	SPACE$	VARPTR$
PRINT#	SPC(	VIEW
PSET	SQR	WAIT
PUT	STEP	WEND
RANDOMIZE	STICK	WHILE
READ	STOP	WIDTH
REM	STR$	WINDOW
RENUM	STRIG	WRITE
RESET	STRING$	WRITE#
RESTORE	SWAP	XOR
RESUME		

BASIC Operators

Arithmetic Operators

- ^ (exponentiation)
- + (unary; the sign used alone with a number)
- − (unary; the sign used alone with a number)
- * (multiplication)
- / (division)
- + (addition)
- − (subtraction)

String Operator

- + (concatenation)

Relational Operators

=	<=
<> or ><	>
<	>=

Logical Operators

NOT
AND
OR

Hierarchy of Operations

1. Exponentiation
2. Unary plus and minus
3. Multiplication and division
4. Addition and subtraction
5. Concatenation
6. Relational operators
7. NOT
8. AND
9. OR

ASCII Table

Below is a list of commonly used ASCII character codes.

CHAR		CHAR		CHAR	
32	**SPC**	64	@	96	´
33	**!**	65	**A**	97	**a**
34	**"**	66	**B**	98	**b**
35	**#**	67	**C**	99	**c**
36	**$**	68	**D**	100	**d**
37	**%**	69	**E**	101	**e**
38	**&**	70	**F**	102	**f**
39	**'**	71	**G**	103	**g**
40	**(**	72	**H**	104	**h**
41	**)**	73	**I**	105	**i**
42	*	74	**J**	106	**j**
43	**+**	75	**K**	107	**k**
44	**,**	76	**L**	108	**l**
45	**-**	77	**M**	109	**m**
46	**.**	78	**N**	110	**n**
47	/	79	**O**	111	**o**
48	**0**	80	**P**	112	**p**
49	**1**	81	**Q**	113	**q**
50	**2**	82	**R**	114	**r**
51	**3**	83	**S**	115	**s**
52	**4**	84	**T**	116	**t**
53	**5**	85	**U**	117	**u**
54	**6**	86	**V**	118	**v**
55	**7**	87	**W**	119	**w**
56	**8**	88	**X**	120	**x**
57	**9**	89	**Y**	121	**y**
58	:	90	**Z**	122	**z**
59	;	91	**[**	123	{
60	<	92	\	124	|
61	=	93	**]**	125	}
62	>	94	^	126	~
63	**?**	95	—	127	**DEL**

Microsoft BASIC on the Macintosh

The implementation of BASIC used on the Macintosh for this textbook is Microsoft 2.0.

Starting the Computer

Turn on the Macintosh power switch, which is located on the lower left side of the back of the computer. Now place the Microsoft BASIC disk in the disk drive. When the screen comes on, you will be in the "Finder" or monitor mode. On the lower half of the screen you will see several icons, or symbols, representing the various forms of BASIC that are available for use; choose the one that best fills your needs. For the programs in this book, Decimal BASIC is the most suitable version. The "mouse," or control box, is a feature of the Macintosh that requires some explanation. It works like a remote control: you move the box in the direction you wish the screen's cursor-arrow to go. Once you have maneuvered the cursor arrow over the appropriate icon, "double-click" the button on the mouse by pressing the button twice, rapidly. The computer will now load the chosen version of Microsoft BASIC. The Command window, appearing at the bottom of the screen, indicates that you are now in BASIC.

As an alternative, the Finder will also display a box at the top of the screen containing the icons of the programs already in memory. To load the program and its appropriate version of BASIC at the same time, simply double-click the program's symbol. The computer will come up in BASIC with the program already loaded.

The Microsoft BASIC Screen

Regions

The Microsoft BASIC screen has four main regions:

1. Menu bar (located at the top of the screen)
2. Command window (appears at the bottom of the screen)
3. Output window (the left portion of the screen)
4. List window (appears on the right side of the screen when activated)

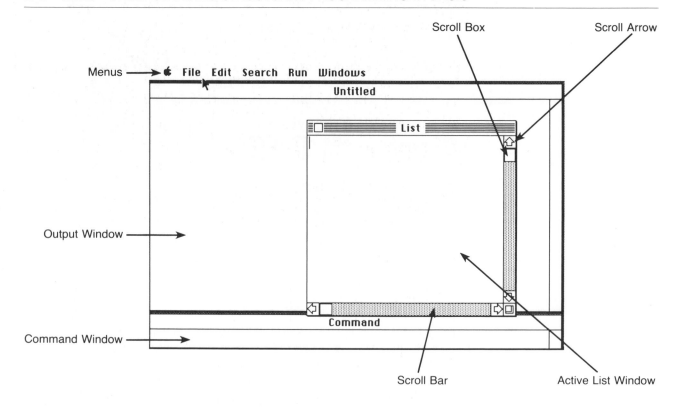

Menu Bar

The Menu Bar allows you to choose one of six menus and to gain access to the commands they contain: Apple, File, Edit, Search, Run, and Windows.

- *Apple Menu:* Contains Macintosh desk accessories.
- *File Menu:* Contains seven BASIC commands that deal with program files.
- *Edit Menu:* Contains three commands used to edit programs.
- *Search Menu:* Contains six editing commands.
- *Run Menu:* Contains six commands concerning program execution.
- *Window Menu:* Contains four commands that open windows.

Windows

To make any of the windows active, you must click the mouse button while the cursor is in the window. To close a window, simply click in the "close box," located in the upper left corner of each window. If you use the mouse to "drag" (to hold the button down while moving the mouse), the title bar will move any window around the screen. In the same way, by dragging the size box (lower right corner of the window), you can change the size of the box.

BASIC commands may be entered in the Command window and will be executed immediately; however, these commands are not stored in memory and are lost immediately after execution. The Output window displays the output of a program when it is run. When the command is given to list a program, the List window appears, displaying the program listing.

Use of the Screen

Many of the commands supplied by the menus for use with the mouse can instead be entered to the computer by manually typing the command in the Command window, with the same results.

Manipulating Programs

Before typing a program, click the File menu and then click the New command, listed under the File menu:

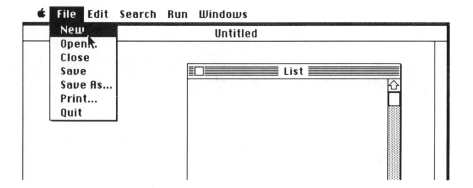

The List window is now active, and you can type your program in this window. You may want to enlarge the List window before typing the program. Another option is to activate the Command window and type NEW in this window:

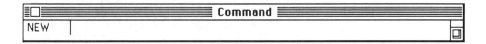

Then press <Return>.

To save a program named Monica, for example, click the File menu and then click the Save As . . . command. A dialog box will appear, requesting a name for the program. At this point, move the cursor into the space provided, type Monica, and press the <Return> key.

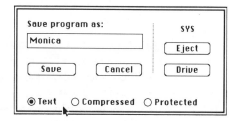

You can also type SAVE "Monica" in the Command window (note that the file name must be in double quotation marks) and press <Return> to get the same results:

SAVE "Monica"

To store the program in protected format, type

SAVE "Monica",P

and then <Return>. This command qualifier prevents the program from being listed at a later time.

To load an old program, click the Open command in the File menu, which will display all the programs in memory. Click the program you wish to load, and then click the Open box again. The program is now loaded and can be listed or run. Optionally, type LOAD "Monica" in the Command window:

LOAD "Monica"

Press <Return>. Type the following statement:

LOAD "Monica",R

Press <Return> to load and run a program automatically.

To list a program, you may want to enlarge the List window first: just click the List window title bar twice. To list a program, click the Window menu and then click the Show List command, which is listed under the Window menu.

If your program is longer than the screen, see Additional Features for scrolling control. Instead of using the Window menu, you can list a program by activating the Command window, typing LIST in the window, and then pressing <Return>.

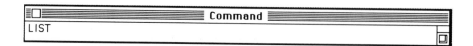

As with the other program-manipulating commands, you have two options to run a program: you can use the mouse and menu features, or you can type the command manually.

To use the menu option, click the Window menu and then click Show Output, which is found in the Window menu:

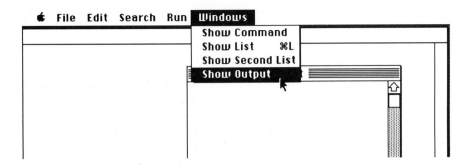

You then need to click the Run menu, and click Start, found in the Run menu.

When the program is running, all windows are hidden except for the untitled window, which is used to display the output.

When the output window is filled with output, it scrolls, eliminating the display of the topmost line of output to make room for a new line of output at the bottom of the output window.

Your other option for running a program is to use the command window and type RUN in the window, then press <Return>:

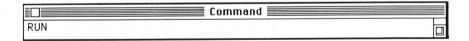

As with the other method, the program's output will be displayed and all other windows will be hidden.

Exiting BASIC

If you are in BASIC and wish to return to the Finder, click the Quit command under the File menu. As an alternative, you may type SYSTEM in the Command window and press <Return>:

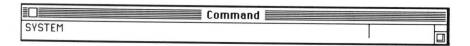

Once in the Finder, double-click the Eject command under the File menu to eject your disk. Turn off the power.

Keyboard

The Macintosh keyboard contains all of the standard keyboard characters. The <Shift> key can be used to enter the upper symbol on those keys that contain two symbols. To type only in uppercase, depress the <Caps Lock> key. Press the <Caps Lock> key once again to return to the lowercase mode.

Specialized Keys

When one of the keys listed in the following box is pressed, BASIC performs a specific function rather than accepting the key as standard keyboard data.

Key	Function
Return	Enters a line to the computer
Backspace	Deletes the character at the current cursor position.
Tab	Can be set to move the cursor to set positions.

Additional Features

Scrolling Control

When a program is listed (and the List window is therefore active), and it exceeds the screen's height, it scrolls off the top of the screen. Likewise, if a line is longer than the screen's width, you cannot see the entire line. In either situation, use of the scroll boxes becomes necessary. The horizontal scroll boxes are located on the right side of the List window, and the vertical scroll boxes are located on the bottom of the List window.

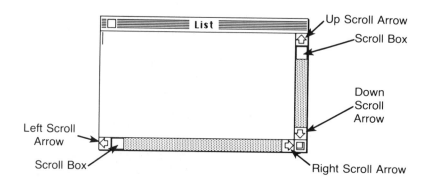

To move up or down in the listing, press the mouse button when the mouse pointer is on the up and down scroll arrow. To move left or right in the listing, press the mouse button on the left or right scroll arrow. To move large intervals (rather than line by line) vertically or horizontally through a listing, press the mouse button on the horizontal or vertical scroll bar and drag the box (still holding down the mouse button).

Output scrolling is controlled in an entirely different manner. To stop scrolling an output, it is necessary to click the Run menu and then click Suspend, which is found in the Run menu.

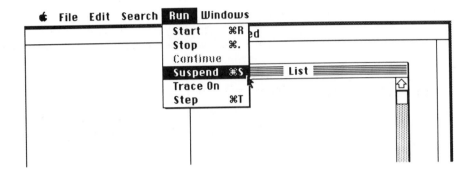

This halts the program output listing. To continue processing, simply click the Run menu again. Then click the command Continue, which is found in the Run menu.

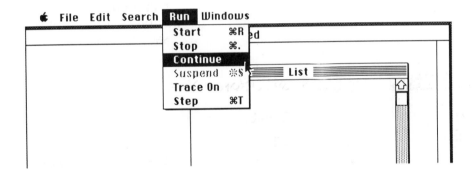

This method applies regardless of whether Run was initiated from the menu or the Command window.

Screen Factor

When a window is enlarged to occupy the entire screen, the screen can display up to 16 horizontal lines. The number of characters that can be printed on one line of the screen varies, because reserved words are boldfaced and thus occupy more space than variable names and numbers. For example, the first of the following two examples will occupy less space than the second, even though each has 24 characters, because IF, THEN, and PRINT will be boldfaced in the second statement, whereas only PRINT will be boldfaced in the first statement:

```
100  PRINT "MY NAME IS SARAH"
110  IF DONE THEN PRINT "YES"
```

A line is not limited to the screen width; it can have up to 255 characters. When a line exceeds the screen width, the Macintosh automatically scrolls to the left.

Line Numbers

Line numbers are optional in Microsoft BASIC on the Macintosh. If line numbers are used, however, the minimum line number is 0 and the maximum line number is 65529.

Print Zones and Width

The Macintosh enables the user to set the print zone width, and in turn the number of print zones per line, via the WIDTH command. Print zone width is entirely up to the user. To set it to 10, you would need to type the following statement:

```
100  WIDTH,10
```

It is possible to specify an output device and a print line width in the WIDTH command. These values default to SCREEN and 255 respectively, which is acceptable for our purposes here. If you wish to change the output device and/or line width, refer to your manual.

The number of print zones per line depends on the value you set for the zone width. Line width defaults to 255, and we set the zone width to 10 in the previous example, so in this case there will be 25.5 zones per line. If zone width is set to 14 (WIDTH,14) there are 18.5 print zones per line, again assuming the line width default value of 255.

When the following statement is executed, the print zone width will become 25 spaces and there will be 10.2 zones per line:

```
100  WIDTH,25
```

Answers to NOW TRY THIS Exercises

Answers to NOW TRY THIS 1–1

1. A program is a list of instructions that work together to solve a problem.
2. A computer system consists of three main components: input devices, a central processing unit, and output devices.
3. Data are facts that have not been organized in any meaningful way.
4. Keyboards, disk drives, and light pens are all examples of input devices.
5. Output that is printed on paper is hard copy.
6. The most powerful computers available today are called supercomputers.
7. Microcomputers are popular because they are relatively inexpensive, small, easy to use, and can run a wide variety of software.

Answers to NOW TRY THIS 1–2

1. A:
2. DISKCOPY A:B:
3. COPY A:B21.B B:B21.B or COPY A:B21.B B:
4. DIR

Answers to NOW TRY THIS 1–3

1. SYSTEM
2. NEW
3. SAVE "B:P21.BAS" or SAVE "B:P21"
4. LIST
   LLIST

Answers to NOW TRY THIS 2–1

1. Software consists of the programs that are executed by the computer's hardware.

2. The only language that computers can execute directly is machine language.

3. Of the three levels of programming languages, the most English-like one is high-level languages.

4. In structured programming, programs are divided into modules, each performing a specific task.

5. Before the computer can execute a BASIC program, the interpreter must translate it into machine language.

Answers to NOW TRY THIS 2–2

1. False. A given problem can have many acceptable solutions.

2. The first step in solving a problem is defining and documenting the problem.

3. The second step in solving a problem is designing and documenting a solution.

4. An algorithm is a sequence of steps needed to solve a problem.

5. False. The steps must be listed in the order in which they are to be carried out.

Answers to NOW TRY THIS 2–3

1. Coding is the process of writing a problem solution in a programming language.

2. Tracing through a program by hand, attempting to locate errors, is called desk checking.

3. A violation of the grammatical rules of a programming language generally results in a syntax error.

4. Debugging is the process of locating and correcting program errors.

5. False. Comments are placed in a program to explain it to humans; the computer ignores them.

Answers to NOW TRY THIS 3–1

1. Line numbers tell the BASIC system that the commands following them are to be executed in indirect mode.

2. True.

3. LIST 120-300

4. a. Hyphens are not allowed.
   c. Commas are not allowed.
5. c. Character strings must be enclosed in double quotation marks.
   d. Quotation marks are missing.
6. True. The first statement entered is lost.

Answers to NOW TRY THIS 3–2

1. The two types of constants are numeric constants and character string constants.

2. A variable is a storage location whose value can change during program execution.

3. A character string variable name must have a "$" as its last character.
4. **a.** Single-precision numeric variable
   b. Character string variable
   c. Double-precision numeric variable
   d. Single-precision numeric variable
5. They are the same. The "!" character denotes a single-precision numeric variable, and when the variable name has no ending character indicating its type, the "default" is also single-precision.
6. Reserved words are also referred to as key words.

Answers to NOW TRY THIS 3—3

1. 100 REM

2. 120 REM *** MULTIPLY SUBTOTAL BY 10.

3. **a.** 200 LET AGE = 17

   b. 210 LET N = 8 ^ 3

   c. 220 LET CAL = 100 + 65 + 305

4. **a.** 130 LET X = ((14 - 10) * 3) / (2 + 2)

   b. 20 LET Y = (6 ^ 3) + (17 / 2)   (Parentheses are optional)

Answers to NOW TRY THIS 3—4

1. 80 PRINT "MY AGE IS",17

2. 50 PRINT 10,20,30,40

3. 50 PRINT 10
   60 PRINT 20
   70 PRINT 30
   80 PRINT 40

4. 999 END

Answers to NOW TRY THIS 4—1

1. 40 PRINT "ENTER THE YEAR YOU WILL GRADUATE"
   50 INPUT GRAD.YEAR

2. 40 INPUT "ENTER THE YEAR YOU WILL GRADUATE";GRAD.YEAR

```
3. 100 INPUT "ENTER THE NAMES OF THE 5 CLASSES YOU ARE TAKING";
       CLASS1$,CLASS2$,CLASS3$,CLASS4$,CLASS5$


4. 100 READ CLASS1$,CLASS2$,CLASS3$,CLASS4$,CLASS5$
   500 DATA "GEOLOGY","GEOMETRY","P.E.","AMERICAN LIT."
   600 DATA "SOUTH AMERICAN HISTORY"


5. 10 READ COMPANY1$,EMPL1
   20 READ COMPANY2$,EMPL2
   30 READ COMPANY3$,EMPL3
   40 READ COMPANY4$,EMPL4
   50 READ COMPANY5$,EMPL5
   600 DATA "E & J Electronics",8
   610 DATA "Best Commercial Cleaning",21
   620 DATA "Toledo Plumbing",13
   630 DATA "M & J Accounting",109
   640 DATA "SKB Communications",34
```

Answers to NOW TRY THIS 4—2

```
1. 100 PRINT TAB(4) "SARA VALENZUELA";TAB(25) "101 W. MERRY"


2. 100 PRINT "SARAH VALENZUELA";" 101 W. MERRY"


3. 100 PRINT SPC(4) "SARA VALENZUELA"; SPC(20) "101 W. MERRY"


4. 100 PRINT "SARA VALENZUELA",,"101 W. MERRY"
```

Answers to NOW TRY THIS 4—3

```
1. 100 F$ = "  #####.##  #####.##"
   110 PRINT USING F$;148.073,70.514
   120 PRINT USING F$;16.1,100
   130 PRINT USING F$;2576.905,3609.95


2. 100 F$ = "  #####.##  #####.##"
   110 LPRINT USING F$;148.073,70.514
   120 LPRINT USING F$;16.1,100
   130 LPRINT USING F$;2576.905,3609.95


3. 100 PRINT USING "#,###.##";4190.03


4. 100 LPRINT USING "$$###.##";AMT
```

Answers to NOW TRY THIS 5—1

1. `240 GOTO 580`

2. `20 ON V - 3 GOTO 400,500,600`

3. `50 ON PRCNT / 100 GOTO 100,200,300,100`

Answers to NOW TRY THIS 5—2

1. If teacher for American Literature = Mr. Ericson
   Then take American Literature

2. `10 IF NME$ = "NORMA JEAN" THEN PRINT "THE NAME IS FOUND."`

3. `100 IF TEMP <= 32 THEN PRINT "IT'S FREEZING OUTSIDE."`

4. `110 INPUT "ENTER PASSWORD";PSWD$`
   `120 IF PSWD$ = "OPEN SAYS ME" THEN PRINT "PLEASE ENTER."`

Answers to NOW TRY THIS 5—3

1. `120 IF NMBR <= 5 THEN CST = NMBR * 5 ELSE CST = NMBR * 4.85`
   `120 IF NMBR < 6 THEN CST = NMBR * 5 ELSE CST = NMBR * 4.85`

2. `80 IF N1 > N2 THEN IF N1 > N3 THEN LRGE = N1`
   `      ELSE LRGE = N2 ELSE IF N2 > N3 THEN LRGE = N2`
   `      ELSE LRGE = N3`

3. `240 IF SX$ = "M" THEN IF WEIGHT > 140 THEN IF GPA >= 2.5`
   `      THEN PRINT "STUDENT IS ELIGIBLE."`

4. `110 INPUT "ENTER PASSWORD";PSWD$`
   `120 IF PSWD$ = "OPEN SAYS ME" THEN PRINT "PLEASE ENTER."`
   `      ELSE PRINT "ACCESS DENIED."`

Answers to NOW TRY THIS 6—1

1. `90    GOSUB 12000`

2. `1000 REM ***********************************************************`
   `1010 REM ***        SUBROUTINE TO CONVERT OUNCES TO POUNDS        ***`
   `1020 REM ***********************************************************`
   `1030 REM`
   `1040 POUNDS = OUNCES / 16`
   `1050 RETURN`

```
3. 1000 REM ****************************************************
   1010 REM ***        SUBROUTINE TO CALCULATE GROSS PAY      ***
   1020 REM ****************************************************
   1030 REM
   1040 INPUT "ENTER HOURS WORKED";HRS
   1050 INPUT "ENTER PAY RATE";RTE
   1060 GROSS.PAY = HRS * RTE
   1070 RETURN
```

```
4. 1000 REM ****************************************************
   1010 REM ***           CALCULATE GRADE POINT AVERAGE       ***
   1020 REM ****************************************************
   1030 REM
   1040 INPUT "ENTER POINTS IN 5 CLASS";P1,P2,P3,P4,P5
   1050 TTL = P1 + P2 + P3 + P4 + P5
   1060 GPA = TTL / 5
   1070 RETURN
```

Answers to NOW TRY THIS 6—2

```
1. 190 ON X/2 GOSUB 1000,2000,3000,1000
```

```
2. 40 IF X = 2 THEN GOSUB 1000
   50 IF X = 4 THEN GOSUB 2000
   60 IF X = 6 THEN GOSUB 3000
   70 IF X = 8 THEN GOSUB 1000
```

```
3. 360 ON X GOSUB 2000,3000,4000
```

```
4. 100 ON QUANTITY - 4 GOSUB 8000,6000,8000,4000
```

Answers to NOW TRY THIS 7—1

```
1. 20 WHILE VLUE <> 9999
   30    READ VLUE
   40 WEND
```

```
2. 40 X = 3
   50 WHILE X < 100
   60    PRINT X
   70    X = X + 3
   80 WEND
```

```
3. 30 INPUT "ENTER THE VALUE";I
   40 TTL = 0
   50 WHILE I > 0
   60    TTL = TTL + 1
   70    I = I - 1
   80 WEND
```

```
4. 400  INPUT "ENTER SAVINGS ACCOUNT BALANCE";BAL
   410  COUNT = 1
   420  WHILE COUNT <= 6
   430     BAL = BAL + BAL * .075
   440     COUNT = COUNT + 1
   450  WEND
```

▬ Answers to NOW TRY THIS 7–2

```
1. 20 FOR I = 1 TO 50
   30    LPRINT I * .05
   40 NEXT
```

```
2. 10 FOR X = 200 TO 100 STEP -4
   30 NEXT X
```

```
3. 100 FOR I = 1 TO 10
   110     INPUT "ENTER COMPANY'S NAME";CMPY$
   120     INPUT "ENTER BALANCE OWED";BAL
   130     BAL = BAL + BAL * .1
   140     PRINT CMPY$;" OWES $";BAL
   150 NEXT I
```

▬ Answers to NOW TRY THIS 7–3

```
1. 100 IF (MNTH$ = "APRIL") AND (DTE = 15) THEN PRINT "TAXES ARE DUE."
```

```
2. 200 INPUT "ENTER YOUR AGE";AGE
   210 INPUT "ARE YOU A RESIDENT? (Y/N)";RES$
   220 IF (AGE >= 21) AND (RES$ = "Y") THEN PRINT "ELIGIBLE TO VOTE."
   230 IF (AGE < 21) OR (RES$ <> "Y") THEN PRINT "NOT ELIGIBLE TO VOTE."
```

```
3. 100 IF DISTANCE <= 800 THEN PRINT "DRIVE CAR."
          ELSE PRINT "TAKE PIPER CUB."
```

```
4. 540 IF (AMT > 1000) OR (OVERDUE > 30) THEN PRINT "SEND BILL."
```

▬ Answers to NOW TRY THIS 8–1

```
1. 10 REM *** READ THREE NUMBERS AND MULTIPLY THEM TOGETHER. ***
   20 READ A,B,C
   30 PRINT A * B * C
   40 DATA 10,15,20
   99 END
```

```
2. 10 REM *** READ LIST OF VALUES UNTIL FIRST VALUE (C) IS ***
   20 REM *** SMALLER THAN SECOND (D).                        ***
   30 READ C,D
   40 WHILE C >= D
   50     READ C,D
   60 WEND
   70 PRINT C " IS LESS THAN ";D
   80 DATA 5,5,4,8,5,5,6
```

```
3. 10 REM *** CONVERT A TEST SCORE  ***
   20 REM *** INTO A PERCENTAGE.     ***
   30 REM
   40 PRINT "ENTER NUMBER OF QUESTIONS CORRECT"
   50 INPUT "OUT OF 100: ";CRRT
   60 REM *** CONVERT TO PERCENT CORRECT. ***
   70 LET PRCT = CRRT
   80 PRINT "YOU GOT ";PRCT;"% CORRECT."
   99 END
```

Answers to NOW TRY THIS 8—2

```
1. 10 RANDOMIZE TIMER
   20 R = RND (1000 - 1) + 1
```

```
2. 20 IF ABS(N) = N THEN PRINT N;"+" ELSE PRINT ABS(N);"-"
```

```
3. 20 IF SGN(N) = 1 THEN PRINT N;"+" ELSE PRINT ABS(N);"-"
```

```
4. 50 PRINT INT(N)
```

```
5. 30 IF N = INT(N) THEN PRINT INT(N) ELSE PRINT INT(N) + 1
```

```
6. 40 IF SGN(N) = 1 THEN PRINT INT(N)
                    ELSE IF N = INT(N) THEN PRINT INT(N)
                    ELSE PRINT INT(N) + 1
```

Answers to NOW TRY THIS 8—3

```
1. 280   LET C$ = CHR$(100)
```

```
2. 100 ST$ = LEFT(ITEM$,4)
   100 ST$ = MID$(ITEM$,1,4)
```

```
3. 60 ST$ = RIGHT$(ITEM$,4)
   70 ST$ = MID$(ITEM$,LEN(ITEM$)-3,4)
```

```
4. 60 PRINT ASC("J")
   70 PRINT ASC("O")
   80 PRINT ASC("N")
```

Answers to NOW TRY THIS 9—1

1. 80 DIM ITEMS$(150)

2. 100 TOTAL = 0
   110 FOR I = 1 TO 10
   120   TOTAL = TOTAL + QUANTITY(I)
   130 NEXT I

3. 100 FOR I = 20 TO 30
   110   PRINT SALARIES(I)
   120 NEXT I

4. 100 FOR I = 30 TO 20 STEP −1
   110   PRINT SALARIES(I)
   120 NEXT I

Answers to NOW TRY THIS 9—2

1. 10 DIM PRODUCTS(40,12)

2. 30 FOR I = 1 TO 20
   40   SUMS(I) = 0
   50   FOR J = 1 TO 15
   60   SUMS(I) = SUMS(I) + X(J,I)
   70   NEXT J
   80 NEXT I

3. 30 FOR I = 1 TO 15
   40   SUMS(I) = 0
   50   FOR J = 1 TO 20
   60   SUMS(I) = SUMS(I) + X(I,J)
   70   NEXT J
   80 NEXT I

4. 30 I = 1
   40 FOUND$ = "N"
   50 WHILE (FOUND$ = "N") AND (I <=20)
   70   IF GRADES(I) = 17 THEN FOUND$ = "Y"
   80   I = I + 1
   100 WEND

Answers to NOW TRY THIS 10—1

1. The data-processing department is responsible for developing and maintaining software.
2. The four components are hardware, software, data, and people.

3. GIGO stands for garbage in–garbage out, which means that program results are only as good as the data entered into the program.

4. Feedback is important to determine how well a system is working.

5. One example of internal feedback is the self-testing that computers perform; an example of external feedback is the testing the programmer performs on program results.

Answers to NOW TRY THIS 10–2

1. A systems analyst meets with the program users to develop the program specifications.

2. In a structured walkthrough, programmers meet to discuss a program currently being developed and share suggestions for improving it.

3. A pilot implementation of a new program involves switching a small portion of the processing to the new program while still performing most processing under the old method.

4. Approximately 80 percent of programmers' time is spent on program maintenance.

```
1. 30 PRINT TAB((80 - LEN("Galena Paint and Paper"))/2) "Galena Paint and Paper"
   40 PRINT TAB((80 - LEN("Employee Payroll"))/2) "Employee Payroll"
```

```
2. 50 PRINT TAB((80 - LEN ("Employee Name      Hours Worked      Gross Pay"))/2)
   "Employee Name      Hours Worked      Gross Pay"
```

```
3. 50 GRAND.TOTAL = 0
   60 FOR I = 1 TO 20
   70    INPUT "EMPLOYEE'S NAME";NAM$
   80    INPUT "GROSS PAY";PAY
   90 GRAND.TOTAL = GRAND.PAY + PAY
   100 NEXT I
   110 PRINT
   120 PRINT "THE GRAND TOTAL IS    $";GRAND.TOTAL
```

```
4. 40 NET.TOTAL = 0
   50 GRAND.TOTAL = 0
   60 FOR I = 1 TO 20
   70    INPUT "EMPLOYEE'S NAME";NAM$
   80    INPUT "GROSS PAY";PAY
   90    GRAND.TOTAL = GRAND.TOTAL + PAY
   100   IF PAY > 400 THEN NET = PAY - 100
            ELSE IF PAY >= 200 THEN NET = PAY - 60
            ELSE NET = PAY
   110   NET.TOTAL = NET.TOTAL + NET
   120 NEXT I
   130 PRINT
   140 PRINT "THE GRAND TOTAL IS    $";GRAND.TOTAL
   150 PRINT "THE NET TOTAL IS    $";NET.TOTAL
```

Answers to NOW TRY THIS 11–1

1. Four ways of entering data into variables are (1) the assignment (or LET) statement, (2) the INPUT statement, (3) the READ/DATA statement, and (4) reading the data from files.
2. Files are divided into records, which are further subdivided into fields.
3. Sequential organization stores records in the order in which they are written to the file, whereas relative organization stores records in numbered locations.
4. False
5. A cylinder is a collection of concentric disk tracks.

Answers to NOW TRY THIS 11–2

1. `100 OPEN "CUSTLIST.DAT" FOR OUTPUT AS #3`

2. `40 OPEN "ADDRESS.DAT" FOR OUTPUT AS #1`

3. `250 CLOSE #1,#3`

4. `300 CLOSE`

Answers to NOW TRY THIS 11–3

1.
```
90 OPEN "BILLING.DAT" FOR APPEND AS #3
100 WRITE #3,"BRYON BOLLINS","418 FAIRVIEW"
```

2.
```
120 OPEN "BILLING.DAT" FOR INPUT AS #3
130 INPUT #3,NAM$,ADDRESS$
140 PRINT NAM$,ADDRESS$
```

3. d

4.
```
120 OPEN "BILLING.DAT" FOR INPUT AS #3
130 INPUT #3,NAM$,ADDRESS$
140 INPUT #3,NAM$,ADDRESS$
150 PRINT NAM$,ADDRESS$
160 CLOSE #3
170 OPEN "BILLING.DAT" FOR INPUT AS #3
180 INPUT #3,NAM$,ADDRESS$
190 PRINT NAM$,ADDRESS$
```

Answers to NOW TRY THIS 11–4

1. `100 OPEN "VENDOR" AS #1 LEN=80`

2.
```
110 FIELD #1,4 AS VENDOR.ID$,30 AS NAM$,20 AS ADDRESS$,14 AS CITY$,
    2 AS STATE$,10 AS ZIP$
```

3. Records in random files can be deleted by replacing the record with a new record or filling each field with blanks or special characters such as asterisks.

4. 100 GET #3,70

5. A random file is more efficient than a sequential file when records must be entered, updated, and printed in any order.

Answers to NOW TRY THIS 12–1

1. 20 LINE (160,100) - (260,100)

2. 30 LINE (0,70)-(319,130),,BF

3. 20 CIRCLE (160,100),25

4. 100 DRAW "R25;F25;D25;G25;L25;H25;U25;E25"

Answers to NOW TRY THIS 12–2

1. 40 SOUND 1200,36.4

2. 50 PLAY "L4G2.E2GGA.G8GE"

3. 100 IF VALUE > 200 THEN BEEP

Glossary

Access method A way in which the computer transmits data between secondary storage and the primary storage unit.

Algorithm The sequence of steps needed to solve a problem. Each step must be listed in the order in which it is to be performed.

Alphanumeric data Any combination of letters, numbers, or special characters.

Argument A value used by a function to obtain its final result.

Arithmetic/logic unit The part of the central processing unit that performs arithmetic and logical operations.

Array *See* Table.

Assembly language A programming language that uses symbolic names instead of the ones and zeros of machine language. It's easier to use than machine language but more difficult than high-level languages.

Assignment statement A statement used to assign a value to a variable.

Audit To test a program using specific sets of input data to determine whether program output is correct.

Auxiliary storage *See* Secondary storage.

Branch To change the normal flow of program execution.

Bubble sort A type of sort in which adjacent table elements are compared and, if they are out of order, switched. This process is repeated until the entire table is in order.

Buffer A temporary storage location used for data being written to or read from a file.

Built-in function *See* Library function.

Call To cause a subroutine to be executed.

Central processing unit The "brain" of the computer, composed of three parts: control unit, arithmetic/logic unit, and primary storage unit.

Character string constant A group of alphanumeric data consisting of any type of symbols.

Code To write a problem solution in a programming language.

Collating sequence The internal ordering that the computer assigns to the characters it can recognize. This ordering allows the computer to make comparisons between different character values.

Command mode *See* Direct mode.

Complete program testing Testing all possible paths of program execution.

Computer An electronic machine capable of processing data in many different ways. Its speed, accuracy, and storage and retrieval capabilities make it extremely useful to people.

Concatenate To join together two or more data items, such as character strings, to form a single item.

Conditional transfer statement A statement in which control is transferred to different locations depending on specified conditions.

Constant A value that does not change during program execution.

Control break The situation in which there is a change in the value of a specified data item.

Control statement A statement allowing the programmer to control the order in which statements are executed.

Control total A subtotal that is calculated until the value of a specified data item changes (that is, until a control break occurs).

Control unit The part of the central processing unit that governs the actions of the various components of the computer.

Conversational mode *See* Inquiry-and-response mode.

Counter A numeric variable used to control a loop. It is incremented (or decremented) and tested each time the loop is executed until the desired number of repetitions is reached.

Counting loop A loop executed a specific number of times. The number of repetitions must be determined before the loop is first entered.

Cursor The blinking rectangle of light indicating where typing will appear on the screen.

Data Facts that have not been organized in a meaningful way.

Data file A file used to store data to be used by one or more programs.

Data list A list containing all the values in the DATA statements in a program. The values are read to variables in the order in which they occur in the list.

Data-processing department The department in a company that is composed of computer professionals who are responsible for the development of new programs and the maintenance of the company's information system in general.

Debug To locate and correct program errors.

Decision structure A structure in which a condition is tested. The action taken next depends on the result of this test.

Descriptive variable name A variable name that describes the storage location it represents.

Desk check To trace through a program by hand to try to locate any errors.

Detail line An individual line in a report.

Direct mode The mode in which commands are executed as soon as <Enter> is pressed.

Documentation Statements or instructions used to explain programs to humans. Documentation can be within a program or written on paper in a separate document.

Double-alternative IF statement A decision statement in which one action is taken if the specified condition is true and another action if it is false.

Driver program A program whose main purpose is to call subroutines. The subroutines perform the processing.

Electronic mail Typed messages sent by cable or telephone lines between computer systems.

Element An individual value stored in a table. Elements are accessed by using the table name with a subscript.

Error trapping The technique of writing a program in such a way that it "traps" or catches input errors, such as invalid data.

Execute To carry out the instructions in a program.

Feedback Information that tells a system how well it is working.

Field The smallest division in a file; it consists of a single data item. Fields group together to form records.

File A collection of related data items kept in secondary storage.

File position pointer An imaginary pointer indicating the file record that will be accessed next.

Flowchart A graphic representation of the solution to a programming problem.

Format To control the order in which program results are output. For example, printing output in a report with headings and columns is a method of formatting it.

Garbage in–garbage out (GIGO) A popular expression indicating that if input data is incorrect, the output of a program will also be incorrect.

Grand total The total value of all items of a specific type.

Graphics mode A mode in which illustrations can be displayed on the screen. The screen is divided into small dots called *pixels* that can be turned off and on.

Hard copy Output printed on paper.

Hardware The physical components of the computer system, such as the central processing unit, printers, and disk drives.

Hierarchy of operations Rules that determine the order in which arithmetic expressions are evaluated. In BASIC, exponentiation is performed first, followed by multiplication and division, then addition and subtraction.

High-level language A programming language that uses English-like statements that must be translated into machine language before execution.

Immediate-mode command A command executed as soon as <Enter> is pressed.

Index *See* Subscript.

Indirect mode The mode in which statements are not executed until the RUN command is executed.

Infinite loop A loop that executes indefinitely. This occurs because the condition controlling loop execution never reaches the value needed for the loop to stop executing.

Information Data that has been processed so that it is meaningful to the user.

Information system A system designed to turn data into useful information. Information systems must have input, processing, output, and feedback.

Input Data that is entered into the computer to be processed.

Inquiry-and-response mode A mode of operation in which the BASIC system asks a question and the user types in a response.

Interpreter A language-translation program that translates each statement in the source program into machine language and executes it before continuing on to the next statement.

Keyword *See* Reserved word.

Library function A function that is prewritten and determines a specific value. It is part of the BASIC system.

Line number An integer value placed at the beginning of a statement to indicate its order of execution. In Microsoft BASIC, line numbers must be between 0 and 65529.

Literal A group of characters containing any combination of alphabetic, numeric, and/or special characters.

Logic error A flaw in the algorithm used to solve a programming problem.

Logical operator An operator that acts on one or more conditions to produce a value of true or false. Examples of logical operators are NOT, AND, and OR.

Loop body The statement(s) that are executed each time a loop repeats.

Loop control variable A variable used to determine whether a loop will be executed.

Loop structure A structure that allows a series of instructions to be executed as many times as needed.

Machine language The only instructions that the computer is able to execute directly; consists of combinations of zeros and ones that represent high and low electrical states. Machine language is different for each type of computer.

Main memory *See* Primary storage unit.

Mainframe A large computer commonly used in business and industry.

Menu A list of the functions a program can perform.

Merge sort A sort that combines two sorted tables into a single sorted table.

Microcomputer The smallest and least expensive type of computer currently available. Microcomputers generally are less expensive, slower, and have smaller primary storage units than other types of computers.

Minicomputer A computer with many of the capabilities of a mainframe, but generally having a smaller primary storage unit and a lower price.

Module A subprogram that is part of a larger program and performs a specific task.

Network A group of computers and peripheral devices joined together by special cables or telephone lines so that information and resources can be shared.

Numeric constant A number (other than a line number) contained in a statement.

Numeric variable A variable that stores a number.

Origin line In a pie diagram, the origin line is a horizontal line extending from the center of the circle to the 3:00 position. All later angular measurements start from this line.

Pixel Short for "picture element." A dot of light that can be turned on or off to create images. In graphics mode the entire screen is divided into a grid of pixels.

Primary storage unit The component of the central processing unit that temporarily stores programs, data, and results.

Priming read A READ statement used to initialize the loop control variable before the loop is entered for the first time.

Program A list of step-by-step instructions that a computer can use to solve a problem.

Program file A file that stores a program.

Program testing The process of systematically checking a program to determine whether it obtains correct results.

Program tracing A method of locating program errors by inserting PRINT statements to check the values of specific variables.

Programming language A language that a programmer can use to give instructions to a computer.

Programming mode *See* Indirect mode.

Programming process The steps used to develop a solution for a programming problem.

Prompt A message telling the program user to enter data at this point. The prompt should indicate the type and amount of data needed.

Pseudocode An English-like description of a program's logic.

Random A term describing a group of values, such as numbers, in which each value has an equal chance of occurring.

Random access Accessing a record directly without accessing any preceding records.

Record One or more fields that together contain the data on a single unit.

Relational operator An operator used to compare two expressions.

Relative organization A method of file organization in which each record is stored in a numbered location in secondary storage.

Reliability The ability of a program to work properly regardless of the data entered to it.

Report heading The title of a report; it is usually placed at the top.

Reserved word A word that has a predefined meaning to the BASIC interpreter.

Ruling A line used to separate two different parts of a report.

Run-time error A logic error that causes program execution to stop prematurely.

Scroll To move vertically off the top of the screen.

Secondary storage Storage that is supplementary to the primary storage unit. It can be easily expanded. The secondary storage most commonly used with microcomputers is floppy or hard disks.

Selective program testing Testing a program by using data with specific characteristics, such as being at the edge of the range of acceptable data.

Sentinel value *See* Trailer value.

Sequence A group of statements that are executed in the order in which they occur in the program.

Sequential access Accessing a record by accessing, in turn, all preceding records in a file.

Sequential organization A method of organizing records in a file in which the records are stored in the same order as they were written to the file.

Sequential search A search that examines table elements, from the first to the last, until the specified value is found.

Single-alternative IF statement A decision statement in which an action is taken if the specified condition is true. Otherwise, control continues to the next statement.

Single-entry, single-exit point principle A rule stating that a subroutine should have only one entry point and one exit point.

Soft copy Output displayed on a monitor screen.

Software A program or a series of programs.

Software development life cycle The steps in the development and maintenance of programs.

Spaghetti program A program with difficult-to-follow logic caused by the use of a large number of unconditional transfers (GOTO statements).

String variable A variable that stores a character string.

Structure chart A diagram that visually illustrates how a problem solution has been divided into subparts.

Structured programming A method of programming in which programs have easy-to-follow logic, use only the three basic logic structures, and are divided into subprograms, each designed to perform a specific task.

Structured walkthrough An evaluation of the design of a program by a group of computer professionals.

Stub A subroutine that has not yet been written and consists only of a PRINT statement indicating that the subroutine has been called. Stubs are used to test the calling program.

Subroutine A subprogram within another program. Subroutines are generally placed after the main program.

Subscript A value enclosed in parentheses after a table name, used to specify a particular element in the table.

For example, NME$(4) refers to the fourth element in table NME$.

Subscripted variable A variable that refers to a specific element in a table.

Supercomputer The largest, fastest type of computer currently available. Supercomputers mainly are used in situations where large amounts of mathematical computations must be performed.

Syntax error An error that occurs when the programmer violates the grammatical rules of a language.

System A group of related elements that work together toward a common goal.

Systems analyst A computer professional who, along with the program user, develops the specifications for new programs. It is the systems analyst's responsibility to make certain the computer programmer adheres to these specifications when writing programs.

Table An ordered group of related data items having a common variable name, all of the same data type.

Text mode The mode in which text characters are displayed on the screen.

Top-down design A method of solving a problem that proceeds from the general to the specific. The major problems are dealt with first, and the details are left until later.

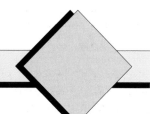

BASIC Reference ▪ Baumann/Mandell

Understanding Structured Programming in BASIC
IBM/MS-DOS Version

BASIC Commands

COMMAND	EXPLANATION
LIST	Displays on screen entire program currently in main memory.
LOAD "program"	Transfers specified program from secondary storage to main memory.
NEW	Clears a portion of main memory in preparation for a new program to be entered.
RUN	Executes program currently in main memory.
SAVE "program"	Writes program currently in main memory to secondary storage under specified name.
FILES	Displays the names of the files on the disk currently being accessed.

Arithmetic Functions

FUNCTION	PURPOSE	EXAMPLE
ABS(X)	Absolute value function.	ABS(-11) is 11
INT(X)	Largest integer less than or equal to X.	INT(16.75) is 16
RND	Random number between 0 and 1.	RND(10)
SGN(X)	Sign of X.	SGN(-12) is -1

String Functions

STRING FUNCTION	OPERATION	EXAMPLE
ASC(string)	Returns the ASCII code for the first character in the string.	If A$ = "DOG" then ASC(A$) is 68
LEFT$(string,expression)	Returns the number of leftmost characters of the string specified by the expression.	LEFT$("ABCD", 2) returns "AB"
LEN(string)	Returns length of a string.	If H$ = "HI THERE", then LEN(H$) is 8
MID$(string,expression1, expression2)	Starting with the character at expression1, returns the number of characters specified by expression2.	MID$("ABCDE",3,2) returns "CD"
STR$(expression)	Converts a real number to a string.	STR$(12.34) returns the string 12.34
VAL(expression)	Converts a numeric string expression to its numeric equivalent.	VAL("12.34") returns 12.34
stringA + stringB	Concatenates two strings.	"NIGHT" + "MARE" is "NIGHTMARE"

BASIC Statements

STATEMENT	EXPLANATION	EXAMPLE
DIM	Sets dimensions for tables.	10 DIM ITEM$(25)
END	Stops program execution.	999 END
FOR/NEXT	Sets up a loop that is executed a stated number of times.	250 FOR X = 1 TO 20 STEP 2 400 NEXT X
GOSUB	Transfers control from the calling program to a subroutine.	260 GOSUB 1000
GOTO	Unconditional transfer of control.	160 GOTO 250
IF/THEN	Executes the clause following THEN if the stated expression is true.	430 IF NME$ = "DONE" THEN PRINT NME$
IF/THEN/ELSE	Executes the clause following THEN if the stated expression is true; otherwise ELSE clause is executed.	430 IF NME$ = "DONE" THEN PRINT NME$ ELSE READ NME$
INPUT	Allows user to enter data during program execution.	50 INPUT NME$,AGE
LET	Assignment statement (the word LET is optional).	100 TOTAL = TOTAL + 1
ON/GOSUB	Transfers control to one of several subroutines, based on the evaluation of a mathematical expression.	250 ON X GOSUB 100,200
ON/GOTO	Transfers control to other statements, based on the evaluation of a mathematical expression.	190 ON X GOTO 120,140
PRINT	Displays the results of computer processing.	130 PRINT "NAME",PAY
PRINT USING	Permits flexibility in formatting output; used with format control characters.	100 PRINT USING A$;PAY
READ/DATA	Reads data from the data list to variables.	100 READ NME$,HRS 800 DATA SMITH,40
REM	Used to indicate documentation.	100 REM COMPUTE PAY
RETURN	Transfers control from a subroutine back to the calling program.	1500 RETURN
TAB	Prints output in a specified column.	100 PRINT TAB(15) "NAME"
WHILE/WEND	Executes a loop as long as a stated condition is true.	150 WHILE COUNT < 50 240 WEND